THE CIA IN GUATEMALA

4/09

THE TEXAS PAN AMERICAN SERIES

The CIA in Guatemala

THE FOREIGN POLICY OF INTERVENTION

by Richard H. Immerman

UNIVERSITY OF TEXAS PRESS, AUSTIN

The Texas Pan American Series is published with the
assistance of a revolving publication fund established
by the Pan American Sulphur Company.

LIBRARY OF CONGRESS CATALOGING IN PUBLICATION DATA
Immerman, Richard H.
    The CIA in Guatemala.
    (The Texas Pan American series)
    Bibliography: p.
    Includes index.
    1. United States—Foreign relations—Guatemala.
    2. Guatemala—Foreign relations—United States.
    3. United States. Central Intelligence Agency.
    I. Title. II. Series.
    E183.8.G9I45   327.7307281   81-16312
    ISBN 0-292-71083-6   AACR2

TO MARION

Contents

Preface

This is a book about United States relations with Guatemala. It is also a book about the United States and Guatemala. I had not intended it to be so when I began the study as a graduate student in 1973. At that time, imbued with the spirit of antiwar protests, I set out simply to expose the perfidy of the CIA. Over the years, however, as I pored over the literature, filed my Freedom of Information Act requests, and spoke with the actors, I realized that to dwell on the CIA would be misleading. The intervention involved much more than a covert operation to defend the United Fruit Company. The basis for the conflict between the two countries was, in sum, this: during the period of cold war tension, neither the United States government nor the public could understand Guatemalans.

The effects of this misunderstanding continue, and subsequent events suggest that the United States success in 1954 may turn out to be one of its most serious failures. I have attempted to explain why. Many people have helped along the way. I am grateful to the staffs of all the archives and libraries I visited, especially those at the National Archives, the State Department, the Truman and Eisenhower libraries, and Princeton University. They not only brought me their documents but also guided me through the intricate declassification process. Peggy Fulton wrestled with my prose, and Jean Wiggs deciphered my scribblings to type clean drafts. Scott Lubeck and Holly Carver of the University of Texas Press turned the manuscript into a finished product.

The list of those who pointed me toward additional material, shared their thoughts, or read the manuscript seems endless. Thank you, Stephen Ambrose, Severyn Bruyn, William Chase, Blanche Cook, Chester Dunning, Lloyd Gardner, Arch Getty, George Herring, Susanne Jonas, Walter LaFeber, Arnold Offner, Alan Rogers, and Martin Sherwin. I would like to extend special thanks to Fred Greenstein. His wisdom, encouragement, and friendship never failed to get me over that last hurdle and then the one after that.

I owe my deepest debt to my family and friends. These wonderful people, including those mentioned above, lived with my toil for close to a decade. I could ask for no more.

RHI
Princeton, New Jersey

THE CIA IN GUATEMALA

My Country, let us walk together, you and I:
I will descend into the abysses where you send me,
I will drink your bitter cup,
I will be blind so you may have eyes,
I will be voiceless so you may sing,
I have to die so you may live.

—GUATEMALAN OTTO RENÉ CASTILLO
KILLED, 1967

1. Truman, Eisenhower, and the Cold War in Latin America

On June 17, 1954, United States Ambassador to Guatemala John E. Peurifoy's son Danny burst into the embassy and gasped to his mother, "There's no school this afternoon because there is going to be a revolution at 5:00."[1] Mrs. Peurifoy was surprised. Her husband had not dared to tell her that, shortly before dawn the day before, a motley band of some 150 Guatemalan émigrés and mercenaries from neighboring Central American countries had crossed the Honduran border to invade Guatemala. They were led by a fugitive Guatemalan colonel, Carlos Enrique Castillo Armas, who, except for his thin mustache, could have easily been mistaken for a native Maya. Castillo Armas and his raggle-taggle army had come to overthrow the revolutionary government of Jacobo Arbenz Guzmán, to liberate their country from the yoke of Communist oppression. They believed Arbenz had become the tool of the Soviet Union, which had used intrigue, deceit, and terrorism to establish an outpost in the western hemisphere. As the world looked on, Castillo Armas and his legions took it upon themselves to restore Guatemala to its place in the Free World. They had the support and blessing of Ambassador Peurifoy.

What happened in the next ten days, however, was anything but a glorious military triumph. Castillo Armas had hoped to be met by throngs of Guatemalans, eager to lend their services to his patriotic cause. In fact he met no one. His forces too weak to approach the center of Arbenz's power, the colonel opted to camp just six miles across the border, at the Church of the Black Christ. There he would wait.

While he waited, a much broader scenario began to unfold. A clandestine radio station, broadcasting from some unidentifiable location, warned the Guatemalan people that a major force was approaching Guatemala City, crushing all opposition that stood in its way. Airplanes circled the capital, dropping any material capable of creating a loud explosion. The government responded by ordering a blackout. In the dark, the few hovering planes gave the impression of a squadron.

Children and parents panicked. Government officials panicked. Guatemala City's streets filled with throngs of people fleeing their homes for the safer recesses of the mountains. There were long periods of silence, followed by the noise of planes, bombs, and sirens, answered by a few impotent machine gun blasts from the National Palace. Armed with a shoulder holster and the only accurate information about what was really happening, the United States ambassador could be seen running around the capital. The regular army officers, fearing for their country and their lives, confronted Arbenz. His nerves shattered, the president addressed the nation by radio at 9:00 on the evening of June 27. He sadly told them that Guatemala was under attack by agents of the United States and the United Fruit Company and that he was turning over the government to his military chief, Colonel Carlos Enrique Díaz. A few short months before its tenth anniversary, the Guatemalan revolution was over.

Nowhere were the events in Guatemala followed more closely than in the United States. For years concerned observers had watched as Guatemala seemed to move closer and closer to the Soviet orbit, and by February 1954 the *New York Times* reported that "the Communists were about ready to assume outright control."[2] The State Department's first formal response to Castillo Armas' invasion declared that the United States government was encouraged, that the outbreak of hostilities "reflected a widely-held hope that these developments may in fact be signs that the people of Guatemala may have begun a movement in earnest against their government."[3] Such an expression certainly did not portray the Eisenhower administration as attempting to be a good neighbor, but the cold war was underway, and sides had to be taken. Florida's Senator George A. Smathers put it bluntly when he declared, shortly before Arbenz capitulated, that a hands-off policy was "unrealistic and naive" and that "we must see that the people opposing communism in Guatemala win this particular battle."[4]

And win the battle the people did, at least according to our administration's official position. Of course there were protests, particularly from Latin Americans, that the Colossus of the North had once again wielded a big stick—but, as the United States ambassador to the United Nations, Henry Cabot Lodge, explained, anyone who had ever had any contact with Secretary of State John Foster Dulles or President Eisenhower ("who is utterly devoted to the principles of democracy, to the rights of man, and who abhors all forms of imperialism") would know that any charges of United States intervention were absurd.[5] Speaking before a radio and television audience on June 30, Dulles proclaimed, "The people of Guatemala have now been heard from. . . . Now the future of Guatemala lies at the disposal of the Guatemalan people themselves."[6] Eisenhower was even more eloquent when he accepted the credentials of Castillo Armas' newly appointed ambassador to the United States, Lieutenant Colonel José Luis Cruz Salazar:

> The people of Guatemala, in a magnificent effort, have liberated themselves from the shackles of international Communist direction, and reclaimed their right of self-determination. For the people of the United States and for myself, I pay tribute to the historic demonstration of devotion to the cause of freedom given by the people of Guatemala and their leaders. It constitutes living proof of the unity of ideals and aspirations which animate and join us together, and which form the basis of our profound faith in the future.[7]

To the administration and to the informed public, the victory of Castillo Armas was "the first clear-cut victory for the West since the battle for Greece."[8] They lauded the Guatemalan people, whose courage put the Soviets on notice that their brand of slavery would not be tolerated by those who loved freedom. State invited Castillo Armas to the United States in order to showcase him before the whole world as a true champion of democracy, as a hero to be emulated by oppressed people everywhere. The House of Representatives conducted special hearings to investigate the event, parading dozens of witnesses from the United States and Guatemala who praised the anti-Arbenz movement and testified to Communist atrocities. On January 19, 1955, when Eisenhower gave his first televised press conference and summarized his initial two years as president, he listed the elimination of the Communist threat from Guatemala as one of his proudest accomplishments.[9] He did not reveal, however, that his administration had played the decisive role in this accomplishment. Later, in his memoirs, Eisenhower would discuss how he had loaned two planes to Castillo Armas.[10] He would never discuss the covert activity of the United States Central Intelligence Agency.

The ease with which Castillo Armas took power has contributed to the lack of any comprehensive analysis of the 1954 coup in subsequent years. Arbenz conceded defeat so readily that there was little time, or apparent reason, for investigation. Except for a few leftist journalists, the press concurred that this was a successful anti-Communist uprising.[11] In the absence of investigative report-ing, United States participation remained secret. The numerous books appearing within the next few years supported this account. Many were written by the same journalists who covered the initial story and accepted the official interpretation, while the more schol-arly studies drew their conclusions from documents supplied by the United States or the Guatemalan government.[12] As the cold war con-test in the 1950s continued to develop, and the United States en-gaged in imbroglios over Suez, Quemoy, Matsu, U-2 surveillance, and Cuba, the victory of Castillo Armas became for the United States public a vague memory. Most even forgot the overarching issue of Communism, recalling the coup as only another banana revolt.

Despite the increasing accumulation of interpretive scholarship on United States involvement in the international arena following World War II, which has led to the evaluation and reevaluation of most episodes in the cold war, the intervention in Guatemala (and the one in Iran the year before) has received strikingly little atten-tion.[13] Writings to date tend to be short on detailed documentation and to treat the coup illustratively. Historians use the episode to pro-vide background material for the escalating cold war,[14] to underscore the inordinate influence of overseas investments on United States foreign policy,[15] or to trace the historical evolution of the Central In-telligence Agency.[16] Most analysts now accept the CIA's involvement in the overthrow, but the antecedents, sequences, and consequences of that involvement remain unclear.

This study argues that the fall of Arbenz was a significant link in the unfolding chain of cold war history. It examines the social and economic conditions in Guatemala which spawned the 1944 revolu-tion, the nature of that revolutionary movement, the effect of the revolution on United States interests, and the steps taken by the Ei-senhower administration, overtly and covertly, to overthrow the rev-olutionary government. But such a study would be incomplete with-out two further examinations: why the intervention took place and what its consequences were. This was not merely another instance of big stick diplomacy, similar to the many United States interven-tions in Latin America characteristic of the earlier years of the twen-tieth century. Rather, this was a critical event in the cold war, an illustration of the cold war ethos and its impact on diplomacy.

The intervention in Guatemala produced lasting effects on United States relations with the underdeveloped nations of the world in general and with Latin America in particular. As will be shown, one major reason for the failure at the Bay of Pigs was the fact that Washington based its strategy on the precedent established in Guatemala, while Castro and his advisers were well versed in their Guatemalan counterparts' experience. Moreover, the present-day revolutionaries in Guatemala are the direct descendants of Arbenz's supporters, and there are strong indications that the success in the 1950s may lead, as in Iran, to a serious failure in the 1980s. Developments in Guatemala, Cuba, and throughout Central America and the Caribbean reveal that, in 1954, the United States cried wolf.

After a detailed study of the overthrow, the connection between the 1954 Guatemalan coup and later events becomes clear. But the contextual framework must be discussed from the beginning. This consists of an underdeveloped country in a region traditionally viewed as vitally important to the United States, a nationalist and reformist political movement, the most powerful capitalist country in the world, and two administrations of that country whose overriding concern was to advance the capitalist system in the face of alleged Soviet expansion. The combination of such forces led to a major confrontation in the cold war.

LATIN AMERICA AND THE COLD WAR: UNITED STATES INTERESTS

Students of foreign policy have written with increasing frequency that, since the Second World War, the center stage for the international drama has shifted to the Third World.[17] Concerns for the traditional loci of United States interests, such as Europe, the Soviet Union, and China, are maintained, but the formerly peripheral areas have come to dominate the headlines. For the United States, Latin America's geographic proximity, along with its historic, economic, and political connections, gives it a position of paramount significance. As the *New York Times* editorialized three months before Arbenz capitulated, the government must make it "clear with finality" that it viewed all forms of Communist activity in the western hemisphere as alien and hostile to its ideals and as intrigue that could endanger the peace. Later that year, in his influential book on what one reviewer called "the most important test United States policy has faced in Latin America in half a century [Guatemala]," journalist Daniel James expanded on the *Times'* perspective:

. . . there can be no battle more decisive than the Battle of the Western Hemisphere. We can "afford" to be defeated in China,

Indo-China, and even perhaps India and Western Europe; but the loss to our cause of the Republics next door would be fatal, for then we should be ringed by hostile nations in our own vicinity.[18]

The reasons for these overwhelming fears are evident. Latin America is contiguous to the United States from Florida to California, including the eighteen hundred–mile open border with Mexico. It contains the Panama Canal, described by former Ambassador to Guatemala Peurifoy as "our greatest strategic installation anywhere in the world," the sites of at least two other potential interoceanic canals, and permanent and emergency military bases. It affords a proven air route to the east and is the source of readily accessible essential strategic materials. In 1952 longtime State Department authority on inter-American affairs Thomas Mann succinctly warned that, in the event of a global war, unobstructed access to Latin American resources "would be essential to the trans-oceanic projection of major United States offensive power."[19]

While Latin America's strategic importance in the immediate postwar years is well known, its economic value is not. There have been numerous accounts of activities by such economic giants as the United Fruit Company, and, along with other underdeveloped regions, Latin America has figured prominently in the myriad dependency models.[20] Analyses of United States economic priorities following World War II, nevertheless, repeatedly concentrate on the Marshall Plan and the development of the European Economic Community. Yet, as a market for commercial exports, Latin America during the early cold war was as important as all of Europe and more important than Asia, Africa, and Oceania combined. Private, long-term investment throughout the region surpassed the amount invested in any other part of the world except Canada. By the end of 1950 this investment had already reached about $6 billion, compared with direct private investments outside the western hemisphere of only $4.6 billion. In terms of the export market, Latin America in 1950 purchased about $2.7 billion worth of United States goods, which amounted to about 50 percent of its total imports from all sources. Dollar investments flowed into Latin America at an unprecedented rate, and experts predicted that this trend would continue to increase. Equally important, statistics for this same period show that about 35 percent of United States imports, valued at approximately $2.9 billion, came from the region, and a considerable part of these were strategic materials. Other imports, such as coffee, sugar, bananas, and wool, were also vital. The dollars provided to Latin America through the purchases of these commodities helped finance its purchase of transportation and industrial equipment, consumer goods, and, of course, the military hardware that the United States sold to all its allies.[21]

Notwithstanding such evidence of Latin America's importance, the conventional view is that both Truman and Eisenhower paid scant attention to their neighbors to the south. As a consequence, compared with the voluminous scholarship on the Monroe Doctrine, dollar diplomacy and the early interventions, the Good Neighbor Policy, the Alliance for Progress, and more recent developments, studies examining United States relations with Latin America from 1945 to 1961 are quite scarce. This relative neglect can be misleading. Neither Truman nor Eisenhower was uninterested in Latin America; economically and strategically it was much too important. If they seemed to lose interest, it was because both presidents grounded their foreign policies on analyses of the cold war. Their strategies accentuated global, not just bilateral or regional, considerations. Latin American policy reflected the overarching objective of containing Communism. Since most Latin American countries, especially the dictatorships, posed no threat to the United States policy, the region generally received less attention and fewer resources than such areas as Europe and the Far East, which appeared more vulnerable to Communist expansion.[22]

THE COLD WAR POLICY

The international cold war policy was outlined in the oft cited National Security Council's "Report by the Secretaries of State and Defense on 'United States Objectives for National Security,'" commonly known as NSC-68. Prepared during the second Truman administration while Dean Acheson and Louis Johnson headed these respective cabinet departments, its basic premise was that the world was divided into two antithetical camps, led by the United States and the Soviet Union. The principal objective of the Soviet camp was to acquire absolute hegemony; thus conflict between the two systems was endemic. Only when one side emerged as the clear victor would this conflict abate.[23] And the struggle would be fierce. Indeed, such diplomatic pundits as John Foster Dulles considered the Soviet threat to exceed even that of Nazi Germany, because, as he explained to representatives of the American republics shortly before the 1954 intervention in Guatemala, Communism constituted "not a theory, not a doctrine, but an aggressive, tough, political force, backed by great resources and serving the most ruthless empire of modern times."[24] This prevalent analysis did not leave much room for considering the specific needs of the underdeveloped areas. No one denied there was a Third World, but, in a bipolar life or death battle, United States policy makers believed only one world could survive.

Dulles and others considered Latin America to be a prime target for the Soviet conspiracy because the region was of crucial importance to the United States; George Kennan feared it was a fertile breeding ground where the Communists could "broadcast their seeds of provocation and hatred and busily tend the plants which sprout in such vigor and profusion."[25] By the 1950s, alarmists claimed that the Kremlin was pouring hundreds of agents into Latin America from the Rio Grande to Tierra del Fuego, agents trained in the theory and techniques of sabotage, espionage, and propaganda at the Institute for the Study of Latin American Relations in Prague. The Communist aim was quite simple: the destruction of Washington's influence in the western hemisphere and the conversion of Latin America into a "hotbed of hostility and trouble for the United States." Then, once the proper environment was established in any of the nations, Moscow could easily send in troops, equipment, and whatever else was necessary to threaten Washington.[26]

The horror with which United States leaders viewed the prospect of the Soviet Union operating in their own backyard can hardly be overemphasized. Their fear stemmed from two primary considerations. First of all, as Dulles explained in 1947, "Soviet policy in South America subjects the Monroe Doctrine to its severest test. There is a highly organized effort to extend to the South American Countries the Soviet system of proletariat dictatorship." In 1954 Dulles simply applied his analysis to the situation in Guatemala, asserting that the "intrusion of Soviet despotism was, of course, a direct challenge to our Monroe Doctrine—*the first and most fundamental of our foreign policies*" (emphasis added).[27] Second, since the sanctity of the Monroe Doctrine and of strategic and economic interests would require the United States to confront the challenge, it might well have to cut back its forces elsewhere in the world in order to take the action necessary. In short, Soviet intervention in Latin America would jeopardize the principles of the Monroe Doctrine and shake the foundation of the global policy of containment. It could readily precipitate a nuclear war.[28]

TRUMAN'S LATIN AMERICAN POLICY

President Harry S. Truman firmly constructed his Latin American policy on this prevailing cold war analysis. He did not merely "mark time," as one former State Department official contended, nor did his assuming the presidency augur the end of the Good Neighbor era.[29] In truth Roosevelt's policies encountered difficulties from their beginning, and this truth became especially evident during the war years. Prior to the outbreak of hostilities, Roosevelt encountered substantial criticism for not doing more to foster Latin America's economic independence, and manifestations of this resentment surfaced with the expropriation of private property in Mexico and Bolivia. The war strained relations still further, for many of the republics viewed the United States efforts to bind the hemisphere together with mutual defense and security pacts as a Yankee attempt to create new structures that would restrict Latin America's autonomy. Truman inherited these deteriorating conditions, in addition to a deteriorating world situation that reinforced the defensive nature of United States–Latin American programs because of the perceived mandates of the cold war.[30]

A recently declassified National Security Council document provides explicit evidence of Truman's concern over reconciling a desire to be Latin America's good neighbor with a commitment to preventing the spread of Communism. Written in 1952 and referred to by one of its authors as "the intellectual last will and testament in this area of security policy of the Truman Administration to the Eisenhower Administration,"[31] NSC-141, which was based on the overall assumptions generated by NSC-68, delineated the task in Latin America:

> In Latin America we seek first and foremost an orderly political and economic development which will make the Latin American nations resistant to the internal growth of communism and to Soviet political warfare . . . Secondly, we seek hemisphere solidarity in support of our world policy and the cooperation of the Latin American nations in safeguarding the hemisphere through individual and collective defense measures against external aggression and internal subversion.[32]

As became uncomfortably apparent with regard to Guatemala, the policy advisers who wrote NSC-141 could clearly stipulate policy objectives, but they could make no new recommendations as to how these objectives could be attained. In the final analysis they only advised the "improvement of present programs" and anticipated results to be no greater than "more rapid realization of our ultimate broad objectives."[33] In retrospect, however, the existing programs were inherently ineffective. The most publicized of these was Point Four assistance. Predicated on the realization that worsening economic conditions could lead to increased social unrest and open the door to Communist subversion, Point Four called for a "bold, new program" of technical cooperation designed to elevate the masses of Latin America (and other underdeveloped areas) out of misery, disease, and illiteracy.[34] It was financially doomed from the start. Since NSC-68 called for the United States to defend the Free World on a global front, it required massive military expenditures. For Truman to have gone before the depression-conscious American public, which was swinging toward Republican conservatism, to ask for the additional nonmilitary funds adequate for Point Four would have been certain political suicide. He had enough difficulty prying money out of Congress without having to explain the need in terms of potential threats.[35]

Truman and those within his administration eyeing developments in Guatemala believed there was a threat to Latin America, even if they did not think they could get public support for more Point Four aid. Therefore NSC-141 outlined the United States "existing" military and political defense programs before it presented Point Four. First, it highlighted the institution of mutual security pacts, such as the Treaty of Reciprocal Assistance, which was signed in Rio de Janeiro at the 1947 International Conference of American States. Second, it summarized the military grant-aid program for Latin America. The Mutual Security Act of 1951 appropriated $38,150,000 for fiscal year 1952 to cover military equipment, material, and training and promised more to follow in fiscal year 1953.[36]

Understanding the ineffectiveness of these Truman programs is a prerequisite to understanding the development of the Guatemalan strategy under Eisenhower. Even if one argues that more extensive Point Four assistance could have alleviated the economic distress responsible for Guatemala's radical reforms, United States domestic considerations precluded this being a viable option.[37] More can be learned by analyzing the military programs. Directed against an armed attack on any signatory nation, the Rio pact, along with the military grant-aid program, reflected the growing fear of Soviet aggression in Latin America. NSC-141 puts forth this position very clearly. The basic Truman policy for resisting Communist aggression was, of course, military containment. Because they believed containment was as appropriate to Latin America as anywhere else, NSC-141 analysts could rely on the continuation of existing programs in spite of Point Four's shortcomings.[38]

But in Guatemala the collective security containment arrangements were inapplicable.[39] Truman officials suspected that Soviet agents were actively subverting the government, but to invoke the Rio pact they had to have proof. The problem of definition compounded the problem of proof. United States policy makers discerned but a fine line separating nationalist reformers from Communist agitators, so fine a line that the distinguishing factor was often the effect of a reform on United States interests.[40] During the Truman administration, the reforms in Guatemala were sufficiently anti–United States to create suspicion of Communist intrigue but insufficiently so to offer proof to many of the Latin American nations fearful of the historic big stick. Hence a military pact against outside aggression was inoperative. By 1951 the quandary had become so frustrating that State considered drafting a proposal for the Consultative Meeting of Foreign Ministers in order to establish a technical staff equipped to study means of identifying subversive elements in the American countries. The plan was rejected because no one knew how to implement it.[41]

EISENHOWER'S DIPLOMACY

NSC-141 might have been Truman's "last will and testament" to Eisenhower, but plainly the new president believed that it needed serious revisions. The New Look strategy which he proposed during the 1952 campaign attacked the Democratic policy of containment, criticizing it for spreading United States resources too thin, accepting the status quo too willingly, and concentrating too heavily on Western Europe. Eisenhower contended that the White House must wrest the initiative from the Kremlin and, if possible, "liberate" areas from Communist control. Eisenhower seemed so much tougher than Truman that, according to the *Nashville Banner*, "the day of sleepwalking is over. It passed with the exodus of Truman and Achesonism, and the policy of vigilance replacing Pollyanna diplomacy is evident."[42]

Yet historians have traditionally depicted Eisenhower as a bland, do-nothing, largely ineffective president. Many scholars see little new in his foreign policy. They contend that the New Look developed out of strategic concepts discussed by the Truman administration after the outbreak of the Korean War and that a 1949 National

Security Council paper concerning Eastern Europe predicted the additional policy objective of "liberation."[43] More important, this argument continues, the critical factor in Eisenhower's diplomacy was the doctrine of massive retaliation, which might have served as a deterrent to Soviet expansion but certainly did not affect those areas already within the Communist orbit. Nuclear weapons could not be used for "liberation."[44] Close scrutiny of recently opened archives, however, reveals Eisenhower in a new light.[45] Massive retaliation was not the only basis for his strategy for combating international Communism. Covert operations also played a major role, and their use in Guatemala represented a significant departure from the policies of Truman.[46]

The covert aspects of the Guatemalan strategy exhibit the personal imprint of the president and, consequently, necessitate another historical corrective. Conventional scholarship almost unanimously attributes Eisenhower's foreign policy to his controversial secretary of state, John Foster Dulles.[47] To contemporary observers and later historians, the indefatigable Dulles appeared to dominate United States diplomacy in the 1950s to so great an extent that "he carried the State Department in his hat." The acknowledged power of his convictions, intellect, and rhetoric gave the impression of Dulles' preeminence with the president, the cabinet, the nation, and the international community. His frequent press conferences and interviews made him a favorite subject of the media,[48] and to most he was the conceptual font and prime mover of United States policy.[49]

Now available evidence seriously challenges this traditional interpretation.[50] Rather than supporting the standard portrait of Dulles leading by the strings a passive president and an overawed collection of advisers, the papers of the Eisenhower administration reveal a foreign policy resulting from a high degree of multiple advocacy, with the final decisions remaining firmly within the Oval Office.[51] Eisenhower and Dulles had a great deal of mutual respect, and no decisions were reached without their having discussed the issues thoroughly during numerous conversations each day. Even when he was away from Washington, Dulles constantly communicated with Eisenhower by telephone or coded cablegram.[52] The National Security Council, the Operations Coordinating Board, and more informal organs carefully reviewed and analyzed all policy proposals and options. Eisenhower and Dulles *agreed* on the fundamental principles of foreign policy. They collaborated; one man did not dominate the other.[53]

Therefore, the final element required to understand the cold war confrontation in Guatemala is a brief synopsis of the views of both the president and the secretary of state. Because he favored summit meetings and pacific programs such as Atoms for Peace and Open Skies, and because he possessed a (generally assumed) amiable and conciliatory nature, Eisenhower is thought to have been much more compromising toward the Communists than was Dulles. In keeping with the conventional wisdom on their relationship, historians consistently contend that Dulles drove the president to emphasize brinkmanship, not negotiation. To support this they often cite the memoirs of Sherman Adams, Eisenhower's chief assistant until forced to resign in 1958. Adams wrote in 1961: "I think that the hard and uncompromising line that the United States took toward Soviet Russia and Red China between 1953 and the early months of 1959 [when Dulles died] was more a Dulles line than an Eisenhower one."⁵⁴

Although in public Eisenhower appeared more inclined to peaceful coexistence with the Communists than did his more vocal secretary of state, the fact is that both men firmly believed in the necessity for constant vigilance against the Red menace. In a diary which reflected his private thoughts, Eisenhower recorded his complete agreement with one of the foremost architects of the United States cold war policies, former Secretary of the Navy and then Secretary of Defense James V. Forrestal.⁵⁵ Shortly after his friend committed suicide in 1949, Eisenhower recalled that Forrestal had been "the one man who, in the very midst of the war, always counselled caution and alertness in dealing with the Soviets." Eisenhower continued his personal eulogy by remembering that on several occasions, while he was Supreme Allied Commander, he had been visited by Forrestal, who carefully explained his thesis that the Communists would never cease trying to destroy all representative government. Eisenhower commented, "I never had cause to doubt the accuracy of his judgments on this point."⁵⁶

Eisenhower's diary entries regarding Forrestal also illustrate how infectious was the latter's cold war ideology, which resembled, in the words of one historian, "Ichabod Crane's terrified flight in Sleepy Hollow."⁵⁷ While president of Columbia University, Eisenhower served as a special consultant to the Defense Department during the early months of its unification. In terms reflective of a national ethos permeated by the beginnings of McCarthyism, he noted that both he and Forrestal agreed that the United States "must wake up to prepare a position of strength," because "the free world is under threat by the monolithic mass of Communist Imperialism."⁵⁸ Eisenhower must have felt that most people in and out of government had heeded the alarm, for six months later he wrote that "those who were then asleep [during the period of the United States–Soviet wartime alliance] now are professional patriots and Russian haters."[59]

Eisenhower's espousal of the cold war ideology relates directly to his approval of the overthrow of the Arbenz government in Guatemala. Similar to but more explicitly than Truman, he confronted the relationship between Communism and nationalism. He well understood that the ultimate struggle between the Communist and Western worlds would occur in the underdeveloped regions. Here nationalist impulses and long years of economic and political repression bred unrest and instability. To Eisenhower the solution was the gradual and orderly transition of the Third World to capitalist democracies. But the people were impatient, and hence the Communists could fill their thoughts with aspirations of instant utopias. Poverty and illiteracy did not create Communists, but they did give the Soviet Union the opportunity to make Communists:

> Nationalism is on the march and world Communism is taking advantage of that spirit of nationalism to cause dissension in the free world. *Moscow leads many misguided people* to believe that they can count on Communist help to achieve and sustain nationalistic ambitions. Actually what is going on is that the Communists are hoping to take advantage of the confusion resulting from destruction of existing relationships and in the difficulties and uncertainties of disrupted trade, security and understandings, *to further the aims of world revolution and the Kremlin's domination of all people.* (Emphasis added.)[60]

A keen strategist, Eisenhower logically concluded that it would be counterproductive for the United States to try to oppose fierce nationalism with inflammatory programs. He recognized the pitfalls of Truman's attempt to contain Communism in the Third World by an overreliance on force. A month after the Guatemalan coup, he wrote his good friend William Robinson, executive vice-president of the *New York Herald Tribune*, that "there is a strong communist leaning among certain groups," and, if the United States pursued policies inimical to their *nationalist* tendencies, "we will almost certainly arouse more antagonism," and the "possibility of these countries turning communist would mount rapidly."[61]

Guatemala presented special problems, because, according to Eisenhower and his advisers, it had already succumbed to Communist intrigue. How could the United States reverse this situation without wielding the type of big stick likely to incur the resentment of others? To someone who had presided over Mark Clark's covert mission to North Africa, the ULTRA secret, and Operation Double-Cross, the answer was evident—you do it clandestinely.[62] World War II made Eisenhower an avid proponent of the intelligence establishment, and one of his initial reorganization projects after becoming president was to solicit his former wartime associate James H. Doolittle to "act as Chairman of a panel of consultants to conduct a study of the covert activities of the Central Intelligence Agency." The president instructed Doolittle to "insure, insofar as practicable, that the field of clandestine operations is adequately covered," and he added, "I desire that your report be made to me personally and classified TOP SECRET."[63] Dwight Eisenhower believed covert operations were a crucial component of realizing United States foreign policy objectives, but they were effective only if they were used correctly and judiciously. Later, with great pride, he would look back at the Guatemalan coup as an operation that had been well conceived and well executed.[64]

The extreme anti-Communism of the other member of the administration's foreign policy–making tandem, John Foster Dulles, has been much more widely noted.[65] His hard-line attitudes developed from deep-seated theological, philosophical, and intellectual beliefs, as well as from profound concern for the political impact of McCarthyism.[66] The son of a Presbyterian minister and former leader of the Federal Council of Churches, Dulles viewed the cold war as a confrontation between two antithetical universal faiths: Christianity against atheism. By the end of the Second World War, he had concluded that there could be no reasonable compromise with the Soviet objective of world domination and, as noted, he was particularly sensitive to the potential threat in Latin America. He assiduously studied the writings of Lenin and Stalin, comparing them to Hitler's *Mein Kampf.* Even after Stalin died in 1953 and his immediate successor expressed an interest in peaceful coexistence, Dulles remained girded for a permanent global struggle. His severe critic Townsend Hoopes is probably not far off the mark when he asserts, "He seemed to require temperamentally a form of communist opposition whose goal was no less than the total conquest of the world in the most literal and physical sense."[67]

Converging with his religious faith was Dulles' sincere faith in the capitalist system. Long one of the highest-paid lawyers on Wall Street, he fervently believed in free enterprise and the expansion of corporate investments abroad. He assumed that these investments were threatened by the Soviet Union, whose agents throughout the world encouraged unwitting nationalists to expropriate property and generally create economic climates detrimental to United States interests. Since a basic tenet of the Eisenhower administration was that security was inextricably linked to economic well-being, Dulles, like others around the White House, viewed the fiscal health of the United States as a crucial component of its defense posture.[68]

Thus, although neither Eisenhower nor Dulles was intimately familiar with Latin America in 1953, the above discussion explains why one of the early objectives of their foreign policy was to devise a more effective program toward that region than Truman's.[69] At a cabinet meeting in the first year of his administration, the president underscored the generally unsatisfactory nature of United States policy toward Latin America, which he said stemmed from past preoccupations with European and Asiatic affairs. He urged the cabinet to remedy this potentially dangerous situation and, toward this end, sent his brother Milton on a fact-finding mission to South America. The purpose of this mission was to acknowledge the importance of hemispheric solidarity to the United States and to sell this importance to all United States citizens.[70]

Milton Eisenhower did not visit Central America; his report, nevertheless, alluded to the developments in Guatemala. When Undersecretary of State Walter Bedell Smith reported the mission's findings to the cabinet, affixed to the document was a memorandum. It read, "The most important question facing the Cabinet was to make up its mind that Latin America is important to the United States" and that "timely action was extremely desirable to prevent Communism from *spreading seriously beyond Guatemala*" (emphasis added).[71] The mission did not have to go to Guatemala in order to investigate Communist infiltration; such infiltration was already accepted as fact. In total agreement with his brother's diary entry almost a year before, Milton Eisenhower's report read:

> The possible conquest of a Latin American nation today would not be, so far as anyone can foresee, by direct assault. It would come, rather, through the insidious process of infiltration, conspiracy, spreading of lies, and the undermining of free institutions, one by one. Highly disciplined groups of Communists are busy, night and day, illegally or openly, in the American republics, as they are in every nation of the world . . . *One American nation has succumbed to Communist infiltration.* (Emphasis added.)[72]

The backdrop has now been provided for studying the steps taken by the Eisenhower administration to obviate this alleged threat to the hemisphere. The reasons for the United States allegations and the sequence of events, as well as their consequences for the future, warrant careful scrutiny. By analyzing the Guatemalan revolution from the viewpoint of the cold war ethos and developing a strategy which went beyond the Truman policy of military containment spiced with Point Four assistance, Eisenhower, Dulles, and the Republican policy makers ushered in a new era in inter-American relations, an era marked by a protracted struggle between the United States and an assumed international Communist conspiracy.

2. Underdevelopment, Repression, and Revolution

United States allegations that Guatemala's political, social, and economic institutions expressed the Communist ideology, and thus posed a threat to the hemisphere's security, arose from the prevailing analysis of the Arévalo and Arbenz revolutionary governments. A study of the causes for the intervention, therefore, requires a study of these governments. But, in the same way that the programs of the Truman and Eisenhower administrations cannot be understood outside of the context of the period's cold war ethos, so the programs of Presidents Arévalo and Arbenz cannot be understood outside of the context of Guatemala's historic conditions. Above all, Guatemala was characterized by a long period of underdevelopment, which led to economic exploitation, cultural repression, and political oppression. The Revolution of 1944[1] responded to these exigencies. In doing so its leaders sought to meet the challenge of Guatemala's historical legacy, not the challenge of the cold war.

THE POLITICAL HERITAGE

Guatemala's "underdevelopment" resulted from hundreds of years of domination and exploitation by the countries responsible for the term's usage in the twentieth century.[2] A region of vast economic potential, Guatemala had been prior to the Spanish conquest a major center of Maya civilization, exhibiting a high degree of advancement in art, science, social organization, and religion.[3] However, it lacked the achievements in military technology of the Europeans. Consequently, beginning in 1523, Hernán Cortés' lieutenant Pedro de Alvarado overcame in only one year an empire that dated back to the fourth century. Not only did Alvarado frighten the Maya by brandishing unfamiliar weapons, but he terrorized the tribal units, hanging or burning alive any local chief who dared to oppose him.[4]

Guatemala's central location and advanced heritage made it one of the most important administrative units of the Spanish Empire, and, in 1670, it became the seat of the captaincy general. In 1821, during the era of struggle for liberation throughout Latin America, the Guatemalans regained their independence. However, in order to acquire the necessary power to do so, the nationalists had to rely on the assistance of Mexico, which soon sought to incorporate Guatemala within its own boundaries. In self-defense the Guatemalans spearheaded a movement among the smaller Central American republics to form a federation that would serve as a bulwark against Mexican aggression. The National Constituent Assembly, convened in Guatemala City on June 24, 1823, under the presidency of El Salvador's José Matías Delgado, lasted some nineteen grueling months. This body was considered the effective government of Central America, and it was charged with drafting a constitution for the permanent republic of Central American states. When the delegates finally completed their arduous work in January 1825, the United Provinces of Central America was duly constituted, with Dr. Pedro Molina of Guatemala elected the first president.

Almost from its inception, the federation encountered severe problems, stemming primarily from internal bickering. Much like the old Articles of Confederation system in the United States, the federal government possessed little real authority to deal with the particularist policies of the individual states. The states were plagued by internal instability, resulting in numerous government changes. The overriding issue was the conflict between the liberals and the conservatives (also known as serviles). The largest and most economically prosperous of the member nations, Guatemala led the conservative movement in advocating increased centralization of power in the federal government. Fearing that powerful Guatemala would use such centralization to exploit the others, the liberals strove to undercut the conservative position by supporting more "federal" principles. Exacerbating the problem was the contest between the newly emergent urban population and mestizos, who claimed the right to participate in the public life of the federation, and the remnants of the Spanish aristocracy, who sought to continue their exclusive political control. Struggles between economic interests and the traditional privileges of class ensued. These political, economic, and social conflicts continued throughout the duration of the federal republic, limiting the opportunity for constructive change in any of the member nations.[5]

The federation period, although a brief interlude in Guatemala's long history, had important ramifications for the future course of the republic's development. The political and economic developments subsequent to the federation's disintegration produced the conditions for the revolution. The concept of a Central American union, moreover, outlived the federation itself.[6] Over a century later President Arévalo drew heavily on the ideas of the 1825 constitution in formulating his own programs. He believed that only a union of Central America's forces—economic, political, cultural, and even military—could achieve lasting independence and progress for each of the nations.[7]

The remainder of Guatemala's political heritage until the revolutionary period can be surveyed quite briefly. Following the disintegration of the federation, save for short periods of relative anarchy, several strong-armed dictators, or *caudillos*, ruled the republic. The first was Rafael Carrera, who came to power in 1838, although his authority was not "legitimated" until 1844. Carrera continued in office until his death in 1865, and, after the short terms of Vicente Cerna and Miguel García Granados, Justo Rufino Barrios became the new autocratic ruler in 1872. This marks the start of the "liberal era" in Guatemala, with the beginning of industrialization, foreign investments, and the development of public services. The "liberals" confiscated the patrimony of the religious orders and divided many of the conservative landlords' holdings among the emerging "middle-class," although this sector constituted only about 30 percent of the population as late as the revolution.

For approximately the next three-quarters of a century, the "liberal" *caudillos* consolidated the hold on land of middle-class parvenus, who merged their economic and political interests with those of remaining old-style conservative landlords. This ruling alliance encouraged the influx of foreign capital into Guatemala, resulting in a genuinely revolutionary situation.[8] Little evidence of this danger appeared during the twenty-two-year reign of Manuel Estrada Cabrera, from 1898 to 1920, but such was not the case when Jorge Ubico's thirteen-year-old government came to an abrupt end in 1944.

THE INDIAN PROBLEM

The shift in power from the old conservative landlords to the emerging middle-class parvenus, or, more accurately, the coalescence of the two classes, took place without concern for the more deprived strata of society. As a result, virtually every political and economic reform throughout this period came at the expense of the lower classes. In Guatemala the lower classes consisted, as they still do, primarily of Maya Indians, who now occupy the mountainous regions and western parts of the country and, at the time of the revolution, comprised some two-thirds of the population. One major reason for the Mayas' vulnerability was their inability to create any united opposition. Divided into numerous tribes, the Maya largely ignored one another. They spoke many different dialects and often lived in isolated districts even within the larger community. These divisions were so extreme that each of the Indian tribes could be considered a virtually independent sociocultural entity based on traditions predating the Spanish arrival.[9]

After the conquest most Indians, distrustful of the newcomers, continued their ancient languages, customs, and traditions, participating only to a limited extent in the economic and political life of the nation. Their main "contribution," apart from their own subsistence agriculture, was to provide a labor supply for the large plantations, or *fincas*, at harvesttime. Although in part dictated by their isolationist tendencies, their marginal societal role also resulted from various government measures which, up until 1944, were clearly designed to force the Indians to depend on the wealthy landlords. For example, in the 1830s the government began a program to "legally" deprive the Indian communities of their communal properties without compensation. Nevertheless, the Mayas' remoteness in the highland regions enabled them to retain a good portion of their lands until the liberal regime of Rufino Barrios in the 1870s and 1880s. Rufino Barrios enacted legislation requiring titles to private property. By doing so his government greatly facilitated the private appropriation of the Mayas' individual and communal holdings. Since many Indians did not understand the system of registration, they allowed their lands to be sold as unoccupied.[10]

The continued expropriation and subsequent subdivision of their lands forced more and more of the Maya to migrate from the highlands to the coffee-growing regions near the coast. Such was the government's intent, for, as the economy became more specialized and commercialized, the guarantee of a permanent supply of cheap labor was necessary to attract foreign investors. As time went on, official legislation defined various categories of forced labor. Debt slavery was revived in the form of the *colono* system, by which hereditary debts to *finqueros* bound the peons to the *fincas*. To insure that this form of bondage continued, the *finqueros'* agents traveled to the Indian villages in the highlands and offered to "lend" the struggling farmers who remained the money they so desperately needed. As repayment, all the Indians had to do was "contract" to work on the *fincas*, especially during harvesttime. With such a cheap labor force so readily available, landowners eagerly appropriated additional holdings for export crops. By 1900 Guatemala had been converted into an importer of staple foods, which drove up prices and created frequent food shortages.[11]

The effects of this system plunged the Maya population into economic dependency and sharpened the division between the upper and lower classes. Prior to 1944 United States State Department official Merwin L. Bohan estimated that the per capita import-purchasing power of the Maya amounted to about $1 per year.[12] Even after the revolution, in 1948, economic experts wrote that the indigenous share of Guatemala's gross national product was about $70 per capita, in contrast with $246 per capita for the nonindigenous population.[13] Malnutrition was widespread and the life expectancy was less than forty years, with an infant mortality rate of greater than 50 percent. Illiteracy, while 70 percent overall, was reported to be 90 to 99 percent in largely Indian communities. When not working on a plantation, the Indians would return to their villages, where they would try to raise enough corn and beans on their small mountain plots in order to survive. Each family often inhabited a small one-room hut with an earth floor, adobe walls, and a thatched roof. Rarely was there any ventilation other than that offered by the door, and the interior was dark and filled with the smoke of the fire used for cooking and warmth. The hut had few furnishings—some grass mats to serve as beds, perhaps a hammock, a box for valuables, and perhaps a makeshift chair for the aged. In most instances all water had to be hauled considerable distances up the steep mountainsides.[14]

The revolutionary governments after 1944 sought to alleviate these conditions. They also sought to alleviate the concomitant to the Mayas' poverty—the racial discrimination which the Indians as a group encountered. Racism in Guatemala was more ambiguous than in certain other societies, since it reflected ethnic and cultural diversities as opposed to strictly physical characteristics. Many generations of intermarriage, and more often rape, had blurred superficial distinctions. Nevertheless, albeit divided among themselves, the Maya viewed themselves as separate from the Europeans. Their resulting distinctive culture and traditions made them the targets of racist attitudes. Attempts to exploit the Maya economically were thus often accompanied by attempts to "deculturize" them, thereby alienating them further and reducing their desire to resist. To a large extent these attempts failed. The Indians became more and more estranged from the social order, for, although the ruling society could command their labor and land, it could not command their loyalty.[15]

A basic feature of the Guatemalan revolution was its effort to integrate the Maya into the social order by constructing policies that were not anathema to their traditional values.[16] One such value is that the Maya, like many indigenous cultures, are noncapitalistic. Their economic goal is subsistence and participation in the community, not capital accumulation. Within the tribal village, displays of wealth are generally scorned, for they upset the balance of "egalitarian poverty." The social ideal is the conformist, not the innovator; the controlled individual, not the power seeker. Historically, the Maya held land primarily on a communal basis, with individual holdings based on land use rather than ownership. These traditions survived the policies of the Spanish conquistadors and the *caudillos* and were considered in the development of such revolutionary programs as agrarian reform.[17]

THE SOCIAL STRUCTURE

Since the Maya constituted such an overwhelming majority of Guatemala's population, their repression and exploitation resulted in an extremely rigid and unbalanced class structure.[18] From the time of the Spanish conquest, Guatemala had been dominated by a tiny aristocracy of landowners.[19] This group did not grow, due to its historic political power, which insured that government policies reinforced the status quo. The upper class consistently constituted only 1 to 2 percent of the population, and, by the twentieth century, very little of it was of indigenous derivation. Rather, the elite was almost exclusively foreign by birth, coming primarily from Europe and the United States. In contrast to the primitive huts inhabited by the Maya majority, the wealthy minority lived in modern homes with Western appliances and furnishings. They wore Western clothes and consumed imported wines, canned foods, and delicacies of all sorts. Most significantly, they owned the land.[20]

Guatemala's middle class is in many respects the most difficult to identify. Its importance to the revolution far surpassed its size and traditional influence within Guatemalan society and government. In fact, the leadership for the revolutionary movement developed from and remained within this middle class. In addition, while the powerful elite predictably opposed the revolutionary changes, and the Maya welcomed the reforms but remained politically inactive, the middle class wavered. To be sure, the revolution might have survived the opposition of the upper class; never could it survive the desertion of the middle class.[21]

Government employees and subordinate officials, clerks, small shopkeepers, skilled and semiskilled workers, administrators, and the like made up about 30 percent of the population. Most of this middle class were categorized as *ladinos*. The term, actually a corruption of the more common *latino*, in Guatemala refers to any ethnic group that adopts non-Indian manners and speaks a European language.[22]

Historically, the *ladinos* were descended from the Spanish landowners, or *criollos*, who were more reluctant to marry Indian women than to rape them. Consequently, *ladinos* and Maya often physically resembled each other, a distinct disadvantage for the *ladinos*. Not only were they sometimes subjected to racist discrimination, but they often had difficulty proving that they were non-Indian in order to be exempted from the tributes imposed on the Maya. They therefore sought to differentiate themselves by accepting Western values and exhibiting Western characteristics. Unlike the Maya, who became indentured to the landowners, the *ladinos* normally worked for a salary or on rented land of their own. Some fortunate *ladinos* even owned land in the fertile lowlands, and many of the more prosperous moved to the urban centers to become professionals, bureaucrats, and technocrats. Others joined the armed services. In this way they accumulated capital, enabling them in the future to become part of the world of their Spanish fathers.[23]

Certain *ladinos* profited greatly during the nineteenth century, with the movement toward capital formation and the more rational exploitation of the land. These individuals were the principal beneficiaries of the liberal agrarian policies, which deprived the Indians of their properties, for the *ladinos* claimed the "titleless" land. Then, in the 1870s, Guatemala increasingly became an export economy based on coffee, which became the economic means for the *ladinos*' rise to power. The tiny *criollo* elite saw that it was in its own interest to include within its power base what was becoming a *ladino* upper middle class, rather than to try to maintain its exclusive position. In this manner the *criollo* elite was not displaced but merely enlarged.[24] The *ladinos* rapidly translated their newfound power into political terms. By the time of the revolution, the highest local officials, even in municipalities predominantly inhabited by Indians, were usually *ladinos* who, all too often, ruled like little dictators, disregarding Indian views and needs. In short, it was through strict and often violent suppression of the Indians that some *ladinos* managed to reach the top and remain there.[25]

The physical similarity between the Maya and the *ladino* sheds much light on the nature of the Guatemalan revolution. It is highly plausible that a Maya dressed in European fashions, speaking Spanish or some other Western language and rejecting the indigenous customs, could have passed for a *ladino* and ascended the social and economic ladder. Neither the Indian nor the *ladino* generally had any documentation of birth. Yet this rarely happened. Even those Maya who somehow managed to acquire enough money to live in a *ladino* community remained within their tribal grouping.[26] If a revolutionary movement really were to reflect the interests of the people, it would have to take into account these strong traditional allegiances of the country's majority. For this reason, certain of the government policies from 1944 to 1954 did not conform to the Western ideal, and within the cold war ethos these were readily interpreted as Communist.

THE ECONOMIC ORDER

The rigidly hierarchical political and social structure in Guatemala gave rise to extreme inequality and poverty, extreme even by Latin American standards. Although the economy generated a great deal of money, and despite its vast potential, Guatemala in 1960 still ranked only fourteenth out of the twenty-one Latin American nations in per capita income.[27] This ranking reflects the social and economic inequities. Some money did filter down from the great landowners and find its way to the cities.[28] At the time of the revolution, however, only about 40 percent of the Guatemalans lived in the district municipalities, and many of these centers were too small to be considered urban areas. Some 77 percent of the people lived in communities of fewer than 2,500, and this figure went as high as 90 percent in a number of departments, since 10 percent of the entire population lived in Guatemala City. Thus, per capita income of the rural regions caused Guatemala's low ranking. In other words, Guatemala itself was not poor, but the majority of its people were.[29]

The economic structure created this lopsided demographic disparity. Although to use the term "feudal" might create confusion with conventional analyses of this premodern system,[30] Guatemala's economy exhibited many of feudalism's most salient features. The racist oppression and economic suppression of the Maya created a virtual serf caste, and in Guatemala class and ethnic origin were virtually synonymous. For this reason, any discussion of the underdeveloped conditions that produced Guatemala's revolutionary discontent must to some extent reiterate the plight of the Indian population.

Prior to Arbenz's land reform in 1952, only 2.2 percent of Guatemala's population held over 70 percent of the land, and less than one-sixth of 1 percent held almost 14 percent. Twenty-two percent of the population, most of whom were *ladinos*, owned another 20 percent of the land, leaving less than 10 percent for the remaining population. About 90 percent of this remainder was Maya. To make matters worse, while an estimated one-third of Guatemala's land was deemed arable, only half of this was in use; the rest was left fallow by the large landowners.[31]

Such general statistics became even more meaningful when translated into specifics. For example, 50 percent of the farm operators occupied the *minifundios*, or small plots of land under four acres, while .03 percent of the operators owned the large-scale holdings, the *latifundios*. These estates constituted over 50 percent of the total farmland. Furthermore, the small holdings were located principally in the less fertile highlands, where the population density reached as high as three hundred inhabitants per square mile. This statistic becomes even more ominous when one considers that Guatemala has one of the highest rates of population growth in the world.[32]

The population density centered around the *minifundios* presented a condition that was detrimental to the country's economic development. Excessive cultivation rapidly exhausted the land, and, since yields were barely sufficient for personal needs, the operators found it financially impossible to afford artificial fertilizers. In addition, due to such topographical factors as multiple varieties of soil in small areas and poor transportation facilities, mechanization was exceedingly difficult, increasing the likelihood of low production and concomitant high costs. This dilemma became more acute because of the often onerous situation of the renters, who frequently had to pay the landlord from 50 to 60 percent of their crops and who constantly faced the danger of having their properties repossessed for failing to pay this rent. Even if it were possible to pay the owner, there usually was not enough left over to cover the cost of production, so more money had to be borrowed in order to buy the minimum requirement of tools, seeds, and other necessities. Consequently many small farmers, no longer capable of sustaining their families, had to take on other part-time work in order to supplement their income.[33]

Predictably, as time went on and the population grew, debts increased and the size of the plots decreased. In purely economic terms, this trend translated by the time of the 1944 revolution into an annual per capita income of only around 180 quetzales (1 quetzal equaled 1 U.S. dollar), with two-thirds of the population earning 70 quetzales. Arévalo's national Economic Program Commission optimistically classified this latter group as existing at the subsistence level.[34] While the commission did not categorize economic level by racial origin, George Britnell, who headed an International Bank for Reconstruction and Development study mission to Guatemala during Arévalo's administration, observed that this two-thirds figure corresponded exactly to the proportion of Indians living in Guatemala.[35]

Not surprisingly, Guatemala's infant mortality rate was the highest in the Americas, for this statistic reflects with the most precision the conditions of life and the economic and physical level of the society. Before the revolution more than 40 percent of those born died in infancy, and, in the rural zones alone, the percentage climbed to 60 percent in some of the Indian communities in the highlands. This meant about fourteen thousand deaths each year, a staggering figure, especially since half of those children who died suffered from an ailment quite common but not nearly as fatal in other areas— measles. Other major causes of death included parasites, malnutrition, and whooping cough. As in most Third World nations, the primary reason for the high number of infant deaths was the lack of health care, in the form of medical facilities or trained personnel. For instance, only 14.3 percent of expectant mothers within the Indian groups received any medical assistance, and only 9.7 percent of their babies were born in hospitals or other equipped facilities.[36]

Inadequate medical attention was only part of the problem. Even should the child survive birth, there were still difficult living conditions to be faced. Several years after the revolution's overthrow, a United Nations survey revealed that only 40 percent of the population lived in housing units, and 43.1 percent of the occupied dwellings had three or more people to a room. In both urban and rural areas, only 33.8 percent of the dwellings had piped water, and only 29.4 percent had flush toilets. As late as 1950, before the agrarian reform bill but after the Arévalo government had begun substantive reforms, such as establishing minimum wages, half the people could still not afford to buy shoes.[37]

What is crucial for our understanding of the direction taken by the Guatemalan revolutionary movement, a direction that created concern within the United States that Soviet Communism had penetrated the western hemisphere, is that, while this "feudalistic" economic system caused severe hardship for the majority of the people, it greatly benefited a fortunate few. These, of course, were the eminent landowners, among whom were giant North American enterprises such as the United Fruit Company. The purpose of any *latifundio-minifundio* system is self-evident: to bring the greatest possible income to the large proprietors at the lowest possible cost. The majority of the people, in Guatemala's case the Maya, are provided with the minimum amount of land to survive, or at least a sufficient number of them survive to insure the system's continuation. The system requires an adequate labor force. Since the Mayas' survival was to a large extent dependent on their ability to supplement their incomes by working on the large *fincas* at harvesttime, the *finqueros* were guaranteed their labor supply when they needed it. But Maya hired hands remained technically independent farm operators who contracted out their labor on a part-time basis. The *finqueros* had no obligation to pay these workers during the off-season, and, of course, they did not.[38]

The majority of Guatemalans suffered additionally from the fact that foreigners owned so many of the *latifundios*. Following the Second World War, when the Guatemalan government confiscated the German landholdings, United States interests predominated. Logically, then, they were targeted by Guatemalan reformers. The foreign elements in Guatemala were far more concerned with the external market than the internal one; thus, as time went on, United Fruit and others devoted increasingly more land to export crops, such as coffee and bananas. By the time of the revolution, these two commodities constituted close to 90 percent of Guatemala's entire agricultural production. Many Guatemalans were thus compelled to purchase imported food, at prices they could ill afford. Variations in the domestic salary levels normally did not reflect variations in the external market. Also, the national income, derived primarily from the export market, was channeled to the upper sector. Wealth was created by and for foreigners, at the expense of nationals.[39]

Because of the nature of the crops, the role of coffee and bananas in Guatemala's export economy aggravated the situation further. Coffee was by far the largest industry, a particularly unfortunate fact, for its market was confined almost exclusively to the United States and Europe. Prices within such a limited, inelastic market fluctuated greatly, depending on the size of the crop, blights, and the overall cost of production for a given year. Moreover, when poor yields necessarily caused very high prices, the market had a tendency to look for substitutes, such as tea. When prices were low, it was easy to saturate the market. The extensive nature of coffee production makes any adjustment of production to demand very difficult, even if the market could be accurately predicted. Hence any coffee economy tends to be highly unstable.[40]

Much the same analysis can be applied to the production of bananas. They were also produced almost exclusively for export, and, being even less essential than coffee, they were subject to even greater variations in demand. Their price depended on the current tastes of the almost exclusive buyer, the United States. Although the economic role of the banana industry was greatly inferior to that of coffee in terms of the gross national product, it had a highly disproportionate effect on the country's fiscal well-being. This influence was due to the large number of employees required by the industry, so that in a given year its activities could have significant repercussions for the overall economic condition of the nation. Banana production became a barometer for Guatemala's economy.[41] For this reason the importance of the country's largest banana producer, the United Fruit Company, is apparent. United Fruit symbolized Guatemala's economic ills—it was the largest landowner, it devoted so much of its land to an unstable export crop, and it represented that country which largely determined both coffee and banana prices, the United States.

THE LAST ARISTOCRAT

The precarious nature of the Guatemalan economic structure became most evident immediately preceding and during World War II. The shock of the world depression in the 1930s was transmitted to Guatemala through the sector most closely linked to the global market: the coffee industry. During the 1930s coffee prices fell to less than one-half their value prior to 1929, and a 1937 price war with Brazil prevented any type of recuperation when the effects of the depression lessened near the end of the decade. Then, the outbreak of war in 1939 effectively halted access to the markets of Europe, forcing Guatemala to depend almost exclusively on the United States for the sale of its most important crop. The United States could not absorb the entire surplus, since the other Latin American coffee-producing nations, experiencing the same difficulty, also turned to the United States. The results in Guatemala were deflated prices, a decreased export volume, and an overall loss of earnings. Domestically, this meant economic stagnation, reduced state spending, rising unemployment, and many of the other features of an economy on the brink of collapse.[42]

Such a bleak economic state frequently has serious political and social repercussions, and, therefore, it is not surprising that the reigning Guatemalan *caudillo*, Jorge Ubico Castañeda, was the "victim" of the 1944 revolution. The spoiled son of an aristocratic lawyer, Ubico had begun his career in 1918 by working for the health board of the Rockefeller Foundation. In his early life he encountered a series of frustrations with his college studies, his military career, and his marriage. A Guatemalan critic of the 1944 revolution wrote that, due to these many early disappointments and a lack of parental guidance, Ubico as a youth led a sterile life, developing a profound sense of inferiority.[43] One thing is certain. He had a legendary temper, and his ruthless insensitivity and excessive display of egotism during a period of severe economic hardship created a climate conducive to revolution.

After his landslide election in 1931,[44] Ubico revealed time and again that he fancied himself as another Napoleon. An ostentatious, albeit fastidious, dresser, he surrounded himself with busts and portraits of the emperor and emphasized the similarity between their appearances. Ubico militarized the post office employees, the schoolchildren, and even the symphony orchestra members, whom he forced to dress in uniforms and to play his personal selections, using the techniques and instruments that he chose. Never one to isolate himself from the people, the dictator habitually paraded around the country on "trips of inspection," bedecked in dress uniform and fully accompanied by a military escort, several cabinet ministers, a mobile radio station, and an official biographer. Ingratiating landlords, assembling their Indian laborers days in advance of his arrival, frequently greeted him with noisy celebrations. At each village Ubico would pause long enough to adjudicate intricate legal cases, fire judges, reverse decisions, release certain prisoners, and sentence others to jail. He believed nothing was beyond his competence or his province. On these trips he broadcast over his portable radio advice on cooking, fishing, engineering, military science, history, economics, and any other subject that came to mind.[45]

In retrospect these actions appear somewhat comical, but for the contemporary Guatemalan people Ubico's rule was anything but a laughing matter. In the words of Ronald Schneider, he was "impulsive, arbitrary, stubborn, opinionated, dominating, energetic, and inflexible . . . a policeman at heart."[46] Ubico's foremost biographer, Kenneth Grieb, writes that he tended to personalize all disputes, becoming vengeful and evoking the popular image of a wild and dangerous beast. According to Guatemalan folklore, Ubico once casually complained to his minister of war that Guatemala no longer had any brave men. The sycophantic official immediately relayed this message to the director of the military academy, who boasted that he could produce ten young cadets who would eagerly uphold the honor of Guatemala's manhood. Ubico ordered the volunteers to come to the National Palace. Without so much as a greeting, he peremptorily directed them to his fleet of limousines so they could proceed to the national zoo. There, he told them to enter the lions' cage. They dutifully obeyed, although clearly frightened by the growling animals surrounding them. At this point, the tale continues, the general-president scoffed at the young men and jumped into the cage himself, gleefully kicking and shouting at the lions until each terrified animal was cowering in the corner. Ubico then stalked out, deriding the cadets for their cowardice. Such folklore contained didactic implications for the Guatemalans.[47]

Extremely conservative, Ubico called anyone a Communist whose social, economic, and political ideologies were more progressive than his own, and he equated Communism with any disobedience to his laws or opposition to his regime. He claimed that the presence of such radicals threatened Guatemala's stability and well-being and that the maintenance of order required that he continue to rule. For Ubico democracy was an unaffordable luxury. He felt that the people could too easily be swayed by radical agitators; he trusted only the army, wealthy indigenous landowners, and foreign corporations. Always on guard against a revolution, he ordered steel shutters for every window of the presidential palace, a uniformed guard for each corner, and an antiaircraft battery and army barracks to surround the palace. He also had his initials stamped on all the government's ammunition, warning publicly that anyone who attacked him or any of his officials would carry his personal emblem into eternity.[48]

As 1944 would prove, Ubico correctly analyzed that, even with his ironfisted control of the state's military apparatus, he would be powerless against a full-blown popular uprising. His loyal following was just too small. His ability to maintain power, therefore, rested on preventing any uprising from becoming widespread. His strategy depended on instilling terror among the people. He knew that his public warnings and heavily garrisoned domicile would frighten many of his subjects, as would the folklore which he carefully cultivated, but he believed that there would be some who required more emphatic discouragement. More frequently than any of his predecessors, Ubico announced the uncovering of subversive plots and the execution of the alleged conspirators. The brutal tactics practiced in his prisons in order to extract confessions from unfortunate suspects were common knowledge in Guatemala. In 1934, in power but three years, Ubico dispelled any doubts as to his determination by ordering the arrest of scores of students, workers, and prominent citizens, charging them with conspiring against his government. Many of these were seized in their homes and summarily killed on the spot. Others confessed after being tortured in prisons, and then they were likewise executed. Even those Guatemalans in the most rural regions, who were normally ignorant of and unconcerned with events in Guatemala City, remembered the events of 1934. The well-known writer Jorge García Granados, later Arévalo's ambassador to the United States, managed to survive the ordeal and flee to Mexico. He described his experience:

> In 1934 [Ubico] uncovered a conspiracy against him . . . Seventeen men were seized, given a farcical trial in which they were not even permitted defense attorneys, and sentenced then to be shot. Although I had no part in the conspiracy, I wrote to Ubico a strong letter charging that the trial was a mockery of the law, and urging him to pardon the condemned.
>
> Ubico replied by sending a squad of police to arrest me in my home, take me to the place of execution, and force me to be an eyewitness to the shooting of the seventeen. Then I was thrown into prison and held in solitary confinement for months.[49]

Linked with his fear of political radicalism was Ubico's conviction that general prosperity bred revolution. He once commented that "if people have money, they will kick me out,"[50] and he characteristically opposed all forms of labor activity. Initially organized in 1921, within a decade Guatemalan unions had become affiliated with the Workers Confederation of Pan-American Labor, a non-Communist movement of Latin American labor leaders based in New York City. Viewed by Ubico as a threat, the unions disbanded during the 1930s, unable to withstand consistent charges of committing treason, of conspiring to commit treason, and sometimes of merely insulting the general-president. The official penal code contained a clause recommending the death penalty for anyone found guilty of union organizing. Nevertheless, there were those who continued labor's struggle. Hoping to take advantage of the economic collapse caused by World War II, they began a concerted effort to demand increased wages. Ubico complained to President Roosevelt, writing that a possible strike would certainly affect Guatemala's defense plants and hurt the war effort. Roosevelt did not respond, possibly because Guatemala's contribution to the Allied cause was as a base for overseas missions, not as a provider of material, but more probably because Ubico's complaints hardly disguised the fact that he feared his own workers as much as he feared the Germans or Japanese. Ubico wrote, "[The workers'] attitudes, adopted collectively, with such lamentable results because of their economic repercussions in time of peace, are still more lamentable in time of war."[51]

Although none of the labor leaders was an Indian, the Maya did comprise the majority of Guatemala's labor force, particularly as unskilled workers, so common in the agrarian economy. The Indians bore a special grudge against Ubico, for he singled them out as a target of discrimination, apprehending and punishing them for minor infractions of the law much more often than the non-Indian population. He also pressed them into a variety of so-called voluntary services, such as carrying the mail from the department capital and acting as messenger boys, and only the Maya were subject to conscription in the army and forced to participate in martial drills each Sunday morning. Ubico rationalized this last requirement by explaining that the Indians were "rude, brutish and with primitive origins."[52] The Maya must understand, he contended, that military training was not a punishment but an educational process which would transform them from this "animal-like" condition into "civilized" individuals, with better personal equipment with which to face life.[53] The Indians did not accept this explanation, and in 1944 they deserted the military en masse.

Ubico had further antagonized the Indian population by removing their last vestiges of self-control. Prior to his regime, the Maya had retained some voice in their own affairs by having representatives in the local government. Normally there had been two *alcaldes*, or mayors, in each village, with a Maya responsible for his people's problems. The Indian *alcalde* might not have had the same influence as his *ladino* counterpart, but at least he administered the purely Indian programs. Immediately upon taking power in 1931, Ubico replaced this dual system with a single *ladino intendente*. This official wielded absolute authority, dictating his orders to all the town's inhabitants, none of whom had any opportunity to express opposition. Any Maya still wishing to participate in the government structure had to accept the role of a minor functionary.[54]

Coupled with such political and social discrimination were Ubico's economic policies, which placed the Indian in an even more vulnerable position than previously. These policies came in the form of the *vialidad* system and vagrancy laws. Their provisions forced those male Indians who could not afford to pay a head tax, which meant practically all of them, to work without wages on road construction. The duration of this forced labor, depending on the individual's financial status, varied from two weeks to one month. The law also required each Indian, even if he were not in debt, to carry a *libreto*, or government book, proving that he had worked for wages a minimum of 150 days per year. Had he not met this quota by the year's end, he would have either been imprisoned as a vagrant or compelled to work on the roads until the fixed number of days was attained. Indians who were in debt did not receive wages at all; their pay was simply deducted from their debt. Since most Indians worked for wages only during the busy harvest season, the state was assured a cheap, in fact a free, labor force for its public works program.[55]

With the onset of World War II and the deepening fiscal crisis in Guatemala, Ubico's program of social, political, and economic repression made his position untenable. As early as 1940 Secretary of State Cordell Hull received a "strictly confidential" departmental memorandum from the United States ambassador to Guatemala, stating that "the president [Ubico] has been so arbitrary, impatient, and grasping in many of his recent acts that a certain amount of resentment has undoubtedly been awakened."[56] Two years later three Guatemalan liberals tried to persuade the Inter-American Congress convening at Rio de Janeiro to recognize their plight. They wrote to the Argentine delegate that Ubico "is not a democratic ruler" and that he "keeps himself in the presidency against the law and against popular sentiment." For the Allies to send him military aid, they continued, would be "truly treason and [would] deceive the miserable public."[57]

Ubico's response to the growing crisis made the situation worse. He ordered widespread arrests of prominent citizens, causing political tension to reach its "highest peak in recent years."[58] He tried to shore up the faltering economy by adopting such deflationary policies as restricting bank credit and balancing the budget. The result was increased unemployment. While the people suffered, he continued to draw his monthly salary, his monthly pension, his monthly entertainment allowance, his monthly food allowance, his monthly "miscellaneous" allowance, and even his monthly allowance for the upkeep of his personal horses. Then, as if this total of more than $215,000 per year were not enough, he blatantly accepted a $20,000 gift and used it to buy up many properties at a price he fixed himself.

In 1941, he also prompted a constitutional congress to extend his term for eight more years, indicative of his intention to rule for life.[59]

For the Guatemalan people, the final straw seems to have come in May 1944, when, in the midst of the mounting dissatisfaction, Ubico issued Decree 2795, which extended the 1935 *ley fuega*. This executive order granted landowners the legal authority to shoot on sight any indigent, which meant any Indian, found hunting for food on private land. Desperate, Ubico hoped that this act would please Guatemala's upper crust to the extent that they would safeguard his regime at all costs. He was not confident of its success, however, for simultaneously he transferred in his wife's name, $50,000 to the Bank of London and South America and ordered his private secretary to destroy all personal and confidential records.[60] A month later the revolution began.

THE OCTOBER REVOLUTION

Ubico's thirteen-year reputation as an authoritarian despot played a significant role in his downfall. Unlike some of the other Latin American leaders, he did not hesitate to declare war against the Axis Powers in December 1941, nor was he reluctant to permit the establishment of a United States air base in Guatemala in order to protect the Panama Canal. But his close cooperation with the Allies did not dissuade many Guatemalans, the liberal intellectuals in particular, from pointedly identifying their president-general with Hitler and Mussolini. As the war progressed, their antagonism toward his authority grew apace. They found in the Atlantic Charter, with its idealistic principles and sublime universal promises, a theoretical framework to guide their struggle against oppression. These dissidents paid special attention to the aspects of the charter which emphasized the universal rights of all individuals and the primacy of democratic institutions. They found it incongruous to permit their country to continue under a government based on fear, misery, and terror after so much blood had been spilled in the global fight against fascism.[61]

Although some United States officials would later claim that Communists inspired the revolution, in truth the liberal middle class and intellectuals provided its impetus. As accurately described by the Guatemalan Manuel Galich, the overthrow of Ubico was another French Revolution under contemporary conditions.[62] That the Guatemalan middle class was relatively small, consisting primarily of students, intellectuals, professionals, small shopkeepers and artisans, underpaid public officials, and junior army officers, and that it consequently depended on the urban and agricultural workers for its support must not obscure the revolution's fundamental nature. In a large part the leaders' forebears were the *ladinos* who had acquired power during the previously described nineteenth-century liberal era, and, like them, the revolutionary leadership promoted bourgeois, not Communist, reforms.[63]

Although its ideology was nonradical, the revolution's leadership did intend to change *for the first time* since independence Guatemala's social, economic, and political class structure. The middle class, squeezed between "the financially powerful upper class and the masses of unscrubbed and unlettered Indians," had long been frustrated by the country's lack of political freedom and economic opportunities.[64] They perceived themselves as speaking for all the hitherto unrepresented segments of society.[65] Although the United States–directed coup thwarted the developing programs, the changes that evolved from the government policies from 1944 to 1954 were substantially more profound than any Guatemala had experienced previously or has experienced since.

Contrary to subsequent attacks upon their character and objectives, the proponents of change in Guatemala did not espouse an overarching philosophy or ideology. There was no single leader or general, nor was there even a coherent body of literature on which the revolutionaries founded their ideas. But it was not merely a romantic movement either. In spite of the absence of a definitive conception of the future, the leadership possessed an inherent program, one which can be summarized as the liquidation of the semifeudal state dependent on the external economies of expansion, the organization of a modern capitalist system, and the rearrangement and revitalization of the social structure. In other words, while specific tactics and strategies were not yet articulated, there was, in the general sense, an overall objective: to modernize and to democratize Guatemala in order to overcome the traditional barriers.[66]

The events of Ubico's ouster can be related quite briefly.[67] In May 1944, nearby El Salvador's dictatorial President Maximiliano Hernández Martínez, who had attained power virtually at the same time as Ubico, resigned amidst violent discontent. Students and young military officers led the opposition. The same month, Ubico witnessed the overthrow of another Latin American ruler, Ecuador's Carlos Arroyo del Río, who was forced by a military junta to relinquish his power to José María Velasco Ibarra. Fearing that these developments might spill over into Guatemala and encourage the revolutionaries within his own country, Ubico increased his control by even more authoritarian methods. He sought to eliminate dissension in the potential centers for insurrection, especially the university in Guatemala City. The academic community vocalized its opposition to his government more stridently than any other sector of society, and it had emphatically proven in El Salvador that it could be a very potent factor in bringing about political change.[68] Therefore, Ubico placed his own followers in high positions within the university structure, suspended constitutional guarantees, and rounded up many of the agitators, especially those on the faculty. Among the persecuted were some of the most prestigious intellectuals found in Guatemala, such as Mario Mendez Montenegro, Manuel Galich, and Alfonso Bauer Paíz, all of whom later played important roles in the Arévalo and Arbenz governments.[69]

Ubico's repressive measures served only to animate student resistance. They resented his attacks on their faculty, and they fully realized that his reactions signified that he feared the growing movement. Rather than being intimidated, the students became even more resolute and bold. On June 23 they presented the dictator with an ultimatum, demanding the university's complete autonomy within twenty-four hours. They held meetings in the streets outside the National Palace and organized marches. Ubico responded by ordering the armed forces to fire on the demonstrators and by placing Guatemala City under martial law. Subsequently, he extended the edict throughout the country. What had begun as a localized and small-scale student movement became a national phenomenon, with lawyers, merchants, and other groups joining the protesters. The leadership called a general strike; people closed their shops, movie theaters shut down, and even some churches locked their doors. Finally, the army, faced with such united opposition, refused to obey Ubico's commands. Within a week, on July 1, he resigned. United States Ambassador Boaz Long had been accurate when he wrote to Secretary of State Hull on June 23, "I do not take an alarmist view of the situation, but the government is known to be nervous and there is a widespread belief that a climax may be approached by June 30 or soon thereafter."[70]

The downfall of Ubico was only the initial step in the ultimate establishment of the revolution. The general-president actually intended to resign the night before, turning the presidency over to General Roderico Anzueto, the former director of police, as a form of trust. However, his advisers convinced him that Anzueto, widely accused of pro-Nazi sentiments, was very unpopular and could not command the support of the army. Concerned that Anzueto might be forced to yield to someone with whom he would have no influence, Ubico consulted with the army's general staff and selected a triumvirate of Major General Buenaventura Piñeda, Major General Eduardo Villagrán Ariza, and General Federico Ponce Vaides to form a new government. This directory promised to convene the National Assembly in order to elect a provisional president. But, as soon as the congresss met on July 3, armed soldiers invaded the hall and dispersed the congressmen. The following day the military leaders summoned the elected officials to the presidential palace and ordered them to vote for Ponce, not for the more popular civilian candidate, Dr. Ramón Calderón. An eyewitness reported to Secretary Hull that, had the electors refused, they certainly would have been "wiped out by the machine guns." Ponce won by an overwhelming majority.[71]

Although Ponce pledged free national elections at an early date, it soon became apparent that he had little intention of holding them; in any event, had he held them, they would have been anything but free. The new regime masqueraded as a legitimate government, but it was merely a pale reflection of the old. Ponce resembled an old skeleton more than a general, having retired years before due to alcoholism. Referred to by a Guatemalan historian as the "Executor of Ubiquism," he transparently took orders from his former chief, who remained in Guatemala, contentedly directing state affairs from the background. Ponce retained in powerful positions many officials who were formerly involved in the Ubico administration, including the minister of foreign relations, José Luis Cruz Salazar, considered by some people at that time to be the most detested individual in the country.[72]

Within a short time the new government dropped all pretense of democracy. It reimposed rigid press censorship, and the mass imprisonments and floggings began anew. Among a great many others, such well-known people as the president of the Association of University Students, the organizer of the Civic Union, and the leader of the National Workers' party were arbitrarily arrested. The government forced the peasants to demonstrate in favor of their new leader and pledged them abundant land for their support. With this last promise, Ponce threatened to unleash a racial war, for he claimed that the only group coming between the Indians and the land confiscated from the Germans during the war was the *ladino* middle class.[73]

In the meantime, the economy continued to falter as unemployment and prices climbed steadily. Opposition groups began to form again, with students and intellectuals reassuming the lead. This time, however, many political and military leaders immediately joined forces, for they understood Ponce's charade and resented their exclusion from the provisional government. They also questioned the constitutionality of the regime, since Guatemalan law stipulated that a leader of a coup d'état was ineligible for the presidency. Among the dissident military leaders was Jacobo Arbenz Guzmán, elected the revolutionary government's second president in 1950. Ubico had fired Arbenz from his post at the Escuela Politécnica, Guatemala's West Point. Since that time Arbenz had been in El Salvador, organizing a band of revolutionary exiles. One of the officers following him to El Salvador was Major Francisco Javier Araña, later to become his chief rival for the presidency.[74]

The precipitating event in the next stage of the revolution came at dawn on October 1, when Alejandro Córdova, the proprietor and editor of the leading daily newspaper, *El Imparcial*, was assassinated in front of his home. Córdova, at one time a staunch supporter of Ubico, had become a vociferous critic of the government. There was also some talk of his possible involvement in another coup, rumored to be under preparation by Ponce's minister of war. When the assassins were captured, they would say only that they were complying with orders from superiors, but many discontented Guatemalans assumed that the murder had been planned in the National Palace and attributed primary responsibility to Ponce and his director of police. The indignation that spread throughout the cities put Guatemala into a state of revolutionary turmoil once more.[75]

Ponce immediately dispatched trucks into the countryside to collect and bring back to Guatemala City many *campesinos* armed with machetes. He then ordered the *campesinos* to march through the streets with pictures of himself attached to their clothes, supposedly demonstrating to the urban populace that the country's majority was on his side. For emphasis, Ponce later transported these peasants to a national *finca* outside the city, where they remained as a constant threat to those in the capital. Lest the Indians forget whom they supported, he sent them truckloads of liquor. Soon after his overthrow, United States observers found many of these Indians dead of poison.[76]

Ponce's tactics of terror were no more effective than had been Ubico's a few months earlier. Even before Córdova's assassination, the situation had become so tense in Guatemala City that stores closed early, their windows barred tightly shut. The United States military attaché reported that Ponce would probably stage some type of incident as an excuse to institute martial law.[77] Then, on the morning of October 19, a small group of army officers led by Arbenz and Araña, along with their student allies, attacked the National Palace. The next day the Honor Guard Battalion (Guatemala's National Guard) revolted. There was little artillery fire, but the rebels' barrage did manage to hit the government's main ammunition arsenal. Badly frightened, Ponce sent an urgent message to the longtime president of Honduras, Tiburcio Carías Andino, requesting a loan of all available aircraft. Carías regretfully replied that conditions in Honduras prevented his compliance and that, furthermore, the lend-lease agreement with the United States prohibited the transfer of military equipment.[78] The United States likewise refused assistance.[79] Never known for his courage, the old general decided to wait no longer. The next day the Mexican embassy granted his request for asylum.

Ponce's capitulation signaled the true end to Ubico's rule. Ubico, following him into exile, found a home in New Orleans by November. There, quite ill, he lived until his death on June 14, 1946, preoccupied (as was his wife after his death) with trying to recover his money and property confiscated by the revolutionary government.[80] Ironically, under the circumstances, Ponce continued the counter-revolutionary struggle. He appealed to President Roosevelt from Mexico City, arguing that the Germans had engineered the coup in an attempt to destroy hemispheric unity and to hinder the transfer of raw materials from South to North America. Secretary of State Hull replied that the United States had no intention of interfering in Guatemala's internal affairs. Ponce thereafter remained in Central America until 1954, organizing antigovernment exiles and claiming that he still maintained the support of the Guatemalan people.[81]

But Ponce had never had the support of the people. It cost the lives of fewer than one hundred men to accomplish his overthrow, and the United States military station in Guatemala reported that "revolutionary troops and civilians continue maintain order with full popular cooperation. This order and calm noteworthy as past army police domination not present."[82] The October revolution was a popular victory, and thousands of Guatemalans spontaneously marched down the streets of the capital, cheering what they hoped was the advent of a new era. The new junta abolished the Court of Instruction, which under Ubico and Ponce had been the institutionalized form for the system of torture, promised a democratic election, and revoked the old constitution in order to write a new one.[83] The overwhelming majority of the Guatemalan people felt that this had been *their* revolution and anticipated a new government dedicated to developing programs in *their* interests. They began the new era by electing Juan José Arévalo Bermej the revolution's first president.

3. The Revolutionary Governments: Communism or Nationalism?

The composition of the junta that preceded Arévalo's election reflected the social and political base of the October revolutionary movement. Arbenz and Araña made up two-thirds of the governing triumvirate. Each had been prominent in the overthrows of both Ubico and Ponce, each came from a middle-class background, and each had the allegiance of the military. This last qualification was essential since, historically, military support has been decisive in the success of Latin American governments.[1] The third member of the junta, however, was a civilian, Jorge Toriello. Toriello's selection signified that, unlike Ponce's junta, the new government was not merely an instance of one military faction replacing another.

JUAN JOSÉ ARÉVALO

The national election conducted before the end of the year was indicative of the revolution's democratic character. That the promised election was held at all was a good portent, for previous administrations had repeatedly reneged on such pledges. Departing from past practices, not one of the junta members sought office himself, and two decades later an American University study group termed the event "the first free election in Guatemala's history."[2] The designation "free" does not mean that everyone participated, and it must be noted that the Indian vote was quite small. But, even when they had previously enjoyed the franchise, the Maya had traditionally chosen to remain outside Guatemala's political arena, having been led to the polls only by bribes or an army escort.[3]

The election soon came down to a contest between two candidates, neither of whom represented the military. Arévalo was, from the beginning, the popular movement's favorite. His victory, in the words of United States Ambassador Boaz Long, was "almost certain."[4] Long might have omitted the word "almost." Not only was Arévalo by himself the strongest candidate, but there were four others splitting the opposition vote. Adrián Recinos, who for some fifteen years had been Guatemala's ambassador to the United States, emerged as Arévalo's chief challenger. A conservative closely identified with the Ubico regime, Recinos gathered around him most of the elements of the old guard. He never sympathized with the revolution's objectives (in 1954 he would head Castillo Armas' delegation to the United Nations) and had no chance of upsetting the movement's candidate. When the ballots were tabulated on the night of December 19, 1944, Arévalo won in a landslide. His total vote was greater than four times that of his combined opposition. Although this margin indicates a lopsided election, it also suggests a competitive campaign compared with prior ones. For example, Ubico won his last triumph by a vote of over 308,000 to 0.[5]

Jacobo Arbenz's preeminent place in the extant literature on the Guatemalan revolution is to be expected, since his controversial programs precipitated Castillo Armas' invasion. But the Arbenz administration, indeed the whole revolution, is incomprehensible without an analysis of Juan José Arévalo. As the revolution's first president and, in many respects, its intellectual font, Arévalo set the tone for the next ten years. His election incarnated the movement's intentions, for he personified change, liberalism, and democracy. His relative anonymity in the United States government underscored his appeal to the Guatemalans—Arévalo was a civilian without previous associations with dictatorships or militarism. Perhaps most important, his background suggested that, unlike his predecessors, he would not seek to maneuver himself into a position of absolute authority.[6]

Born in 1904 into a middle-class family, Arévalo was an educator and an intellectual. After receiving his doctorate in philosophy and the science of education from the University of La Plata in Argentina, he returned to Guatemala in 1934 to work within the Ministry of Public Education. However, his outspoken criticism of Ubico necessitated his going into self-imposed exile in 1935, so he went back to Argentina to accept a faculty position at the University of Tucumán. During this time he published a number of works dealing with the psychology of development and the concept of social integration. Hence he was absent from Guatemala throughout most of the unpopular Ubico regime and avoided any identification with it. He did return to Guatemala following the initial stage of the revolution, one week before his fortieth birthday, but Ponce forced him once again into hiding. He emerged after the October revolution, and the movement's leadership quickly selected him as their presidential candidate. His inauguration on March 15, 1945, marked the beginning of a new era in Guatemalan politics, an era of social and economic reform.[7]

Arévalo's nonmilitary background and lengthy absence from his homeland were not the only determinants in his election. Nor should one overemphasize his appeal as a campaigner, although he was a dynamic and articulate speaker, capable of capturing the Guatemalans' imagination. The essence of Arévalo's popularity derived from his ideas. Above all he was a democrat; he believed democracy to be the crucial component in human progress and relationships. Long before he became president, Arévalo's extensive writings were well known within Guatemala's literate community, the foundation of the movement for reform. His primary concern was with the potential of each individual, with constructing a government program that accounted for the diverse needs of all Guatemalans—Indians and non-Indians. During his campaign, aware that only a small minority had read his books, he continually reiterated these moralizing concepts. If, as one sympathizer remarked, Arévalo was too idealistic, a sort of contemporary Don Quixote, his idealism coincided with the revolutionary fervor so prevalent in his country.[8]

As opposed to "ubiquism," "arévalism" was not a political machine but a vigorous popular movement proposing to liberate the citizens from rigid authoritarianism and, subsequently, to free Guatemala from its dependence on the more developed nations. An early foe of fascism, which he believed surfaced in Central and South America more than a century before Hitler and Mussolini, Arévalo asserted over and over again that the government of Guatemala must be run for the people and by the people. This philosophy might sound somewhat trite by North American standards, but it was alien to Guatemala's entire political history. To Arévalo, the death of European and Asiatic fascism signaled the beginning of the death of fascism in Latin America and, concurrent with the October revolution, the beginning of Guatemala's salvation. His would be a government of peace, of work, of material and spiritual prosperity: an expression of the people's free will.[9] He used these words, and they do sound like idealistic rhetoric. Yet Arévalo was not a politician, and his administration revealed his intention to put theory into practice.

Whereas Arévalo's political philosophy started from this North American perspective, he added to it a number of less familiar concepts, which, along with the programs they spawned, initially made some United States observers uneasy and soon made almost all of them critical. Arévalo conceived of the state as an aggregation of collective interests and values; he viewed the function of government within a democratic society as serving equally the individual and the collectivity. He did not take it for granted that an individual's gain necessarily implied society's gain. He stressed that all citizens must control their own future, but he did not stress the primacy of the individual. To Arévalo, the foundation of human development was freedom, but a freedom that coincided with the aspirations of the community. Democracy was a social, not an individual, system.[10]

The president warned that particular interests must not become obstacles to the necessities and progress of society as a whole. Political rights must complement social, cultural, and economic objectives, and to assure justice and harmony individual liberty must be exercised only within the limits of social order. Arévalo went so far as to state that, if necessary, civil rights might have to be restricted to protect majority rights and national security.[11]

Arévalo's willingness to subordinate civil rights to societal requisites seems to contradict his dedication to establishing a government that expressed the people's free will. Indeed, there was a statist component of his philosophy. The apparent paradox stemmed from his rejection of classical Western liberalism or, at least, his rejection of its applicability to Guatemala. Arévalo believed that to develop their potential the backward Guatemalans, especially the Maya, needed the assistance that only government could provide. Government intervention in the country's economic and social life would create the conditions necessary for the expression of the majority's free will. Such thinking reflects a certain romanticism, yet it was a romanticism firmly rooted in Latin America's intellectual tradition.[12]

Arévalo likewise rejected classical Marxism. He used phrases like "socialist mentality," but only to convey that each citizen had a responsibility to Guatemala and that the government had a responsibility to each citizen. He rejected class struggle and emphasized the ideal of social harmony, fraternity, and the reconciliation of antagonistic interests. He found the Marxist concept that human nature is essentially materially predetermined either invalid or, at the very least, extremely limited, and he believed that a genuinely democratic government must represent the legitimate aspirations of all classes: the capitalists, the professionals, and the workers. Property rights must be respected, as long as they are always subordinated to the social necessities and interests of the nation as a whole. Arévalo never supported the confiscation of private property; rather, he recommended reform of the capitalist system so that production would be more beneficial to society and improve the situation of the working majority.[13]

Arévalo called himself a socialist, but he defined his philosophy as "spiritual socialism." Again taking issue with traditional Marxists, he opposed the "ingenuous distribution of material goods for the silly economic leveling of men who are economically different."[14] Spiritual socialism was concerned primarily with what he described as "the psychological freedom of the individual." He wanted to develop within all Guatemalans the "psychological and moral integrity" which he believed had been neglected by both conservatives and liberals in the past. In more specific terms, this meant that all citizens should have the right to their own thinking, their own property, and their own way of life. If the government could guarantee these rights, he believed Guatemalans would then have faith in their institutions and each other, allowing for the development of a harmonious and progressive society.[15]

THE ARÉVALO ADMINISTRATION

Arévalo explicitly espoused his views on the individual, society, and the role of government in his early writings and throughout the electoral campaign. Perhaps because they sounded vague and idealistic, they did not seem to frighten many in the United States. Even during this early cold war period, analysts tended to overlook Arévalo's socialism, perceiving him as some kind of starry-eyed reformer. Yet these views became the cornerstones for the specific programs developed during Arévalo's presidency, as well as for those of his successor, Jacobo Arbenz. Arévalo had mentioned virtually every one of these programs in his 1944 campaign; there was no radical shift to the left, as commentators would later write. As the revolutionary program progressed, it necessarily threatened traditional interests, among which were those of the United Fruit Company. When this happened, United States observers took another look at spiritual socialism and this time interpreted it as radical Communism. Guatemala became a threat to the Free World.

Guatemala's National Assembly ratified the new constitution soon after Arévalo's inauguration. A progressive statement reflecting most of the president's ideas, it contained over sixty provisions for strengthening the democratic process, for initiating social reform, and for establishing governmental agencies and programs. Drawing on the theories of Montesquieu, Thomas Jefferson, and others, the framers emphasized a decentralization of power, a shift away from "monostructure," or the *caudillo* system, with all the power vested in the executive, to a "polistructure," which divided authority among the executive, legislature, and judiciary. The new constitution granted universal suffrage to all adults, except illiterate women, and guaranteed freedom of speech, the press, and assembly. There were even provisions for the organization and free functioning of political parties—except Communist and other "foreign or international" parties—thereby encouraging a greater choice in the elections. To many liberal commentators the 1945 constitution was the most enlightened throughout Latin America, with its system of checks and balances safeguarding against the types of abuse so characteristic of Guatemala's political tradition.[16]

The administration's international outlook also reflected the government's emphasis on democracy and reform. Warning of future developments, some of its foreign policies conflicted with the objectives of its neighbors and the United States. One of President Arévalo's initial acts was to break diplomatic relations with Spain, and he soon launched an all-out effort to eradicate dictatorships in both Central and South America. At the inter-American conference on problems of war and peace, held at Chapultepec, Mexico, the month before Arévalo's inauguration, the Guatemalan delegation recommended to the American republics that "they abstain from recognizing and maintaining relations with anti-democratic regimes . . . especially with regimes which might come to power through a *coup d'état* against a democratically elected government legitimately constituted." Many of the conference's voting members were themselves dictatorships and, therefore, could not accept such a recommendation. In response Guatemala severed relations with the two most notorious authoritarian governments—those of Anastasio Somoza in Nicaragua and Rafael Leonidas Trujillo Molina in the Dominican Republic. Arévalo explained, "While we should not meddle in the internal affairs of countries . . . we cannot be forced to maintain friendship with governments that have transformed republican practices into those of monarchy."[17]

At the ninth International Conference of American States in Bogotá the following year, Guatemala again proposed that democracy in America be "defended and preserved in the face of the establishment of anti-democratic regimes in the Western Hemisphere," but the Latin American dictatorships once more defeated the effort. Frustrated by its failure to get satisfactory results through such legitimate channels, the Arévalo government began supporting the recently organized Caribbean Legion. Founded by a group of radical democrats, the legion sought to oust the existing dictatorships, by force if necessary. Its membership consisted primarily of Nicaraguan and Dominican exiles, with some British and United States zealots, and, although it rarely totaled more than 125 individuals, it did have some impact. It contributed to the 1948 military overthrow of Teodoro Picado in Costa Rica[18] and generally created concern among all Central American and Caribbean *caudillos*, who reacted by branding the legion and its supporters—including Arévalo—as Communist. Officials in Truman's State Department would not go this far. They did feel, however, that Arévalo's policies encouraged the chaotic conditions which promoted Communist influence and that the support of the Caribbean Legion was "inconsistent with United States objectives."[19]

Perhaps Arévalo can justifiably be criticized for interfering in the affairs of his neighbors. Yet the Central American dictatorships also deserve criticism, because they actively strove to undermine the Arévalo administration from its inception. Guatemalan leaders believed that the welfare of the revolution required more sympathetic governments on Guatemala's borders. Additionally, Arévalo advocated the creation of a Central American union. He felt that Guatemala could not progress divided from those countries with which it had natural and historical ties. A confederation would both lessen the opportunity for a single ruler to obtain excessive authority and offer economic remedies by facilitating the interchange of products and the establishment of common industries. Political and economic cooperation would provide the best protection against domestic instability and foreign domination. Each country would benefit immeasurably while losing nothing, for each would maintain its autonomous congress and fundamental institution. Since Arévalo predicted that the power-hungry dictators would never permit such a union, he sought their elimination.[20]

The resurrection of the Central American federation figured prominently in Arévalo's inaugural address, and he quickly tried to find support for his project outside of Guatemala. In May 1945 he traveled to San Cristóbal, El Salvador, to discuss the possibilities with President Castañeda Castro. He invited the other Central American nations, but they declined. Accompanying Arévalo were both Arbenz and Araña, already considered the two most likely candidates to become Guatemala's next president. Castro was receptive to the idea. He and Arévalo appointed a temporary federal council to set up technical committees in order to work out the details. The council's first step was to establish a mechanism for economic cooperation, for its members felt that such a move would make political unification easier. Experts from both nations recommended the removal of all customs barriers, the elimination of immigration restrictions, and the merger of the banking, other monetary, and educational systems. Both governments approved the recommendations, and a month later Arévalo and Castro jointly announced that the five million citizens of Guatemala and El Salvador, more than half the population of Central America, would combine to form a single political unit. They intended their agreement to be formalized within the United Nations, but developments never reached this stage. Difficulties within each of the nations delayed effective action, and in 1948 the Castro government fell to a military junta led by Oscar Osorio. This was the closest Arévalo ever came to realizing his dream of union, although he never abandoned the idea altogether.[21]

While Arévalo felt that a Central American confederation was the ultimate solution to Guatemalan underdevelopment, he fully understood that the country's conditions required immediate attention. His campaign platform promised an active program of social, economic, and political reform, including an end to the persistent exploitation of the Indian majority. Although emphasizing that change would be gradual, Arévalo left no doubt that it would be far-reaching and based on government participation and supervision. His program, nevertheless, received support from leading capitalist economists. For example, partway through his administration, he invited the International Bank for Reconstruction and Development (IBRD) to tour the country and make policy recommendations. The mission, headed by Canadian economist George Britnell, concluded that "under existing circumstances the state must assume the major role in the advancement of the underdeveloped segments of the Guatemalan economy." These existing circumstances—an underdeveloped economy and widespread poverty—created the need for government guidance.[22]

Accepting the government's responsibility for Guatemala's economic progress, the Arévalo administration immediately established agencies to promote reform. The framers of the 1945 constitution established the Ministry of Economy and Labor and the Department of Cooperative Development, launching an active program to develop the country's productive potential. Soon afterward the government set up the Bank of Guatemala and the Institute for the Development of Production. Their purpose was to diversify Guatemala's economic base by providing financial stimulation and agricultural assistance, primarily in the form of accessible credit, and by, for the first time, encouraging technological and industrial growth. Funded by the government, the institute conducted experiments, studied new systems of credit, and statistically examined the various sectors of the economy.[23]

Arévalo and his subordinates were well aware that his interventionist government activity might lead to charges of Communism, and they therefore made a concerted effort to avert such criticism. For example, when it announced the creation of the Institute for the Development of Production, the administration was most explicit about its objective: the institute's purpose was to "promote the agricultural and industrial development of the country by the direct action of the state and the participation of private enterprise, which must be the determining stimulus."[24] Also, contrary to traditional Communist practices, the government stated its intention to leave foreign investments intact. The goal was economic reform, but the administration publicly asserted that Guatemala would encourage outside capital to continue to flow into the country. Arévalo perceived foreign investment and expertise as a vital component of his program for achieving economic development.[25]

Any program to reform the economic structure in Guatemala had to concentrate on the agricultural sphere, which, as has been pointed out, was among the least satisfactory in Latin America. Agrarian reform in an underdeveloped nation is mandatory in order to raise the standard of living and the purchasing power of the populace, to free a sufficient number of rural laborers so that they can form the basis of an industrial work force, and to produce enough food to sustain growing urban centers. In short, agrarian reform is a prerequisite for industrialization. It was for this reason that Arévalo requested IBRD advice and that IBRD president John J. McCloy recommended that a study mission be sent.[26]

The government immediately addressed the problem of the country's agricultural system. The constitution of 1945 contained provisions to restrict the growth of *latifundios* and to formally nationalize the German plantations that had been confiscated during World War II. These properties would be rented out to individuals, cooperatives, or joint-stock companies, thereby providing employment for thousands of workers and affording opportunities for experimentation and diversification. The administration organized technical services for farmers, promoted legislation to support soil and forest conservation, and established research centers to study commodities such as wheat, corn, and sugarcane. The National Assembly sponsored programs enabling Guatemalans to learn modern techniques in the United States. State-financed farms provided scientists with laboratories to develop improved breeds of horses, mules, cows, and other livestock. The legislature created the Commission of Agricultural Studies, which made general tax lists of rural and municipal property; studied the annual internal migration of day laborers; compiled bibliographies of works concerning agrarian reform in

England, France, and Spain; critiqued agrarian reform in Romania, Italy, and Mexico; and investigated Guatemala's agricultural production and export industry. The most radical measure was the Law of Forced Rental, which sought to control land rents and to compel large landowners to rent uncultivated lands at rates not to exceed 5 percent of the value of the crops produced. All these programs were in addition to those of the Bank of Guatemala and the Institute for the Development of Production.[27]

In a nation with as large an agricultural problem as Guatemala's, these programs, however impressive, hardly scratched the surface. Arévalo, as the president of the initial revolutionary government, had to concern himself with so many diverse aspects of Guatemalan life that he could not concentrate on agrarian reform to the extent that he might have liked. Perhaps he also feared doing too much too soon, possibly alienating some of the economic sectors whose support he needed for his entire program. Arévalo realized that certain interest groups, the large landlords in particular, would be hostile to even the most moderate reforms, and hence the middle groups would play a significant role in insuring against a conservative backlash. These factors, along with bureaucratic inefficiency, made the evolution and implementation of a broad reform difficult. Arévalo's agrarian program proceeded only in fits and starts, and invariably its measures fell short of their objectives. It was left to Arbenz to enact more comprehensive legislation.[28] Arévalo did, nevertheless, lay the groundwork for the 1952 agrarian reform bill and, in doing so, dramatically altered the course of Guatemala's social, economic, and political development.

The vast agricultural enterprises employed most of Guatemala's workers, so that agrarian and labor reform were inextricably intertwined. For the first time in Guatemala's history, the government passed laws to protect employees. The new constitution abolished the vagrancy laws and all other forms of forced labor, and in December of 1945 the National Assembly enacted a statute that permitted employers to dismiss workers only for acts of violence, drunkenness, willful injury to property, or four unexcused absences in one month; specifically forbade employers from firing workers for refusing to accept an assignment that necessitated their prolonged absence from home; and required employers to pay additional compensation to those employees resigning due to management's abusive practices, breach of contract, or neglect of safety precautions. Thus began a program of labor legislation that attempted to reverse conditions which had persisted since the time of the conquest.[29]

Over a year later, in February 1947, after much careful discussion and analysis by both the executive and the congress, Arévalo promulgated the much needed Labor Code. Clearly articulated, the code unequivocably asserted the fundamental rights of all workers in Guatemala, regardless of their ethnic origin or place of employment. It called for compulsory labor-management contracts, requiring collective bargaining in good faith and establishing a system of labor courts; it expressly acknowledged the right to organize, thereby rectifying one of Ubico's most repressive policies; it established the principle of minimum salaries, although no specific figures were mentioned, and the principle of equal pay for equal work; and it set guidelines for better working conditions. Not content with these provisions, the congress amended the code the following year, specifying the minimum schedule of severance payments, mandating preferential hiring of Guatemalan workers if all other conditions were equal, and providing protection for women and children workers. Provisions were also added concerning benefits, medical assistance, and workers' compensation.[30]

The purpose of the Labor Code and related legislation was to guarantee Guatemalan workers rights which they had been denied in the past. George Britnell described the code as "a very important and necessary step toward defining the relationship between employers and employees."[31] The results rapidly became apparent. Whereas the average salary for an agricultural worker in 1944 ranged from five to twenty-five centavos per day (one centavo equaled one U.S. cent), by the time Arévalo left office in 1951 the figure had risen to close to eighty centavos. Even with adjustments made for inflation, this increase was dramatic. Large employers like the United Fruit Company charged that the government intended the Labor Code to harass foreign investors, but their arguments ignored these positive results. The United States ambassador to Guatemala, Edwin Jackson Kyle, Jr., emphatically upheld the code's benefits when questioned about the program. He responded that it "provided for the moral and economic improvement of the workers of Guatemala and definitely had not been aimed against the foreign interests in the country."[32] The code did not discriminate against any particular company, but it redressed employment grievances that had been ignored by the previous dictatorships.

The plight of the poor in Guatemala required more than agricultural and labor reforms, although economics might have been the root of the problem. Arévalo understood that, in order to revitalize Guatemalan society from the lowest class on up, his program would have to include massive social legislation. In his first year in office, he created the Commission of Social Security, responsible for developing mechanisms capable of extending benefits even to the remote tribes in the highlands. Such a comprehensive program posed innumerable problems due to Guatemala's complex ethnic, linguistic, and economic structure. The administration proceeded methodically, taking into account differences in occupation, regional characteristics, tribal arrangements, and other salient aspects of the Guatemalan people which influenced their personal life styles and needs. The result was the Guatemalan Institute for Social Security, inaugurated in 1948. Financed by the workers contributing 25 percent of the total cost, the landowners and industrialists 50 percent, and the state the remaining 25 percent, the institute initially covered approximately seventy-five thousand individuals. Within two and one-half years, the number had risen by more than 100 percent and included all state employees. The social security system was one of the revolutionary government's proudest accomplishments. In the last year before the Castillo Armas coup, it paid out well over two million dollars in benefits.[33]

Recognizing that the Indian majority suffered from wretched medical facilities, the Arévalo administration reorganized and expanded the Ministry of Public Health and Assistance. Year by year, depending upon the availability of funds and personnel, the state financed new hospitals, and Guatemala's Roosevelt Hospital became the largest in Central America. Again the government approached the program systematically, tailoring facilities to suit urban centers, regional zones, rural services, and emergencies. The ministry installed nurses in White Cross clinics in the crowded districts of the cities, thereby helping to improve urban hygiene. It initiated campaigns to combat epidemics through vaccination programs and other preventive measures. Engineers introduced water-filtering systems throughout the rural areas, and they built new sewer systems in the cities. Although these measures were only a modest beginning in the attempt to ameliorate Guatemala's severe plight, the country's mortality rate constantly decreased by an average of 2.5 percent each year during the revolutionary period.[34]

Educational reform was undoubtedly Arévalo's pet project. Formerly a professor, he was painfully aware that Guatemala's illiteracy rate of over 70 percent ranked second only to that of Haiti among the countries of Latin America. This figure would have been substantially higher had only the rural areas been considered: illiteracy in Indian communities reached over 90 percent.[35] Hence the government devoted tremendous efforts to improving the country's academic system, and rural school construction and literacy programs flourished. In the last year of his administration, Arévalo spent over seven million dollars on educational projects alone, which was greater than one-half of all state expenditures in Ubico's final year.[36]

The progress was striking. Arévalo created the National Literacy Committee and, in 1949, replaced it with regional organizations. He built normal schools, special technical schools, municipal primary schools, kindergartens, adult night schools, industrial centers, and rural schools, until about six thousand places of learning were functioning throughout Guatemala. Teachers, whose pay prior to 1945 was so little that many had to moonlight, and who generally had only a few years of higher education themselves, were given substantial salary increases and greater opportunities to earn their full teaching degrees. A more decentralized educational system emphasized regional identity; model schools were established in some twenty different regions to improve the quality of rural education and to help integrate it more fully into the life of the community. Mobile cultural missions contacted those Guatemalans above school age and taught them history, health care, legal rights, and elementary education. Government expenditures for education rose, in real terms, some 155 percent from 1945 to 1950.[37]

Although the Maya directly benefited from these programs, the government leaders knew that the Indians' historic circumstances needed special attention in order to eliminate their racial stigma and their sense of exclusion. Within the first six months of his administration, Arévalo formed the National Indian Institute in order to introduce the isolated Maya to modern developments without forcing alien ways upon them. The institute studied the characteristics that defined each tribe; statistically analyzed the rural nutrition of the country; founded the first regional rural school based on social, economic, and linguistic factors; published maps of the various linguistic groupings; and investigated the social organizations, economies, customs, politics, and religions of the diverse communities. A major drawback of the government program was that it made no attempt to unify the Balkanized Maya nation, which would have promoted group cohesiveness. But, in these early years of reform, the explicit recognition of the Indians' acceptance in the new order was a marked improvement over the past.[38]

Although many in the United States later contended that the Indians paid little attention to the change in Guatemala's government, Arévalo's concern for the Maya communities did leave a lasting impression.[39] One journalist traveled extensively in the Guatemalan highlands after the revolution, canvassing the Mayas' reactions to the reforms. He reported this repeated response: "Now we are free. We are equal to the ladinos . . . Now no one can force us to work on a coffee plantation far away against our will. We will go only if we want to."[40] The Indians demonstrated their appreciation by beginning, for the first time since the conquest, to show an active interest in the affairs of the nation. They organized political parties and revitalized the pattern of self-government that had been destroyed under Ubico and previous *caudillos*.[41] The Maya probably never understood all the ramifications of the Guatemalan revolution and its relationship to the cold war. But they welcomed the reforms and the government which enacted them.

The significant accomplishments of the Arévalo administration were only the initial stages of a comprehensive revolutionary program. Susanne Jonas, one of the foremost historians of Guatemala, concludes that the early reforms were not as extensive as those of Roosevelt's New Deal or Britain's postwar Labour government.[42] Arévalo chose to proceed incrementally. Part of the reason was the solidified structure of Guatemalan society. Long accustomed to their privileged position, upper- and upper-middle-class Guatemalans resented any change. With each reform their resistance increased. But another part of the reason was Arévalo's own outlook. He remained a spiritual socialist, concentrating more on intellectual than on structural changes. In comparison with his educational program, Arévalo's agrarian reform was most moderate. He believed that, once "spiritually liberated," the *finqueros* would accept reform as beneficial for all Guatemala. To Arévalo, there was "no agrarian problem; rather, the peasants are psychologically and politically constrained from working the land." Spiritual socialism would rectify this condition "without harming any other class."[43] For the most part Arévalo left the power and property of the great landlords alone, whereas the demands of revolutionary change required redistribution. The landlords understood this requirement and prepared to fight against it. Arévalo gave them time.

COUNTERREVOLUTION AND THE ELECTION OF ARBENZ

Despite Arévalo's conciliatory rhetoric and moderate policies, supporters of the traditional order in Guatemala perceived the revolutionary program as tantamount to class warfare.[44] Arévalo had not been in power one month before he faced his first revolt, and by the time he ended his six-year term as president he had successfully survived over twenty-five attempted coups.[45] The leaders of these attempts were Guatemala's minority property holders, described by

Ambassador Kyle as the "so-called better elements." They were businessowners, importers, agriculturists—virtually the entire upper class. Voicing their opposition through organs like the Society of Agriculture and the Chamber of Commerce and Industry, they tirelessly attacked Arévalo as a Communist and organized vigilante committees in self-defense. To this conservative upper crust, the administration's program was unreasonable and unfair, too expensive for Guatemala's economy, and too radical for stability and development. Condemning government officials as inexperienced, incompetent, and easily corrupted (and, of course, Communist), they predicted widespread rioting and looting, rampant inflation, and social and political chaos. In a fascinating illustration of their single-minded perceptions, they refused to acknowledge the popular movement of 1944 and warned in 1948 that conditions were "ripe for revolution."[46]

Criticism is healthy for a democratic society, but open insurrection, as Arévalo remarked in a 1946 address to the National Assembly, is "sad and destructive."[47] The president's opponents never gave his programs a chance. After Ubico died in exile, they sent envoys and secret messages to Ponce in Mexico. Encouraged, Ponce roamed throughout Central America trying to raise arms and troops, and at one point he told a United States State Department official that his invasion was only two months away. Ponce was dreaming. Counterrevolutionaries realized that to launch an invasion of Guatemala they needed more than a figurehead: they needed a dynamic leader. Yet State reported in 1948 that a successful plot against Arévalo's government had become "a growing possibility."[48]

The State Department based its judgment on the reports that it periodically received.[49] Over time these reports indicated that, while initially divided, the conservatives in Guatemala seemed to have found someone they could all back—Arévalo's chief of armed forces, Francisco Javier Araña. He would be more acceptable to the Guatemalan people than Ponce because of his role in the 1944 revolution, when he had been considered the counterrevolutionaries' enemy. Potentially he could also lead the military to desert Arévalo. Always one of the more conservative members of the government's inner circle, Araña by 1947 had become increasingly critical of administration policies. His personal ambitions added to his growing alienation—he wanted to be Guatemala's next president but knew that the more liberal Arbenz stood in his way. Bitter rivalry developed between the two of them, a situation exacerbated by Arbenz's appointment as minister of defense. Time and again they clashed over proposed projects, with Arbenz normally winning out because of

Arévalo's support. Araña began to fear for his position, and, as rumors circulated that he might emerge as the leader of an attempt to overthrow the government, he began to fear for his personal safety. He believed, perhaps accurately, that, if Arévalo and Arbenz decided such rumors were true after so many previously attempted coups, they would take forceful action against him.[50]

This volatile political situation could not continue, and, as the 1950 national election approached, tensions within the administration became almost unbearable. The campaign promised to be more explosive than that of 1944. Never before had a Guatemalan president abided by a one-term limitation, and many feared that conditions were too unstable to permit a peaceful succession. To add to the concern, unlike the previous contest when Arévalo was the odds-on favorite, there now were two strong candidates, each of whom commanded loyalty within the critically important army. When it became apparent, however, that Arbenz's liberal support was too much for Araña, a coalition of conservatives and reactionaries indiscreetly urged the army chief to mount a revolt before the election could take place. Prompted by enough observers who believed that this was precisely his intention, the United States embassy reported, "It is difficult not to attach significance to rumors that [Araña] is seeking the right opportunity and a reasonable excuse for a military coup d'état."[51] The National Assembly attached a great deal of significance to the rumors. Its members voted overwhelmingly to impeach Araña for treason and then ordered his arrest.[52]

Araña refused to accept his indictment. Still with enough powerful allies in the military to prevent his imprisonment, he traveled around Guatemala City, charging that he was the victim of Communist intrigue and that Arbenz was the real traitor. Then, on July 18, 1949, he went to nearby Lake Amatitlán, announcing that he had information that the Caribbean Legion hid their cache of arms there and that Arbenz planned to use them once he gained power. However, no one was to find out if Araña's claims were true. As his limousine approached the Chalet Morlon, purportedly the arms' hiding place, a car blocking the road forced it to stop. Immediately some twenty men jumped out from under a bridge, riddling the limousine with submachine gun fire. Araña died instantly.[53]

The role of the revolutionary government in Araña's assassination remains undetermined. A "reliable" informer told the United States embassy that Araña's killer was a subdirector of the police who died in the ensuing gunfire. The CIA assumed Arbenz's complicity when planning his 1954 overthrow, and, before it had been in power a week, the Castillo Armas government charged the former president with murder.[54] The major evidence used against Arbenz was the testimony of Araña's chauffeur, Lieutenant Chico Palacios. Palacios claimed that among the assassins were Aníbal Gramajo, Arbenz's wife María's chauffeur, and Lieutenant Alfonso Martínez Estévez, who occupied several influential positions in Arbenz's administration. But Palacios could not directly connect Arbenz with the plot, nor could he explain (although he was not asked) how he alone managed to survive the barrage of bullets.[55] This question presents the possibility that Guatemalan counterrevolutionaries, realizing that Araña stood no chance of winning, actually arranged his assassination in an attempt to incite a rebellion.

The Araña assassination did give Arbenz's opponents another opportunity to try to take power before the election. This was the most violent of the attempted coups. The fighting raged over two days, with the rebel forces using heavy artillery. Government casualties reached an estimated 150 dead and 300 wounded. Many of the capital's buildings, including the National Palace, were practically demolished. The situation became so grave that new United States Ambassador Richard Patterson, Jr., finally had to flee Guatemala City for the countryside, taking refuge in roadside ditches along the way. Arévalo's forces prevailed, but only after receiving the assistance of students and workers who organized themselves into a popular militia. With their defeat Guatemala's conservatives all but gave up hope of overthrowing the government before the election. They made one last attempt, but it was significant only because two United States pilots were arrested for alleged participation and because the leader was Carlos Castillo Armas.[56]

With Araña's elimination, Arbenz's election as Guatemala's next president was virtually assured. The campaign, nevertheless, was extensive and heated. Two candidates emerged as Arbenz's chief opponents. The upper middle class, most of whom were professionals who supported some change from the prerevolutionary order but thought that Arévalo had gone too far too quickly, championed Jorge García Granados.[57] García Granados came from one of Guatemala's oldest and "best" families. At first he actively worked for the revolution, helping to draw up the 1945 constitution and serving as Arévalo's first ambassador to the United States. He hoped that by being elected president he could prevent the revolutionary program from moving more to the left.[58]

The hard-line opponents of the revolution selected a former *ubiquista*, General Miguel Ydígoras Fuentes, as their standard-bearer. During his long military career, Ydígoras had earned a reputation for dishonesty and cruelty. According to the noted scholar of

Latin America Samuel Guy Inman, an old friend of Roosevelt's Undersecretary of State Sumner Welles and one of the architects of the Good Neighbor Policy, Ydígoras, on at least one occasion, ordered the rape of Indian women and the capture and imprisonment of their children.[59] His principal assignment during Ubico's government had been to administer the vagrancy laws and generally to oversee the Maya majority. He was brutally efficient. He imprisoned those Indians whom he suspected of shirking their state service and instructed his agents to shoot any Maya found crossing the border to Mexico in order to earn extra money by selling handicrafts. Ydígoras knew that he was unacceptable to the poor, or even to the moderate middle class, so he appealed exclusively to Guatemala's conservative and reactionary elements. His platform called for saving the country from the Communists, which he proposed to do by reinstituting an authoritarian government.[60]

Arbenz received his support from practically the entire remaining population. This included those still active in the parties that had comprised Arévalo's coalition,[61] organized labor, and the whole agricultural community with the exception of the great landholders. Arbenz campaigned throughout Guatemala as the candidate of national unity, repeatedly emphasizing how far the revolution had come and how far it still had to go. He discussed the need to improve transportation, to study regional problems, and to introduce scientific and technological innovations. Most important, he talked of the need to expand the reforms and programs which had begun under Arévalo. When the election was held in November 1950, Arbenz received more than 60 percent of the votes cast.[62] Ydígoras came in a distant runner-up, followed by García Granados. For the first time in the 130-year history of the Guatemalan republic, executive power had passed peacefully and on schedule from one man to another.[63]

THE ARBENZ ADMINISTRATION

Jacobo Arbenz's inauguration as president of Guatemala at age thirty-seven made him the youngest head of state in the Americas. Nothing in his background had suggested that he would have such a noteworthy career. His father, a Swiss druggist who had emigrated to Guatemala in the hopes of finding better financial opportunities, married a *ladina* and for a while prospered. But with the coming of the depression his pharmaceutical business collapsed, and, unable to provide for his family, he committed suicide. The Swiss community in Guatemala was small and tightly knit, and an influential

friend of the family managed to secure young Arbenz an appointment to the national military academy, the Escuela Politécnica. Tall,
good-looking, and motivated by an intense desire to make up for his
father's failure, Arbenz studied long and hard, receiving the highest
grades in the school's history. Ubico's military structure, however,
severely limited the advancement opportunities for those officers
with lowly social and economic backgrounds. Frustrated, Arbenz
came to hate the system that denied success to an individual simply
because he was from the wrong class. He gravitated toward the revolutionary movement, and, after Ubico forced him into exile at the
age of thirty, he became one of the leaders of the opposition. An en-
gaging personality with a vibrant voice and fluent diction, Arbenz
became the movement's primary spokesman for freedom and reform, an avid nationalist whose critical assessment of national conditions articulated the grievances of the Guatemalan majority. As
Arévalo's chief supporter throughout the first administration, Arbenz was the popular choice to continue the government's revolutionary program.[64]

In addition to his personal attractiveness, rhetorical skills, and
ideological appeal, Arbenz had another political asset—his beautiful
wife, María Cristina Villanova. María Arbenz accompanied her husband on practically all his public appearances, as did his two equally
beautiful daughters. To many Guatemalans the family personified
the vitality and youthfulness of the revolution. But, even more, they
represented change and an intense opposition to oppression. The
Villanovas had been one of El Salvador's wealthiest and most influential families. María's father was associated with the government's
1931 massacre of nearly twenty thousand Indians and *mestizos*.
Horrified by what she had witnessed, the young María adopted an
almost parental concern for the Maya peasants.[65] María Arbenz
spoke out in favor of the revolution as often as did Jacobo. By the
time of his election, she had become a national figure in her own
right.[66]

Having worked so closely with Arévalo during the first six years
of the revolution, Arbenz had formulated specific opinions regarding
the course the government's program should take. His overriding
objective was to build upon the ongoing reforms and to establish
Guatemala's independence in relation to the international political
and economic structure. He felt this could be accomplished only by
developing an autonomous domestic economy. Foreign interests
would not be excluded, but they would no longer be granted the special concessions which permitted the great landholders to avoid paying the taxes necessary for the country's social reforms and which

provided for an inequitable division of land. Advancing the majority's standard of living was, of course, one of Arbenz's primary goals. Yet equally important was the promotion of Guatemala's autonomy. Arbenz was not a Maya, but he studied the Maya culture and sent government representatives to their communities to find out what they wanted. He learned that the Maya still retained their traditional values emphasizing dignity and self-determination, not material acquisitions. Arbenz referred to this sentiment when he outlined his administration's program: "[If] the independence and prosperity of our people were incompatible, which for certain they are not, I am sure that the great majority of Guatemalans would prefer to be a poor nation, but free, and not a rich colony, but enslaved."[67]

Arbenz explicitly stated how he intended to promote this independent development. While not abandoning spiritual socialism, his emphasis would be on capitalist modernization, relying essentially on the recommendations made by the IBRD study mission. In his inaugural address, he explained that the basic policy of his administration would be "to convert Guatemala from a country bound by a predominantly feudal economy into a modern, capitalist one."[68] He would encourage private initiative, he would encourage the accumulation of private capital, and he would encourage the influx of foreign investments and technology. This was virtually the same program announced by Arévalo at his inauguration. If there were any differences, it was that Arbenz went even farther than Arévalo in accentuating the role of the government in supervising this modernization.[69]

Arbenz's inaugural remarks dealt exclusively with the need for the government to participate actively in Guatemala's economic development. He stressed that prosperity had to be accompanied by social progress. His program called for additional agrarian reform and new industrial growth. Arbenz warned that there would be a difficult period of transition, during which many Guatemalans would have to readjust their lives. Some would have to learn to manage a farm rather than just work on one; others would be relocating in cities, where they would need to acquire new skills and build good housing. There would have to be more educational programs, more health programs—more social programs of all kinds. To Arbenz, the responsibility of the government was to assure that this transformation did not create massive economic chaos and discontent, for not only would such conditions prevent most Guatemalans from enjoying the economic improvements, but they would give the counterrevolutionaries more opportunities. Arbenz knew that there were factions which would continue to oppose the reforms and that they could take advantage of any disorder to subvert, and even overthrow, the still precarious revolution.[70]

Having dedicated his government to the ambitious task of modernizing Guatemala, Arbenz put together a comprehensive legislative program. This included the transformation of practically the entire economic infrastructure: the construction of factories, the improved exploitation and acquisition of mineral resources and other raw materials, the building of avenues of communication and transportation, and the development of modern banking institutions and systems of credit. Above all Arbenz proposed large-scale agrarian reform. He realized that Arévalo had left this essential feature of Guatemala's economy intact. A select minority of *finqueros* continued to control a great percentage of the land, using it almost exclusively for the extensive cultivation of export crops. Arévalo's administration parceled out some of the land confiscated from the Germans during World War II and initiated a number of experimental and educational programs. He did very little, however, to change the overall system.[71]

Arbenz's reform bill sought to destroy the *latifundio-minifundio* structure. Devoting so much of the country's rich agricultural potential to raising bananas and coffee severely limited long-range growth. What was needed was to free the tremendous numbers of workers these crops required at harvesttime so that they could form an industrial labor force. More land had to be used to grow staple foods, for otherwise reliance on imports would continue to drive prices in the cities higher and higher. Technological innovations had to be introduced in order to increase yields, and the traditional practice of leaving hundreds of acres fallow so that the soil could be naturally replenished had to be discouraged if not totally eliminated. By diversifying Guatemala's agricultural production and redistributing the land more efficiently, Arbenz hoped to promote a more rational economy and a unified, interdependent state.[72]

The Arbenz agrarian reform resulted from careful government study. In addition to using the information collected during the preceding administration, agricultural advisers sought the opinions of many leading Latin American economists. They all agreed that the outmoded methods of agricultural production had to be replaced by a system more conducive to capitalist development. Certain of the measures recommended would cause little controversy. They were to institute accessible credit facilities, carefully monitor prices, adjust tariff regulations, provide tax incentives, and expand research programs. The inherent problem was how to mandate the necessary land redistribution without creating widespread opposition and violating the principle of private ownership.[73]

Administration officials believed they came up with a solution or, at least, a workable compromise. The plan was to divide and distribute only the idle land of those *latifundios* with more than 223 acres, which amounted to a substantial area. According to the Arévalo studies, in 1950 the thirty-two largest *fincas* totaled 1,719,740 acres, of which 1,575,181 acres were not under cultivation. So as not to be accused of being unjust, Arbenz decided that the reform should permit those proprietors with holdings between 223 and 669 acres to keep one-third of the total fallow, and it would exempt permanent pastures and woods which were being economically exploited and those lands which had a slope in excess of thirty degrees. Consequently, the land which was expropriated came primarily from the 1,059 properties whose average size was 4,300 acres.[74]

The government program stipulated that the land would be distributed to as many peasants as possible, the determinant being that each tract be of sufficient size to permit viable agricultural exploitation. The allocated plots varied in size from 8.5 to 17 acres if the land had previously been under cultivation (the cultivated land was distributed from the national *fincas* which had been expropriated from German coffee growers during World War II) and from 26 to 33 acres if the land had been fallow. The administration established that the annual rents would be at the rate of 5 percent of the value of the produce derived from land that had previously been in private hands and 3 percent if the land had been government-owned. As for the owners of holdings which were expropriated, they would be compensated through government bonds at 3 percent interest to be paid over a twenty-five-year period, the amount of which was predicated on the *finqueros'* own tax declarations recorded in the Register of Immovable Property before May 9, 1952. In this regard, and in terms of the extent of the expropriations, the Guatemalan agrarian reform was far more moderate than either the Mexican reform which preceded it or the Cuban measures which would come a few years later.[75]

The National Assembly unanimously enacted the agrarian reform bill on June 17, 1952, and the program began almost immediately. The results were dramatic. By May 1953, the government had redistributed 740,000 acres from the 107 state farms that had been formed following the World War II expropriations. Close to 8,000 small farmers divided 61 of these properties, while the remaining 46 became cooperative enterprises. By June 1954, despite the strong opposition of the large landholders and an often confused and inefficient administrative machinery, a total of 917,659 additional acres of idle land had been expropriated from over 1,000 plantations and distributed to 87,569 Guatemalans in the form of either freeholds or peasant cooperatives. This averages out to about 10.5 acres per individual. In sum, approximately 100,000 *campesino* families, or about 500,000 individuals, received some land under the program, land that otherwise would have remained predominantly idle. Virtually all of those who benefited from the redistribution were Indians.[76]

Within this brief period the Arbenz agrarian reform provided more land for small farmers and peasants than had been available in the previous years of the republic. The program also guaranteed that the new landowners or occupants were supported, as much as possible, by a system of financial credit. The principal agency for this was the government-sponsored National Agricultural Bank, instituted in early 1953. The bank, after only a few months, approved $195,894 in provisional credits to agricultural cooperatives, plus another $189,030 to individual farmers who had received national lands. As its capital grew, so did its operations. In July alone, 14,011 farmers received credits amounting to $2,641,546, which meant an average of over $188 per person. Although this amount might appear modest by United States standards, struggling Guatemalan farmers considered it a small fortune. By the time Arbenz's overthrow brought an end to agrarian reform, the National Agricultural Bank had provided $8,500,000 for loans and credits and other investment opportunities, and the capital of the bank had risen to another $8,000,000. The Arbenz administration also saw to it that thousands of farmers received technical aid, and thousands more benefited from in-the-field demonstrations of recommended agricultural practices.[77] Whether the agrarian reform would have accomplished all Arbenz intended remains in question. It did, however, go far beyond any other program in Guatemala's history.

The official name for Arbenz's agrarian reform was Decree 900. It evolved from the provisions of the 1945 constitution, intended to overcome the causes of Guatemala's underdevelopment and to restructure the hierarchical organization of society. Reflecting their middle-class origins, the constitution's framers wanted to raise the standard of living of the country's majority and establish juridical equality among Guatemalan nationals and foreign entrepreneurs. Agrarian reform began this process. While many Maya chose to maintain their traditional isolation, communally farming their newly acquired land, others opted for integration. They began to grow their

own food and sell their surpluses at local markets. The price of food
went down, and the per capita purchasing power rose.[78] An increasing percentage of the population could afford radios, shoes, small appliances, and even automobiles. Rural Guatemalans started to come
to the cities, first to sell their produce and then to shop for themselves. Some set up small businesses, while others found work in
the nascent factories. These trends should not be exaggerated, but
subtle changes could be seen throughout the country. Guatemala remained underdeveloped, but there was discernible progress.[79]

4. The View from the North

The progress that resulted from Arévalo's and Arbenz's programs ended with the CIA-orchestrated invasion by Castillo Armas. As will become apparent from the remainder of this study, the Eisenhower administration approved the CIA operation because all concerned officials believed that Communists dominated Guatemala's government and leading institutions. The year 1950 marked a watershed in the growing estrangement of Guatemala from the United States. Washington analysts viewed, for example, Guatemalan labor's increased hostility toward the United Fruit Company (UFCO) and the International Railways of Central America (IRCA), the formation of the Workers Revolutionary party of Guatemala, and the publication of the leftist newspaper *Octubre* as indications that the Communists were coming out into the open.[1] The expropriation of UFCO's property, beginning in late 1952, solidified this view. This action opened a new phase in United States–Guatemalan relations, for it brought to the public's attention the irreconcilability of their respective policies.

THE UNITED FRUIT COMPANY IN GUATEMALA

United Fruit had long occupied a central position in Guatemala, as it did throughout Central America and the Caribbean. In many respects the company's development paralleled that of Guatemala's liberal era, when enterprising agriculturists acquired an increasing amount of the country's land and devoted it to export crops. Among those entrepreneurs who took advantage of Guatemalan—and for that matter Central American and Caribbean—conditions was Minor C. Keith, an "apple-headed little man with the eyes of a fanatic" who came from an industrious Brooklyn family. In 1871, when he was only twenty-three years old, Keith and his two brothers pooled their resources, hired a crew from the toughest sections of New Orleans, and commenced construction of a railroad in Costa Rica from Puerto Limón to San José. The project cost the lives of hundreds of men, including his brothers, but it began a career that would earn Keith the title of the Uncrowned King of Central America. He would do anything to expand his interests; he even married the daughter of Costa Rican President Rafael Iglesias Castro.[2]

In order to finance his railroad concerns, Keith started to sell bananas. By 1883 he owned three banana companies, and he had had the good fortune to meet a Cape Cod sailor, Captain Lorenzo Dow Baker, and a Boston businessman named Andrew Preston. Together the three men found enough backers to form the Boston Fruit Company, which merged into the United Fruit Company in 1899. At the turn of the century UFCO was already the world's largest producer of bananas, owning land in Costa Rica, Nicaragua, Panama, Colombia, Santo Domingo, Cuba, and Jamaica; operating a Great White Fleet consisting of eleven steamships which it owned and twelve to thirty others which it rented or chartered; and holding the title to 112 miles of railroad, most of which linked coastal banana property to the sea.[3]

Two years after its formation, United Fruit, or La Frutera as it came to be known in Latin America, obtained from the then current Guatemalan dictator, Manuel Estrada Cabrera, the exclusive concession for transporting the country's mail between Guatemala's Puerto Barrios and the United States. Thus began over fifty years of unbroken and prodigious profit making. Since Guatemala offered an "ideal investment climate," Keith envisioned huge development potential. Under the laws of the state of New Jersey, he incorporated the Guatemalan Railroad Company as a subsidiary of United Fruit and capitalized it at $40,000,000. Then, in 1904, he negotiated a contract with Estrada Cabrera to complete a railroad connecting Guatemala City to Puerto Barrios. Puerto Barrios, which became virtually a United Fruit city, was the nation's only port on the Caribbean coast. The railroad link with Guatemala's capital had been planned since the administration of Rufino Barrios, but until this time there had been little progress on it. Not content with just the railroad, Keith also extracted from Estrada Cabrera the concession for telegraph lines between the two cities, the purchase at a nominal price of urban lots in Puerto Barrios on which to construct UFCO installations, and the grant of a stretch of land one mile long and five hundred yards wide on each side of the city's pier.[4]

Through its transportation monopoly and its control of Puerto Barrios, La Frutera became a dominating factor in Guatemala's banana industry. Not only did it carry a high percentage of the export traffic, but, by charging excessive rates or refusing to transport their produce, it ruined local companies or forced them to sell out. In addition, United Fruit began its own banana farms, for at the same time it acquired the railroad concession it received, as an incentive, 170 acres of prime banana land. The tract may not appear very large, but it was just the beginning. Estrada Cabrera exempted this land from almost all Guatemalan taxes and, along with the railroad and port, it provided Keith's empire with the requisites for rapid expansion. And expand it did. As one historian of the banana industry, Charles Morrow Wilson, aptly commented, "The Guatemalan venture proved to be an oversized show window for a new era of tropical agriculture and a working model for still bigger divisions to come."[5]

In spite of the swift growth of his enterprise, Keith was far from satiated. In order to realize the great banana empire he envisioned— Guatemalans were soon calling the company El Pulpo (the octopus)—he needed to continually expand his landholdings and, just as important, to formalize his special relationship with the Guatemalan government. At this time his possessions in Guatemala came under the legal title of the Guatemalan Railroad Company; the United Fruit Company itself had no formal standing. Although this arrangement did not prevent the acquisition of additional agricultural property, it did complicate negotiations. Keith's opportunity to remedy this situation came a short time after Estrada Cabrera's overthrow in 1920, when, under the name of the Agricultural Company of Guatemala, he negotiated a new contract with the next president, José María Orellana. United Fruit obtained legal status in Guatemala. It also acquired a twenty-five-year, tax exempt lease on additional territory on the Caribbean coast along the Motagua River and the corresponding monopoly of that region's maritime trade. Freed from all restraint, El Pulpo's acquisitive tentacles soon began to reach for the Pacific coast. Keith set his sights on some 181,000 acres of extremely fertile land in the zone of Tiquisate, Escuintla, owned by the independent California-Guatemala Fruit Company. A small company, California-Guatemala Fruit could not compete with powerful United Fruit, especially since UFCO could arbitrarily increase the costs of all its competitors by raising transportation rates. California-Guatemala Fruit sold out at a tremendous loss, establishing La Frutera as dominant on both of Guatemala's coasts.[6]

United Fruit's next big opportunity came with the arrival of the Great Depression. By this time Keith had died and had been succeeded by a Bessarabian Jew named Samuel Zemurray. Commonly known as Sam the Banana Man, Zemurray became involved with bananas in 1895, when he was only eighteen years old; within fifteen years he had formed the successful Cuyamel Fruit Company. Based in New Orleans, Cuyamel Fruit had its primary interests in Honduras, where it had played a role in Manuel Bonilla's successful coup in 1911. Under the protection of Bonilla and his successor, Francisco Bertrand, and the occupying United States Marines, Zemurray's Honduran enterprise flourished. He then sold the company in 1929 to United Fruit for a great fortune. Actually it was more of a merger than a sale—in return for his properties, Zemurray received United Fruit stock, making him its largest shareholder, and became a director. When he told the other directors he wanted to be managing director, no one disagreed. The president, Victor Cutter, resigned; although his successor was Francis Russell Hart, Zemurray unquestionably took charge.[7]

It was more than just a coincidence that Zemurray's rise to power in United Fruit paralleled the inauguration of the Ubico regime. Orellana died in 1926, and Guatemala's next president was General Lázaro Chacón. In 1930, hoping to induce UFCO to use its influence to guarantee his presidential succession, Chacón negotiated another contract, this time granting the company the exclusive right to build a Pacific port. But Zemurray, aware that Chacón was seriously ailing, opted to remain neutral so as not to antagonize any of his potential successors. In the ensuing scramble between 1930 and 1931, Chacón, Baudilio Palma, General Manuel Orellana, and José M. Reyna Andrade held power successively until Ubico finally emerged the enduring victor.[8] Zemurray had influenced the other great landholders to support Ubico, and, in 1936, Ubico consented to renegotiate United Fruit's contract. Represented by the prestigious law firm of Sullivan and Cromwell (whose executive partner was John Foster Dulles), United Fruit extracted concessions so beneficial that no further negotiations were required—until the 1944 revolution. It received a ninety-nine-year lease on more land on both coasts, bringing its total property to more than the combined holdings of half of Guatemala's landholding population. The contract specifically exempted United Fruit from virtually all taxes and duties, including import duties on such items as food for the company's commissaries and construction materials. The export tax on bananas was insignificant—one and a half cents per bunch—which meant that practically none of the profits found their way into the official coffers. It was thus extremely difficult for Ubico to counter the fiscal crisis of the depression.[9]

Other aspects of the contract enriched the United Fruit Company at the expense of the Guatemalan economy. Ubico guaranteed that there would not be any regulation of United Fruit's transportation rates, nor would any other companies be granted competing charters. He permitted UFCO unlimited profit remittances, the right to construct at its own discretion, and to charge for their use, new communication and transportation networks, and the freedom to expand its operations wherever it chose. And, as if all these concessions were not enough to insure United Fruit's support, Ubico agreed to a property tax scale that enabled the company to greatly undervalue its holdings. In short, combined with glaring loopholes that made it easy for UFCO to declare fictitious profits on overseas sales in order to conceal domestic profits, the 1936 contract enabled the company to evade almost the entire Guatemalan tax burden.[10]

In return, United Fruit's contract promised nothing that would substantially benefit Guatemala's development. As a matter of fact, it even suspended the provision of the 1930 contract that required UFCO to build a new port on the Pacific coast with a railroad connection to Guatemala City. Being relieved of this obligation played a significant part in UFCO's future profit making. Almost all of Guatemala's commerce already had to pass through the company-controlled Puerto Barrios, so United Fruit saw no financial gain in building an alternative. On the contrary, such an expensive project would have cut deeply into its profits. Through its subsidiary, the International Railways of Central America (formed by Keith in 1923 to incorporate his Guatemalan Railroad Company), United Fruit owned all but twenty-nine miles of Guatemala's tracks. IRCA's rail lines extended from Puerto Barrios over the central mountains to the Pacific plain and then crossed the border into El Salvador. This monopoly enabled it to reap huge profits from the long-haul business of transporting produce from the Pacific to the Caribbean. Any inconvenience or added expense to UFCO's own Pacific operations was more than offset by IRCA's practice of charging competitive banana and coffee growers approximately ten times the rate it charged its parent company to carry produce over the same distance and by the assurance that, once the crops arrived at Puerto Barrios, their only means of export was the Great White Fleet. UFCO repeatedly claimed that all of its funds—and those of IRCA—were tied up in capital investments and that, therefore, there were no liquid assets with which to finance a new port and railroad lines. Ubico accepted this explanation without argument.[11]

When United Fruit came under attack by Guatemalan nationalists and labor organizers following the 1944 revolution, its representatives argued that the banana-growing industry was so costly that, even with the favorable concessions, profits were marginal. Statistics indicate otherwise. Capitalized at $20 million when it was initially formed in 1899, the company's value by 1920 had risen to $150 million. Thirty years later it reported an annual profit exceeding $65 million—more than twice the ordinary revenues of the entire Guatemalan government—and the following year, in spite of serious windstorm damage to the plantations, United Fruit's ledgers still showed net earnings of greater than $50 million.[12]

These profits may be translated into other statistics. United Fruit exported almost one-third of all the bananas that traveled from Latin America to the United States and Europe, and it was the leading banana grower in every Central American and Caribbean country. It produced four times the volume of its closest competitor, the Standard Fruit Company of New Orleans. Although United Fruit's corporate statistics during this time were not broken down, one can deduce from its annual report that Guatemala's contribution to UFCO's overall earnings was about 25 percent. The enterprise in the Pacific region of Tiquisate constituted the largest mechanized farm throughout Latin America.[13] United Fruit's complaints of financial difficulties in the context of its massive operations were therefore unacceptable to Guatemala's revolutionary leaders who pledged themselves to the country's comprehensive development. To them, and to all Latin American nationalists, El Pulpo was the very symbol of Yankee imperialism.[14]

When leaders of a nationalist movement apply the term "Yankee imperialism" to criticize a North American business concern or government policy, outraged United States citizens react by calling them programmed Communist agitators or fanatical guerrilla warriors. The nationalists' criticism has been so overused that often it is dismissed as polemical propaganda, devoid of any substantive meaning. But to Guatemalans the meaning was clear, the evidence tangible. While they conceded that United Fruit provided its employees with living quarters, the natives merely had to peer over the high wire fences separating their dwellings from those of their employers. To poor Guatemalans, "Yankee imperialism" meant the workers' three- to five-family buildings juxtaposed with the splendid single-family houses, theaters, swimming pools, and golf courses "next door"—the exclusive preserve of the managerial command. It meant the Guatemalans' inescapable opportunity to look through the wire fences every time they walked to the outhouse located behind each of the barracks. It meant knowing that, should they somehow acquire a white-collar job, they could be assured a much lower salary than their North American counterpart with a dozen years' less experience.[15]

"Yankee imperialism" to the Guatemalans also meant United Fruit's long-held reputation for bribing politicians, pressuring governments, and intimidating all opponents in order to gain political and economic concessions. That United Fruit paid so few taxes on its huge holdings was well known throughout Guatemala, as was its fiefdomlike power over its properties. Because UFCO had been closely associated with Ubico's oppressive regime, Guatemalan revolutionaries perceived the company as a major roadblock to their objective of establishing democracy and enacting social and economic reforms. Guatemalans did not believe that United Fruit officials—indeed, that officials of the United States government—paid adequate attention to their country's needs. Observers from the United States often agreed. For example, in 1945 a college professor touring Guatemala complained to the State Department that United Fruit was "totally indifferent to the economic welfare" of Guatemala's native population. He received the reply that the continuation of such correspondence "would not serve any useful purpose."[16]

Another cause for United Fruit's being called "Yankee imperialist" was the institutionally racist policies of its Guatemalan representatives. The overseer of the Bananera plantation decreed that, in order to "avoid complications," company policy would require all nonwhite persons to yield the right of way to whites and to remove their hats while talking to them. Another rule forbade any Indian laborer to enter the front yard of a white residence. United Fruit personnel acted as if they were masters, not just employers. Interestingly, this condescending attitude of racial superiority so infected company officials that they delayed in treating the Guatemalans' unrest as a serious matter. Spruille Braden, who, after leaving his post as assistant secretary of state for inter-American affairs in 1947, went to work for Zemurray, complained that United Fruit's directors in Guatemala were ignoring a potentially dangerous situation. These complaints came during the early 1950s, when UFCO's public relations counsel, Edward L. Bernays, was voicing similar concerns. Zemurray's response revealed UFCO's prevailing racist approach. Bernays recalled, "Zemurray kept pooh-poohing this warning. The Indians, he said, were too ignorant."[17]

In sum, United Fruit's ostentatious opulence, its overt support of unpopular governments, and its blatant racist policies all contributed to an upsurge of anticompany feeling. But, at its most fundamental level, the resentment toward La Frutera stemmed from the harsh economic realities of its workers. UFCO boasted that it paid the highest wages in Guatemala. These wages, however, were for seasonal work, and it was extremely difficult for a Guatemalan to support a family on an intermittent salary of $1.36 per day. UFCO's boast becomes less accurate after examining the workers' real disposable wages. As in many company towns in the United States, the cost of living on a United Fruit plantation was the highest in Guatemala. Company stores charged expensive prices, and the hospital service cost employees 2 percent of their salary. No employee could afford not to purchase this service. There was neither workers' compensation nor any guarantee of safe working conditions, and, because the frequent use of insecticides and other toxins commonly caused tuberculosis and various stomach ailments, workers who tried to save money by not paying for the hospital service were playing Russian roulette with their only means of income.[18]

Being the wealthiest and largest employer in Guatemala, United Fruit was logically targeted as the most oppressive villain. This dubious distinction, however, was not merely the result of its size. Historically, United Fruit had exhibited less consideration for its workers than had many smaller concerns. After Ubico began to enforce the vagrancy laws, which required peasants to grant the state their free labor, a number of landlords allowed them to grow their own food on small family plots. This was small compensation, but nevertheless it assured many peasants of at least one daily meal. UFCO made no such allowances. Perhaps because most of its workers were employed 150 days a year, or perhaps because it felt that its salary levels were sufficiently high, La Frutera, without any explanation, refused to make any special provisions for its less fortunate employees.[19] When the agricultural workers organized unions following the 1944 revolution, they referred to this seemingly callous attitude. In addition, one of the intents of Arévalo's 1947 Labor Code was to guarantee that workers were cared for, since past practices indicated that companies like United Fruit would not make such guarantees on their own.

GUATEMALA REACTS TO UNITED FRUIT

In view of United Fruit's historical legacy in Guatemala, it should come as no surprise that the company became a focal point for much of the revolutionary activity—both governmental and popular. But the leaders did not indiscriminately harass United Fruit, as would later be charged. Rather, their intention to develop Guatemala, to bring about social and economic reforms sufficiently comprehensive to reach the two-thirds of the population that had for so long been poor, made a confrontation with the largest landholder inevitable. Significantly, the initial assaults on the privileged position of United Fruit came from its own workers, those who had suffered most directly from its long-standing practices.

In 1946 came the first of what would be a number of strikes against La Frutera. The demands dealt primarily with a salary increase; United Fruit's initial reaction was to discharge the most actively involved workers. Explaining that this was an unfair method of handling a labor dispute (the Labor Code was not yet enacted), Arévalo intervened by threatening to confiscate property if UFCO did not rehire the workers. The company conceded, although it did not meet the demands and publicly criticized the government for its interference. Negotiations between United Fruit and its workers dragged on, with UFCO officials becoming increasingly disgruntled after the Labor Code's passage. They protested that it directly discriminated against their company by requiring that agricultural operations employing over five hundred people give their employees ten vacation days each year (smaller companies had to give only five), pay time and a half for overtime (as opposed to time and a quarter), and treat unions as if they were industrial or commercial concerns. More to the point, the code permitted strikes against larger firms during harvesttime but not against smaller ones. United Fruit complained to the United States State Department that it might be economically unfeasible to continue its operations in Guatemala under such restrictions, an argument that appeared vacuous after all the other twenty-nine agricultural firms employing more than five hundred workers fulfilled the Labor Code's provisions without protest.[20]

Convinced that it was being unjustly persecuted, United Fruit refused to compromise with the workers. Negotiations broke down. In 1948 and 1949 came another strike, with the union reiterating its demand to increase wages to $1.50 per day. This time, however, the strikers asked United Fruit for more than money. Among the issues they raised were free medical care and a permanent medical facility in Puerto Barrios, where the ill or disabled could get continued treatment, new housing, better and safer working conditions, a month of paid salary in the event of injury or sickness, compensation for families whose members died from work-related incidents, and a special allowance for funerals. United Fruit, again refusing to accede to the demands, threatened to terminate operations (it did basically close down Puerto Barrios) and to lock out the workers. Rather than deal with the issues presented by the union, UFCO concentrated on attacking the Labor Code for being discriminatory. In the end, primarily through the efforts of Arévalo and his economic minister, Alfonso Bauer Paíz, United Fruit agreed to accept arbitration and the conflict was settled. However, the terms of the eventual contract hardly augured well for the future. It stipulated that the United Fruit workers would collectively receive an increase of $1.5 million by the end of 1949, but this raise was quite modest considering the large number of employees (over fourteen thousand before World War II). Nothing was done concerning the issues of benefits and working conditions.[21]

By June of 1949, only three months after the new contract was signed, another dispute erupted between United Fruit and its work force. Storms had damaged several of the company's farms in the Caribbean region of Bananera in April and June. UFCO's general manager in Guatemala, William Taillon, ordered that fifteen hundred employees be laid off, insisting that these disasters gave him the right to do so although the dismissals were in direct contravention of the recent agreement, which guaranteed existing jobs for at least one more year. Then, in September 1951, a hurricane hit the Pacific plantation of Tiquisate, leading to the discharge of half of the seven thousand workers there. Lest Arévalo attempt to intervene once again to force a settlement, United Fruit repeated its threat to discontinue operations if conditions did not improve.[22] It is instructive that, in its 1951 annual report, United Fruit did not indicate that it planned to withdraw completely from Guatemala. The report does discuss the financial loss suffered from the storm damage and, most revealingly, analyzes this loss in the context of the continuing labor turmoil. Its author, President Kenneth Redmond, left no doubt that UFCO was more concerned with the labor unrest than with the climactic conditions. Undoubtedly his representative in Guatemala told Arévalo the same thing:

Unusual losses from windstorms were the primary reason for failing to realize anticipated production. The plantations in Guatemala were most seriously disturbed . . . Ordinarily, losses from windstorms are transitory, but because of certain conditions existing in Guatemala . . . the Company has decided not to rehabilitate the blown down acreage in Guatemala until such time as operating conditions in the country become more stable . . . During recent years extremists who are not employed by the Company [an obvious reference to the Communists] have kept the laborers in a constant state of unrest. The Company has been endeavoring to negotiate a settlement which would provide sufficient stability of costs to warrant the Company in rehabilitating the damaged plantations. These negotiations have been unsuccessful thus far . . .[23]

Negotiations continued, with United Fruit refusing to rehire the workers. A viciously circular argument evolved. UFCO explained that it did not need the workers since the damaged portions of its properties were not operating. It would make no attempt to put these properties back into operation until the labor dispute was settled. But the workers made the reinstatement of those fired a quid pro quo for any settlement. Again United Fruit warned that it would shut down completely and buttressed its threat by beginning to sharply curtail the Guatemalan traffic of its Great White Fleet. Finally, in January 1952, the Guatemalan labor court ordered United Fruit to take back the dismissed workers and pay them close to $650,000 in back wages or have all its properties confiscated, as was compulsory under the law. The company refused, and the court at Escuintla scheduled an auction of the Tiquisate holdings. United Fruit relented, and both sides signed a new agreement. UFCO would rehire the workers with the stipulation that they would receive their back pay over the next three years. Employees would not, however, get any pay increases during this entire period. The 1952 annual report read, "Very little fruit was shipped from these areas [in Guatemala] during 1952, but the area is rapidly coming back and increasing amounts of bananas are being harvested, and the area should be in full production again in the spring of 1953."[24]

Concurrent with the unrest on United Fruit's plantations, its subsidiary, the International Railways of Central America, began to experience labor difficulties of its own. A strike broke out in late 1950 when IRCA accused seven union members of stealing from the company and subsequently dismissed them without proving the charges. The controversy started at the railroad's terminal point in Puerto Barrios, but the strike rapidly spread along the entire line. Following Arbenz's election, the labor court ruled that the charges could not be substantiated and, thus, that the alleged offenders deserved their jobs back. The strikers, on the other hand, received only three-quarters of their pay for the time they refused to work, and the court denied their demand that IRCA select a native Guatemalan to be its local master of transportation.[25]

Conditions went from bad to worse for the company. Arbenz began construction of a highway paralleling the IRCA route to the Caribbean and terminating at a new port, Santo Tomás. In 1952 the railroad, however, claimed that it was facing bankruptcy due to increased labor costs and the cutback in revenue that resulted from United Fruit's curtailment of its banana shipments. Had the highway been completed (which it was not), such an alternative means of transporting produce would have seriously undercut IRCA's monopoly and forced it to lower its rates, which in 1951 were the highest in the world. Simultaneously, the government impounded the railroad company's assets on the grounds that it owed $10.5 million in back taxes. IRCA joined its parent company in threatening to leave Guatemala.[26]

UNITED FRUIT AND THE AGRARIAN REFORM

The decision of the Arbenz government's labor court to compel IRCA to rehire the seven workers indicated to the United Fruit Company that the new administration would be no more sympathetic to its deteriorating position than had that of Arévalo. UFCO's concerns took a quantum leap in June 1952, with Arbenz's enactment of the agrarian reform law. The agricultural decree came as no surprise to the company—its officials realized that the revolutionary program of developing and modernizing Guatemala required a comprehensive reform that would better redistribute the land. Public relations counsel Edward Bernays, after learning of Iran's expropriation of the British-owned Anglo-Iranian Oil Company property in 1951, suggested to Zemurray that United Fruit retain a distinguished lawyer to write a brief for the Senate Foreign Relations Committee condemning expropriation and that a conference of legal experts be convened to air the problem publicly. Bernays also recommended that Zemurray influence "a high official of a democratic Latin American nation to make a public pronouncement against expropriation" and, if possible, persuade the president of the United States to issue a statement, comparable to the Monroe Doctrine, which expressed the dangers of expropriation to international amity and commerce.[27]

Bernays' suggestions were never effected.[28] Even if they had been, it is doubtful that the course of events would have been different. Being the largest landowner in Guatemala, United Fruit could not possibly have avoided the government programs which were necessary for substantive reforms. Both United Fruit and State Department officials understood that the requisites of Guatemalan development demanded these modifications. Nevertheless, UFCO's uncompromising negotiations during the labor strife proved that only the government's intervention could get the company to alter its traditional policies.

UFCO and State had been cautioned. Forward-looking analysts understood that United Fruit's historical relationship with Guatemala had bred a high degree of nationalistic antagonism. In 1950 John F. Fishburn, the State Department's labor officer for the Office of Regional American Affairs, predicted in a memo to Assistant Secretary of State Edward G. Miller that "as a foreign owned corporation and as a large and financially successful one, United Fruit must anticipate a certain amount of anti-company feeling" and that "the Company will be fortunate if it is able to continue operations over a lengthy period without being expected to do more than grant higher wages and better working conditions." Fishburn advised that United Fruit should not "fight this inevitable trend and argue that there is unfair discrimination."[29] Neither United Fruit nor the State Department heeded Fishburn's warnings. When the inevitable expropriations came, the decision was made to fight.

There can be little doubt that the anti-UFCO sentiment so prevalent in Guatemala spurred the Arbenz government to include the company's holdings among those affected by the agrarian reform law. But this emotional factor should not be overemphasized. The mandates of the decree—intended to redistribute the country's idle land among the propertyless population—left the law's administrators no alternative. At the time of the law's enactment, only 15 percent of United Fruit's more than 550,000 Guatemalan acres were under cultivation. The remaining acreage was idle land. Company representatives argued that the banana industry required that these huge amounts of land be held in reserve, for the tracts had to be flooded periodically in order to drown out the fungus-caused Panama disease to which bananas were prone. Agricultural authorities in Guatemala rebutted this argument—maintaining that, since this fungus takes 10 years to appear on uninfected land, even if the company doubled its banana acreage it would still have sufficient reserve land for another 110 years. Given these figures, Guatemalan government officials confidently asserted that not only was the expropriation of United Fruit's surplus property nondiscriminatory, but the failure to expropriate would have discriminated against the country's less powerful elements. Decree 900 explicitly recognized that all landowners were legally equal.[30]

The sequence of expropriations began in December 1952, when, as provided by law, the Regional Peasant Confederation (one of the reform's administrating units) recommended the redistribution of 55,000 acres of United Fruit's uncultivated land in the Pacific region of Tiquisate. The government's agrarian committee reviewed this recommendation and approved it. A short time later, on February 25,

1953, the agrarian committee approved a similar claim, bringing the total to 234,000 acres of United Fruit's Pacific holdings. By November of that year, all this property had been parceled out to over twenty-three thousand previously landless peasants. On February 24, 1954, the government expropriated more of UFCO's land, this time 173,000 acres from the Caribbean coast's Bananera plantation. The total expropriation was now over 400,000 acres of United Fruit's holdings or approximately one-seventh of all the arable land in Guatemala.[31]

The amount of land turned over to the peasants might seem extreme, and certainly it was viewed that way by the United Fruit Company and by many within the United States. They viewed as a further outrage the Guatemalan government's offer to compensate the company by paying it a total of $1,185,000—the exact figure at which United Fruit valued its property for the Guatemalan tax records—through twenty-five-year, guaranteed 3 percent bonds. United Fruit protested vehemently, as did the State Department, which in an aide-memoire wrote that "the fixing of the amount of the bonds on the basis of tax value of the properties . . . bears not the slightest resemblance to just evaluation," and, thus, the government's offer of compensation "represents a mere gesture."[32] Then, on April 20, 1954, the United States formally submitted to the Guatemalan government in the name of United Fruit a bill for $15,854,849, the largest claim presented to any foreign country on behalf of a United States firm since the 1938 oil expropriation in Mexico.[33] The Arbenz administration never paid this bill. Arbenz had followed the letter of the law—the compensation offered United Fruit was its land's declared value on the tax records. Meanwhile, as the countries were still disputing the issue, the CIA completed its plans to overthrow Arbenz.

The expropriation of United Fruit property was just one of many controversies that arose subsequent to the Guatemalan revolution. Shortly following Ubico's collapse, an influential circle within the United States began to suspect that Communist elements had subverted the revolutionary leadership. As the reform program broadened its scope and Guatemala's popular sentiment for change increased in intensity, this circle widened appreciably. The expropriation convinced them—if they had not been convinced previously—that their suspicions were correct. Products of the cold war ethos, they believed it axiomatic that no government would take such a radical measure against a United States business if it were not dominated by Communists. This was the cold war, when a Communist was defined as anyone who opposed United States interests. Willard Barber, Truman's deputy assistant secretary of state for American republic affairs, succinctly applied this definition to Guatemala when he wrote that Communist influences were those which were "alien to American ideals and which have adversely affected Guatemala as a place for capital investment."[34]

Barber was explaining in 1949 that Washington viewed government programs such as agrarian reform bills, which damaged United States investments, as symptoms of a much larger problem. They were "secondary problems," Assistant Secretary of State John Moors Cabot explained to Guatemala's ambassador to the United States, Guillermo Toriello Garrido, in 1953. The larger problem was Communism. When the issue was Communism, there could be no negotiation. Communism, in the words of Cabot's deputy Thomas Mann, "was not any economic, doctrinal, or even military matter, it was a political one. This government knew that communists the world over were agents of Soviet imperialism and constituted a mortal threat to our own national existence."[35] John Foster Dulles put it best: "If the United Fruit matter were settled, if they gave a gold piece for every banana, the problem would remain just as it is today as far as the presence of communist infiltration in Guatemala is concerned. That is the problem, not United Fruit."[36] Slightly over a week after Dulles uttered these remarks over national television, Castillo Armas invaded Guatemala.

THE UNITED STATES IDENTIFIES INTERNATIONAL COMMUNISM IN GUATEMALA

Official United States concern over the possibility of Communist penetration of Guatemala surfaced well before the Arbenz government's expropriation of United Fruit property. Because of long-standing economic—as well as political and strategic—interests in this critical Central American republic, makers of United States foreign policy carefully eyed the events preceding and following the 1944 upheaval. The United States did not ultimately intervene in Guatemala to protect United Fruit. It intervened to halt what it believed to be the spread of the international Communist conspiracy.

Since the 1920s, when New York replaced London as the principal market for Guatemalan bonds, Guatemala had been the United States' most important outlet for Central American trade and investment. During that decade, over 60 percent of Guatemala's imports came from the United States, and more than two-thirds of its exports were sent to its North American neighbor. United States private investment in Guatemala grew from $6 million in 1897 to close to $59 million by the beginning of the depression, with almost all of this increase accounted for by UFCO, IRCA, and Empresa Eléctrica, a subsidiary of the American and Foreign Power Company. Empresa Eléctrica, which produced over 80 percent of Guatemala's electricity, had initially been a German company, but after World War I it was purchased by the United States concern for only $300,000. In order to protect their investments, the large firms dispatched numerous economic experts to Guatemala to advise the government. Among these experts was Princeton University's E. M. Kemmerer, who recommended sweeping reforms of the country's banking and other monetary systems. To their credit, the various *caudillos* of the 1920s initiated almost all these recommendations.[37]

The investment trend increased during the years preceding World War II, as depression-ridden companies in the United States looked for moneymaking outlets for their capital. W. R. Grace and Company, Pan American World Airways, and a number of smaller investors in mining and foreign telecommunications eagerly entered the Guatemalan market. Through its courtship of United Fruit, the Ubico regime demonstrated that Guatemala provided profitable opportunities, with its orderly and tranquil political situation and its cheap and docile work force. Ubico granted so many monopolies that, by the time of the 1944 revolution, United States companies virtually dictated Guatemala's economic life. In addition to the previously mentioned monopolies of the country's transportation and power systems (not to mention United Fruit's influence on agricultural jobs), United States interests controlled the airways, the communications networks, such recreational activities as movies, and even a large portion of the press. When the revolutionary junta took over at the end of 1944, investments had reached ninety to one hundred million dollars.[38]

Since, as reflected in Barber's 1949 memorandum, a goal of United States foreign policy was to insure that Guatemala remained "a place for capital investment," the official attitude toward the repressive *caudillos* was toleration if not benediction. The State Department's primary concern was that Guatemala remain stable, and its best guarantee of this stability was to support the status quo. The propensity to overlook successive governments' strong-armed tactics reached its zenith during the early years of World War II. At that time, Guatemala City's and San José's importance as fueling stations for air connections with the Canal Zone and for long-distance patrol and bombing missions added to the country's overall value as an investment opportunity, as did its proximity to the new atomic installations in New Mexico.[39]

In many respects, the United States support for Ubico typified its traditional policies toward the Latin American dictatorships. Despite Guatemalan complaints that "Washington is the author of all these little rulers of America," Ubico continued to receive military supplies from the United States, which he used both to fight the Nazis and to suppress his own people.[40] Neither the government nor the public was oblivious to Ubico's excesses, yet both rationalized their look-the-other-way attitude in terms of the requisites of hemispheric defense and a prevalent paternalistic analysis. A noteworthy example is a 1942 article in the influential *Harper's Magazine*. After praising Ubico for "working hand in glove with us in the common cause," the piece goes on to describe him in such euphemistic terms as a dictator "who hates to be called one" and an "honest admirer of democracy in a country that has never known the meaning of the word." This last description was a necessary ingredient for the United States rationale. Sure, the article continued, Ubico was often harsh, but then he was "Tata," the father to the Indians, who, like a stern parent, forced his "children" to do what was in their best interests. Ubico might have been despotic, but he was an "enlightened," "benevolent" despot, just the sort of leader that a country like Guatemala needed.[41]

This line of thinking engendered a most curious—and almost incomprehensible—demeanor on the part of those State Department officials charged with Guatemalan policy. Although they were fully cognizant that opposition to Ubico pervaded the country, they seemed incapable of conceiving that his "children" might really oust him. How else can one reconcile, in retrospect, the practically cavalier attitude of Roosevelt's ambassador to Guatemala, Boaz Long, who had over thirty years' experience in Latin America, including previous ambassadorships in El Salvador, Nicaragua, and Honduras? Despite his own concerns over the possibility of antigovernment activities, and despite reports of the impending revolt that flooded the United States embassy, Long planned a vacation to his home in Missouri! He later wrote Roosevelt, perhaps to excuse this negligence, "The farthest thing from my thought when planning to visit the middle west this fall was that Ubico, firmly seated here for thirteen years, should give up the Presidency so unexpectedly."[42] When Ponce succeeded Ubico, Long appears to have been reassured that the Guatemalan people had regained their reason, having once again placed their trust in a powerful father figure so that "the machinery of government is continuing to function smoothly and the outward life of the country has apparently settled back to normal."[43] Long carried out his vacation plans soon after the United States government extended Ponce its official recognition. The October revolution, therefore, also caught this State Department veteran by surprise, as he again explained to Roosevelt: "Conditions in Guatemala seemed calm . . . Unfortunately, my stay [in Missouri] was short-lived for the unexpected revolution calls me back all too soon."[44]

Long's lackadaisical and naïve behavior is understandable only in the context of United States ignorance of Guatemalan conditions. Ignorance, actually, is not the precise description, because United States policy makers knew of the conditions. They just could not comprehend their implications or their seriousness. In short, as will become increasingly evident, throughout the revolutionary period officials failed to adequately consider the causes and forces of Guatemalan nationalism and the anti–United States sentiment that this nationalism spawned. This failure led to a misguided policy that, under Truman, widened the gulf between the two countries and, under Eisenhower, precipitated a diplomatic war and a surrogate invasion.

Since the State Department, as epitomized by Ambassador Long, was so totally unprepared for the 1944 revolution, it approached the subsequent provisional junta and the election of Arévalo with both confusion and apprehension. Ubico may not have comported himself in accordance with all Washington's standards, but he certainly had promoted United States interests and been a good neighbor. Official analysts knew little about the new Guatemalan leadership, and any change in the status quo raised the possibility of less friendly government policies. There were some who feared that the United States had been too closely identified with the fallen dictatorships and that now it might be treated as a kind of accessory or even accomplice. Concern mounted when Long reported some scattered anti-Yankee incidents, such as a March 1945 parade in which students carried placards picturing Uncle Sam condescendingly dispensing chewing gum to his tiny neighbors, cracking a whip over the small American republics, or, more familiarly, stretching his octopuslike tentacles throughout the hemisphere. One poster graphically portrayed a series of United States Army activities at its Guatemala City base, including a scene of a star-spangled bomber dropping a load of babies onto a nursing home.[45] Government onlookers hoped that this demonstration did not represent a widespread or longlasting sentiment, but they could not be sure.

Most indications were, however, that, once the initial revolutionary fervor quieted down, Guatemala's relationship with the United States would return to normal. By the end of October 1944, the State Department determined, after a good deal of deliberation, that the junta should be recognized, and this recognition came on November 7. More to the point, while extremely anti-Communist experts like Assistant Secretary of State Spruille Braden feared that Arévalo's connections among the Latin American intelligentsia made his political inclinations suspect, the majority opinion within the State Department was that the new Guatemalan president "desired a moderately liberal and constitutionally stable form of government" that would not run counter to United States interests.[46] To satisfy Braden's misgivings the State Department consulted John F. Griffiths, chargé d'affaires of the United States embassy in Argentina, where Arévalo had spent most of his academic life. Griffiths responded:

> [Concerning] the suspicions that might be had about Arévalo
> . . . it is my considered opinion that anyone even reasonably
> well informed about his teachings, writings and general ac-
> tivities would be inclined to pass over such suspicions as being
> so utterly without foundation as to call for no response.[47]

As developments in Guatemala unfolded, the United States assessment of Arévalo and the revolutionary movement changed drastically. In 1945, however, most informed observers perceived him as a "man who does believe sincerely in the United States," and State recommended that Roosevelt invite the new president for an official visit. By the end of Truman's administration, Arévalo was more typically described as "an enemy of the United States," Guatemala as "the only country in the hemisphere . . . in which the Communists have penetrated within the inner circle of government."[48]

This changing analysis corresponded with the developing cold war ethos and an increasing number of United States–Guatemalan controversies. Many of the two countries' sources of friction exclusively concerned economic disputes. The first of these arose in February 1945, prior to Arévalo's inauguration, when the provisional junta expropriated Guatemala Airways. Alfred Denby, who owned 80 percent of the airline's stock, and the other major stockholder, Pan American Airways, complained to the State Department that the expropriation was unjust and that the government had not made any move toward offering compensation. The junta argued that Denby was not entitled to compensation since he had embezzled funds from Guatemala Airways and what was more, having left the country after Ubico's overthrow, he continually schemed to bring the former dictator back. Following Arévalo's inauguration, the new government agreed to a compromise settlement, with Pan Am assuming control of the company. Nevertheless, the affair alarmed officials like Nelson Rockefeller, who became more and more uneasy over perceived Guatemalan trends.[49]

The Truman administration's alarm grew concurrently with the enactment of Arévalo's Labor Code and the rising number of strikes involving United Fruit and International Railways of Central America. A State Department memorandum to Ambassador Edwin Kyle called attention to the code's provisions, which appeared to "discriminate in practice against U.S. companies." By 1950, Guatemalan experts were so disturbed by the "continued mistreatment of U.S. business concerns" that Kyle's successor, Richard Patterson, warned Arévalo that "cordial relations between Guatemala and the United States cannot continue if the persecution of American interests does not cease."[50] Assistant Secretary of State Edward Miller prompted Patterson's warning. Miller had written the ambassador a year earlier that the analysts in Washington doubted that a United States firm could receive any justice in Guatemala, because the Arévalo government seemed to "condone obviously improper activities." Also in 1949, the fledgling CIA assessed the Guatemalan administration as "distinctly unfriendly to U.S. business interests."[51]

In issuing his warning to Arévalo, Patterson reflected a growing consensus within United States government circles. The consensus among the leaders of those business concerns with large Guatemalan investments had already been formed. These leaders had met with Patterson shortly after his appointment in 1948 to let him know exactly how they felt. Among those present were UFCO's Zemurray and its president, Thomas Dudley Cabot; J. L. Simpson, president of the board of IRCA; and several representatives of Electric Bond and Share, the subsidiary of the American and Foreign Power Company, which owned Empresa Eléctrica. Acting as spokesman for this distinguished group, Simpson told Patterson that Guatemala was "not a place to invest American dollars until such time as they were assured that the discriminatory Labor Code would be done away with." Each company official recounted his headaches to Patterson, who relayed them to Arévalo.[52]

Arévalo did not have to be told that the United States business community in Guatemala was upset. In February 1947, he had invited Truman to Guatemala in an effort to restore harmony between the two countries. Ambassador Kyle urged Truman to accept the invitation, but Truman explained that he was too busy. When he contemplated making the trip the following year, Patterson strenuously objected. He wrote Truman that, given the "difficult situation" for United States businesses in Guatemala, the visit might be misinterpreted as a gesture of support or goodwill. Truman did not go.[53]

The above evidence clearly indicates the extent to which the Truman administration sympathized with the investors' plight in Guatemala. It must not be interpreted, however, as evidence that the government policy was merely to protect the exposed flank of big business. Neither Patterson's warning to Arévalo nor Truman's refusal to accept the Guatemalan president's invitation was a contemporary extension of Taft's dollar diplomacy. Both were, rather, manifestations of the cold war ethos. Willard Barber's definition of Communist influences—those "which have adversely affected Guatemala as a place for capital investment"—provides a more fundamental basis for understanding the government's opposition to Arévalo's programs. From this perspective, when the business leaders told Ambassador Patterson that Guatemala was "not a place to invest American dollars," they were in effect telling him that Guatemala had gone Communist. Similarly, when United Fruit threatened to cease all its Guatemalan operations after the labor strikes and the expropriations, it convinced Eisenhower officials like John Foster Dulles that Guatemala had become the western hemisphere's outpost for the international Communist conspiracy. The leaders of the 1944 revolution founded their economic and social programs on their analysis of Guatemala's developmental needs. In doing so, they unwittingly turned their country into a battleground of the cold war.

It did not take long for the Truman administration to begin to investigate the possibility of Communist inroads into Guatemala. Even before the first strike against United Fruit and the passage of controversial reforms like the Labor Code, the Federal Bureau of Investigation, which during this period was the agency charged with Latin American intelligence, ordered its agents in Guatemala to check carefully for any radical influences. From 1945 on, these agents sent a constant stream of secret diplomatic correspondence to the Washington headquarters. Contained in these dispatches were accounts of events as they developed, biographies of both prominent and minor individuals within the government and labor organizations, and conclusions about the extent of Communist infiltration. As sources, Hoover's agents used Guatemalans who had provided information during the Ubico regime. The results were a large number of dossiers, most of which detailed the lives of labor organizers. The profiles generally concluded that the suspected individuals had a

long history of activism—many having been imprisoned by Ubico—
and tended to have leftist political inclinations.[54]

In addition to the FBI dispatches, the State Department received
disquieting reports from foreign embassies. Representatives of Guatemala's surrounding dictatorships were "tireless in their condemnation" of the Arévalo administration as Communist.[55] A particularly critical report came from the chief of the American section of
the Spanish Foreign Office—Generalissimo Francisco Franco's government was "closely following events in Guatemala since it considers that country an increasingly important center for Communist
activity in the Caribbean area." The Foreign Office claimed that
Arévalo's program was meant to foment class warfare in Guatemala
and destroy all private initiative.[56] The State Department decided it
needed its own study. In fact, as early as October 1947, Undersecretary of State Robert Lovett cabled the United States embassy in Guatemala that "no adequate study on Communism in Guatemala is
available." He requested that the embassy prepare a comprehensive
report, covering all aspects of possible Communist subversion and
activities.[57]

On May 6, 1948, Milton K. Wells, first secretary of the embassy
in Guatemala, sent Secretary of State George Marshall a twenty-
eight-page report entitled "Communism in Guatemala." The report
included the embassy's opinions on the leadership of the Guatemalan Communist movement, that movement's international connections, its objectives, and its prospects for the future. This report,
along with similar material, will be cited over the following pages in
order to document the dominant United States analysis of conditions in Guatemala and to illustrate the line of reasoning that contributed to this analysis. It began by summarizing the situation:

> Communist penetration made startling progress during the im-
> mediate post-revolutionary period (1944–47), as evidenced by
> the radical nature of social, labor, and economic reforms, ac-
> companied by strong overtones of class warfare. Infiltration of
> indoctrinated communists, fellow-travelers, and Marxist ideas
> unquestionably reached dangerous proportions.[58]

Almost all critiques of Communist activity in Guatemala began
with evaluations of the growing labor movement. This is to be
expected, since the strikes against UFCO and IRCA, if not the first
indications of the country's mounting unrest, certainly focused
United States attention on Guatemala's changing conditions. Em-

bassy officials rapidly concluded that there was "undoubtedly a connection" between the strikes and Latin American Communism.[59] The State Department explicitly explained the reason for its mention of Latin American Communism, not just Guatemalan. According to the scenario that experts like Wells outlined, when the Cuban Communist Blas Roca visited Guatemala in 1946, he was "supposed to have left a plan of action for local Communists to follow."[60] To make sure the Guatemalans followed through, Mexico's Vicente Lombardo Toledano, president of the Confederated Workers of Latin America, which contained a large number of Communists, personally supervised all union organization. Citing the findings of the FBI and the Spanish Foreign Office, the department predicted that Toledano—presumed to be Moscow's most seasoned emissary in the western hemisphere—and his allies would try to pose as friends of Guatemalan labor in order to transform the movement from an organization concerned with defending workers' rights into an instrument of political warfare. Their master plan presumably called for a mass strike that would produce conditions sufficiently chaotic for a Communist seizure of state power.[61]

The State Department's characterization of the Guatemalan labor movement added to the Truman administration's worries. Because Ubico's regime had outlawed all forms of labor organization, the masses of Guatemalan workers were, according to the officer in charge of Central American and Panamanian affairs, W. Tapley Bennett, "young and vastly inexperienced," with "no particular ideology."[62] This situation made them extremely vulnerable to the advice and organizational skill of veteran Communists like Toledano. To make matters worse from Washington's standpoint, the ranking hierarchy of Guatemala's native labor leaders all appeared to be Communists or, at least, crypto-Communists. This group included Manuel Pinto Usaga, the secretary general of the Syndical Federation of Guatemala, and Víctor Manuel Gutiérrez, the secretary general of the Confederation of Workers of Guatemala.[63]

Gutiérrez, whose body was found in the ocean in 1966, headed all lists of native labor organizers, and later the House of Representatives subcommittee which held hearings on the events leading to Arbenz's overthrow described him as "the real brains of the Communist movement in Guatemala."[64] Having been a brilliant young college professor before the revolution, when he was nicknamed the Franciscan because of his humility and ascetic manner, he turned his attention to building a teacher's union after 1945. He developed an excellent reputation and later served as a representative to Guatemala's National Assembly. The FBI investigation of Gutiérrez could find "no direct evidence of Communist affiliation or activity," but it did report that he "frequently expresses the Communist line in public speeches."[65]

As would become increasingly evident, the early concern that Communists had penetrated the Guatemalan labor movement was for United States officials only part of a much broader concern. Certainly, they ideologically opposed a Communist presence in the unions, believing that this philosophical thrust was anathema to a free enterprise system. But their major feats stemmed from their firm conviction that the Communists would use their influence among the workers to exact political leverage and eventually to control the Guatemalan government. State Department analysts well understood that Arévalo's primary support lay with the young intellectuals and the masses of illiterate or semiliterate Indian laborers.[66] These were precisely the individuals active in the labor organizations. Conversely, the government's chief opponents were the small number of wealthy business owners and landowners who perceived each of the reforms as a further erosion of their traditionally privileged status. The greater their opposition—as manifested by the numerous attempted coups—the greater Arévalo's dependence on his majority. Control of the government's major sources of support would consequently place the Communists in a position to pressure Arévalo into granting them high administrative and decision-making appointments. In short, observers of Guatemalan developments interpreted the spread of Communist influence in the unions as merely a prelude to its complete domination of the country. Appropriately, it was labor leader George Meany who best reflected this view when he wrote in 1951, "The Communists can neither capture nor hold power in any country without first controlling its labor unions."[67]

Almost as if the fear of a proliferation of Communist influence generated a self-fulfilling prophecy, concerned United States analysts began to detect Communists throughout the Guatemalan infrastructure. In its 1954 report, the House subcommittee on Communist aggression claimed that Communists and Communist sympathizers came to dominate all of Arévalo's propaganda outlets, including the information offices, the official newspapers, and the government-owned radio stations. But, even in 1947, State Department representatives perceived what they discerned to be the beginning of this subversive trend. In explaining to the secretary of state the reasons for the outburst of labor unrest on United Fruit plantations, Milton Wells blamed Arévalo's minister of labor, Augusto Charnaud MacDonald. Wells did not brand Charnaud as a Communist, but he did label him as "extremely pro-labor and hostile to foreign enterprises." According to Wells, while Charnaud was not in a position to lead the workers' strike against United Fruit, he did encourage it by expressing his ministry's sympathy and influencing the government not to defend the company's interests.[68]

Wells was more explicit when identifying Carlos Manuel Pellecer, who held several important government posts. Pellecer first came to the United States embassy's attention in 1945, when, after having been a labor organizer for agricultural workers on Guatemala's Pacific coast, he became the secretary of the legation in Moscow. Robert Woodward, then first secretary to the United States embassy in Guatemala, believed this appointment to Moscow resulted from Arévalo's desire to remove from Guatemala all persons he considered too extreme. Embassy officials followed Pellecer to Paris in 1947, where he served in his country's mission to France. Wells noted to the secretary of state that the Guatemalan was publishing a number of articles which parroted the Communist party line, particularly in denouncing Yankee imperialism, and that he should be "clearly marked . . . as an extreme leftist, if not actually a Communist party member."[69] The tone of Wells' 1949 report to the secretary of state on Pellecer was more urgent. Arévalo had brought him back to Guatemala to head the traveling cultural missions, the mobile units that went into the outlying regions to educate those Indians who had no other available facilities. Wells lamented that these missions had been suspected of radicalism since 1945, but now that their chief was "a Communist in heart if not fact . . . at the same time these backward Indians get their A.B.C.'s, they get a shot of communism." The State Department introduced its history of Communism in Guatemala by identifying Pellecer as the "most fiery and least inhibited of the young Communists."[70]

As the cold war intensified, so did Truman officials' alarm over Guatemala's international policies. In a bipolar world they could ill afford a Communist satellite so close to Washington's doorstep. After carefully scrutinizing Arévalo's foreign ministry, they arrived at the unsettling conclusion that pro-Communists had infiltrated the government's foreign service. Foreign Minister Enrique Munoz Meany's continued opposition to Franco strongly suggested to Wells "the possibility of Communist tendencies," although he admitted that "the evidence is not conclusive."[71] More revealing of the State Department's line of reasoning was its analysis of Jorge García Granados, the Guatemalan ambassador to the United States. The FBI investigation did not substantiate the Spanish government's claim that García Granados was the secretary of Spain's Communist party, but it did identify the ambassador as a Communist. Without revealing its sources, the FBI wrote a secret dispatch to the State Department claiming that it had evidence that García Granados had assumed a new name; drawing on a traditional anti-Semitic aspersion, it further substantiated its argument by asserting that he was part Jewish and operated under the front of various unnamed Jewish organizations.[72]

The allusions to Munoz Meany's anti-Franco attitudes and García Granados' alleged association with the Spanish Communist party indicate one of State's primary indictments against the Arévalo foreign ministry. As early as 1946 and 1947, it began to express concern regarding an apparent pervading sympathy in Guatemala for the Spanish republican movement. Embassy officials reported that Pellecer was using his position as secretary to Guatemala's legation in Paris to funnel exiled Spaniards into Guatemala. When thirteen exiles arrived in Guatemala City in April 1948, Wells reported that "such information as the Embassy has been able to gather from reliable sources regarding these immigrants warrants our previously expressed apprehension over the possibility that this mass migration scheme will result in Communist infiltration." The next month, in his report to the secretary of state, Wells added that after the revolutionary government first came to power it "promptly demonstrated its leftist inclinations by breaking diplomatic relations with Spain and reorganizing the Spanish Republican government-in-exile," and he repeated that there was a "danger of Communist infiltration because of this close affinity with Spanish Republicans." Wells conceded that part of this affinity resulted from the "anti-fascist political philosophy which dominated the political orientation of the new regime," but he underscored the associations that prominent Guatemalans had with the Spanish exiles. A State Department memorandum a year later claimed that it was a Spaniard living in Guatemala City, known only by the name of Aguado, who was the brains behind the Communist establishment throughout Central America.[73]

This alleged link between Guatemalan radicalism and the Spanish republican movement illustrates how deeply the cold war ethos affected the United States analysis of Guatemala's foreign policy. Repeatedly government experts used McCarthy-like inferences rather than facts to find evidence of Guatemalan Communism. They inferred that any policy opposing that of the United States, or even independent of it, was inherently pro-Soviet. On certain occasions they omitted relevant details in order to make their inferences stronger. As a case in point, Guatemala was the only Central American nation not to sign the previously discussed 1947 Rio pact. In his 1950 State Department memorandum, Tapley Bennett interpreted

Guatemala's refusal as "a pertinent example of the influence on government thinking by Communist-minded individuals."[74] Bennett neglected to mention that Guatemala's opposition to the Rio pact stemmed from its long-standing controversy over control of the territory of Belize. In fact, Guatemala was the second country to ratify the pact, only it added the reservation, "Guatemala refuses to recognize British sovereignty over Belize." The majority of the other signatory nations would not accept this proviso, although they did agree to similar ones involving boundary disputes which Honduras, Mexico, and Chile proposed. Guatemala then withdrew its ratification. After Arbenz's overthrow, the Castillo Armas government voted to join the pact, but only after it appended, "The present Treaty constitutes no impediment preventing Guatemala from asserting its right with respect to the Guatemalan territory of Belize by any means by which it may deem most advisable."[75]

In other words, at virtually the same time that Senator Joseph McCarthy was "discovering" Communists throughout the State Department by castigating its policies—such as allowing China to "fall"—State Department experts were applying these same principles to Guatemala. The events of the Korean War provide a good illustration. When the war broke out, the State Department seemed satisfied with the Guatemalan position. Arévalo issued a statement affirming his country's solidarity with the United States, and Munoz Meany's successor as foreign minister, Ismael González-Arévalo, spoke in support of the United Nations resolutions. But, like most Latin American nations, Guatemala did not send troops to Korea. Assistant Secretary for Inter-American Affairs Edward Miller acknowledged that the United States military policy stipulated that no contributions from the armed forces of any country would be accepted unless they were at least the size of a brigade, fully equipped and trained, and able to remain in Korea for a minimum of ninety days. He understood that very few of the Latin American countries could fulfill all these requirements. The CIA concurred with Miller and added that, since none of the Latin American nations considered themselves in immediate danger, it would be most unexpected for them to burden themselves with this substantial military and financial responsibility.[76]

Yet by the signing of the 1953 armistice Washington officials had become highly critical of the Guatemalan posture. Indeed, for President Eisenhower, Guatemala's stance on Korea was perhaps even more damaging evidence than were the expropriations from United Fruit. "Expropriation in itself," he wrote in his memoirs, "does not, of course, prove Communism; expropriation of oil and agricultural properties years before in Mexico had not been fostered by Communists." As "proof" Eisenhower cited the Korean War, during which Guatemala not only did not participate, but "it accepted the ridiculous Communist contention that the United States had conducted bacteriological warfare in Korea."[77]

Eisenhower was not alone in emphasizing the alleged use by the United States of bacteriological warfare in Korea. Early in his well-publicized 1953 lecture at Dartmouth College, appropriately entitled "Syllabus on the Communist Threat in the Americas," Truman's former assistant secretary, Spruille Braden, indicted Guatemala for not banning a film that charged the United States with conducting an inhumane war. Miller's successor, John Cabot, also highlighted the Korean controversy when he spoke against Communism in Guatemala. The tenuous logic of his argument underscores the prevalent line of reasoning:

> We find it difficult, for example, to be patient, after all the blood and treasure we have poured out in Korea to safeguard the Free World, when the official Guatemalan newspaper follows the Communist line by accusing us in effect of bacteriological warfare just after our airmen have returned to tell us of the tortures to which they were subjected to extract fabricated confessions.[78]

The discussion of United States concern over the Arévalo government's support for the Caribbean Legion now comes into sharper focus. From their cold war perspective, analysts perceived the legion not as an antidictator organization, and a small one at that, but as a sinister vehicle by which the "seed [of Guatemalan Communism] will spread to all Latin American countries."[79] The State Department held that the Communist strategy was to divide and subvert all Guatemala's neighbors. The desired effect of this strategy would be the weakening of each country, of hemispheric solidarity, and eventually of the United States. In other words, the alleged Communist presence in Guatemala could leave the entire hemisphere open to attack.[80]

One State Department memorandum after another implicated the Guatemalan government in a plot to overthrow one or another Caribbean or Central American dictatorship. Among those countries Arévalo purportedly conspired against were Nicaragua, Honduras, the Dominican Republic, and Costa Rica.[81] According to Richard Patterson, Arévalo once remarked to Edwin Kyle that after he had served out his term of office he would like nothing more than to devote the rest of his life to eliminating the Latin American dictators.[82] From his initial campaign speeches he made clear his opposition to Somoza, Trujillo, and others of their ilk. Sympathetic governments joined with Arévalo until, as the CIA reported, the Caribbean became divided into two "mutually hostile alignments," with Guatemala, Cuba, and Venezuela opposing Nicaragua, Honduras, and the Dominican Republic. This contest between what the CIA called the democracies and the dictatorships jeopardized the political stability of the region, but, the agency added, "Communists are not a major factor."[83] Nevertheless, when the National Planning Association published its findings in 1953, it reflected the overwhelming consensus in the United States that the Guatemalan government used the Caribbean Legion as "a major instrument of ambitious Communist plans."[84]

Observers throughout the White House, State Department, Congress, and the informed public[85] found other indications of Communist activity in Guatemala. Missives like those by Milton Wells prominently mentioned the visits of the Chilean poet Pablo Neruda to Guatemala, and in 1950 *New York Times* correspondent Crede Calhoun reported that Neruda's visits received wide acclaim in the newspaper *Nuestro Diario*, "which frequently speaks for the government." While these allusions to Neruda highlighted his Communist beliefs, they omitted any reference to the Chilean's reputation as Latin America's greatest living poet.[86] State Department officials carefully chronicled each time a Guatemalan journeyed behind the Iron Curtain, whether it be to study the various land reform programs in Eastern Europe or to negotiate trade agreements with the Balkan countries.[87] One memorandum concluded that this boundary between the Free World and the Communists "can only be crossed by agents of, or outstanding sympathizers with, communism."[88]

As was the case with the Korean War analysis, a high proportion of the indictments against Guatemala emphasized the anti–United States thrust. In 1947, to commemorate the growing success of the labor movement in Guatemala, the unions sponsored a May 1 parade through the capital city. Although this date is traditionally the international labor day, and therefore an appropriate time for this demonstration, United States observers commented only that it was a major holiday in the Soviet Union. They also noted that several Guatemalans carried placards criticizing the recently announced and controversial Truman Doctrine. Guatemala's union leaders took this occasion to issue a statement regarding their objectives, which the State Department described as a criticism of the American Federation of Labor and a "curiously confused but acceptably Marxian resume of some phases of economic and political history."[89]

What Washington interpreted as official Guatemalan snubs also came under the heading of evidences of Communism. Ambassador Richard Patterson complained bitterly to Arévalo's minister of health when, at the 1949 dedication of the new wing of the Roosevelt Hospital, he was not invited to say one word, the United States flag was not flown, and only after his personal request did the Guatemalan president agree to play *The Star-Spangled Banner*. The following year there occurred a more serious incident. The Arévalo government proudly sponsored the Central American and Caribbean Games, which were held in Guatemala City's Olympic Stadium. The United States did not participate in these games, but Puerto Rico did. Guatemalan officials, therefore, felt it was fitting that Puerto Rico should be allowed to carry its own flag at the inaugural ceremonies and that its athletes should be greeted by "La Borinqueña," a Puerto Rican dance tune, rather than the United States national anthem. Since Arévalo had gone on record as a firm opponent of all forms of colonialism, Secretary of State Dean Acheson perceived this gesture as another instance of Guatemala's parroting the Communist line and declared that its government "appears to consider that it has a mission to obtain—the complete separation of Puerto Rico from the United States."[90]

The most publicized anti-Yankee episode during the Arévalo administration concerned Ambassador Patterson himself. It may not be just to label Patterson "a businessman before he was a diplomat," as did the *Nation* in 1950, but the liberal journal was correct in calling him "an unfortunate choice as ambassador to a country engaged in a social revolution."[91] A midwestern businessman who had made his mark as an executive with the RKO and Du Pont corporations, Patterson had little diplomatic experience and knew virtually nothing about Latin America. His success in the financial world led to his selection as Roosevelt's assistant secretary of commerce, and, as a reward for his dedication to both the government and the Democratic party, he received the ambassadorship to Yugoslavia in 1944. He was miscast. In spite of the increasing signs of Tito's disenchantment with the Soviet Union, Patterson, whose career had represented the benefits of a free enterprise system, could not refrain from openly criticizing Yugoslavian economic practices. His repeated interference into what Tito considered the internal affairs of his country drove the marshal to request Patterson's recall, and in 1947 he returned to the United States.[92]

Patterson's recall coincided with Ambassador Edwin Kyle's resignation. Like Patterson, Kyle was not a career diplomat—for thirty-three years he had been dean of the Agricultural and Mechanical College of Texas. Roosevelt's understanding that Guatemala's problems stemmed primarily from its agricultural economy prompted his appointment of Kyle, and Truman hoped that by retaining Kyle he could establish good relations with the Arévalo government, regardless of other contravening factors. Indeed, during the first few years of the revolution, Kyle's sympathetic attitude toward the re-, form programs made him, in the words of Latin American expert Samuel Guy Inman, "the most popular man in Guatemala."[93] Inman undoubtedly exaggerated, but Kyle was given the country's highest decoration, the rank of Grand Commander of the Order of the Quetzal,[94] because, according to the government, "he understood us."[95] One prominent agriculturist earlier praised Kyle for having "done more for us in Guatemala . . . than any of your [United States] ambassadors you have sent us in the past 100 years," a remark that prompted Kyle to write a friend that "these people down here seem to appreciate an Ambassador who is not interested in politics but who is anxious to help them in the development of their natural resources, which are largely agricultural."[96]

When Kyle agreed to Truman's request to continue his mission after Roosevelt's death, the ambassador stated that because of personal considerations he would prefer not to remain in Guatemala too much longer. As events transpired, it is unlikely that Truman would have permitted Kyle to stay on in any case. By 1948 the State Department felt it needed someone who *was* interested in politics. In this sense, Patterson's sudden availability seemed fortuitous. Here was a man who had proven in Yugoslavia that he would not tolerate any form of Communism. Whereas someone like Edwin Kyle might have excused Arévalo's programs as necessary reforms, Patterson, Truman confidently believed, would not be so naïve. His long corporate experience guaranteed that he would follow attentively such indications of Communism as government and labor criticisms of United States companies, and in fact, on making the appointment, Truman wrote Patterson that he was "fully aware of the effective manner with which you carried out your duties as Ambassador to Yugoslavia . . . For these reasons I am pleased to welcome you for an assignment . . . where the interests of the United States need the services of a successful businessman and an experienced diplomat."[97] Patterson understood his task and agreed that he was well prepared. Writing to Miguel Ydígoras Fuentes, that staunch opponent of the revolution, the new ambassador explained, "I feel that I know many of the tricks of international communism, and my three years of experience with Marshal Tito should be helpful in my future work."[98]

Patterson hardly let any time elapse before coming directly to the point. At a dinner hosted by Arévalo to honor his arrival in January 1949, the new ambassador stated bluntly that his job was "to protect and promote American interests in Guatemala."[99] Lest his words not be taken seriously by the administration, he repeated them exactly in August, adding that "these interests had been persecuted, prosecuted, and unmercifully kicked around over the past two years and that personally I was fed up and the patience of my government nearly exhausted."[100] Early the next year, Patterson demanded that Arévalo dismiss from his government seventeen officials, all of whom he accused of being Communists. If Arévalo refused, the ambassador warned, the United States government would deny Guatemala any further assistance.[101]

It was the patience of the Guatemalan government that became exhausted first. Arévalo complained to Inman that "you do not have an Ambassador of the United States here, but a representative of United Fruit."[102] Then, on March 24, 1950, the Guatemalan president sent Foreign Minister Ismael González-Arévalo to Washington to join with Ambassador Antonio Goubaud-Carrera in formally protesting Patterson's actions. In a conversation with Willard Barber and Thomas Mann of the State Department's Latin American division, the two Guatemalan envoys stated that Patterson had overstepped all bounds of propriety by demanding the resignation of their government's officials. Furthermore, his incessant criticisms had "resulted in the crystallization of personal animosities which were directed not against the United States but against the Ambassador personally. This made it unsafe for him to remain in Guatemala." Goubaud-Carrera then presented Barber and Mann with a brief note requesting Patterson's recall.[103]

This request instigated a flurry of activity in Washington. Rumors circulated that, if Patterson were not removed immediately, he would be officially declared *persona non grata*. On March 25, Secretary of State Acheson wired Patterson to cancel all his scheduled appearances and return to the United States as soon as possible. After replying that the Guatemalan government's alleged concern for his safety was a crude attempt to silence him, Patterson reluctantly consented. Giving the excuse that he required special medical attention, he left for the United States on April 6. On that day the *New York Times* praised him for having taken "an outspoken position in opposition to the Communist element in Guatemala" and reported that "it is generally assumed here that the moving force behind the demand for his recall came from that quarter."[104]

Although the Arévalo government never did officially declare Patterson *persona non grata*, the State Department decided that he should remain in the United States.[105] Categorically denying the contention that Patterson had been guilty of intervening in Guatemala's internal affairs, the official Washington position was that Communists had "influenced the government to expel Ambassador Patterson on trumped up charges that he was the agent of United States imperialism."[106] The case against Guatemala now seemed conclusive. Representative Monroe M. Redden of North Carolina, referring to the Central American republic as "the Communist haven of the Western Hemisphere," described the Patterson incident as "a story of personal and official resistance to Communist intrigue and chicanery, and of bluntly spoken protest against acts harmful to the United States and to United States commercial interests in Guatemala."[107] Perhaps most important of all, President Truman himself acknowledged for the first time that he accepted the indictments. In March 1951 he appointed Patterson ambassador to Switzerland, thanking him "on behalf of the American people" for his "no compromise policy on Communist influence and aggression. You have set an example that others may very well emulate."[108] After Eisenhower succeeded Truman, Ambassador John Peurifoy would do more than just "emulate" this "no compromise policy."

5. From Truman to Eisenhower: The Road to Intervention

The evidence provided thus far documents the increasing concern with which United States observers viewed what they perceived to be the spread of Communism throughout Guatemala and the means by which they reached their conclusions. The final chapters maintain that these conclusions were greatly exaggerated and unfortunately led to short-sighted policies. These exaggerations and misperceptions did not result from lunatic paranoia. Most of those who postulated that Guatemala was becoming Communist-dominated were not extremists in the mold of Joseph McCarthy. Their view was the majority view, accepted by both liberals and conservatives within the governmental, journalistic, and academic communities. Furthermore, Communists did exist in Guatemala, even if, as Milton Wells reported in 1948, their estimated number was only two hundred.[1] To understand why so many misinterpreted the Guatemalan situation, we must analyze their assessments in the context of the cold war ethos. In the previously cited 1949 words of Dwight Eisenhower, practically all United States citizens were "professional patriots and Russian haters," and so they remained into the 1950s.[2] They firmly believed that a Soviet-masterminded international conspiracy threatened the Free World and that the Communist agents were almost impossible to identify.

THE THREAT OF GUATEMALAN COMMUNISM: THE COLD WAR FRAMEWORK

The identification of Communists presented particular problems to United States analysts. As mentioned in chapter 1, at the 1951 Consultative Meeting of Foreign Ministers the State Department had to abandon its proposal to establish a technical staff in order to identify subversive elements in the western hemisphere. It knew of no method by which this could be done; certainly effective conspirators wouldn't reveal themselves in public. The period's broad definition of Communism—as the opposing of United States interests—made matters even more difficult. This definition produced a range of subversive classifications, including Communists (card-carrying members of the Communist party), fellow travelers, Communist sympathizers, crypto-Communists, and other similar labels. And Ubico and then Ponce commonly branded all their opponents as Communists, further complicating the task in Guatemala.[3]

The results of this imprecision are all too familiar to the contemporary public. The excesses of Senator McCarthy and the loyalty and security programs of both the Truman and the Eisenhower administrations need not be repeated here. It is essential, however, to emphasize that within the framework of the cold war ethos, when the fear of Communist aggression dominated the foreign policy community, United States officials who themselves suffered from McCarthy's indictments applied the same practices to the international arena.[4] On-the-spot observers like Ambassador Patterson did not consider it necessary to prove a Guatemalan was a Communist. They believed that, by understanding the nature of Communism, they could identify Communists. Patterson called his method of detection the duck test, and he explained it to a 1950 Rotary Club audience:

> Many times it is impossible to prove legally that a certain individual is a communist; but for cases of this sort I recommend a practical method of detection—the "duck test." The duck test works this way: suppose you see a bird walking around in a farm yard. This bird wears no label that says "duck." But the bird certainly looks like a duck. Also, he goes to the pond and you notice that he swims like a duck. Then he opens his beak and quacks like a duck. Well, by this time you have probably reached the conclusion that the bird is a duck, whether he's wearing a label or not.[5]

The identification of the Soviet Union as the mastermind behind the Guatemalan conspiracy presented much less of a problem. In the bipolar world of the cold war, United States leaders used "Communist" and "Soviet" interchangeably. In the words of the Eighty-third Congress' Senate Foreign Relations Committee chairman, Alexander Wiley, "There is no Communism but the Communism which takes orders from the despots of the Kremlin in Moscow. It is an absolute myth to believe that there is such a thing as homegrown Communism, a so-called native or local communism."[6] Convinced that the Communist world was hegemonic and that Guatemala was becoming Communist-dominated, Washington logically concluded that this small American republic, so close to the United States and so close to the Panama Canal, was on the brink of becoming another arm of the Soviet state. The State Department's Thomas Mann put it best: "This government [the United States] knew that Communists the world over were agents of Soviet imperialism . . ."[7]

Herein lay the grave danger of Guatemalan Communism. If the Soviet Union established an outpost in the western hemisphere, it could undermine Washington's position more seriously than could a Communist take-over of any other region of the globe. It could use Guatemala as a base to extend its subversive operations throughout Latin America, disrupting the United States' lifeline to markets and essential raw materials. More threatening were the strategic implications of a Soviet beachhead. By infiltrating neighboring governments and creating unstable or even anarchic political conditions, the Soviet Union could shatter hemispheric defense arrangements like the Rio pact, the key to Truman's Latin American program, and could penetrate the vital Panama Canal Zone. Eventually the Kremlin would no longer have to act through proxies; it could simply move its weapons to the Caribbean. In its white paper on the Communist penetration of Guatemala, the State Department succinctly summarized the international aspects of this Communist challenge:

> The Guatemalan PGT [Partido Guatemalteco de Trabajo, the Guatemalan Labor party, which was controlled by Guatemalan Communists] acted within a global, not a local Guatemalan context. It conceived of the ultimate triumph of communism in Guatemala as part of a successful world wide advance of the Communist [that is, Soviet] forces, and as a disciplined battalion in advance of an army. It adjusted its tactics and objectives to support the main effort.[8]

The department's synopsis reveals a critical element in its concern over Guatemalan developments—the alleged Communist penetration of Guatemala had international implications. Rejecting the notion of an indigenous Communist movement, United States observers likewise viewed local, or nationalist, movements for reform as mere fronts for the Kremlin's intrigues. Even those native reformers who sincerely sought to improve their country's conditions became, perhaps unknowingly, dupes of the Soviets. Neutrality, as John Foster Dulles would later make clear and, in fact, as United States policies insured, was impossible within a bipolar world.

Because United States policy makers believed that the real problem stemmed from Moscow, not Guatemala City, they adroitly developed an analysis applicable to any underdeveloped region. Not surprisingly, their analysis began with the "fall" of China, considered the most demonstrable evidence of past failures to understand the Communist mind. Whereas few in Washington had the intellectual discipline to wade through Stalin's *Problems of Leninism*, Eudocio Racines' *The Yenan Way* provided a much less demanding means of comprehending Soviet strategy.[9]

Racines, a native Latin American, had spent many years within Communist circles before becoming disillusioned just prior to World War II. His 1951 memoirs presented a convincing exposé of the international Communist conspiracy. Racines reported that, while in the Soviet Union in 1934, he discussed the "Road of Yenan" with several Chinese Communist dignitaries. They planned to ally themselves with middle-class politicians and ambitious army officers who were frustrated by Chiang Kai-shek and his corrupt Kuomintang. Eventually they would work themselves into situations of power, winning election to influential positions within local communities and becoming indispensable to their non-Communist allies. Racines quoted from a conversation he claimed to have had with Li Li Siang, the founder of the Chinese Communist party: "[The allies] will help to make the name of the party popular and they will protect us so that the party shall have men in office." Racines alleged that Mao himself told him that, once the Communists had become sufficiently entrenched, they would turn on the "petit bourgeois" and "strike him hard. He must be really destroyed with every arm at hand, be left a wretched tatter at the end."[10]

To Free World leaders still reeling from the loss of China and now faced with what they felt was naked aggression in Korea, *The Yenan Way* both explained the current predicament and presented a grim prospect for the future. From their vantage point, it also coincided with what was occurring in Guatemala. After all, Racines implied that he had been instructed to transport the strategy back to his native continent. Fortified with their past successes, including the theft of the atomic secret, the Soviets apparently were ready to begin their move toward world domination. According to the experts, the Kremlin felt sufficiently confident not only to order the attack on South Korea but also to establish an outpost in the United States' backyard.

Shortly after the publication of Racines' book, policy makers began to apply his analysis to conditions in Guatemala.[11] By the time of Arbenz's fall, it had become the official explanation for what had happened. As a matter of fact, Raymond G. Leddy, State's officer in charge of Central American and Panamanian affairs, remarked that the subversion of Guatemala required special study since the Communists had distinctly improved the "Yenan Way" so as to produce the "Guatemalan Way." Testifying before the House of Representatives hearing on Communist aggression, Leddy maintained that in Guatemala the infiltrators had not needed military force, as in Eastern Europe, nor had they depended on massive shipments of arms and supplies from the Soviet Union, as in China.[12] Had the Soviets succeeded in Guatemala, their triumph would have been even more devastating for the Free World than previous ones. They would have established a puppet government in the western hemisphere solely by political infiltration—by seizing control of a nationalist movement and perverting its purposes to their own ends.[13]

The acceptance of such an analysis made it easy for observers to interpret virtually every Guatemalan measure as further illustration of the success of the "Guatemalan Way." The interpretation resulted from a simple syllogism. Since there were some Communists in Guatemala, they must be following Moscow's orders and worming their way into the policy-making elite. The results were the Labor Code, agrarian reform, and eventually strict censorship, suppression of dissonance, and virulent anti-Yankee attitudes and policies. Not only Washington officials advanced this tendentious argument. Within the cold war ethos, it ultimately dominated contemporary literature, and both journalists and academicians accepted its logic. As epitomized in the writings of Professor Robert Alexander of Rutgers University, a leading authority on Latin America who worked informally with the government in its campaign against Guatemala, the consensus in 1954 was that "Guatemala presents an interesting case study of how a Communist party, starting with nothing, can in a short period of time rise to a position of great influence in the public life and government of a nation."[14]

BUILDING THE CASE AGAINST GUATEMALA

Patterson's controversial departure from Guatemala in 1950 indicated to the United States that a sufficient number of Communists had penetrated the Arévalo government to permit the Soviet agents tremendous leverage. In spite of their obvious uneasiness about the

leftist direction of Guatemala under the first revolutionary government, many pundits in the United States had felt—or hoped—that
Arévalo would prevent the country from swinging entirely into the
Soviet orbit. Embassy officials in particular, while acknowledging
that the Guatemalan president recognized the purported Communist leanings of many of his associates, maintained that "on balance
. . . despite these disturbing circumstances, the record does not
make a closed case against Arévalo for alleged communism."[15] Certain of his executive measures, such as the dissolution of the labor
school Escuela Claridad for being "international or foreign in character" and the dismissal of radicals from influential government posts,
suggested that Arévalo would not tolerate extremely pro-Soviet influences.[16] While State Department officers would have preferred
that he be less liberal in his acceptance of alleged Communists,
most opined that he was not a Communist, that his liberal attitudes
toward Communists resulted from an ill-advised confidence that he
could enlist their aid for his reform programs without jeopardizing Guatemala's non-Communist alignment. Milton Wells reflected
this sentiment when he wrote, "It is felt that [Arévalo] is more of
a political opportunist of the extreme left than a Communist, who
admits the fallacies of Marxism, but who believes that the chief
function of the State is to champion the under privileged and force
needed social and economic reforms upon the intransigent conservatism and 'reaction.'"[17]

With the change of administrations, many at Foggy Bottom predicted that the United States would be pleased with the answer to
what Wells called the "big question on everyone's mind . . . Will Arbenz divorce his administration from the strong Communist influences which have compromised the present government?"[18] Assistant Secretary of State Edward Miller testified before the Senate
Foreign Relations Committee that Arbenz's military background enabled him to understand "the realities of life better than Arévalo
does." Miller believed that Arbenz was not a Communist and that,
although he would have a difficult time changing the pro-Soviet
course of Guatemala's government, he would "work in that direction . . . and be successful over the long term."[19] Wells wrote the
State Department that the United States embassy in Guatemala held
the opinion that "the coming Arbenz administration will veer somewhat toward the center and that the Communists will be quietly
pushed aside even if not entirely eliminated from their present positions of influence."[20]

Miller and Wells evidently reflected the department's majority
view in 1950. This would soon change. As a matter of fact, even at

this early date a strong minority felt otherwise. Senior official Tapley Bennett described Arbenz as a ruthless opportunist with no political convictions of his own who was, therefore, unlikely to challenge the powerful Communist elements. Ambassador Patterson concurred, as did such influential publications as the *New York Times* and *Newsweek*. *Intelligence Digest*, a private British journal read by President Truman and other Washington policy makers, contended that Arbenz "has been approved by Moscow and has the support of all Communist controlled organizations."[21] The CIA and military intelligence charged that Arbenz did orchestrate Araña's assassination, predicting that "all the government structure . . . will follow more than ever a Communist line policy." The FBI advised that in 1948 he began to actively propagandize the Communist cause within the army.[22] By the time of Arbenz's overthrow, this minority opinion had become a unanimous conclusion—even the reservation that he was a tool of the Communists had been ruled out in favor of the conviction that he was a card-carrying member of the party. Ambassador Peurifoy went so far as to testify in 1954 that evidence uncovered by his embassy months prior to Castillo Armas' invasion identified the former president's Communist code number as 44.[23]

United States policy makers revised their assessment of Arbenz by extending the analysis they had applied to Arévalo: they perceived each new development as a further manifestation of Communist subversion. A month before the November 1950 national election, the State Department Office of Intelligence Research completed a report titled "Guatemala: Communist Influence." Approved by the CIA station chief in Guatemala, Collins Almon, and praised by Milton Wells as "an excellent piece of work" that "deserves to be commended highly," the report traced the "rather steady progress" of the Communist movement since the 1944 revolution. For 112 pages it recapitulated almost all the arguments advanced in the United States over the past years, asserting at the end that, due to the attitudes and policies of the Arévalo administration, Communists now dominated the labor movement and had obtained influential positions in the government and political parties. The authors predicted Arbenz's election but would not speculate about what he would do. With ominous overtones, however, they wrote that "the future of communism in Guatemala depends much on the 1950 election and the man who succeeds Arévalo as President."[24]

In short, because Washington had concluded by the time of Arbenz's election that Arévalo's policies, intentionally or not, had prepared the ground for Communist penetration of Guatemala, the only way that the new president could have won the approval of the Truman administration would have been to have disavowed his prede-cessor's programs and rejected most of his party's staunchest supporters. Not only was this politically unfeasible but also, as has been noted, Arbenz's interpretation of the revolution's mandate was identical to Arévalo's. During the campaign he had pledged his government to bring to fruition the reforms that had been initiated since 1944. Hence, despite the guarded optimism with which the majority of United States observers viewed the 1950 election, it seems highly improbable that they could have found the new regime any more satisfactory than the preceding one. In fact, within a few months of Arbenz's March 15, 1951, inauguration, the State Department was already discouraged. As Tapley Bennett wrote in his continuation of "Some Aspects of Communist Penetration in Guatemala" (he called the new paper "A Review of Communist Influence in Guatemala"), "The two-and-a-half-month period since the inauguration of Arbenz as President of Guatemala provided few indications to bear out hopes that the new President would take action to reduce the influence on the Government and life of Guatemala of known Communists and leftist extremists."[25]

According to Bennett, Arbenz had appointed a number of Communists to strategic positions in his government, had permitted an increase in the volume of Communist propaganda activities in Guatemala, had supported the Communist labor leaders, and had pursued foreign policies paralleling those of the Soviet Union. If anything, Bennett charged, Communist elements had consolidated their economic and political bases: "The ascending curve of Communist influence has not even tended to level off, but has inclined upward on an accelerated incline."[26] In acknowledging the study Assistant Secretary Miller wrote, "I think the attached [study] is an excellent factual presentation," and he requested that Bennett summarize it for the next undersecretary's meeting so that the department could better plan steps "to put the squeeze on the Commies in Guatemala."[27]

The 1952 agrarian reform bill, therefore, was merely the *coup de grace* as far as Truman's advisers were concerned. Throughout 1951 and 1952 they monitored with increased apprehension the policies of the Arbenz government toward United Fruit, fearing the confrontation that seemed inevitable. Diplomatic dispatches and memoranda repeatedly linked the labor disputes, the government position, and the possible closure of UFCO operations in Guatemala to the influence of Communist subversives. Long before the first expropriation, but a month before Truman left office, his administration had indicted and convicted the Guatemalan revolution for having become permeated by Communism. It would be up to Eisenhower, Dulles, and the Republicans to devise a suitable sentence.[28]

THE GENESIS OF A POLICY

To decide that the Communist influence in Guatemala had grown to dangerous proportions is one thing; to develop policies to counteract this influence is quite another. Truman and his advisers relied on traditional diplomatic and economic mechanisms to maintain the stability of the Latin American nations and to guarantee their adherence to the objectives of the United States. The Democratic policy makers did not lose interest in their neighbors to the south but assumed that, relative to other troubled regions of the globe, Latin America was safe; given certain political and fiscal limitations, expediency required that the bulk of United States resources and attention be committed to Europe, Asia, and the Middle East. Consequently, while such dramatic initiatives as the promulgation of the Marshall Plan, the construction of the NATO alliance, the formulation of the Truman Doctrine, and the dispatch of troops to Korea highlighted Truman's foreign policies, for Latin America there were only a modest military aid program and ineffective Point Four assistance.

By 1950, convinced as they were that the situation in Guatemala necessitated greater involvement, Truman's officials attempted to establish some means by which, without "risking improper identification, even by implication, with any movements in Guatemala against Arbenz," they could better control the direction of the government. Unable to take really positive steps, they relied on negative ones, or, as Raymond Leddy later wrote, "we have steadfastly maintained a policy of withholding favors from the Guatemalan Government."[29] The first of these favors was military equipment. Traditionally the United States had supplied Guatemala with arms and munitions, but the Truman administration instituted a boycott. On the surface the boycott might appear to have contradicted the administration's emphasis on hemispheric defense, but it was consistent with the prevailing fear of Communist aggression. The criticism that arose over Arévalo's failure to sign the Rio pact and his support for the Caribbean Legion, coupled with the assumption that the Soviet Union intended to use Guatemala as a station from which it could launch incursions throughout the hemisphere, makes Washington's reluctance to provide Guatemala with arms understandable. Not long after Eisenhower took office, when Arbenz became convinced that plans for an invasion of Guatemala were underway, his ambassador to the United States, Guillermo Toriello Garrido, repeatedly requested that the new administration lift the boycott. On one occasion Assistant Secretary of State for Inter-American Affairs John Cabot responded bluntly, "We had to be sure about the orientation of the people who were getting the arms." State took Toriello's request "under study."[30]

Washington officials felt the denial of economic assistance would have a more immediate impact than the arms boycott. They contemplated withholding Point Four assistance, canceling the agricultural research program that the United States had planned in Guatemala, discontinuing the educational exchange, and similar measures. Also, because the State Department felt that the Arévalo administration exhibited a hostile attitude toward any United States business concern, it considered presenting its case before the Organization of American States and even instituting unilateral economic sanctions. While not ruling out such a course of action, officials decided to delay these measures. Despite having been attacked by allegedly discriminatory reforms and worker agitation, United States interests had not yet suffered any serious harm, and Washington predicted that too forceful a policy might lead to extreme retaliation. Furthermore, Truman's advisers still hoped that the Communists could be isolated, and they feared a policy that might drive moderates into the radical camp. Perhaps the newly elected president and National Assembly would understand the wisdom of conciliation.[31]

The Truman strategy through 1950 was to be patient, to wait and see what transpired under Arbenz. The Latin American desk, nevertheless, had recommended a year before the election that "it would not be rational to go ahead and confer additional benefits before we have some reliable assurances as to the treatment American capital will receive in the future." Washington decided that existing assistance programs should be continued but that no new ones would be authorized. The approximately $850,000 that had been allotted for future use in Guatemala would be set aside as a reserve contingency for fiscal 1951, if the situation improved. Relatedly, in 1949 Paul C. Daniels, the director of American republic affairs, had instructed Ambassador Patterson to "speak to the President again of the contributions that United States private capital is making to the Guatemalan economy and the role it could play in future development." Patterson, rejecting this positive approach, harangued Arévalo for Guatemala's harassment of private capital. Official policy now coincided with Patterson's negativism. Department representatives would hold "frank and open discussions of the problems" with the new Guatemalan president and his top officials, "making moderate groups aware of the real harm being done to United States–Guatemalan relations by present trends in that country."[32]

GUATEMALA AND PUBLIC OPINION

At the same time that the department would be presenting its case to the Guatemalan government, it hoped that the press would be presenting a similar case to the United States populace. Actually, Washington would do more than hope, for another component of the Truman policy called for conducting a campaign through the newspapers and magazines to bring the situation in Guatemala to the public attention. The mechanism for such a campaign had just been established. The postwar emphasis upon "the battle for the minds of men" underscored the need for more direction and coordination of the government's dissemination of information. In 1950 the administration set up the Psychological Operations Coordinating Committee, composed of representatives from the Defense and State departments, the CIA, and the Economic Cooperation Administration. But its effectiveness was suspect, prompting Truman in 1951 to establish the high-level Psychological Strategy Board. Its first head, former Secretary of the Army Gordon Gray, later became Eisenhower's special assistant for national security affairs.[33]

In fact, the government's effectiveness as a propagandist did not significantly improve until the Eisenhower administration, when the National Security Council's Operations Coordinating Board subsumed the Psychological Strategy Board and the State Department established the United States Information Agency. However, in regard to publicizing Guatemalan conditions, the Truman administration received tremendous help from the United Fruit Company. Although Edward Bernays, United Fruit's public relations counsel, could not get UFCO's Zemurray and his lobbyists to use their influence with the Truman White House to persuade the government to institute more activist policies, Bernays himself did take active steps. Referred to in the field as "the father of public relations" and an "institution," Bernays, beginning in the late forties and early fifties, launched a campaign to publicize the Communist menace in Guatemala. He was extremely successful and, in reality, accomplished for the State Department the propaganda component of its own Guatemalan strategy.[34]

Bernays' task was less difficult than one might have expected. First, although the public normally paid little attention to the Central American republics, during this period newspapers and magazines found any item concerning the danger of Communism highly newsworthy. Second, Bernays received the independent assistance of *New York Times* publisher Arthur Hays Sulzberger. Sulzberger, a classmate of Richard Patterson at Columbia University, had visited the ambassador in Guatemala in 1949. While he was there, presumably listening to Patterson's own analysis of Guatemalan conditions, his car was mysteriously set on fire. After his return to New York, Sulzberger dispatched Crede Calhoun, the *Times'* Central American correspondent based in Panama, to investigate the situation in Guatemala. Calhoun could not obtain any more information than that given him by the resident reporter, Mrs. Alfred de Ham. Hence, Sulzberger assigned Will Lissner, a Russian specialist who had written a great deal about economic development, to the story. It was Lissner's reporting that broke the news of the events in Guatemala to the United States public.[35]

While Lissner's articles in the respected *New York Times* were probably the most influential, other leading newspapers and magazines published similar accounts. In 1949 Bernays contacted the *New York Herald Tribune*, resulting in Fitzhugh Turner's five-part series on Guatemala in February 1950. The alleged activities of Communists and mistreatment of United Fruit also received continuous coverage in such prestigious publications as the *Chicago Tribune, Time, Newsweek, U.S. News & World Report*, the *Atlantic Monthly*, and the *Saturday Evening Post*. When the controversy intensified following Arbenz's election, and the enactment of an agrarian reform seemed imminent, Bernays invited a number of important editors and publishers to be UFCO's guests on a fact-finding junket to Guatemala. Among those who accepted were William Bowen, contributing editor for *Time*; Ludwell Denny, Scripps-Howard foreign editor; James G. Stahlman, *Nashville Banner* publisher; Gene Gillete, UPI day manager; Roger Ferger, *Cincinnati Enquirer* publisher; *Newsweek* publisher Theodore F. Mueller and his Latin American associate editor, Harry B. Murkland; Scott Newhall, *San Francisco Chronicle* Sunday editor; John D. Pennekamp, *Miami Herald* associate editor; J. David Stern III, *New Orleans Item* publisher; and William Stringer of the *Christian Science Monitor*. United Fruit's hospitality paid large dividends. Referring to the episode in his memoirs, Bernays wrote, "After their return, as I had anticipated, public interest in the Caribbean skyrocketed in this country [the United States]."[36]

The above narrative is not meant to imply that Bernays or the United Fruit Company intentionally misled the public. The objective of the public relations campaign was, in Bernays' words, "to present the facts to the American public."[37] Even one of the few journalists critical of the prevailing view of Guatemala, Herbert Matthews of the *New York Times*, wrote of Bernays in 1966, "I did not admire United Fruit's previous record in Guatemala or some of the things they were doing in the 1950's, but they had . . . a legitimate story and I could always get [the facts] honestly and straight from the Bernays office."[38] Bernays undoubtedly exaggerated when he termed the coverage of Guatemala "masterpieces of objective reporting," yet Matthews' opinion that the press arrived at its conclusions "no doubt honestly" is a fair assessment.[39] Certainly, the press corps obtained most of its information from United Fruit officials, and its host in Guatemala selected the attractions on the tours. Reporters like Will Lissner, however, spent a month in Guatemala largely independent of the UFCO guides. Their opinions reveal that the press, as well as United Fruit, was infused with the cold war ethos: they assumed that, since there were Communists in Guatemala, they must dominate the country.[40]

Coverage of the events in Guatemala was so unfavorable that, Arévalo recalled bitterly, "the large newspapers, magazines, and radio agencies unleashed a publicity offensive that pulled out all the stops in bombarding defenseless Guatemala."[41] He had reason to complain. To use only the *Times* and the *Herald Tribune* as examples, journalists repeatedly charged that following Arévalo's election Guatemala moved decidedly to the left, increasingly falling under the domination of Communist elements. Since the equation of Communism with Soviet totalitarianism penetrated all reporting, the articles described a discernible trend away from democracy toward dictatorship. Correspondents made no attempt to describe the prerevolutionary political system. Referred to in a *Times* editorial as the "Guatemalan Cancer," Communists were portrayed as responsible for the disruption of the country's previously friendly relations with the United States and, just as important, for the apparent discrimination toward United Fruit.[42] As this "discrimination" intensified, so did press criticism. Correspondents like Sydney Gruson, later a *Times* editor, and his successors wrote that whereas UFCO paid the highest wages in Guatemala, put the Indians to work, built schools, hospitals, and houses, and "tamed the jungle for them and has brought a measure of prosperity, it had become the whipping boy for the Communists, the pawn in the Soviet's vast conspiratorial design."[43] Gruson and NBC's Marshall Banner were so stridently critical that, in February 1954, the Guatemalan government requested their removal for writing articles that Arbenz claimed "defamed and offended" Guatemala (Gruson wrote that Arbenz was "a prisoner of the Communists"). In Senator Alexander Wiley's opinion, the expulsion was "the latest sickening demonstration of the Communist octopus at work," while the *Times* broadened its emphasis by editorializing that the "constant harassment here [in Guatemala] to which the company now is being subjected is largely a Communist tactic."[44]

These evaluations underscore that, in the context of the cold war ethos, it was sufficient for Bernays to "let other people view the facts and present them to the public." United Fruit officials understood that their interests would be served better by letting the press draw its own conclusions than by exerting undue influence. Knowing full well that the media tended to reflect rather than oppose the dominant societal values, which were anti-Communist, not pro-UFCO, Bernays never saw any reason to issue press releases.[45] The editors of the leading publications instituted their own screening process. For example, on his 1950 tour of Guatemala, Samuel Guy Inman conducted a lengthy interview with Arévalo, during which the president distinguished his views from the Communists' and lamented the slanted reporting in the United States. The reputable Inman tried to get the Associated Press, United Press International, the *New York Times*, the *Herald Tribune*, *Newsweek*, and several other journals to run a story based on his findings, but none agreed.[46] The fear of Communist subversion during this period was so strong that editorial staffs, in the mainstream of contemporary thought, shared all the cold war assumptions. They must have thought that dissenters like Inman had been duped. They did not need Edward Bernays or anyone else to tell them that what was occurring in Guatemala was Communist-inspired; they could see it for themselves.[47]

Although opinion analysts did not poll the United States public, one can assume that those who read the journalistic accounts of the Guatemalan government's policy and the trials of United Fruit concurred with the view that the country had become, or was becoming, a threat to the hemisphere. It is logical also to conclude that a direct connection exists between public opinion and official policy. In 1928, Bernays wrote in his seminal study *Propaganda*, "The conscious and intelligent manipulation of the organized habits of the masses is an important element in democratic society. Those who manipulate this unseen mechanism of society constitute an invisible government which is the true ruling power of our country."[48] More recently, especially in the wake of Vietnam and Watergate, we take it as axiomatic that a leading publication's editorial policy, by influencing voter opinion, influences the behavior of a representative government. Just as important, but perhaps less known, is the extent to which elected officials rely upon primary newspapers and journals for their personal information. A leading authority on the press, Bernard Cohen, has written that State Department staff members often remark that their jobs would be impossible were it not for the *New York Times*, a paper described on Capitol Hill as "everyone's Bible of Information" and "every man's CIA."[49]

That State agreed with the journalistic assessments has already been demonstrated. Congress agreed also. Before Arbenz enacted the agrarian reform, the House Committee on Foreign Affairs' subcommittee on the western hemisphere began to devote increasing amounts of time to "the problem that has been most under discussion in the last few months, the problem of Guatemala, which is the only country in the Western Hemisphere where the Communists have made serious inroads into the upper spheres of government." In the other chamber, the influential Senator Wiley, consistently at the forefront of the anti-Arévalo, then anti-Arbenz forces in the United States (he visited Guatemala several times), requested his colleague on the Foreign Relations Committee, Theodore F. Green of Rhode Island, to call his Latin American affairs subcommittee into special session so that it could investigate the Guatemalan situation too. Wiley was certain of what the investigation would reveal. He wrote Green, "It seems to me that Guatemala is going to be a source of Red infection throughout Central America and the sooner we help sterilize that source, the better."[50]

Wiley came from Wisconsin, whose junior senator's electoral success was derived almost exclusively from his unmasking of Communists. But the fact that Wiley's constituency paralleled that of Joseph McCarthy did not signify an ideological identity. In fact, on the issue of Guatemala, McCarthy was uncharacteristically silent. Congressional criticism of the Guatemalan government, and a concomitant sympathy for the United Fruit Company, was not confined to McCarthyite extremists or to any one political party. To illustrate, on March 13, 1952, again before any expropriations, the Democratic senator from Louisiana, Allan Ellender, took the floor to condemn Guatemala's "fanatical and determined" Communists, who have "cunningly devised to identify themselves as the champions of the social justice and nationalist aspects of the Guatemalan Revolution."[51] Almost two weeks later, California's Republican Representative Donald Jackson lashed out at Arbenz, who, the Foreign Affairs Committee member claimed, "endorsed and abetted coercive efforts against the United States and foreign operators almost to the point of rendering successful operations impossible . . . the aggression of the Soviet Union is no less malignant and no whit less dangerous because it is not borne on the tips of Soviet bayonets."[52]

Along with its public relations campaign, UFCO employed several prominent lobbyists on Capitol Hill, headed by former Roosevelt aide Thomas C. Corcoran. The brilliant Corcoran, widely known as Tommy the Cork, had been on Zemurray's payroll since the 1930s. When Ubico expressed an interest in having some of his young cadets meet Roosevelt, Corcoran used his considerable influence to obtain ten thousand dollars from Congress to pay for expenses and also took care of all arrangements. Also on the lobbying staff were former Assistant Secretary Braden and Robert La Follette, Jr., son of the well-known progressive and himself a four-term senator from Wisconsin until defeated by McCarthy in the 1947 primary.[53] The dominant view within Washington suggests that congressional opinion would have favored UFCO's position without these eminent lobbyists, but the tactic was certainly consistent with contemporary business practice. Indeed, a few months before his return from Guatemala, Ambassador Patterson wrote Zemurray:

> With the present severe political instability in this country and the persecution of American interests, my suggestion is that there be an all-out barrage in the U.S. Senate on the bad treatment of American capital in Guatemala. This takes the onus off the UFCO, and puts it on the basis of a demand by our Senators that all American interests be given a fair deal.[54]

Among those targeted for the company's lobbying efforts were Senator Henry Cabot Lodge and Representative John McCormack, both from United Fruit's home state of Massachusetts. United Fruit's difficulties were naturally significant to the congressmen (the Lodge family held UFCO stock for many years) because of the company's critical position within the state's economy. Nevertheless, it would be unfair to longtime public servants like Lodge and McCormack to interpret their utterances as merely reflecting their ties, political or economic, to the United Fruit Company. Each demonstrated on countless other occasions his acceptance of the cold war axioms and undoubtedly would have adhered to the consensus regarding Guatemala under any circumstances. The lobbyists knew that they did not have to approach the two state leaders from the perspective of UFCO's self-interest. Rather, much as Bernays did with the press, they presented the facts, letting the cold war ethos do the influencing for them.

The Massachusetts representatives did tend to emphasize the plight of United Fruit in their general remarks on Guatemalan conditions. Lodge began the senatorial barrage in 1949, charging that Arévalo's Labor Code discriminated against the company and was a tool of the Communists to cause "a serious economic breakdown" of UFCO's Guatemalan operations.[55] A week later McCormack expanded on this theme in the lower chamber. The future Speaker of the House reminded his colleagues that he represented a region that "has made a speciality of Latin America" and that "over 90% of New England's foreign investment is in Latin America, a large part being Boston's United Fruit Company." Now, McCormack argued, this investment was being threatened by the Communists. Whereas United Fruit had brought its technical skills to benefit Guatemala and employed more native workers than any Guatemalan corporation, it was being subjected to wanton attacks from "the foolish tactics of a minority of reckless agitators," and it faced Communist-initiated legislation that virtually divided "all Guatemalan companies into two classes, the United Fruit Company and the rest."[56]

Over the next years McCormack was among the most vocal critics of the Guatemalan government. As United States policy toward the country stiffened, he became a liaison between the State Department and Congress. He cautioned that United Fruit must be viewed not as a local problem but as one that endangered the entire nation. UFCO's only "crime" was that it was a United States company, and Guatemala represented the "malignant growth" of the "Soviet menace in the Western Hemisphere," a menace that must be thwarted before it spread. Should Communist influence increase, and by 1951 McCormack lamented that it was all but dominant, the government's entire program would become "subservient to the Kremlin's design for world conquest." According to the majority leader in 1952, the confiscation of United Fruit's property symbolized the "growth of a Soviet beachhead"; Guatemala had developed into a "situation of great peril."[57]

Representatives of United Fruit also discussed this "situation of great peril" with those directly responsible for constructing United States policy. Their access was not difficult, recalling that Braden had formerly served as Truman's assistant secretary for Latin American affairs. Thomas Dudley Cabot provided another ready channel. Cabot, who had been a director and president of United Fruit and its registrar bank, the First National Bank of Boston, served as director of the State Department's Office of International Security Affairs. Braden's successor, Edward Miller, came to Washington from the Wall Street law firm of Sullivan and Cromwell, United Fruit's legal representative in Guatemala. In 1950 Miller candidly commented to Undersecretary of State James Webb that the department had "a good working relationship with the top people [of United Fruit] in the United States."[58] In fact, throughout the final years of the Truman administration, UFCO executives sent a stream of correspondence to and held numerous conversations with State Department officers concerning Communist activities in Guatemala and their effect on company operations.[59]

Again, however, too much should not be made of UFCO's lobby or its other connections on Capitol Hill. Much has been written about these connections and about those during the Eisenhower administration. Yet United Fruit lobbyists needed to do no more than publicize the accounts presented in the press and Congress, accounts that coincided with the information gathered by Truman's own sources. By cold war standards, the evidence amounted to such an overwhelming indictment of Guatemala that, even without the lobby, a government response was predictable.

THE FIRST ATTEMPT

Following the enactment of the agrarian reform law, Truman's advisers concluded that their policy of moderation and "frank discussions" with Guatemalan representatives had not produced the desired results. The month of the first expropriation of UFCO property, Deputy Assistant Secretary for Inter-American Affairs Thomas Mann sent a memorandum to Truman's Special Counsel Charles Murphy recommending a more forceful alternative. Mann, who would later contribute substantially to the interventions in Cuba and the Dominican Republic, had been moving toward a more active policy for several years. In 1951 he had headed Truman's delegation to Arbenz's inaugural ceremony. Included with his ceremonial tasks was the additional assignment of collecting information on the new president's political inclinations. After talking with several of his Guatemalan acquaintances and some members of the United States embassy, he concluded that Arbenz was indeed a Marxist. Some months earlier, while director of the Office of Middle American Affairs, Mann had met with United Fruit's lobbyist Thomas Corcoran. Corcoran told him that the "die was already cast" between the Guatemalan government and UFCO and that he had been "turning over in his mind the possibility that the American companies might agree between themselves on some method to bring the moderate elements into power in Guatemala." In Corcoran's opinion, "Arbenz, like Macbeth, could not last and . . . something ought to be done by American companies to bring a measure of political stability and social tranquility."[60]

It is impossible to gauge how much his earlier conversation with Corcoran influenced Mann's views in 1952. Certainly it could not have had more impact than his own trip to Guatemala. In any case Mann, a rising young star in the State Department and a consummate believer that instability and nationalism in Latin America bred Communism, undoubtedly shared Corcoran's assessment.[61] The State Department in 1950, nevertheless, was undecided about the direction Arbenz would take, and Assistant Secretary Miller was one of those who still considered the possibilities good for more conciliatory relations. Also, as yet there was no definite candidate to replace Arbenz. Mann told Corcoran at the time of their meeting that the United States government was not willing to go along with any company-sponsored method of bringing about a change in Guatemala's government. But, in his 1952 memorandum to Murphy, Mann himself proposed a method. While not going so far as to suggest any type of clandestine operation, and conceding that "our ability to exert leverage is limited," he advised that "we should make it clear, by our acts rather than words, that cooperation begets cooperation; that all the United States is capable of reacting when unfairly attacked; and above all, that [Guatemala's] own self interest is best served by cooperating with the United States." Mann was vague about what these acts should be. Generally he favored an increased economic boycott, and the United States did refuse Arbenz any aid and withdrew its remaining technical assistance missions. According to Mann, "Our refusal to extend favors will create serious problems for the government."[62]

Given that Mann wanted the government to move more decisively against Arbenz, he might have known of another plan being hatched in 1952. This plan was kept secret, so secret that the primary source of documentation is Herbert Matthews' report of a conversation he had with Edward Miller in 1953. Unfortunately Miller is dead, but Matthews' reputation for accuracy, the assistant secretary's high regard for him, and the circumstances of the plan make his account highly plausible and, therefore, in need of discussion. Miller would have had no reason to concoct the story, and Matthews has no doubt that it is accurate. Furthermore, a recently declassified State Department document does substantiate part of Matthews' account.[63]

Miller told Matthews that the plan surfaced in the summer of 1952, when Nicaragua's ironfisted ruler, Anastasio Somoza, visited Capitol Hill. Somoza, educated in the United States and perhaps Washington's best friend in Latin America (the son of a notorious bandit who had been publicly hanged in Managua, Somoza rose to power as a result of the marines' occupation of his country), traditionally eschewed any pretense of democratic governance and had actively opposed the Guatemalan revolution from its inception.[64] At a meeting with Miller and several unidentified State Department officials during this visit, Somoza boasted that, if the United States would supply him with sufficient arms, "I'll clean up Guatemala for you in no time." Miller did not take the dictator seriously, so a few days later Tacho, as Somoza was called, went to see Truman himself. Along with the President, present in the Oval Office were Secretary Acheson, Undersecretary of State Robert Lovett, Truman's close military aide and friend General Harry Vaughan, and another aide who Matthews thinks was named Marrow. In March 1953 Somoza's son, Anastasio, Jr. (whose 1979 ouster ended the family's close to forty-year rule), confirmed in a conversation with the first secretary of the United States embassy in Nicaragua that this meeting with Truman did occur and that "his father proposed that he take action to bring about the downfall of the Communist government in Guatemala."[65]

Because the proposal was so secret, and neither Miller nor the younger Somoza was privy to all the conversations, the subsequent details are hazy. Evidently the plan called for a united effort on the part of Guatemala's neighbors. Truman felt it worth exploring, so he instructed Marrow to accompany Somoza to Central America to ascertain how much support could be mustered among the other nations. Miller emphasized to Matthews that, when Marrow returned to Washington, he reported directly to Truman that the Somoza plan could work. Truman bypassed the Bureau of Inter-American Affairs and, without any consultation, approved the report and sent it to CIA Director General Walter Bedell Smith, Eisenhower's World War II chief of staff.

Miller and Somoza, Jr., differ as to what happened next. Miller recalled that, given the green light from Truman, the Nicaraguan dictator stepped up his effort to enlist the support of other countries. He had no difficulty in Colombia, the Dominican Republic, or Venezuela but found Cuba's Batista wary and uninterested. Whether

Honduras' José Manuel Gálvez and El Salvador's Oscar Osorio joined the conspiracy is unclear. Apparently Somoza felt that his alliance was sufficiently strong, for he began to question Miller about when he would receive arms. The assistant secretary, not knowing that Truman had agreed to support the plan, consistently told Tacho that he knew nothing of any arms agreement. In the meantime, Bedell Smith and the conspirators decided that an exile living in Honduras, Castillo Moreno, should become Guatemala's liberator. The CIA arranged for a United Fruit freighter to transport the arms in cases marked "agricultural machinery." But, a few days after the ship sailed for Nicaragua, Miller received an authorization request from the department's munitions division. He suddenly realized what had happened and, taking State Department officers Freeman Matthews and David Bruce with him, immediately confronted Acheson. Acheson, who also might have been kept in the dark, presented State's case to Truman, who aborted the plan. To the best of Miller's knowledge, the United Fruit freighter was redirected to Panama and the armaments were unloaded in the Canal Zone.[66]

It seems probable that this basic scenario is accurate. After all, this would have been a low-risk operation for the United States and would have resolved a very thorny problem. All the United States would have done was supply the arms; Somoza pledged to do the rest. Truman, while clearly not the master of covert operations that Eisenhower was, must have found such a seemingly simple solution most appealing. Why then did he call it off so abruptly? Was it because he feared his circumvention of Miller would cause irreparable damage to his relations with the State Department? And was the State Department so dovelike? Neither of these explanations seems adequate.

More likely, certain advisers involved in the project, perhaps Bedell Smith, convinced Truman that an anti-Arbenz invasion had little chance for success at this time. Arbenz was in total command of Guatemala's military, and, as would be seen in 1954, a successful coup required intricate preparations. A defeat could embarrass the United States and, even worse, further solidify support for the Guatemalan revolution. Moreover, Somoza's son, who acted as his father's liaison during the negotiations, reconstructed a slightly different picture. He stressed the reservations of Honduras. Tachito maintained that, unlike the presidents of Peru, Panama, El Salvador, Venezuela, and the Dominican Republic, Gálvez wanted State Department assurances before he made any commitment. When Somoza, who would not have known that State had been excluded and hence believed that the department had not "fully understood the plan his father had in mind," could not get Miller to agree, even to the request that the United States do nothing but look the other way, Gálvez backed off. Since Honduras was strategically critical to any successful invasion, the plan became too risky.[67]

Neither Miller's nor Somoza's account precludes the other; in fact, combined they present a convincing narrative. Truman might have dropped the project because he, and the CIA, knew of Honduras' reluctance, and Miller's continued pleas of ignorance concerning Somoza's queries on the arms shipment could have easily been interpreted by Gálvez as a lack of commitment. What is clear is that, by the end of the Truman administration, at least some officials as well as the CIA had become convinced that a policy of conciliation toward Guatemala was unproductive. More had to be done, and perhaps the answer lay in a clandestine operation in conjunction with Guatemala's surrounding dictatorships. The stillborn project foreshadowed the events two years later and represents the continuity of the cold war ethos.

THE TRANSITION

While the election of Dwight David Eisenhower did not guarantee a United States intervention in Guatemala, it pointed in that direction. Eisenhower could justifiably interpret his overwhelming victory as a mandate for the more actively anti-Communist foreign policy on which he campaigned. To be sure, the liberationist rhetoric of the Republicans lacked real substance, and the popular hero of World War II probably could have been elected as either party's candidate. He had, after all, been wooed by the Democrats as well. But the United States public was tired of such cold war defeats as had occurred in China, just as it was tired of the stalemated Korean War. And it was none too pleased with Truman's recall of General Douglas MacArthur. With MacArthur gone, the people felt comfortable having the other five-star general lead them in the new war. Not only did another global conflict seem almost inevitable, but in 1949 the Soviet Union broke the United States atomic monopoly, for which many blamed Truman and the Democrats' "twenty years of treason." The Red scare was a dominant facet of political life, transcending the person of Joseph McCarthy.[68] Eisenhower radiated the confidence the public so eagerly sought, and he was a proven leader.[69]

That Eisenhower believed in a vigilant policy toward the Soviets is clear from prepresidential entries in his private diary. He concurred with Truman's critics that the Communist take-over in China had resulted from the Democrats' ambivalent policies and firmly warned that only unequivocal resistance on the part of the United States could prevent future incursions. Always the strategist, he attempted to predict Soviet movements. While not as intellectual as his secretary of state, he reached the same conclusions as Racines in *The Yenan Way*, and for this reason he never doubted his advisers' opinions concerning the threat in Guatemala.[70]

If Truman never received any advice challenging the prevalent analysis of Guatemalan conditions, it is hard to imagine finding any mavericks in the Republican administration. Eisenhower's chief opponent for the nomination had been Mr. Republican, Robert Taft; there was no Henry Wallace. McCarthy's censure came following Arbenz's overthrow, and, even after McCarthy, Republicans in Congress forced Eisenhower to depend on Democratic support for his more moderate foreign policies. But, most important of all, Eisenhower's chief diplomatic adviser—the foreign policy spokesman for both the president and the party—was John Foster Dulles.[71] Dulles never dominated Eisenhower, but he did earn the respect and trust of his superior, and only on the rarest occasions was his counsel not followed. As a rule the two men agreed on matters of principle and strategy, and the formulation of a policy toward Guatemala was no exception.[72]

While it is misleading to claim that the Eisenhower administration only spoke with the voice of big business, in fiscal matters it certainly reflected Republican conservatism. Not only did such leaders of commerce and industry as George Humphrey, Charles E. Wilson, and Sinclair Weeks join Dulles in the cabinet, but the president devoutly believed that the nation's security required a sound economy and, if at all possible, a balanced budget. United Fruit's protests found a receptive audience. Eisenhower and his advisers unquestionably assumed that the Guatemalan treatment of UFCO and other foreign interests had to have been instigated by the Communists. Otherwise, Arbenz would have been promoting a variant of Engine Charlie Wilson's dictum: what's good for United Fruit is good for Guatemala.[73]

The official line of Eisenhower's policy defended United Fruit's interests so avidly that political scientist and former State Department member Cole Blasier wrote that the United States government entered into the controversy as a virtual speaker for the company.[74] This analysis is an oversimplification, for it has already been shown that, within the context of the cold war ethos, to defend UFCO in Guatemala was tantamount to defending the hemisphere against the

Communists. Yet, United Fruit's connections within the Eisenhower White House cannot be ignored. They epitomize the genre of individuals charged at this time with constructing foreign policy. These people thought like representatives of United Fruit because they had the same backgrounds. They did not have to be persuaded by company lobbyists. There was no conspiracy.[75]

To begin at the top, Secretary Dulles serves as a prime example of both the direct connections and the ideological affinities that existed among many government and company officials. Through the intervention of his grandfather, former Secretary of State William Foster, Dulles joined the prestigious Wall Street law firm of Sullivan and Cromwell in 1911. Considered "probably dollar-for-manhour the world's most lucrative law firm," Sullivan and Cromwell had for many years represented United States enterprises in Latin America. In his noted study *Lions in the Street*, Paul Hoffman describes one of the firm's founders, William Nelson Cromwell, as "a bachelor recluse who will go down in history as the mastermind behind the international intrigue that led to the Panamanian revolution and the construction of the Panama Canal."[76] On assignment for Sullivan and Cromwell, Dulles went to Central America in 1917; after his return, he urged President Wilson to recognize Costa Rica's pro-UFCO, dictatorial Tinoco government, which had just seized power. Of more significance was his involvement with Guatemala's Ubico. As the firm's executive partner in 1936, he had been instrumental in drafting the contract that gave United Fruit its exceptional status for the next ninety-nine years. Dulles' evaluation of the Arbenz government reflected his steadfast anti-Communism; as Hoffman writes, corporate lawyers tend to identify with their clients, becoming "businessmen with law degrees."[77]

Dulles' background resembled that of many other influential government figures. His brother, Allen, director of the CIA during the Castillo Armas invasion, had also been a partner with Sullivan and Cromwell and had vast experience dealing with United States investors in Latin America. Before World War II, Allen became a director of the J. Henry Shroeder Banking Corporation, another of the firm's clients, which helped finance German economic penetration of Guatemala and in the process acquired a strong interest in International Railways of Central America. John Cabot, who became assistant secretary of state for inter-American affairs in 1953 and had served earlier as ambassador to Guatemala, held a substantial amount of stock in United Fruit. As noted, his brother, Thomas, had been a director and president of both the company and its registrar bank. Another director of the bank was Sinclair Weeks, the secretary of commerce. General Robert Cutler, first special assistant to the president for national security affairs and thus head of its planning board, had been board chairman of the company's transfer bank, Old Colony Trust, which also made him board chairman of United Fruit. Shortly before Arbenz's overthrow, Dulles, after confirming over the phone that Cutler had "pretty close relations with the United Fruit Company," summoned him to the State Department for a private meeting on Guatemala.[78]

The list of officials with UFCO-government connections continues. Former High Commissioner of Germany John J. McCloy, Eisenhower's close friend who as president of the International Bank for Reconstruction and Development had ordered the study of Guatemala's agrarian difficulties, was a United Fruit director. Ann Whitman, the president's personal secretary, was the exwife of United Fruit's director and then vice-president for public relations, Edward. Ambassador Robert Hill in Costa Rica, part of the diplomatic team that participated in the CIA project, was a former vice-president of W. R. Grace and Company, which had large Guatemalan interests, and later became a director of United Fruit. Walter Bedell Smith became a director immediately upon resigning from the government in October 1954. On the Council on Foreign Relations, Whitney H. Shephardson was an IRCA officer, and Robert Lehman served on the UFCO board. Lehman was related by marriage to Frank Altschul, the council's secretary, who was responsible for the influential National Planning Association report that contended that the Communists were in complete control of Guatemala.[79]

Bernays stepped up United Fruit's press campaign to coincide with the change of administrations. To again use the *New York Times* as an example, its journalists portrayed the Arbenz government as being in full partnership with the Communists. The objective of the revolutionary programs was to squeeze UFCO, IRCA, Empresa Eléctrica, and other United States interests. According to the reports, by 1953 opposition to Arbenz had all but collapsed, so that in the National Assembly "Communist sway is no longer disputed and . . . the immediate aims of the government and Communists are indistinguishable." The expropriation of UFCO's uncultivated land was inexcusable, given the precarious nature of the banana industry and the benefits which the company had brought to Guatemala. By developing the land and providing employment, United Fruit had begun the process of modernization, but now "the jungle creeps back."[80] In Herbert Matthews' opinion, Bernays' campaign was on target: the press "saw and wrote exactly what the State Department wanted to see."[81]

Company representatives like Spruille Braden took UFCO's case directly to the United States public. Braden's experience in Latin America was long and controversial. Before becoming Truman's assistant secretary of state, he had numerous clashes with Juan Perón as ambassador to Argentina. In 1953 only John Foster Dulles' intervention averted the display in the Dominican Republic's Ciudad Trujillo of a bronze plaque defaming Braden.[82] "Bradenism" came to be the term applied to particularly undiplomatic negotiations with Latin American dignitaries. Dean Acheson described him as "a bull of a man physically and with the temperament and tactics of one, dealing with the objects of his prejudices by blind charges, preceded by pawing up a good deal of dust."[83] When it came to Communists, Braden was as prejudiced as anyone. Consequently, it struck Adolf Berle as "funny" that Franco's government attacked Braden as a Communist in 1954. Berle wrote a friend, "Spruille Braden is a friend of mine and former colleague. Don't however hold me responsible for all his views. The last time he joined anything it was one of those extreme rightist McCarthyite things."[84]

Braden's proclivity not to mince words and his vehement anti-Communism made him an ardent crusader for United Fruit. In all likelihood he would have criticized the Arbenz government even had he not been in direct contact with UFCO President Kenneth Redmond. Also, he would not have been content with the information supplied by the *New York Times*, a paper he later called "the Mid-Town Daily Worker" and "the New York Tass."[85] But his involvement with United Fruit lent special meaning to his cause. As he told a Houston gathering of the United States Inter-American Council in April 1952, UFCO was the "first victim" of the Communists in Guatemala, where "party members, fellow travellers, demagogues, gunmen and killers, have joined with opportunists, extreme nationalists, some of the military, and a few misguided idealists, to make a beachhead for international Communism." This was Braden's initial speech on the Communist menace in Guatemala, and it set the tone for his future, more publicized statements. United Fruit had to be the Communists' target, he explained to his audience, because, had the company been able to earn a reasonable profit in Guatemala and reinvest millions of dollars in the country's development, "the resultant increases in production, employment, government revenues and general well-being for Guatemala would have obstructed, if not ruined, the Politburo's schemes to spread poverty and chaos in the Western World." Braden concluded by warning that the danger had become so grave that "collective or even unilateral intervention" was not inconceivable.[86]

A year later Braden repeated his warning in a lecture before the great issues course at Dartmouth College. He reiterated many of the same phrases he had uttered in Houston, but he had developed a more dramatic presentation. Rendering a short history of the alleged Communist take-over in Guatemala, he described how Araña had been eliminated from the 1950 presidential election by as "bloody and messy an assassination as can be imagined. So riddled was his body by sub-machine gun bullets, that his insides oozed forth from countless wounds." Braden maintained that he had sworn testimony proving that Arévalo and Arbenz had instigated the murder. He continued by quoting himself regarding the persecution of United Fruit, adding that other United States enterprises operating in Guatemala had been similarly victimized. "Clearly," he lectured, "this particular 'good neighbor' has travelled far down the 'Yenan Way.'" He then called upon the new administration to repudiate Truman's patient diplomatic handling of Guatemala, because "diplomatic 'finesse and patience' are all right under the Marquis of Queensbury rules, but they may bring defeat if applied in a bar-room brawl, such as we are engaged in with the Kremlin." In short:

> Frequently it is necessary to fight fire with fire . . . No one is more opposed than I to interference in the internal affairs of other nations. But . . . we may be compelled to intervene . . . I should like to underscore that because Communism is so blatantly an international and not an internal affair, its suppression, even by force, in an American country, by one or more of the other republics, would not constitute an intervention in the internal affairs of the former . . . I pray that the new Administration will attack this danger rapidly, intelligently and energetically.[87]

Although Braden proposed intervention only as a last resort, the acidity and context of his remarks created a stir in both the United States and Guatemala. He had challenged the Eisenhower administration to take strong measures, to put into action the Republican campaign promises. If the situation required forceful intervention, so be it. The *Times* highlighted this portion of his speech, as did the Guatemalan congress, which revoked the Order of the Quetzal that had been bestowed on him by Ubico.[88] Some United Fruit officials, such as the more liberal Edward Bernays, objected to the choice of words, but even Bernays could not deny that Braden brought added publicity to the Guatemalan controversy.[89]

Evidence exists of Braden's more direct impact on Eisenhower's policies. Beginning in October 1952, he chaired a series of six Council on Foreign Relations study groups titled "Political Unrest in Latin America." Although the council has no official position on Capitol Hill, its influence is well known.[90] Since the group's purpose was to "formulate a new policy toward Latin America to be recommended to the incoming administration," not surprisingly the topic of the initial session was Guatemala. The minutes of the session reflect that Braden's connection with United Fruit compromised his position as chairman. Moreover, he asked his friend John McClintock, formerly of the State Department and currently UFCO's assistant vice-president, to serve as discussion leader. Some of the participants, particularly such Latin American scholars as Columbia's Frank Tannenbaum and Rutgers' Charles Cumberland, tried to direct the forum to distinguish between Communism and nationalism and to analyze Guatemalan conditions historically. Braden and McClintock, however, controlled the meeting. To them, social and economic factors had little to do with the unrest. The problem was Communist subversion, not the maldistribution of land. Braden expressed the prevalent feeling: "Perhaps we are getting to the point where actual armed intervention is the only solution."[91]

The first months of the Eisenhower administration did not assuage the group's concern that more needed to be done—its consensus was that the Republican policies were foundering. The members decided to invite John Cabot, the new assistant secretary for inter-American affairs, to the final session. Their advice to Cabot, succinctly contained in a preparatory paper written by Adolf Berle, was unequivocal: "The Guatemalan situation . . . is quite simply the penetration of Central America by a frankly Russian-dominated Communist group . . . There should be no hesitation in tackling diplomatic exchanges with surrounding governments, in quite overtly working with the forces opposed to Communism, and eventually backing a political tide which will force the Guatemalan government either to exclude its Communists or to change."[92]

Berle's role in insuring that the impetus for an aggressive policy toward Guatemala passed smoothly from Truman to Eisenhower transcended his involvement with the council. The former New Deal brain truster, for many years instrumental in formulating Latin American policies, had close contacts within the countries' ruling elites. In June 1952 he discussed Guatemala with Luis Manuel de Bayle, Somoza's brother-in-law, concluding that "the Communist cell has gotten control of the Guatemalan government."[93] Then in October—around the time that Somoza made his overture to Truman—Berle held a similar conversation with the secretary general of El Salvador's Democratic Revolutionary party, Miguel A. Magaña.

Magaña, who feared that it was only a matter of time before Guatemalan Communism spread throughout the entire Central American region, asked Berle whether he thought the United States would sympathize with an effort by Guatemala's neighbors to overthrow Arbenz. By this time Washington's sympathies had been made abundantly clear, so Magaña must have been seeking the type of commitment that had apparently eluded Somoza and trying to determine how much assistance, if any, he could expect. Berle could not speak for the government, and his reply to Magaña was appropriately circumspect. He agreed that conditions in Guatemala were disturbing and, moreover, constituted a clear-cut case of intervention by the Soviet Union. For this reason, he felt that the 1945 Act of Chapultepec, which stipulated that aggression against one American state was tantamount to aggression against all states, and the 1947 Rio pact, which called for a meeting of foreign ministers to consider collective action against an outside threat, could be invoked on perfectly sound grounds. Berle assured Magaña that he would discuss the matter of ousting Arbenz with Nelson Rockefeller, another longtime Latin American specialist, and Democratic presidential hopeful Adlai Stevenson. He could not guarantee anything, but he encouragingly added, "I think we would welcome it, and if possible guide it into reasonable channels."[94]

Later that day Berle wrote Arthur Schlesinger, Jr., whom he considered the "head of Stevenson's 'Brain Trust.'" Referring to the possibility of an attempt to oust Arbenz, he suggested that Stevenson's advisers immediately set up "some sort of machinery" to work on a program that could be put into operation as soon as Stevenson took office. Stevenson's defeat, of course, made Berle's suggestion irrelevant, and there is no record of his bringing up the subject with the Republican Rockefeller.[95] But, not long after election day, he presented Magaña's views to future CIA Director Allen Dulles and the agency's western hemisphere chief, Colonel J. C. King.[96]

Berle's next step was to initiate a conversation with José Figueres, soon to be elected president of Costa Rica. While Figueres listened, Berle explained that the United States would not tolerate a Communist government in the hemisphere and that some policy had to be devised to eliminate Arbenz. The Costa Rican Social Democrat, himself suspected of being a Communist by some in Washington, concurred that a potentially dangerous situation was developing in Guatemala. Nevertheless, he ruled out military intervention, since he felt it might very well arouse Latin American nationalist reactions and make martyrs out of the Guatemalan revolutionaries. He preferred that Arbenz be induced to get rid of any Communists in his administration. This resolution, however, seemed extremely remote. Figueres was left with one option: wait until the Guatemalan people resolved the problem themselves, by force if necessary. In the meantime, he recommended that the United States organize a massive propaganda campaign to encourage the Guatemalans—but it had to be carefully planned. For example, corrupt reactionaries who resisted all the Guatemalan reforms, and Figueres specifically mentioned Anastasio Somoza, should be excluded from all anti-Arbenz propaganda.[97]

On March 31, 1953, a week after his meeting with Figueres, Berle submitted a sixteen-page memorandum on Guatemala to Eisenhower's Jackson Committee, the abbreviated title for the International Information Activities Committee, chaired by former Deputy Director of the CIA William Jackson but directed by State Department representative Charles Douglas Jackson. C. D. Jackson had been central to the draft-Eisenhower movement and had taken time off from Henry Luce's Time, Incorporated, to serve as the president's special assistant, primarily concerned with cold war strategy. His experience in psychological warfare went back to World War II, and he had worked closely with Berle on the CIA-financed National Committee for a Free Europe, an organization devoted to liberating Eastern Europe from Soviet domination. Less than a month after his election, Eisenhower asked Jackson to produce a "dynamic plan" to "push the Russians back." Jackson immediately solicited Berle's assistance. Within four days the former brain truster responded with an "Outline of Political Counterattack against Soviet Aggression." Berle emphasized that the "primary target (not secondary as commonly thought) will be disorganization and seizure of portions of the Western hemisphere." Jackson required only four more days to send Eisenhower his initial recommendations.[98]

Berle's memorandum on Guatemala essentially inserted his previously reached conclusions into the outline. After acknowledging that the Jackson Committee was fully aware that "Guatemala presents a genuine penetration of Central America by Kremlin Communism," it focused on the "precise problem of how to clear out the Communists." In more specific terms than those in his later paper to the Council on Foreign Relations, Berle listed the possible alternatives. He discounted armed intervention by the United States, positing that such action would "raise immense complications" throughout the hemisphere. Another possibility was for Washington to organize a countermovement, capable of using force. This operation also presented difficulties. The movement would have to be based in a cooperative neighbor of Guatemala. El Salvador, Honduras, and Costa Rica could help, but the logical leader was Nicaragua. In Berle's opinion, while Somoza would "be quite willing (perhaps anxious)" to volunteer his country, it would be unwise for the United States to become identified with this "symbol of corruption"; if the plan failed, the dictator himself might be overthrown. A variant of this strategy, Berle mentioned in passing, would be "American support of a Guatemalan group which would do its own work."[99]

Berle did not feel that he had "adequate information to include or exclude" this last alternative, so he advised the administration to take another tack. The State Department should arrange a Central American "political defense" action to effect Figueres' recommendations. A coalition from all the surrounding countries, including Nicaraguans without official ties to Somoza, would condemn the situation in Guatemala in a "smashing declaration," quickly followed by an "equally forthright declaration by the United States." If such "moral intervention" were combined with economic pressure, Berle predicted that in twelve to eighteen months Arbenz would be forced to expel all Communists or resign, with a moderate like García Granados succeeding him as president. The State Department would direct its embassies in the region to coordinate the campaign under one "theater commander," and the coalition's agents, assisted by experts from the United States, would establish bases within Guatemala. These agents would be able to utilize the native dissidents and do "a good deal of quiet work" in the Guatemalan army.[100]

Berle discussed his recommendations with Jackson the following weekend, and in May he and Figueres met with Jackson, Cabot, and Thomas Mann. The impact of his memorandum, nevertheless, cannot be determined. While it is true that Eisenhower's policy closely resembled that in the memorandum, although the emphasis was on "support of a Guatemalan group" as opposed to relying on moral intervention, Arbenz's opponent Miguel Ydígoras Fuentes contends that actions were already underway. Ydígoras wrote that in early 1953 UFCO executive Walter Turnbull, along with two men who introduced themselves as members of the CIA, offered to assist him in organizing a counterrevolution. In return, he would have to promise to enact legislation favoring UFCO and IRCA, outlawing the radical labor unions, and establishing a strong-armed government along the lines of Ubico's. The future Guatemalan president maintained that he refused this bargain, feeling that the conditions ran counter to his country's interests. He told Turnbull and company that he needed time to suggest an alternative. The three men left and did not return.[101]

Ydígoras' account cannot be substantiated. Turnbull has since died. Braden commented that he knew nothing of the proposition, but he thought it possible. He added, "It might have been Turnbull going off on his own. He was down there, and he was powerful."[102] E. Howard Hunt, who ultimately played an important role, likewise could not support or deny the narrative. He remembered only that during the operation Turnbull proved to be very valuable to the CIA. Before that, "We had to isolate Turnbull from events because he was very anxious, of course, to run his own show."[103]

In retrospect, it seems unlikely that Ydígoras would have turned down an invitation to lead the insurrection. The alleged CIA operatives have never been identified, and, as will be explained, the agency did not want Ydígoras to head the coup. What is certain is that within the initial months of 1953 the new administration received a stream of advice advocating the elimination of Arbenz's government, and this advice reached the individuals who constructed the eventual policy. Assistant Secretary Cabot attended the Council on Foreign Relations study group and met with Berle and Figueres. Several months later he publicly remarked, "We should not assume that the anti-bodies which exist in the Latin American body politic will always repel an intrusion of the Communist virus. Indeed, in Guatemala they have not done so."[104] By this time, members of the Eisenhower administration were privately working on a way to produce the antibodies.

6. Project PBSUCCESS:
The Preparation

Eisenhower had been in office only about six months when Washington began to prepare for the overthrow of Arbenz's government. Exactly how much knowledge the president had of the Guatemalan situation in early 1953 cannot be known. But his remarks at the 1953 cabinet meeting and the haste with which he sent his brother Milton to study Latin American conditions testify to his intense interest in the region and his desire to remedy the shortcomings of the Truman policies; and, at a staff meeting in March, he specifically brought up Guatemala. This same month the State Department underscored the fact that the National Assembly had observed a minute of silence to mark Stalin's death, and some eighty Guatemalans had demonstrated in front of the United States embassy on behalf of Julius and Ethel Rosenberg. In August Secretary Dulles asked former Republican standard-bearer and New York Governor Thomas Dewey to represent the administration at Figueres' inauguration in Costa Rica and Panama's fiftieth-anniversary celebration. Dewey's real assignment was to monitor the Guatemalan delegation. Evidently, even without the input of individuals like Braden and Berle, the issue for the new administration was not the extent to which Communists dominated the country. As Milton Eisenhower's report reflected, the consensus was that it had already "succumbed to Communist infiltration." The issue was what policy to follow.[1]

INITIAL PLANNING

Planning took place with the utmost stealth. Only Eisenhower, the Dulles brothers, and a few other top-level members of the White House, State Department, and Central Intelligence Agency knew that an operation was even being considered, let alone were privy to its details. The CIA transmitted its communications to the president and secretary of state "top secret Ita," a superclassification that permitted a document to be read only by the select group stipulated on its heading. The agency burned most of its papers in a massive furnace. Any operative brought in on the project was sworn to secrecy. In all likelihood, a good deal of the discussion took place in Eisenhower's study late in the afternoon, when the president would meet with the secretary over cocktails, or at the Sunday lunch that Eleanor Dulles hosted for her two brothers each week.[2]

Although a recent study of the coup contends that the decision to intervene resulted from a high-level meeting in early August 1953, no evidence exists to pinpoint the project's inception so precisely.[3] Everyone who participated in the initial planning is now deceased. In Spruille Braden's opinion, while Central American efforts to build an anti-Arbenz coalition continued, the United States did not become involved until the beginning of 1954. Braden heard from some of his Nicaraguan friends that at this time Somoza again solicited Washington's help to launch an invasion of Guatemala. According to this version, the dictator convinced the Colombian ambassador in Washington and several other Latin American envoys to meet with Undersecretary of State Walter Bedell Smith. Bedell Smith, of course, had been director of the CIA when Somoza allegedly made his first proposal. The diplomats told him that all their sponsors needed to overthrow Arbenz was money and military equipment. Shortly thereafter, if Braden's informants were correct, the United States actively joined with Somoza.[4]

Howard Hunt, who, unlike Braden, participated directly in the project, believes that Eisenhower's decision to develop a covert plan for Guatemala came in the summer or early fall of 1953. The CIA had assigned Hunt to Mexico during the last years of the Truman administration. From his contacts throughout the Central American universities, he learned that Arbenz might be vulnerable to some type of paramilitary operation and recommended that action be taken. He doubts that his recommendations ever reached Washington. The CIA station chief in Guatemala, Collins Almon, had placed a bug in the headquarters of the Guatemalan Labor party that was discovered by the party's workers. When Ambassador Rudolf Schoenfeld, Patterson's successor, found out, he ordered Almon to keep a low profile and transmit all messages through the embassy. Almon, an aging FBI retread with little experience or interest in paramilitary endeavors, complied with Schoenfeld's wishes and, Hunt alleges, censored CIA missives. Birch O'Neill eventually replaced Almon, but he proceeded just as cautiously. Then, according to CIA scuttlebutt, United Fruit lobbyist Tommy Corcoran enlisted the support of Bedell Smith to have Allen Dulles name John Doherty station chief in Guatemala. This shift in personnel signaled the beginning of the operation.[5]

Without impugning Braden's sincerity, his credibility on this matter is suspect. He was far removed from Eisenhower's national security apparatus, and those familiar with the procedures involved in planning an operation of this magnitude assert categorically that the process required more than just a few months. Unknown to Braden, in November 1953 officials of the United States embassy met with representatives of Nicaragua and Honduras. Their report to the Latin American desk read, "The only means of overthrowing the Government [Arbenz's] was through a decision of the United States Government to do so." Moreover, when Assistant Secretary of State Cabot reluctantly conceded to Bedell Smith in September that a "CIA-organized coup was the only solution [to the Guatemalan dilemma]," the undersecretary "nodded and smiled," giving Cabot the impression that the agency had already begun working on it. Somoza's agents might have met with Bedell Smith, but by 1954 the CIA project was well underway. Braden, long impatient over what he considered Washington's laxity in dealing with the Guatemalan Communists, probably exaggerated the government's procrastination.[6]

Likewise, Hunt's frustration regarding the Truman administration's failure to accept his recommendation would make him susceptible to the hypothesis that an outside factor—the United Fruit Company—intervened to influence policy makers. His chronology of the events seems accurate, but for the wrong reasons. Hunt overlooks the change in administration, a change that brought to the White House a president who highly valued covert tactics. And, at the time that he opined that the CIA project in Guatemala began, a successful precedent was established in Iran. Whereas the Democrats wavered regarding a British proposal to overthrow Mussadegh, the Republicans brushed aside all reservations and virtually jumped at the opportunity to return full power to the shah. As the chief operative for Project AJAX, Kermit ("Kim") Roosevelt, recalled, the CIA's success in Iran so inspired Eisenhower and Dulles that they wanted to duplicate it in Guatemala. Roosevelt goes so far as to assert that Allen Dulles offered him the assignment.[7]

Several other indicators suggest the middle months of 1953 as the period when Washington strategists began to plot the intervention. In August Ydígoras and Castillo Armas met in Tegucigalpa, Honduras, to unify the anti-Arbenz forces. The two men had never been on close terms—each was jealous of the other's claim to being the leader of the Guatemalan exiles. They nevertheless signed a gentleman's pact, promising to cooperate in the future. In fact, relations remained strained, the rivalry being fueled by Ydígoras' complaint that Castillo Armas reneged on a pledge not to seek the presidency. What is significant for the chronology is that, at Tegucigalpa, Castillo Armas told Ydígoras that the United States government had already assured him of its support. This boast might be dismissed as a mere ploy to win the respect of his rival were it not for some correspondence that fell into the hands of the Guatemalan government in January 1954. The previous September, Castillo Armas had written Somoza. The letter, although omitting any explicit reference to United States participation in a plan to oust Arbenz or to the role of the CIA, reported that "I have been informed by our friends here that the government of the North, recognizing the impossibility of finding another solution to the grave problem of my country, has taken the decision to permit us to develop our plans." A month later the opposition chief wrote Somoza's son, "Our work with our friends from the North has ended in complete triumph in our favor . . ." Castillo Armas was confirming to his Nicaraguan allies that the United States had finally extended the guarantees that Somoza had sought for such a long time. The younger Somoza replied by offering Castillo Armas "machine guns, mortars, napalm bombs, and Vampire Jet aircraft."[8]

It is doubtful that even Castillo Armas knew everything being planned in Washington. As will become clear, a crucial component of the United States plan was the teamwork that existed between the State Department and the CIA. A suitable ambassador had to be selected who could coordinate this cooperative effort in the field. Schoenfeld had acquired some experience dealing with Communists when he had been the representative to Poland's government-in-exile during World War II and then minister to Romania, but as his experience with the CIA bug attests, he did not have the temperament for such a delicate assignment. As longtime State Department hand Eleanor Dulles told brother Foster, Schoenfeld was "first class" and "intellectual" but "a bit cautious."[9] Dulles transferred Schoenfeld to Colombia, and the search began for a less conventional individual for the Guatemalan post. From April through July 1953, C. D. Jackson met with CIA Deputy Director of Plans Frank Wisner and Bedell Smith to discuss the candidacy of Whiting Willauer. While General C. L. Chennault's right-hand man with the Flying Tigers in China, Willauer had distinguished himself as an active opponent of Communism. But he was a Republican, and the administration evidently wanted a Democrat who could take the blame should the project fail. During the August recess, the State Department and the White House decided to send Willauer to Honduras and switched its initial choice for Honduras, John E. Peurifoy, to Guatemala. Peurifoy was identified with the chief architect of Truman's foreign policy, Dean Acheson.[10]

Peurifoy's appointment is perhaps the best evidence that by summer's end the United States project was gaining momentum. As the *New York Times* wrote in December, shortly after his arrival in Guatemala City his selection as ambassador "means a change in the asserted passivity with which the United States has watched the growth of Communist influence."[11] Dynamic, a sports car enthusiast, and given to wearing a flamboyant green Borsalino in place of the traditional black homburg, Peurifoy had built a solid reputation as a plainspoken, forceful diplomat. He was a man of action, neither profound nor intellectual. As the columnist Drew Pearson wrote, Peurifoy "did not seem to have much imagination."[12] He left his native South Carolina to attend West Point from 1926 to 1928 but for financial reasons dropped out; in 1935 he came to Washington to study business administration at American University. Once in the capital city, he found the glamour and excitement of the diplomatic corps irresistible. Unfortunately, he lacked the educational background to pass the foreign service examination and the privileged status which permitted a select few to bypass it. He temporarily settled for a job as an elevator operator in the House of Representatives. Yet the lure of foreign embassies remained, so he enrolled in law school at George Washington and found new employment as a clerk in the State Department. His hard work attracted the attention of then Undersecretary Acheson, who made Peurifoy his special assistant. Peurifoy played a large part in the prosecution of Alger Hiss, and, even though Acheson was Hiss' friend, he recognized the former elevator operator's competent work and appointed him assistant secretary in charge of administration.[13]

Peurifoy now had the connections he needed, and in 1950 he received the ambassadorship to Greece. There he acquired the expertise for his later assignment in Guatemala. He actively intervened in the troubled Greek political situation in order to consolidate the anti-Communist elements and exclude all Communist participation in the government. Peurifoy's formula was to be firm, frank, and unyielding in a fight. Further, in these efforts he collaborated with CIA personnel, proving himself a most willing and able ally. Peurifoy's exploits were brought to Eisenhower's attention. Pennsylvania's Republican Congressman James Fulton commented to the House Committee on Foreign Affairs' subcommittee on the western hemisphere, "I came back from Greece and saw Eisenhower . . . I said what a good job Jack had done in Greece against the Communists. He said, 'Well, that's fine. That's interesting. I'll remember that.' So they pulled him out of Greece and put him in Guatemala."[14]

On October 29, the day of his arrival in Guatemala City, Peurifoy pointedly remarked to Arbenz's outgoing foreign minister (he delayed seeing Arbenz because "I have psychological advantage of being new and government feels I have come to Guatemala to use the big stick. We have been letting them stew") that "agrarian reform had been instituted in China and that today China was a Communist country." His interview with Arbenz produced an even more ominous report: "In view of inadequacy of normal diplomatic procedures in dealing with situation, there appears no alternative to our taking steps which would tend to make more difficult continuation of [Arbenz's] regime in Guatemala." In January 1954, much to Washington's dismay, Peurifoy wielded the threat of the big stick in public. He told a *Time* correspondent, "Public opinion in the U.S. might force us to take some measures to prevent Guatemala from falling into the lap of international Communism. We cannot permit a Soviet Republic to be established between Texas and the Panama Canal."[15]

LAYING THE FOUNDATION

Once it received the go-ahead from the White House, the CIA rapidly began to prepare for Arbenz's overthrow. The project was given the code name PBSUCCESS, and operational headquarters was set up at Opa Locka, Florida, a hamlet on the outskirts of Miami. Estimates of the intervention's cost range from five to seven million dollars, and it involved some one hundred CIA agents and contract operatives. The agency also enlisted the services of scores of recruits, mostly mercenaries, from Guatemala and the neighboring Central American nations, especially Nicaragua, Honduras, and Panama. During the operation's early days, the United States government flew personnel, aircraft, and other supplies to France's Field, an abandoned airstrip in the Canal Zone which provided a safe base from which they could be transported under cover to opposition camps in Nicaragua and Honduras. For the first time the CIA organized a clandestine unit distinct from one of its regional divisions. Agency heads reasoned that PBSUCCESS was of such magnitude that it would be extremely confusing and inefficient to have the same desk officers handling other assignments simultaneously with those concerning Guatemala. The unit received its own communication facilities, financial officers, support people, cover agents, and special authority to requisition confidential funds. PBSUCCESS became the CIA's highest priority.[16]

Virtually all the agency's chief officials played important roles. At the top was Allen Dulles. An imposing man with a Teddy Roosevelt mustache, Dulles communicated constantly with his brother throughout the operation and, according to Richard Bissell, his special assistant during PBSUCCESS and deputy director of plans for the later attempt to oust Castro in Cuba, he "was closer to the Guatemala operation than he was to the Bay of Pigs."[17] As the CIA director, nonetheless, Dulles had to attend to other matters as well, including the growing crisis in Indochina, so he placed Frank Wisner directly in charge of Guatemala. Born in Mississippi and a former assistant secretary of state, Wisner had headed the OSS missions in Istanbul and Bucharest during World War II. A pugnacious workaholic with remarkable retentive powers, he had the mind of a trial lawyer. His profound concern for the security of the nation and zealous attention to his work eventually caused a nervous breakdown and his suicide in 1965. In 1953 and 1954, however, his dedicated approach to PBSUCCESS made for an extraordinarily well executed effort.[18]

At a critical juncture in the project's progress in early 1954, when difficulties began to arise over coordination, Tracy Barnes and Richard Bissell joined the team. Barnes, formerly a Wall Street lawyer and member of the OSS with many acquaintances among those listed in eastern social registers, became the liaison between Washington and Opa Locka, so distinguishing himself that Bissell later selected him to head the day-to-day operations of the Bay of Pigs. Bissell was one of the few ranking CIA officers who had not served in the OSS. The son of a Connecticut insurance magnate, he had impressive credentials—Groton, Yale, the London School of Economics, and professorships at Yale and MIT. His friendship with Wisner and Barnes promoted his entry into the CIA's elite, whereupon he immediately took on the PBSUCCESS assignment. Wisner's successor as deputy director of plans and the mastermind of U-2 surveillance as well as the Bay of Pigs, in 1954 he was simply assistant to the director. He had an anomalous role in the project, helping out where needed and generally supervising operations. Bissell, Barnes, and the others on the project's directory would meet three times a week in Dulles' office and almost daily in Wisner's.[19]

The two major figures in the field were Colonel J. C. King and Al Haney. At the outset King, as chief of the western hemisphere division, had supervisory responsibilities. But, like former station chief Collins Almon, he was a holdover from the period when the FBI conducted Latin American surveillance, and he preferred espionage and intelligence gathering to paramilitary operations. His lack of enthusiasm led to organizational difficulties, requiring Dulles to shift the bulk of his functions to Wisner, Barnes, and Bissell. This shift suited Haney well, for as the field commander he found his relations with King much less harmonious than with the others, especially Barnes. Haney's authority extended over all the agents outside Washington. Because of the project's delicacy, however, Dulles created a special position to take charge of political action. The man who filled it was E. Howard Hunt.[20]

In an oft cited pioneering study of the Guatemalan project, David Wise and Thomas Ross quote testimony given by Whiting Willauer in 1961 before the Senate's subcommittee to investigate the administration of the Internal Security Act as evidence that a team of United States diplomats assisted the CIA operatives. Willauer testified that in addition to himself and John Peurifoy, the leader, the team included the minister to Nicaragua, Thomas Whelan, and Robert Hill in Costa Rica. Journalists Wise and Ross had no reason to doubt Willauer. His participation appears certain. Describing his primary duty as making sure that the Honduran government fully cooperated with the operation, he apparently also supervised the landing of equipment earmarked for Castillo Armas' forces. Further, he had previously worked with General Chennault's Flying Tigers, which performed many functions for the CIA. Years later, on an NBC television special, a United States air attaché stationed in Guatemala during the invasion referred to Willauer's involvement in PBSUCCESS and association with Chennault by commenting, "I am quite sure that if any of the pilots flying for the liberation army [of Castillo Armas] had been shot down, some of those pilots could have spoken Chinese."[21] Willauer, in fact, wrote the general in May 1954, cryptically explaining, "We have a helluva situation down here and unless really forceful action is taken we are going to have a little Commie Chine [sic] right in our own backyard . . . I am literally working night and day on the problem and am hopeful that a solution will develop. Unfortunately, I can't tell you any more than that."[22]

Peurifoy's role is also certain. As the ambassador to Guatemala, he served as a liaison between CIA and State Department personnel who were privy to the clandestine activities. When the CIA wished to instruct Peurifoy from Washington, it would contact Undersecretary Bedell Smith to insure coordination. The State Department would then transmit a message over the CIA's channel to the agency's station in Guatemala. To guarantee that there were no leaks or misunderstandings, an agent would carry the instructions by hand to the ambassador. In April 1954, Peurifoy returned to Washington to iron out last-minute details. Satisfied, he responded to a press query regarding the future of Arbenz's regime by remarking, "We are making out our Fourth of July reception invitations, and we are not including any of the present administration." Two days after Arbenz's resignation he quipped, "People are complaining that I was forty-five minutes off schedule."[23]

Willauer may have been inaccurate when he included Whelan and Hill as participants. Whelan was a Truman appointee who had been kept on in Nicaragua only as a favor to North Dakota's Senator William Langer. Since there was now no question of Somoza's cooperation, State and the CIA might not have deemed the Nicaraguan post critical enough to let Whelan in on the secret. No evidence exists of his involvement. Hill's participation is more ambiguous. His financial interests in Guatemala and his influential position within the Republican party (from 1965 to 1968 he chaired the Republican National Committee Foreign Policy Task Force) would seem to qualify him for membership on Peurifoy's team. Yet he denies any covert activities, and in 1954 there were some Republicans on Capitol Hill who did not fully trust him. Furthermore, while documents refer to him in connection with the Guatemalan project, he apparently did not meet the administration's expectations or those of the Latin Americans. For example, after Hill's transfer to the embassy in Mexico, Willauer praised his work to C. D. Jackson. Jackson, who recalled that "dear Amb. Hill was the character who made so much trouble for us in his previous post [Costa Rica], and someone whom we did not consider the darling of the Latinos," then wrote his former *Time* associate and Eisenhower speech writer Emmet Hughes. Reviewing his conversation with Willauer, Jackson's 1958 letter went on, "All I did was to nod sagely, because I remembered all the trouble we had with Hill when he was in Guatemala . . ."[24]

Although the State Department's input, with or without Whelan and Hill, was unquestionably substantial, the CIA held the ultimate responsibility for PBSUCCESS. Once the operational apparatus was established, the agency's first task, as presaged in Berle's memorandum, was to select a leader from among the Guatemalan opposition. This proved to be quite complicated. Many of the opposition favored Ydígoras, the conservative candidate in the 1950 election, regarding him as the rightful heir to the presidency. But CIA political experts like Howard Hunt rejected Ubico's former henchman as being too reactionary and apt to incur the hostility of both the international community and the Guatemalan people. Ydígoras also resembled a Spanish noble, which agency pundits considered a defi-

nite liability. Hunt explained: "These were the little things we had
to take into consideration. You don't rally a country made up of *mestizos* with a Spanish don."[25]

With the most obvious choice thus ruled out, the CIA searched
elsewhere. The first alternative was Juan Córdova Cerna, the brains
of the counterrevolutionary movement. Born in 1899, the prominent coffee grower had headed the influential General Association of
Agriculturists and served briefly as Arévalo's minister of the inte-
rior. He resigned the post to become the native legal adviser for the
United Fruit Company. Following the death of his son in a 1950 antigovernment uprising, he turned sharply against the revolution. After
an abbreviated voluntary exile in New York City, Córdova Cerna returned to assume an active role in plotting Arbenz's overthrow. In
1953 he helped organize another coup, this time in Salamá, after
which he fled to Honduras. Here he joined forces with Castillo Armas, although the two men never agreed about the ultimate dis-
position of power. Those among the opposition and the CIA who
advocated that Córdova Cerna assume the movement's leadership
believed that, as a distinguished civilian, he would be more acceptable than someone with a military background. But the question
became academic, for a routine physical examination uncovered
throat cancer, and the wealthy Córdova Cerna flew to New Orleans
for treatment.[26]

With Ydígoras deemed inappropriate and the civilian candidate
unavailable, the CIA decided on the forty-year-old Carlos Enrique
Castillo Armas. His father was a fairly well-to-do landowner, but
since Castillo Armas was illegitimate he could not inherit his father's estate. He therefore chose a career in the military, ironically
attending the Escuela Politécnica at the same time as Arbenz. After
the 1944 revolution the colonel spent eight months at the United
States Army Staff School in Fort Leavenworth, Kansas, and then returned to his native country to become director of the Escuela. He
firmly sided with Araña during the latter's power struggle with Arbenz. Interpreting the 1949 assassination as evidence of the revolution's corruption, Castillo Armas organized an attempt to overthrow
the government. Its failure cost him his military career but made
him into something of a folk hero. He was so severely wounded that
the medical squad pronounced him dead and carried him off to be
buried. A fortuitous moan changed his destination to a hospital. Following his release the government sent him to prison, and, according to Guatemalan lore, on June 11, 1951, he made a dramatic escape
by hand-digging a long tunnel.[27]

Castillo Armas initially went to Colombia but, after a short stay, realized that the heart of the counterrevolutionary movement had settled in Honduras and Nicaragua. So in 1952 he successfully requested asylum from the Honduran government and, in September, took up residence in Tegucigalpa. From this strategic locale he contacted such exiled leaders as Ydígoras and Córdova Cerna, along with such sympathetic organizations as the influential Committee of Anti-Communist University Students. Within a year he had joined the same country club as Central America's most prestigious officials, and he became a frequent visitor to the United States embassy in Honduras. He made no attempt to conceal his objectives. He requested Washington's assistance with his plans to overthrow Arbenz and thanked it for the support it had already extended, including the arms embargo. The embassy reported, "[Castillo Armas] believes that the only way to obliterate Communist influences in Guatemala is by military action carefully planned and carefully carried out." The CIA concurred and sent its representative to see him. While suspicious of his charismatic appeal, the agency considered him honest. Unlike Ydígoras, he did not look like an aristocrat, nor did he have an ultrarightist reputation. Approved by the CIA, Castillo Armas boldly announced that he would "return very shortly" to Guatemala.[28]

PROPAGANDA AND THE CARACAS CONFERENCE

Policy makers in Washington considered it essential that they establish the proper international climate for an anti-Arbenz coup. They certainly did not want world opinion—especially that of the other nations in the hemisphere—to sympathize with the struggling Guatemalan revolution. Nor did they want the coup interpreted as merely one more internecine conflict within the Latin American military or, even worse, a surrogate invasion sponsored by the United States and the United Fruit Company. The actions of the Arbenz government had to be incontrovertibly tied to the Kremlin, and Castillo Armas and the other opposition leaders had to appear as the representatives of Guatemala's popular sentiment. The objective of PBSUCCESS was not just to effect Arbenz's overthrow but also to put the Soviets on warning that the people of the Free World would not tolerate their conspiratorial designs.

The State Department's United States Information Agency (USIA) undertook this critical assignment. As the USIA summarized to the National Security Council's Operations Coordinating Board immediately following Arbenz's overthrow, "Our principal information effort was directed toward creating greater awareness through-out the Hemisphere of the real threat to peace and security posed by the verifiable communist penetration of the Guatemalan govern-ment." The appropriateness of the adjective "verifiable" is dubious. The USIA's summary continued by reviewing how it established a re-gional service operation to collect, prepare, and place anti-Arbenz press material in Central American publications, tailoring the sto-ries "to meet the specific needs in individual countries." While the agency stopped short of making any direct accusations that could be traced to the United States, it did distribute unattributable articles labeling certain Guatemalan officials as Communists or actions by the Arbenz government as Communist-inspired. For example, the summary described "a successful project" in January 1954, in which the USIA wrote a series of accounts critical of Víctor Gutiérrez and the secretary general of the Guatemalan Labor party, José Manuel Fortuny, planted them in a Chilean newspaper, and then arranged for reprints to be circulated elsewhere with Chilean attribution.[29]

This same month the USIA conducted another project not in-cluded in its summarizing missive. Due to the increasing indica-tions of an impending invasion, Arbenz ordered the arrest of a num-ber of antigovernment agitators. Among these were some of the most strident opponents of the Guatemalan labor movement. The USIA, after conferring with Peurifoy's embassy, orchestrated the "prompt-est press, radio coverage without official attribution." The coverage implied that these were arbitrary arrests with the sole function of intimidating Arbenz's opposition. No mention was made of any pos-sible connection between the arrested individuals and the schem-ings of Castillo Armas and Ydígoras, which Arbenz had recently revealed by publicizing the former's correspondence with the Somo-zas. Yet the next day the embassy in Guatemala informed the State Department that those arrested were "apparently materially in-volved in plots by Colonel Carlos Castillo Armas and General Mi-guel Ydígoras Fuentes, the exiled Guatemalan anti-Communist leaders, to overthrow the Arbenz Administration."[30]

Although the State Department propaganda campaign benefited greatly from the USIA activities, its most concerted effort came at the tenth Inter-American Conference, held in Caracas from March 1 to 28, 1954. The name and location of the conference reflect the shortcomings of United States policy toward Latin America. Ini-tially, formal meetings of all the American states had been termed "international" or, more commonly, "Pan-American." But over the years, particularly following the successive interventions during the twentieth century's first quarter, Latin Americans came to interpret "Pan-Americanism" as a euphemism for United States dominance. Consequently, the 1948 charter of the Organization of American States stipulated that subsequent assemblies be termed "Inter-American." The name change, however, did not disguise the differences between the United States attitudes and those of its neighbors to the south. A number of Latin American leaders opposed the selection of Venezuela as the host nation, since its ruler, Marcos Pérez Jiménez, ranked with Somoza as one of the hemisphere's most ruthless dictators. In fact, Costa Rica's José Figueres and Rómulo Betancourt, Pérez Jiménez's major opponent in Venezuela, attempted to line up the democratic republics to boycott the conference unless the dictator agreed to pardon the thousands of political prisoners that filled Venezuelan jails. United States State Department representatives took the contrary view, regarding the dictator as a firm ally in the struggle against Communism, and threatened to deny assistance to countries that participated in the boycott. The conference convened in Caracas on schedule, with only Costa Rica declining to attend.[31]

The controversy over the conference's site revealed a sharp divergence between the objectives of the United States and those of most members of the OAS. As Secretary Dulles remarked at a February 1954 cabinet meeting, "The major interest of the Latin American countries at this conference would concern economics whereas the chief United States interest is to secure a strong anti-Communist resolution which would recognize Communism as an international conspiracy instead of regarding it merely as an indigenous movement."[32] To the secretary of state, the problem of Latin America's development was secondary to that of Guatemala.

The State Department planned its Caracas strategy very carefully. Despite the United States' membership on the committee on preparations for the conference, which began planning the agenda in 1951, its representatives did not propose the inclusion of an anti-Communist resolution until late 1953. Hence minimal time existed for any organized opposition. Moreover, when State discovered that the agenda listed those items under the heading "Economic Matters" as the conference's first order of business and its resolution as the last item under "Juridical and Political Matters," it protested to the OAS council. When the final agenda appeared, the United States proposal headed the topics to be discussed.[33]

An impressive array of dignitaries comprised the United States delegation. Dulles went, as did Henry Holland, who officially became the new assistant secretary for inter-American affairs while the conference was in progress, his predecessor John Moors Cabot, and Thomas Mann. Other delegates included Merwin L. Bohan, United States representative of the Inter-American Economic and Social Council; Samuel W. Anderson, assistant secretary of commerce for international affairs; W. Randolph Burgess, deputy to the secretary of the treasury; John C. Dreier, representative to the OAS council; Herman Phleger, Dulles' legal adviser; the ambassador to Venezuela, Fletcher Warren; Andrew N. Overby, assistant secretary of the treasury; and Samuel C. Waugh, assistant secretary of state for economic affairs. Senators Bourke B. Hickenlooper and Theodore F. Green, members of the Foreign Relations Committee, accompanied the delegation, as did United Nations Ambassador Henry Cabot Lodge. Their mandate was clear. In the words of one congressman, "Nothing short of positive expressions of disapproval will serve to indicate that this hemisphere and the people of the other republics do not propose to stand idly by while the Red tide engulfs Guatemala and its people, and constitutes a threat to the sovereignty of every republic of the hemisphere. A showdown is imminent."[34]

While a showdown was imminent, State Department advisers wanted to avoid the appearance of one. They feared that other nations might interpret the resolution as a means of bullying Guatemala or perhaps even as the first step toward armed intervention. "A timely, hard-hitting speech by the Secretary at Caracas would take the communist conspiracy (Kremlin) off balance . . ." a State Department memorandum read. "It should be remembered, however, that the 'big power' concept is anathema to the Latinos who take seriously the legal doctrine of equality of states."[35] Indeed, the department deferred its announcement of a pending military assistance pact with El Salvador lest Guatemala or any other country claim that the United States was preparing for a joint invasion. Washington hoped that Dulles and the other delegates could prevent any discussion of possible intervention until Guatemala brought up the subject, which it invariably would. Then, "The United States should immediately cause [the intervention] to be linked with the subject of Communist penetration, and prevent return to the topic of alleged intervention."[36]

As soon as the committee charged with examining juridical and political matters came to order, Dulles introduced the draft proposal "Declaration of Solidarity for the Preservation of the Political Integrity of the American States against International Communism." Commonly known as the Declaration of Caracas, the resolution eclipsed all other items on the conference's agenda. For the next seven sessions, the committee devoted its entire attention to the resolution and the more general issue of the Communist threat to the hemisphere. Dulles, who had consulted his brother about the phrasing of his introductory speech, so impressed Hickenlooper that the senator described it to his Foreign Relations Committee colleagues as "one of the most clear, powerful, and concise speeches, laying down exactly what the situation was, that I have ever heard in my life." To Eisenhower Hickenlooper wrote that Dulles did "a brilliant job."[37]

The secretary denounced international Communism as "alien intrigue and treachery," as the form of foreign intervention that posed the most severe danger to the peace and security of the entire hemisphere. Referring to the Rio pact, which called for a meeting of consultation in the event of aggression, armed or not, Dulles concluded by proposing that Communist domination or control of any country would justify "appropriate action in accordance with existing treaties."[38] But he heeded the State Department's warning—at no time did he mention Guatemala or the possibility of military intervention. He even deleted from his original draft a passage that could be construed as specifically aimed at Guatemala: "The United States considers that we are not here engaged in an academic or philosophical exercise, but that we are taking action of a momentous nature."[39]

Dulles had carefully chosen his words. Nevertheless, a number of Latin American nations voiced the apprehension that the resolution might be used to sanction intervention in the internal affairs of a state. Colombia included a meeting of consultation in the final clause to make certain that this aspect of the "existing treaties" was not overlooked. To insure approval, Dulles himself offered an amendment to emphasize that the United States designed the resolution to protect, not impair, the right of each nation to select its own form of political and economic system. He added at the beginning, "This declaration of foreign policy made by the American Republics in Relation to Dangers originating outside this Hemisphere . . ." However, since the secretary of state had already explained that indigenous Communism did not exist, by his logic no country in Latin America could voluntarily embrace Communism—it would have to originate "outside this Hemisphere."[40]

This last point was not missed by the head of the Guatemalan delegation, Foreign Minister Guillermo Toriello Garrido. He immediately denounced the resolution as "merely a pretext for intervening in our internal affairs."[41] The debate predicted by the State Department ensued, as both veteran diplomats jockeyed for an advantage. At one point Toriello bluntly asked Dulles, "What is international Communism?" Dulles' response was equally blunt: "It is disturbing if the foreign affairs of one of our American Republics are conducted by one so innocent that he has to ask that question."[42] Toriello won this round. As Dulles himself admitted, the foreign minister drew the most applause from the other delegates by meeting the secretary of state head-on. He accused the United States of returning to the tradition of waving a big stick and dollar diplomacy and charged that the declaration was an example of the "internationalism of McCarthyism." If the resolution passed, he cautioned,

> Pan Americanism would become an instrument exclusively in the service of monopolistic interests and a weapon of coercion to strangle any attempt at political and economic liberation of the oppressed peoples of Latin America. They [the United States] wanted to find a ready expedient to maintain the economic dependence of the American Republics and suppress the legitimate desires of their people, cataloguing as "Communism" every manifestation of nationalism or economic independence, and desire for social progress, and intellectual curiosity, and any interest in progressive or liberal reforms . . . any nation which expresses these desires will be accused of being a threat to the continental security and making a breach of continental solidarity.[43]

After Toriello's audience applauded, the resolution passed by an overwhelming majority. Only Guatemala voted in opposition, with Mexico and Argentina abstaining.[44] The vote, nevertheless, fell short of "positive expressions of disapproval." Only the most dictatorial nations, including Nicaragua, Colombia, Paraguay, and the Dominican Republic, unreservedly accepted the proposal as the best means to combat Communism in the hemisphere. The others put through a parallel resolution (the real Declaration of Caracas) which stated that the antidote to Communism was the promotion of human rights, the effective exercise of representative democracy, and social and economic development. Another approved resolution, sponsored by Panama, advocated the abolition of racial discrimination to neutralize the Communists' appeals.[45]

In truth, the United States resolution passed because, as Roy Rubottom, who became Eisenhower's final assistant secretary of inter-American affairs, commented, "[Dulles] spared no effort and spared no blandishment to get this Caracas Resolution through." Rubottom termed it the low point in United States relations with Latin America during the Eisenhower years, and John Cabot, despite his firm opposition to the Arbenz government, left the Latin American desk because he disagreed with Dulles' approach.[46] The United States delegation at Caracas not only subordinated the other twenty-seven items on the conference's agenda to the anti-Communist declaration but also used the threat of economic reprisals to assure its passage. Dulles, the delegation's chief, refused to be briefed on the pertinent economic issues, and immediately following the declaration's passage, in Cabot's words, he "went streaking off" to Washington and then to Geneva in his continuing effort to keep the French fighting in Indochina.[47] The *Christian Science Monitor* wrote that many of those delegates who voted for the resolution "were not completely convinced that Communist influence in Guatemala was really a threat to the United States or to hemispheric solidarity," and the *Hispanic American Report* quoted Uruguay's Dr. Justino Jiménez de Arechaga, who lamented that his country had acquiesced to the proposal "without enthusiasm, without optimism, without joy, and without the feeling that we were contributing to the adoption of a constructive measure."[48] In Paris *Le Monde* summarized:

> Those who supported [the declaration] most enthusiastically were just those dictatorial governments whose power rests on a military junta and on the official representatives of the great United States companies. These governments owe their existence solely to the protection of the United States.[49]

But, for Eisenhower and Dulles, Caracas was a success. Economic and social issues could be dealt with at any time, but Communism in Guatemala was a problem about which "something had to be done quickly. The first task was to marshal and crystallize Latin American public opinion on the issue."[50] This was the declaration's purpose. The USIA sent a special team to the conference to cover the debate, resulting in a continuous flow of news, backgrounders, photos, and tape recordings. Field officers disseminated these materials throughout the hemisphere via the agency's direct wireless file. The State Department produced a documentary film on the resolution that emphasized such highlights as Dulles' speech and made it available to movie and television outlets. Also available were briefings and conversations with editors, commentators, and other public opinion leaders. Small wonder that the *New York Times* ignored any adverse reaction and editorialized that Caracas was "a triumph for Secretary Dulles, for the United States, and for common sense."[51]

Whether Eisenhower and Dulles ever intended to invoke the Caracas resolution remains problematic. By this time PBSUCCESS was well underway, so much so that Arévalo later drew a parallel between the United States conduct at Caracas and Japanese negotiations in Washington on the eve of the attack on Pearl Harbor.[52] Bitter, the former Guatemalan president obviously assumed that Dulles' proposal had been nothing more than a public relations charade, an empty gesture advanced with the sole purpose of establishing the proper climate for Castillo Armas' invasion.

Arévalo's analogy is certainly stretched. While publicizing the Communist threat in Guatemala was the major objective of the United States delegation to Caracas, many State Department officers sincerely hoped that the declaration could be an effective anti-Communist doctrine. Some, like Assistant Secretary Holland, later regretted that the execution of PBSUCCESS obviated the opportunity to test the proposal's efficacy; shortly after the conference's adjournment, he began to solicit OAS support in an effort to "move toward application of the Caracas Resolution to Guatemala."[53]

In early April Holland discussed applying the declaration with both Foster and Allen Dulles. The two brothers then held a carefully worded telephone conversation, during which each referred to items contained in a "special black book," probably referring to the black book the Operations Coordinating Board had prepared for Caracas in February. They wondered whether the Caracas resolution was sufficiently broad to be applied to Guatemala, musing that perhaps some specialized machinery could be invoked. The secretary of state admitted that he was unsure of all the declaration's legal fine points, but he did believe that, at a minimum, proceeding along the lines of the resolution (that is, calling a meeting of consultation) would give a subsequent armed intervention a more legitimate appearance. He explained to the CIA director, "If something like this ["some action along the lines of the resolution we passed down there"] got underway, it might make other things more natural."[54]

In all probability Holland never learned of this telling conversation. A number of Dulles' assistants knew of PBSUCCESS, but they were unaware of all its specifics. And probably only the secretary was privy to the decisions being made by Eisenhower and his top security managers. The skeletal outline for a delicate operation like PBSUCCESS would have been worked out in the National Security Council and smaller high-level meetings, but the president discussed details only with his secretary of state, the director of the CIA, and a few others in the privacy of the Oval Office. At the time of Caracas this inner group had not yet decided to implement PBSUCCESS fully, although it clearly viewed the chances for a diplomatic settlement as extremely remote. Yet even a remote chance is a possibility, and, while the Dulles brothers may have thought of the Caracas resolution primarily as a precursor to the intervention, they had not yet given up all hope. It was not until April 19, almost two weeks after the phone conversation between the Dulles brothers, that State Department intelligence concluded that the resolution had had minimal effects on Arbenz's strength or on the formation of any unified opposition to him.[55]

CONGRESSIONAL INVOLVEMENT

The Caracas meeting also served as a catalyst for Congress to escalate its involvement in the Guatemalan controversy. As noted in chapter 5, a number of congressional leaders publicly harangued Arbenz's government during the several weeks preceding and following the conference. In February, Republican Senator Margaret Chase Smith from Maine took a more definitive tack. Charging that the "Communist movement has gained such economic and political strength within the Republic of Guatemala that it now largely dominates and controls economic and political affairs," she noted that the price of Guatemalan coffee imported into the United States appeared to have risen substantially. Implying that the reason for the price increase rested with the Communists (she mentioned neither the increase in Guatemala's minimum wage scale nor the tropical storm damage that caused low yields), the senator proposed that the United States government investigate Communist control of the Guatemalan coffee industry to determine the extent to which the increase was justified. Evidently Smith did not feel it necessary to wait for the investigation's findings. She also suggested that concurrent with the investigation President Eisenhower take the required steps to ban coffee imports from Guatemala until he was satisfied that "(1) the economic and political affairs of that country are no longer dominated and controlled by the Communist movement, and (2) the unjustified prices for coffee imposed by producers in that country have been reduced to reasonable levels."[56]

Referred to the Foreign Relations Committee, Smith's resolution never reached the Senate floor. Her speech, however, put her on record as advocating action against the Arbenz government. The next month she went farther. Writing "A Woman Senator's Views—It Is Time to Stifle Guatemala's Reds" for the *Newark Star-Ledger*, she encouraged the United States public to "face the fact" that the Communists in Guatemala had begun their "assault on the freedom of this hemisphere." "Surely," she added, "we have by this time learned the folly of delaying a facing up to danger—look at the tragedy of China, Korea, and Indochina." Smith was not a saber-rattling anti-Communist like Spruille Braden. Yet her article paralleled the latter's much publicized Dartmouth speech by asserting, "We might well do away with the diplomatic niceties right away."[57]

Along with the sentiments expressed by other senators and representatives, Smith's resolution and article influenced the Eisenhower White House to take, within limits, more congressional leaders into its confidence. Security requirements, of course, dictated that most of the plans remain secret. Nevertheless, in early 1954 Eisenhower's staff started to leak indications that action was in the offing. For example, in February California's Senator William Knowland, the conservative majority leader, called the president to discuss the Bricker Amendment. Named for the senator from Ohio, the amendment sought to limit executive authority over foreign policy relative to that of the legislature.[58] Eisenhower's reply to Knowland's advocacy of the amendment was, "What I am concerned about [is] recognizing new government (Guatemala for example)." In this abstruse manner he informed Knowland that he anticipated Arbenz's overthrow.[59]

Because both Eisenhower and Dulles believed that an effective foreign policy depended on cordial relations with Congress, they strove to keep the Senate majority leader informed. The documents do not reveal whether Eisenhower's allusion to Guatemala whetted Knowland's appetite for more details, but a month later Dulles phoned the senator to report his most recent conversations with the CIA regarding Guatemala. Knowland asked if he could obtain additional information, particularly a history of the controversy. After agreeing, Dulles immediately called Assistant Secretary Holland, who promised he would send the material to Knowland's office.[60] A month later it was Undersecretary Bedell Smith who spoke with a congressional leader about Guatemala, in this instance with Styles Bridges of New Hampshire, the Senate's senior Republican. In his report to Eisenhower, Bedell Smith did not recount Bridges' end of the conversation. The senator must have suggested that some type of belligerent statement be issued against Arbenz, for Bedell Smith "told him that it was not a matter that we wanted to make an explosion about just now." With the preparations for PBSUCCESS almost complete, Bedell Smith wanted as little diplomatic turmoil as possible.[61]

Bridges, like so many others in Congress, wanted a more dynamic policy toward Guatemala. His dissatisfaction stemmed from the meeting of the legislative leaders he had attended earlier that morning. In an effort to assure the leaders that he was in full control of the Guatemalan situation, Eisenhower had requested that the State Department prepare a memorandum for presentation. Holland prepared it in April, with the help of Raymond Leddy of the Middle American bureau, the CIA's Frank Wisner, and Ambassador Peurifoy. The result was a laundry list of what must be done: "By every proper and effective means we should demonstrate to the courageous elements within Guatemala who are trying to purge their government of its Communist elements that they have the sympathy and support of all freedom loving people both in the United States and elsewhere." At the same time, the memorandum continued, "We must assemble evidence of a kind that would convince the minds of reasonable men, and showing the extent of Communist penetration of the political institutions of Guatemala." Referring explicitly to Caracas, the document went on, "We must be prepared to invoke the consultative procedure contemplated by the Rio Treaty." In relation to all these steps, Holland concluded, "I think it very important that all action by the Executive and by the Congress in this field should be carefully coordinated."[62]

Holland did not mention PBSUCCESS, reflecting the limitations of executive-legislative coordination. Within this context Bridges' frustration is understandable. Congress had grown impatient with the official policy of sympathy, fact finding, and consultation. Eisenhower's announcement at the May 24 gathering of the legislative leaders that "we will move on Guatemala under the Caracas and other agreements" failed to assuage their restlessness.[63] As late as June 23, Congressman Charles J. Kersten sent off a three-page memorandum to the State Department, criticizing it for not taking more direct action. Reasoning that the Guatemalans had a right to revolt against the Communists, the representative from Wisconsin argued that the United States had a right to assist the revolt. This assistance, he specified, should not be restricted to moral support or even indirect aid. Such aid was an "honorable act," and the United States should openly send the rebels whatever they needed. As for invoking agreements like the Rio pact and the Declaration of Caracas, Kersten opined that the "United States cannot escape into a pious neutrality by claiming it must follow determinations of the UN, the OAS, or other body." Actions taken by these organizations constituted "legalistic folderol," and "the U.S. is a competent sovereign nation responsible for its own actions." In summary the memorandum read, "It could be argued that aid to rebels should be undercover. This may be so. But I believe we should not make any attempt to disguise the fact that we are helping the Guatemalans regain control of their country."[64]

Dulles' assistant, Roderic O'Connor, forwarded the memorandum to Holland and the State Department's assistant secretary for congressional affairs, Thruston Morton. His cover letter concluded, "I am sure that you are aware of this line of thinking which I suspect is held by a number of other Congressmen." Earlier memoranda reveal that State closely followed congressional reactions to events in Guatemala and welcomed such hard-line opinions.[65] If Eisenhower saw Kersten's criticism, he might well have smiled. By this time, with all the assistance he required, Castillo Armas had already entered Guatemala. The president concurred with the congressman's view but he felt it essential that the aid be disguised. Such criticism was a small price to pay for keeping the operation secret, thereby adding legitimacy to what the administration would later call an outstanding expression of the Guatemalans' love for freedom.

Kersten would have had no quarrel with the State Department had he known all that was going on behind the scenes. After the Caracas conference the White House, the State Department, and the CIA carefully monitored all public statements in order to emphasize official opposition to the Arbenz government without revealing the administration's hidden hand. Attempting to capitalize on the Caracas declaration, Washington charged that Guatemalan Communists were creating instability throughout Central America. For example, when the Gálvez government claimed that a massive strike against United Fruit's Honduran division was the result of Communist subversion, the State Department heartily agreed. The strike began in early May, shortly after three new Guatemalan consuls arrived in Honduras' capital. Gálvez (and Eisenhower) blamed the consuls and declared them *personae non gratae.* Although Holland was reluctant to make an issue of the incident, Dulles saw it as an opportunity "to spread the atmosphere there are indications [of Communist influence] etc."[66] Careful to avoid any comment that might imply that Eisenhower would consider the use of force, the secretary suggested at his next press conference that the "so-called strike in Honduras is not entirely a domestic phenomenon" and termed its relationship to the Guatemalan consuls "an interesting coincidence."[67] There was another coincidence: the State Department concluded negotiations on a military pact with Honduras (in April it had concluded one with Nicaragua) that it had been seeking for a year. Soon tanks and long-range strategic bombers assigned to the Strategic Air Command as well as smaller weapons were airlifted to both countries to signify the seriousness of Washington's commitment. The *Times* editorialized: "Militarily the United States is doing its utmost to draw a circle around this spot of Communist infection . . . the charter aircraft business at Toncontin [Honduras] boomed so that it was virtually impossible to hire a private plane."[68]

ARMS TO ARBENZ AND THE FINAL DECISION

While providing Guatemala's neighbors with direct military assistance had been on the White House's agenda for a long time, it was the arrival of a shipment of arms in Guatemala that occasioned the airlift's commencement. Arbenz firmly believed that Castillo Armas' invasion was only a matter of time. Before Caracas he had repeatedly implored the United States to lift its boycott.[69] He had also suggested that he and Eisenhower agree upon a neutral commission to arbitrate the dispute with United Fruit, hoping to avoid a confrontation.[70] Unsuccessful and increasingly desperate, the Guatemalan president now risked infuriating both the United States and his own military officers (rumors circulated that he intended to form a peasant militia) by soliciting assistance from behind the Iron Curtain. The Soviet Union jumped at the opportunity to embarrass, at the very least, the United States. The Czechoslovakian government transported some two thousand tons of small arms and light artillery pieces from its Skoda factory to the Polish port of Stettin on the Baltic. After being registered with Lloyd's of London, the merchandise was listed as optical supplies on the manifest of Sweden's *Alfhem*, a freighter cleared for Dakar, Africa. Communist agents must have bribed the captain, for the ship sailed directly for Puerto Barrios.[71]

The CIA discovered the *Alfhem*'s real cargo before it arrived on May 17. Posing as a bird-watcher, the agency's operative in Stettin spied what he believed to be arms. He then wrote a seemingly innocuous letter to a Parisian automobile parts concern. He meticulously pasted a microfilm dot over one period. The agent in Paris translated the microfilm message into code and immediately transmitted it by shortwave to Washington. The message read like the twenty-second prayer of David in the Book of Psalms: "My God, my God, why hast thou forsaken me?" Decoded, this meant that military supplies were on board the ship. Allen Dulles ordered another agent, stationed at the Kiel Canal, to surreptitiously inspect the *Alfhem* as it passed from the Baltic to the North Sea. The inspection confirmed the cargo, as did information pried loose from a senior officer on Arbenz's staff by yet another operative. The CIA director wanted to intercept the *Alfhem* en route, but the ship charted such a circuitous course that for a time it seemed to have vanished. When it did reach port, John Peurifoy and his staff were waiting on the dock.[72]

As might be expected, Capitol Hill erupted in an uproar. No one was prepared for such an audacious move. Dulles immediately decided that the Swedes were innocent of any wrongdoing—the problem was to find some grounds on which to declare Guatemala guilty. Allen Dulles conceded that "there is nothing illegal about what they are doing," and Senator Knowland asked how the United States could be upset that arms were entering Guatemala when its official military mission was still there ostensibly to train Arbenz's army how to use them! Secretary Dulles' reply that the CIA considered the mission a valuable intelligence asset hardly solved this dilemma.[73]

Incapable of arriving at an immediate solution, the Dulles brothers decided that the best short-run expedient would be to fan the public's fury. Allen became a legislative liaison, encouraging congressional leaders to speak against this most recent Communist outrage. In response came charges like those of Senator Wiley, who called the shipment "part of the master plan of world Communism," and of California's Representative Patrick J. Hillings, who claimed that the arms "were to be used to sabotage the Panama Canal."[74] On May 19, at the early morning White House staff meeting, the secretary and the president decided that during his press conference later that day Eisenhower should underscore the gravity of the situation. As if reading from a prepared script, Eisenhower responded to the inevitable question about his reaction to the *Alfhem*'s cargo: "Well, it is disturbing. I think that above all, it highlights the circumstances, the background, that led to the adoption of the resolution at the Caracas conference regarding communism in this country." He added in his memoirs, and as the former Supreme Allied Commander his opinion carried considerable weight, "This quantity [of arms] exceeded any legitimate, normal requirements of the Guatemalan armed forces."[75]

The State Department's press release on May 17 was equally damning. Accepting Allen Dulles' suggestion that the as yet undetermined quantity of arms be termed a "very large shipment," the department contended that Guatemala had become the most heavily armed nation in Central America, with more than three to four times the equipment of Nicaragua, Honduras, and El Salvador. The release left it up to Secretary Dulles to draw the proper conclusion. At his press conference the next week, he asserted that "a government in which Communist influence is very strong has come into a position to dominate militarily the Central American area."[76]

These statements collectively point toward one of the strategies adopted by Washington. As the president explained to the legislative leaders on May 24, the importation of arms into Guatemala exemplified the potential for aggression that had induced Dulles to work so hard in Caracas. The United States was "not going to sit around and do nothing on this but was going to move in to try to stop these shipments under the Caracas agreement."[77] In particular, Eisenhower informed the leaders that he had directed the State Department to take action conforming to the UN Charter and the Caracas resolution and arrange a meeting of the OAS as soon as possible. He added that Honduras and Nicaragua had already requested United States help. That same day the National Security Council's Planning Board drafted a statement recommending that Eisenhower's directive become official policy. Four days later the council adopted the statement.[78]

As would become apparent very shortly, the decision to invoke the Caracas resolution was but one of several courses agreed upon by the White House and, in fact, was the least coercive. As Ambassador Willauer cabled Dulles on May 21, the concept of a united front against Guatemala had certain benefits, but "probably situation requires some stronger action."[79] The primary benefit was derived from the publicity that would result from an attempt to convene another meeting of the OAS so shortly after Caracas. This would emphatically demonstrate that the inherent dangers described by the secretary of state when he introduced the resolution had become an actuality.

The State Department's tactic of repeatedly postponing the date for the meeting indicates, however, that Washington had already decided upon "some stronger action."[80] Dulles was more reluctant to settle on a specific time than Holland, but neither man would commit the United States to a firm schedule.[81] The meeting was not to be held until at least two-thirds of the member nations had consented *in advance* to support a resolution "calling only for the prevention of movement of arms and agents," a policy "believed to be the minimum step in the present circumstances." "The matter was given pretty thorough consideration at the highest levels here," Raymond Leddy wrote Peurifoy on June 5. "There is one thing which I think you can be assured of, and that is that we are on the road to settling this problem . . . There is 100 percent determination here, from the top down, to get rid of this stinker [Arbenz] and not to stop until that is done."[82] After Arbenz's overthrow, Holland agreed with Dulles that he should "postpone [the meeting] for 30 days and then call it off—but he is not telling anybody that."[83]

While the State Department saw little need to push for a rapid convocation of the Latin American nations, it did vigorously pursue the public relations angle. The USIA's memorandum to the Operations Coordinating Board read, "The Communist shipment to Guatemala in mid-May marked a definite turning point."[84] Domestically, *Time's* assessment that the shipment of arms "amounted to the Red bloc's first public display of big-brotherly trust and confidence in Guatemala" typified the press coverage.[85] Later a journalist writing for *Harper's Magazine* claimed he had uncovered the Soviet plot. According to Keith Monroe, the Kremlin intended that only one-third of the *Alfhem's* cargo would remain in Guatemala, to be used by Arbenz to create an irregular militia composed of "phalanxes of peons and Indians who were already drilling openly on the golf courses around Guatemala City." Monroe alleged that another third was earmarked for Nicaragua, where Communist agents were planning to assassinate Somoza and take over that government as well. Communists in Honduras, who had already begun their effort to unseat Gálvez by instigating the strike, would use the final third to complete their assignment.[86] Monroe never revealed the sources of his information, nor did he write his story until Arbenz's government had become history. Except for a few scattered Guatemalans writing from exile, no one refuted his charges. Similarly, Washington's proposal for an emergency OAS meeting under the guidelines of the Caracas resolution indicted Guatemala on the grounds of "Communist domination or control." Since the meeting was stillborn, this indictment also went unchallenged.

Given the prevalent domestic press opinion prior to this time, the USIA did not need to pay much attention to journalistic reaction in the United States. It concentrated most of its efforts elsewhere in the hemisphere and overseas. The agency immediately began an aggressive information campaign to discredit the Arbenz government, to dramatize the threat to hemispheric security, and to encourage action by all nations of the Free World. Despite the lack of lead time, the USIA boasted that, during the month following the *Alfhem's* arrival, it prepared two hundred articles and backgrounders, designed some twenty-seven thousand anti-Communist cartoons and posters, and developed both films and scripts for media outlets. By means of wireless file, cable, and fast pouch, this propaganda blitz expeditiously reached all parts of the globe. The CIA worked closely with the USIA, pointing out areas where reports criticizing the United

States for overreaching had to be countered. Action against Arbenz required a conducive international climate, and the State Department succeeded in establishing it.[87]

Establishing a proper climate of world opinion was especially important to Washington in the context of its other tactics. The ethics of its propaganda campaign are problematic. The components of the rest of its strategy were unquestionably illegal. Shortly after the State Department confirmed the shipment of arms, it began to explore the possibility of blockading major ports and searching foreign vessels destined for Guatemala. As Secretary Dulles soon discovered, the department's legal advisers could find no basis for such measures under international law. Perhaps the United States could unilaterally enact temporary sanctions, including cutting off the importation of such strategic materials as oil, but there was no legal justification for banning arms from entering Guatemala. Furthermore, to conduct surveillance of naval traffic outside United States waters violated a fundamental principle of maritime trade. Holland wondered if the navy could delay Guatemala-bound ships on the pretext that they might be transporting atomic weapons, but Allen Dulles' opinion that no one would find the excuse credible torpedoed that idea. The CIA director further considered it highly unlikely that Arbenz would attempt to smuggle arms into Guatemala on an Iron Curtain vessel, which meant that the United States would have to intercept ships belonging to its allies.[88]

The Eisenhower administration could find no other way to guarantee that Arbenz would not receive additional military supplies. In spite of the State Department's final legal opinion that interception could not be justified under either the Rio treaty or the UN Charter, on May 21 Holland ordered the surveillance of ships bound for Guatemala. At the next legislative meeting, Eisenhower read from a memo written by his special assistant for national security affairs: "To prevent further Communist arms build-up in Central America, U.S. Navy will stop suspicious foreign-flag vessels on high seas off Guatemala in order to examine cargo. If such vessels will not voluntarily cooperate, they will be taken forcibly to Panama for examination."[89]

The order came as a shock, even to some of Eisenhower's supporters. State Department veteran Robert Murphy secretly wrote Dulles on May 25, "I believe the philosophy back of the action is wrong . . . to resort to this action confesses the bankruptcy of our political policy vis-a-vis that country . . . Our present action should give stir to the bones of Admiral von Tirpitz . . ."[90] Dulles ignored Murphy's reservations. He personally presented the United States case to British Ambassador Sir Roger Makins but, as might be expected, to no avail. In the opinion of Foreign Minister Anthony Eden, Dulles exaggerated the threat of a Communist buildup in Central America. Eden agreed to do whatever was practical to discourage British shipowners and merchants from bringing arms to Guatemala, but under no circumstances would he acquiesce to the interception of one of Her Majesty's vessels. The other European nations followed Britain's lead.[91]

From the administration's perspective, the attempt to stop any further arms from reaching Guatemala, even had it been successful, could only have prevented an already intolerable situation from getting worse. When the *Alfhem* docked in Puerto Barrios, Eisenhower and his advisers decided that they could no longer delay the authorization to effect PBSUCCESS. Castillo Armas' invasion had to begin before Arbenz distributed the new supplies, either to the peasants or to his cohorts elsewhere in Central America. The only real question was whether it was already too late, whether this unforeseen variable had, as Foster Dulles feared, "invalidated" or "knocked the props out" from under "the program." Allen Dulles assured his brother that this was not the case, although he doubted that "we can pull it off next month."[92] The CIA director remarked that success depended on Arbenz's army not supporting the president. Soon thereafter one of his agents, disguised as a German businessman, managed to gain the confidence of the regular army's senior staff. He reported that many officers were disloyal to Arbenz. The CIA decided that "Arbenz would not be backed by his army in the event of an anti-communist revolution."[93]

7. Project PBSUCCESS: The Coup

For close to a year the Eisenhower administration laid the ground-work for overthrowing Arbenz's government. The arms shipment from Czechoslovakia forced its hand, and on June 18 the invasion began. Nervously the CIA monitored the progress of the tiny "Army of Liberation"; there was not much to watch. Encountering no re-sistance, Castillo Armas crossed the Honduran border, moved six miles into Esquipulas, and established camp at the religious shrine of the Church of the Black Christ. The colonel called for Arbenz's unconditional surrender, but, severely outnumbered, his army went no further. Castillo Armas claimed that he had not yet completed the organization of his forces and that the heavy rains prevented his driving deeper into Guatemala. A CIA memorandum to Eisenhower revealed the true reason. "The action of Colonel Castillo Armas," the memorandum read, "is not in any sense a conventional military operation . . . As of 20 June the outcome of the efforts to overthrow the regime of President Arbenz of Guatemala remains very much in doubt." The agency's acting assistant director for current intelli-gence explained to the president that the loyalty of regular army of-ficers was the "controlling factor." If Arbenz's regular forces elected to fight, they could repel the invasion without any difficulty. In sum, "The entire effort is thus more dependent upon psychological im-pact rather than actual military strength, although it is upon the ability of the Castillo Armas effort, to create and maintain for a short time the *impression* of very substantial military strength that the success of this particular effort primarily depends."[1]

THE INVASION BEGINS

The CIA memorandum reflected the high risk of the operation. When Eisenhower had initially authorized the agency to devise a plan to overthrow the Guatemalan government, his guidelines were that there was to be no direct United States intervention. This directive compelled the operation's planners to come up with a scheme that did not rely on military force. After all, even before the *Alfhem*'s arrival, Arbenz commanded the most formidable army in Central America. Without massive external assistance, including foreign troops, Castillo Armas could not possibly win an armed confrontation. Consequently, Allen Dulles and the other top CIA officials based their strategy on the assessment that both Arbenz and his military staff could be deceived into believing that Castillo Armas was at the head of a major insurrectionary force and that, if necessary, direct United States support waited in the wings. Perceiving such a challenge, the strategists predicted, the military would desert the revolution and Arbenz would resign. The actual scenario followed the CIA prognosis almost exactly. Not until years later would evidence reveal that Castillo Armas never possessed sufficient military power to oust Arbenz or that the Eisenhower administration never intended to commit United States troops or substantial equipment to the effort.[2]

The preparations of the previous months contributed to the psychological war. Dulles' speech at the Caracas conference, the USIA's propaganda campaign, and all the other expressions of United States opinion inexorably highlighted the alleged Communist penetration of Guatemala, as well as the administration's determined opposition to the revolutionary government. But, for the strategy to work, Arbenz had to believe that Castillo Armas could realistically take on the regular government forces. Hence the CIA furnished the opposition leader with all the requisites for an invasion. In need of an army, the colonel received sufficient money to recruit mercenaries from among the Guatemalan exiles and neighboring populations. Evelyn Irons, a reporter from the United States, hired a donkey and visited Castillo Armas' camp in Honduras. She witnessed many of the troops "receiving wads of dollar bills passed out by men who were unmistakeably American."[3] This "rag-taggle" band comprised the Army of Liberation. Unknown to Arbenz and his officers, at the time of the invasion it consisted of about 150 troops, most of whom had little or no military experience, and another 150 advance agents who had already entered Guatemala. Castillo Armas probably could not have won a battle, let alone a war.[4]

So that the Army of Liberation could resemble an effective fighting unit, CIA agents established training centers in both Honduras and Nicaragua, one of them at El Tamarindo, an estate owned by Somoza. There the troops learned to march in single file and similar rudimentary maneuvers. Into these camps flowed shipments of rifles and other small arms, machine guns, and ammunition from the agency storehouse at France's Field. United States flyers piloted several obsolete bombers to an airport in Nicaragua, where they became Castillo Armas' instant air force. These planes were slow and cumbersome but perfectly acceptable for a war of nerves. As the invasion became imminent, and the administration signed the military pacts with Guatemala's neighbors, the CIA no longer had to use its former circuitous supply route through the Canal Zone. Along with the strategic bombers and tanks that the United States sent Nicaragua and Honduras came Bren guns, mortars, flamethrowers, and other heavy armaments. Castillo Armas never obtained the bombers and tanks, but the other material became a threatening addition to his arsenal.[5]

The CIA wanted Arbenz to know what was going on across Guatemala's border. Indeed, it is more than likely that the agency planned for him to discover Castillo Armas' correspondence with the younger Somoza. The revelation of the correspondence did not prove United States complicity, and it reinforced the Guatemalan government's growing conviction that a Washington-supported invasion was soon to be launched.[6] This conviction was the key to PBSUCCESS. Policy makers did not really delude themselves. They had few expectations of the army's deserting Arbenz out of anti-Communist fervor, nor did they forecast that the masses would rally to the counter-revolutionaries' cause. Instead, the Army of Liberation was intended to frighten both the government and the people into accepting a Castillo Armas victory as a *fait accompli*. If the Guatemalans thought that the Army of Liberation was invincible, if they thought that the bombers and tanks poised in Nicaragua and Honduras were prepared to support the invasion should the regular army offer resistance, they would abandon Arbenz and force his resignation.[7]

While the CIA was putting together a force ostensibly capable of overthrowing the Arbenz administration, it began a concerted psychological offensive within Guatemala itself. Part of its effort focused on the country's majority. Most of the population, particularly the Indians, still played but a small part in the nation's political life, but there was always the possibility that the government could initiate a popular ground swell to defend the revolution. United States commentators could allege that the reform movement was merely a vehicle for Communist subversion, but they could not deny that the reforms benefited a great number of Guatemalans. And, since some two-thirds of the citizens could read neither the articles fed to the Latin American press by the USIA nor the anti-Arbenz literature that the agency paid pilots to drop throughout Guatemala City and the countryside, the CIA needed to implement a more universally accessible propaganda technique. Hence, with the help of the Catholic church, the agency arranged for clandestine meetings with the native clergy. The impact of the resultant anti-Communist messages delivered nearly each Sunday from Guatemalan pulpits cannot be determined, but the peasants were more likely to listen to their pastor than to other speakers for or against the government.[8]

The main target of the propaganda activities, however, was the wealthier group of urban Guatemalans, many of whom comprised Arbenz's officer corps. If this segment of the population continued to support the government, PBSUCCESS was doomed to failure. From its recent success in Iran, the CIA borrowed the formula of preparing the population for a military operation so that it would interpret any sign of force as the beginning of a massive effort. The agency grafted this formula onto a black propaganda technique which had been successful in World War II, "the Big Lie."[9] On May 1, the international labor day, when an unusually large number of Guatemalans were at home, a team of Guatemalan exiles trained and financed by the CIA began to transmit anti-Arbenz, counterrevolutionary broadcasts from the neighboring jungles in Honduras and Nicaragua. The Voice of Liberation, as the station called itself, adopted the slogan "Trabajo, Pan y Patria" (Work, Bread and Country) and announced that it was the mouthpiece for Guatemalan exiles who would shortly return to free their country. Castillo Armas, the broadcasters contended, had everything he needed to oust Arbenz. He only awaited an auspicious moment. The station claimed to be located not too far from Guatemala City. As proof, it would simulate a raid by government officials and return to the air the next day from a fictitious new location. In reality, it remained protected across Guatemala's border. How could Arbenz stop Castillo Armas, the station jeered, when he could not even shut down the broadcasts of a few isolated patriots? The Voice of Liberation sounded so authentic that many foreign correspondents accepted it as the most accurate source of information.[10]

The broadcasts produced the desired effect. Almost all Guatemalans with radios, including Arbenz and his military command, regularly tuned in to the Voice of Liberation channel. By the end of the month, after Washington had reacted so vociferously to his attempt to increase his military capability, the Guatemalan president desperately tried for the last time to reach an accommodation with the United States. On June 1 he renewed his suggestion that his country's dispute with United Fruit be placed before an independent arbiter, this time offering to visit Eisenhower personally in order to demonstrate his good faith. It was too late. Peurifoy replied to Foreign Minister Toriello that Eisenhower's sole interest was in Guatemalan Communism and immediately wired Dulles that the proposal was "obviously designed to gain time to permit lowering of local tensions." The ambassador recommended that the White House arrange for an appropriate question at Eisenhower's next press conference which would permit him to state that, as long as the Communist problem persisted, a meeting between the two presidents could not accomplish anything. Dulles disagreed. He did not want a question planted concerning Arbenz's offer. In fact, he urged Press Secretary James Hagerty to have Eisenhower duck the whole issue. With Castillo Armas' invasion but a few weeks off, the less said about any possible reconciliation the better. Eisenhower opened his conference with a statement on his loyalty-security program. The subject of Guatemala never came up.[11]

The president continued to remain silent while Secretary Dulles spoke for the administration. On June 8 he issued his well-known statement differentiating between Guatemala's problem with United Fruit and its problem with the United States government. Two days later he repeated the difference in a major policy speech on international unity. Then, on June 15, he had his final press conference before the invasion. Brother Allen wanted him to say that the situation had become very critical and that the United States hoped and expected that Guatemala's anti-Communists and army would "clean their own home." They agreed to omit "expected" and "army," since the words might imply that the secretary wanted a revolution. Assistant Secretary Holland felt that the statement was still too incriminating and that it should be amended to say that the Guatemalans had the "capability of peacefully cleaning their own house." Allen did not consider it necessary to qualify the statement. Foster compromised. He told the press, "There is no doubt in my opinion but that the great majority of the Guatemalan people have both the desire and capability of cleaning their own house."[12]

Allen Dulles had intended Eisenhower to make the comment at his press conference on the sixteenth. On the fourteenth he had told Press Secretary Hagerty that the situation was coming to a head and that, by the time of the president's conference, a statement would be in order. Events moved too quickly, however, and on the morning of the fifteenth he advised Foster to make the statement. That afternoon the CIA director sent Hagerty a revised memorandum for Eisenhower. Again Holland felt that it was overly suggestive of United

States involvement. Foster agreed. Since he had already gone as far as would be prudent in issuing the call to arms, he urged Eisenhower to say only that he found conditions within the Guatemalan government disturbing and that the Communist infiltration and arms shipment constituted a serious threat to the hemisphere which would be discussed at the proposed OAS meeting. The State Department's final draft of its suggestions for the conference noted at the bottom, "The President can express hope Guatemalans will solve their problem but should carefully avoid any statement which could be interpreted as an invitation to the Guatemalan people to revolt."[13] Eisenhower artfully followed this advice, concluding his brief comments with the remark, "I couldn't go beyond that in talking about the situation."[14] He had to be evasive, because two days later Castillo Armas would cross the border into Guatemala. Hagerty entered in his diary, "Officially we don't know anything about it."[15]

As its memorandum to Eisenhower reflected, the CIA fully understood the task still remaining. It had to maintain the fiction of Castillo Armas' invincibility, even though the entire Army of Liberation was now out in the open. And because the United States "officially" knew nothing about the invasion, and because Arbenz lost no time in blaming "representatives of the American multimillionaires, such as Messrs. McCarthy, Wiley, and Foster Dulles" for the conspiracy, CIA assistance had to be more covert than ever.[16] The world was watching the developments too closely for the field operatives to risk detection. The CIA hoped that the Army of Liberation would not have to fight. But, if it did, it would have to fend for itself.

Yet the CIA had no intention of idly watching the events run their natural course. It still had its two most potent weapons: the bombers flown by United States pilots that comprised Castillo Armas' air force and the well-camouflaged Voice of Liberation radio station. The agency had hired a number of expert pilots, all capable of flying the cumbersome planes on daring sorties over Guatemala's urban centers. Since the weight of an F-47 bomber (some believe the planes were P-47s) restricts maneuverability, and sufficient fuel had to be carried to allow the pilots to fly back and forth from Managua's international airport, such former barnstormers as Jerry DeLarm substituted blocks of dynamite attached to hand grenades and gasoline-filled soda pop bottles—anything capable of causing a loud explosion—for heavy conventional bombs. They dropped their cargo on parade grounds, ammunition depots, and other highly visible targets. In his zeal one pilot inadvertently bombed the British freighter *Springfjord* moored off the port of San José, an embarrassing happenstance which the CIA's Richard Bissell dismissed as an unfortunate "subincident"—a subincident that cost the agency one million dollars in compensation.[17]

To the frightened city dwellers, Guatemala's capital resembled London during the Battle of Britain. Guatemalans later called the planes *sulfatos*, their word for laxative, due to the debilitating effect upon the government and general population. One commentator has compared this effect to that of Cortés' horses on the sixteenth-century Aztec. Following the conclusion of the operation, the CIA arranged for Castillo Armas' markings to be removed from the *sulfatos* and for the pilots to whisk them out of the country.[18]

The Voice of Liberation enhanced the effectiveness of the bombing raids. The CIA jammed native radio communications, thereby preventing accurate information from reaching the capital city. Instead, Guatemalans heard only the agency's broadcasts, which reported major government defeats in the countryside and the relentless advances of well-equipped divisions of rebel troops. In an effort to silence the transmissions, Arbenz ordered the major electrical company to shut down operations. The ensuing blackout heightened the tension. Hundreds began to flee the city amid rumors of Castillo Armas' imminent arrival, rumors seemingly confirmed by those who continued to receive the CIA station by using batteries or gasoline-powered generators. Incessant police sirens and curfew bells exacerbated the atmosphere of crisis.[19]

CIA strategists feared that Arbenz would expose their charade if his air force could not be neutralized. The government planes were easily capable of intercepting the handful of obsolete bombers as they overflew the cities. Aerial surveillance would reveal Castillo Armas' actual position and impotence; a few well-placed bombs might annihilate the entire Army of Liberation. Hence, the Voice of Liberation expanded its program to include allegedly true-to-life accounts of Soviet aviators who had defected to the West with their aircraft. By June 20 the romantic narratives succeeded in seducing at least one Guatemalan to desert Arbenz, taking his plane with him. The Voice of Liberation's management tried to persuade him to encourage his compatriots to follow his lead. At first he refused, but, after being plied with alcohol, he consented to make an imaginary appeal in the privacy of the station's hideout. As the naïve pilot acted out his part with dramatic flair, the agents secretly recorded his ramblings. A painstaking editing session produced a convincing appeal, which the station promptly aired throughout Guatemala. The results were almost too good to be true. In the words of CIA veteran David Phillips, "From that moment the Guatemalan air force was grounded. Arbenz, fearing his pilots would defect with their planes, did not permit the flight of a single military aircraft for the duration of the conflict."[20]

Had the CIA-sponsored "blitzkrieg" not accomplished the desired psychological effect, and had the Guatemalans not fallen for the Voice of Liberation's ruse, Arbenz's government undoubtedly would have survived. The air attack was so crucial to PBSUCCESS, and Eisenhower was so proud of its effectiveness, that the president referred to it in his memoirs. It was his only admission of his administration's covert assistance. Within the first few days of the invasion, government antiaircraft fire had shot down the rebels' bombers, in one case forcing a wounded pilot to land his crippled plane in Mexico. Castillo Armas urgently requested replacements. Eisenhower, the two Dulles brothers, and Assistant Secretary Holland met in the Oval Office. Holland advised against sending any more planes, insisting that all the Latin Americans would know that they came from the United States. Allen Dulles, on the other hand, informed the president that, with the planes, Castillo Armas' chances of success were no greater than 20 percent. Without them, they were zero. In his own words, Eisenhower "knew from experience the important psychological impact of even a small amount of air support, . . . our proper course of action—indeed my duty—was clear to me." He replaced the planes. This was war, when the exigencies of battle precluded normal diplomacy. The CIA director remarked to the president on their way out of the White House, "When I saw Henry walking into your office with three large law books under his arm, I knew he had lost his case already."[21] Eisenhower had once again become a general.

CONTROVERSY IN THE UNITED NATIONS

Sending the additional planes to Castillo Armas illustrates the extent of Eisenhower's commitment to overthrowing Arbenz. Despite Holland's well-founded reservations, the president willingly risked unmasking the operation. In an equally significant decision, he risked jeopardizing United States relations with its most valued allies and the future utility of the United Nations. The day following Castillo Armas' invasion, Foreign Minister Toriello sent telegrams to the president of the UN Security Council (United States Ambassador Lodge) and Secretary Dulles, charging that "there is a manifest aggression on the part of the Governments of Honduras and Nicaragua, instigated by the interests of foreign monopolies that have been affected by the progressive policy of my government" and requesting that the council convene in order that "it may proceed to take the necessary measures to prevent a breach of international peace and security in this part of Central America." The same day the Guatemalan chargé d'affaires in Washington, Alfredo Chocano, dispatched a note to the president of the OAS Inter-American Peace Committee, requesting that it also call a meeting "to prevent the continuance of the aggression against Guatemala."[22]

Arbenz's official reaction came as no surprise. As noted, in April of 1953 his government had used the UN as a platform to denounce the conspirators preparing to invade Guatemala from across its border. That same year, in support of a resolution to establish a United Nations day, Carlos Manuel Pellecer had ominously advised the National Assembly that "we must support the U.N. so that later we can request its support against the aggression of which Guatemala is the victim."[23] Similarly, at Caracas, in its final statement after the declaration's passage, the Guatemalan delegation wrote that it would interpret any attempt to intervene in the country's internal affairs as an "imminent threat" to its peace and security; in the event of such an attempt, Guatemala would immediately present its case to the UN.[24]

The Eisenhower administration adamantly opposed bringing Guatemala's complaints before the Security Council. Consistent with its previous position, it maintained that this was an internal dispute between Arbenz and Castillo Armas which should therefore come under the aegis of the OAS. Toriello was just as adamant. In his telegrams of June 19, he traced the events leading up to the invasion. He repeatedly provided evidence that the present crisis constituted an external attack, not a civil war. He complained privately to Peurifoy that the Caracas conference had already demonstrated Washington's leverage over the OAS and that his government would never receive an impartial hearing before that organization. The State Department, also privately, heartily concurred. Acting for Dulles, Robert Murphy wired the United States embassies in Nicaragua and Honduras that the administration did not even want the Guatemalan allegations aired before the OAS organ of consultation. Although both the Rio pact and the Caracas declaration stipulated this procedure, there was concern that Toriello might be able to convince the other foreign ministers that the matter should be included on the agenda for the next meeting of the entire body. Murphy explained that the preferred forum for discussion was the Inter-American

Peace Committee, whose members "generally share U.S. views" and where a "greater degree of control exists."[25]

The Security Council considered Guatemala's complaints at an emergency session on June 20. As is customary in such special cases, the council president invited representatives of Guatemala, Nicaragua, and Honduras to attend the meeting. Lodge opened by reminding the members that Brazil, Colombia, and Cuba had already recommended that the complaints be referred to the OAS. He then recognized Arbenz's envoy, Eduardo Castillo-Arriolla. In a lengthy speech, Castillo-Arriolla expanded upon the Toriello cablegrams, underscoring the hostility encountered by both the Arévalo and the Arbenz governments from the revolution's inception. On his list of Guatemala's enemies were not only Nicaragua and Honduras but also the United States and the United Fruit Company. After bringing the council up to date on the most recent happenings, Castillo-Arriolla informed its members that his country respectfully declined the OAS offer to consider the situation, which was Guatemala's prerogative according to OAS rules. Instead, he formally requested that the Security Council send an observation team to Guatemala and, if necessary, to the surrounding countries to verify "the fact that the countries which my Government accuses have connived at the invasion."[26]

The ensuing debate was both heated and predictable. Nicaragua's and Honduras' representatives denied any wrongdoing and advocated a change of venue to the OAS. Only the Soviet Union spoke in favor of the Guatemalan position, although France and Great Britain acknowledged that the UN had a responsibility to attempt to reestablish peace and expressed their willingness to support *any* constructive proposals in that direction. Finally Lodge took the floor as the spokesman for the United States. He quickly dispatched of Guatemala's request, asserting that the situation was precisely the kind of problem that should be dealt with by the OAS. The remainder of his remarks defended the United States and, in particular, Dulles and Eisenhower. Dulles, he said, was well known to practically everyone in the room, and "the merest inference that he could be actuated by any consideration other than that of duty [such as the interests of UFCO] is one which certainly reflects no credit on him who utters it." As for Eisenhower, "He is a man who led a great army in World War II against Nazi imperialism and who has shown by every word and deed of his life, since the day when he was a small boy in Kansas, that his heart is always on the side of the little man who is trying to get by in life." Lodge ended by pointing an accusing finger at the Soviet Union: "Stay out of this hemisphere and do not try to start your plans and conspiracies over here."[27]

The members voted 10 to 1 in favor of referring Guatemala's complaints to the OAS. The veto, however, came from the Soviet Union. While not unexpected, this complicated the administration's plans because the Arbenz government continued to press for a Security Council investigation, despite the fact that the Inter-American Peace Committee, acting at the request of Nicaragua and Honduras, set up a fact-finding team to visit the troubled region. The committee hoped Arbenz would accept the OAS delegation, but instead he sent the Security Council additional telegrams reporting new attacks. He also repeated his request that the council place the Guatemalan complaints on its agenda. To the surprise of both the White House and the State Department, Great Britain and France now favored the Guatemalan request. Upon learning of this serious reversal, Assistant Secretary Holland immediately instructed Lodge to do everything possible to keep Guatemala off the Security Council's agenda. Lodge knew what to do. He told Dulles that he would delay calling a council meeting until the United States had sufficient votes to defeat the proposed agenda. The State Department began to line up support.[28]

Neither Dulles nor Lodge could understand the behavior of Great Britain and France. They were outraged. Of perhaps even more significance, so was Eisenhower. When the president became angry his face would grow red and the veins would protrude from his forehead and neck, prompting his longtime assistant Bryce Harlow to liken his temper to a Bessemer furnace.[29] One can imagine his explosion after learning of the newest crimp in his Guatemalan policy. At a top-level meeting with his advisers, he thundered that we have been "too damned nice" to our European allies. He singled out the British, who, he fulminated, "expect us to give them a free ride and side with them in Cyprus and yet they won't even support us on Guatemala." He would teach them a lesson and show them that "they have no right to stick their nose into matters which concern this hemisphere entirely."[30] Then, on June 24, for the first time in the UN's history, a United States president authorized his Security Council delegate to exercise a veto against the British and French.[31]

Other heavy-handed tactics obviated the need to use the veto. The British and French took the position that OAS jurisdiction was permissive, not mandatory; since articles 34 and 35 of the UN Charter gave any member the right to bring "any dispute, or any situation which might lead to international friction" to the Security Council's attention and authorized the council to investigate the dispute or situation, they saw no reason why they should not grant Guatemala's request.[32] As noted above, the United States had a very good reason. Lodge summoned the French and British representatives to his UN office to tell them so in no uncertain terms. After mentioning the possibility of a veto, he announced that he had been instructed by Eisenhower to inform them that "if Great Britain and France felt that they must take an independent line backing the present government in Guatemala, we would feel free to take an equally independent line concerning such matters as Egypt and North Africa." According to Lodge, "My announcement was received with great solemnity."[33]

Lodge then suggested to Dulles that he have the United States ambassadors in London and Paris reiterate the threat personally to those countries' foreign offices, lest its impact be "lost, garbled or distorted in transmission."[34] His suggestion was not necessary. By a fortunate circumstance, Churchill and Eden arrived in Washington on the morning of June 25—the day Lodge had scheduled the Security Council meeting—to discuss the beleaguered Geneva talks on Indochina. Dulles met them at the airport and immediately raised the Guatemalan question. Eden offered a compromise. The agenda should be adopted, and Lodge would then tell the members that the Inter-American Peace Committee had already selected a team of observers to visit Central America. This information would preempt the Guatemalan request, so that the council could adjourn by a procedural vote which would not be subject to veto. Dulles insisted that the agenda must not be approved and that any attempt to do so would be a "body blow to the rights of the American Statesmen."[35] He told Lodge that if "we split on this, they better pack up and go home."[36]

They drove to the White House, where the secretary and the president "talked cold turkey" to Britain's two leading statesmen. Neither Englishman "was entirely happy about these proceedings," but they could not ignore the administration's threats. They reluctantly agreed to abstain from the vote and recommend to the French that they do likewise. Just to make sure, Dulles phoned Paris to report the conversation. That afternoon the Security Council met for the 676th time. Lodge ruled that Guatemala could not be represented, and the council rejected the agenda by a one-vote margin, with Britain and France abstaining. Secretary General Dag Hammarskjöld wrote Lodge that the United States position could have "serious consequences" for the UN's future.[37]

A NEW GUATEMALAN GOVERNMENT

At a cabinet meeting shortly following Arbenz's overthrow, Eisenhower and Dulles noted with great satisfaction the British "willingness to cooperate in regard to the u.n. aspect" of their Guatemalan policy without requiring the use of the veto. They added that the "cooperation" had contributed to the present "happier situation in Guatemala."[38] Indeed, having overcome this final obstacle, the administration brought pbsuccess to a triumphant conclusion without further interruption. In his June 21 telegrams to the embassies in Nicaragua and Honduras, Murphy revealed the State Department's intention to delay the Inter-American Peace Committee's fact-finding mission as long as required to avoid the possibility of any embarrassing discoveries. Arbenz's government, by refusing to sanction the mission until after the Security Council's final rejection of its request, ironically served the United States purpose.

The observation team left New York on June 28. By this time, there was little for it to observe. The day before, Arbenz had resigned. Yet, until it had safely installed Castillo Armas in the National Palace, Washington still wanted no outside observers. Holland called the commission in Mexico City and persuaded it not to continue on to Guatemala until the provisional junta renewed Arbenz's invitation. He then phoned Peurifoy to suggest that the ambassador "cause the Junta" to cable the commission's head, Luis Quintanilla, that it preferred the trip be postponed until all the fighting was over. The group never left Mexico City. The Central American desk's monthly summary for July read, "The Inter-American Peace Committee fact-finding group . . . was informed early in July [July 2] by the authorities of all three Governments [Guatemala, Nicaragua, and Honduras] that the controversy no longer existed. Since the purpose of the Committee was to clarify the facts of the situation in order to assist in a peaceful solution, there remained no further basis for action on its part."[39]

Had the committee reached Guatemala, it is doubtful that it would have been able to "clarify the facts." The final stages of pbsuccess were meticulously concealed. When the controversy with Britain and France erupted, the Eisenhower administration judged the international political situation as too volatile to prolong the operation. Encouraged by the reports coming in from Peurifoy and the cia, it opted to launch an all-out effort. To demonstrate United States solidarity and resolve in the face of potential allied defections, the State Department orchestrated resolutions in both houses of Congress. Except for one vote, each passed unanimously. Their wording was virtually identical: the United States could not and would not tolerate Communism in the hemisphere. The Senate version passed on the day of the Security Council vote.[40]

In Guatemala, CIA agents met with the rebel high command. They arranged a Voice of Liberation broadcast, also to coincide with the Security Council vote, announcing the convergence of two divisions on Guatemala City. Simultaneously, Jerry DeLarm, the most adventurous of the pilots paid to fly for Castillo Armas, strafed the capital, blowing up the government's oil reserves. Appropriately frightened, Arbenz committed his ultimate error: he ordered his army officers to distribute arms to local peasants and workers. They balked, demanding instead that the president resign or come to terms with Castillo Armas. Arbenz knew that he could not continue without the army's support and that either alternative in the ultimatum amounted to total defeat. On June 27 he met with Chief of Armed Forces Colonel Carlos Enrique Díaz. Visibly tired, he told Díaz that he would peacefully turn the government over to him if he received the guarantee that there would be no negotiations with Castillo Armas. Díaz, who had supported the revolution all along and opposed the invasion as much as Arbenz, readily consented. At 9:00 that evening, Arbenz publicly announced the agreement. Whiting Willauer wrote his former boss with the Flying Tigers, "For a while it was a very close thing but as you can expect, air power did the trick."[41]

Arbenz's resignation presented Washington with another unexpected problem. Castillo Armas was still nowhere near the National Palace, and Allen Dulles did not trust the presidency to the man who had been the revolutionary government's chief army officer. It had been Peurifoy who encouraged Díaz to accept Arbenz's resignation. Although on two previous occasions the ambassador had told Toriello that he had "no control" over Castillo Armas' actions and that only by landing the marines could the United States hope to put an end to the hostilities, he assured Díaz that he would try to contact Castillo Armas to arrange a cease-fire.[42] Peurifoy had not known, however, that Díaz intended to form a junta that would enable him to keep fighting should Castillo Armas continue his assault. The provisional president—pledging never to surrender to the rebel invaders—immediately sought the support of the military by appointing as part of his governing body Colonels Elfego H. Monzón and José Angel Sánchez. The Dulles brothers decided that they had to "get [Díaz] out and get a better army officer in."[43]

Thus, early on the morning of June 29, Peurifoy, who through-out the invasion had been a familiar sight as he ran back and forth among Arbenz's military with a shoulder holster slung over his arm, paid another visit to Díaz. Eager to prove himself worthy of Washington's confidence, the unsuspecting colonel greeted the ambassador with a summary of his first day in office, highlighting his arrest of numerous supporters of the previous government. Peurifoy was not impressed. He castigated Díaz for having permitted Arbenz to use his resignation speech for one final attack on United States policy. He then added, according to his report to Dulles, that "this being his first act, I did not see how we could work together toward bringing about peace." Lest his meaning not be clear, Peurifoy suggested that Díaz designate Monzón as president.[44] Outside, Jerry De-Larm got back into his plane to drop one more bomb—on the main army powder magazine. Díaz got the message; Washington would not tolerate his continued opposition to Castillo Armas. Wearily, he told Peurifoy that he and Sánchez would withdraw from the junta. At this point, Monzón, who had been waiting outside, joined the meeting. His armed guard escorted Díaz from the room. Monzón followed them out, announcing, "My colleague Díaz has decided to resign. I am replacing him." He would form a new junta.[45]

For the second time in as many days, Peurifoy had, to use Drew Pearson's word, "persuaded" a Guatemalan military officer to assume the presidency.[46] But the ambassador's work was far from over. Still undecided was whether the State Department would support a Monzón government or engineer the formation of a third junta with its man—Castillo Armas—at the head. Much could be said for continuing to back Monzón. He was already entrenched in Guatemala City and, unlike Díaz, had not made any deals with Arbenz. In fact, months earlier Peurifoy had singled him out as "an individual who might prove of value."[47] Monzón, who had been a prominent force in keeping the army loyal to the government following Araña's 1949 assassination, resented the fact that he had never been given what he considered to be adequate recognition. Peurifoy liked him. "I am sure that results of years of Communist infiltration will require more than 24 hours to eradicate," the ambassador cabled Dulles on June 30, and "I am convinced Monzón and associates are sincerely anti-Communist and are doing best they can in short time to clean up Communist mess in Guatemala."[48]

Eisenhower's secretary of state was not so sure. Monzón had never proven himself the type of dynamic leader demanded by the situation. There was also the question of Castillo Armas' voluntarily accepting a subordinate role. Dulles did not think the United States could risk alienating the leader of the opposition forces, and Peurifoy doubted that Monzón could maintain control without the exiles' acquiescence. Thus far they had shown no indication of a willingness to acknowledge any government other than one of their own. Under the circumstances, Dulles and his brother decided that Monzón and Castillo Armas should hold a conference. Monzón immediately agreed to the proposal, so Assistant Secretary Holland phoned Ambassador Willauer in Honduras, instructing him to have a Honduran official contact Castillo Armas to urge him to meet with Monzón. Holland then called the ambassadors in Nicaragua and El Salvador to get them to arrange for a cessation of all hostilities. The embassies reported that everything had been done. So, on June 29, Holland phoned Peurifoy to go ahead and have Monzón extend the invitation.[49]

Initially both Dulles and Holland feared that Peurifoy's presence at the meeting could be interpreted by other countries in the hemisphere as undue interference by the United States. The publicity surrounding the ambassador's activities caused even Peurifoy to acknowledge that his position had been compromised. State induced El Salvador's President Oscar Osorio to lend his good offices for the conference and provide a papal nuncio to act as mediator. On June 30, both Monzón and Castillo Armas flew to El Salvador, the latter accompanied by Córdova Cerna. But Dulles wired Peurifoy that "if in your judgment conference agreement and consequent stabilization anti-Communist government can only be assured by exercise your personal influence on the spot, you may proceed to participate." Holland ordered that a plane be placed at the ambassador's disposal in the event of an impasse.[50] The two Guatemalan colonels met for two and one-half hours the first day. That evening Holland dictated a message to the CIA's Frank Wisner, explaining that, according to El Salvador Ambassador Michael McDermott's account, a rapid settlement would be difficult and Peurifoy would have to fly in from Guatemala City. Early the next morning, Peurifoy arrived at Osorio's palace.[51]

The ambassador had not even had time to discuss the progress of the negotiations with El Salvador's president when he received a call from Dulles. The secretary told him that he had Eisenhower's full support and that he should take a strong line if necessary. In Peurifoy's words, "I was authorized to 'crack some heads together.'"[52] As might be expected, his biggest problem was with Castillo Armas. After spending the last three years preparing for the invasion, the Army of Liberation's leader felt that he was entitled to the Guate-

malan presidency and wanted nothing to do with someone tied to
the Arbenz regime. Peurifoy did not disagree. He took Castillo Armas aside and told him confidentially that he would do everything
possible to help him get elected but that, for the time being, he
should simply join Monzón's junta. When the colonel replied that
his legions would never accept such a bargain, the ambassador re-
torted that he thought he was speaking with the top man. Castillo
Armas needed some time to digest this last remark, so Peurifoy went
off to talk to Monzón. This tête-à-tête led to Monzón's agreeing to
take Castillo Armas into his junta and hold elections within a short
time of their joint return to Guatemala. The concession broke
the deadlock. Peurifoy's embassy wired Washington, "Without actually stating it, the implication was that Castillo Armas would be
elected."[53]

Peurifoy had done his job masterfully. Castillo Armas joined
Monzón's junta and triumphantly marched up the steps of the National Palace. On July 7, the junta elected Castillo Armas Guatemala's provisional president and Monzón resigned to head the armed
forces. Elections for the permanent government came in early October. Castillo Armas' National Committee for Defense against Communism screened all potential candidates and banned all political
parties. Only the provisional president received its official sanction.
Government officers staffed the polling places; there was no secret
ballot. The final tally showed Castillo Armas with 99 percent of the
vote. Of the more than 486,000 ballots tabulated, only 400 were
negative. The counterrevolution had succeeded completely, and the
largest military encounter had cost but seventeen lives. Arbenz lived
in exile until 1971, when, at the age of fifty-seven, he was found dead
in his bathtub in Mexico City. Officials listed the cause of death as
drowning.[54]

THE COVER-UP

By the time of Castillo Armas' election, Peurifoy was already
gone. Dulles considered it best to remove the controversial ambassador from the scene and replace him with the department's most
experienced diplomat, Norman Armour. The secretary knew that
Armour, who had already retired once, would agree only to a short
stint in Guatemala. He felt, nevertheless, that the prestige which
the venerable old man would bring to the appointment would "build
that situation up." As he confided to Senate majority leader Knowland in August, "We picked Armour because it would be evidence of

our willingness to put our best foot forward and would show our great concern." He intended to rely on the embassy's newly appointed second-in-command, Thomas Mann, to do the real work.[55]

As for Peurifoy, Dulles and his brother decided he was perfect for the ambassadorship to Thailand. They transferred him to Bangkok, where he could lend his expertise to the fight against Communism in Southeast Asia. A year later, while speeding down a narrow rural road in his blue Thunderbird, the flamboyant ambassador and his son were killed in a head-on collision with a heavy truck. The CIA believed his death the revenge of the Communists, but no evidence could be found. Despite questions of official propriety, the White House sent a military plane to bring the bodies back to the United States.[56]

Washington never publicly acknowledged a possible political motive for Peurifoy's death. To have done so might have reopened conjecture regarding its complicity in Arbenz's overthrow. Indeed, PBSUCCESS remained one of the administration's best-kept secrets. But it was also one of its greatest triumphs. Accepting Hagerty's and Dulles' advice that he initially moderate his reaction, in his first press conference after the coup Eisenhower said only that it would be "just deceitful" for him to conceal his satisfaction over the turn of events. Later, at the Illinois State Fair, he elaborated: "In Guatemala, the people of that region rose up and rejected the Communist doctrine, and said in the terms of the spirit of the agreement at Caracas, 'You shall not come here and establish yourselves.'"[57] In conjunction with his dramatic acceptance of Lieutenant Colonel José Luis Cruz Salazar's credentials as Guatemala's ambassador to the United States (Salazar occupied the same post under Ubico), when the president asserted that, "the people of Guatemala, in a magnificent effort, have liberated themselves from the shackles of international Communist direction," Eisenhower's expressions regarding the coup left no doubt about his position.[58]

Dulles echoed Eisenhower's sentiments. For several weeks prior to the coup's completion, the secretary and his staff had labored over the speech he would deliver if the meeting of the OAS foreign ministers were held. It would have to be an exceptional speech, for the State Department deemed it imperative that the secretary go down to the meeting with the full weight of United States public opinion behind him. He might have to do some hard selling in order to convince the other ministers that the OAS should take concerted action against the Guatemalan government. Castillo Armas' victory, of course, obviated the need for the meeting, and Assistant Secretary Holland arranged to "postpone it for 30 days and then call it off."[59]

But Dulles now felt that it was more important than ever to address the public. Telling his press secretary Carl McCardle that "this is the chance to talk about the biggest success in the last five years against Communism," on June 29 he instructed him to line up all the television and radio networks.[60] He wanted to make his remarks on the same day as Eisenhower's press conference, because he could express the enthusiasm that the president could not.[61]

That evening Dulles was at his oratorical best. With his characteristic certitude, he proclaimed that "the people of Guatemala have now been heard from." They had "cured" their country of "an alien despotism which sought to use Guatemala for its own evil ends." For this "new and glorious chapter" in the "already great tradition of the American States," Dulles thanked the OAS, the United Nations Security Council, and, above all, the "loyal citizens of Guatemala who, in the face of terrorism and violence and against what seemed insuperable odds, had the courage and the will to eliminate the traitorous tools of foreign despots." He did not thank the CIA.[62]

Since it viewed Castillo Armas' triumph as the "biggest success in the last five years against Communism," the administration wanted to play it up with more than just words. It also sought to put an end to any speculation regarding United States involvement. State recommended that the White House officially invite the new Guatemalan president to visit the United States. This could not be done immediately: Castillo Armas had to remain in his country to solidify his control and oversee the government's campaign to root out all the alleged Communists. Moreover, Washington had to be careful not to do anything that might suggest his indebtedness to the United States. "Offhand," Eisenhower wrote a friend on July 6, "I would foresee problems [concerning an invitation to Castillo Armas] in connection with neighboring, consistently friendly Latin American countries"; the next day he wrote Dulles, "I can think of a number of pitfalls in the idea."[63] A year seemed an adequate period of delay, so in the spring of 1955 preparations for the visit began. Upon learning that State intended Castillo Armas to come the next fall, Senator Alexander Wiley complained to the president. He felt that too much time had already elapsed and that the visit should take place before the current Congress adjourned. If the timetable were moved up, Wiley wrote Eisenhower, the Guatemalan hero could be scheduled to address a joint session of Congress, so "we would be able to convey to the world by one of the most dramatic, sincere, and forthright means possible how free men join together in brotherhood with a proud people which had the courage to overthrow a Red regime."[64]

Although Eisenhower promised Wiley that he would consider the suggestion and thanked the senator for his substantial role in exposing the Arbenz government, Castillo Armas did not arrive until October 31. There is no definite evidence concerning why the administration rejected the senator's proposal, but a handwritten notation on Acting Secretary of State Herbert Hoover's memorandum to the president suggests that the July summit in Geneva precluded an earlier date.[65] In any event, by October Eisenhower had suffered his first heart attack, and Vice-President Nixon had to fill in as chief of state. The substitution did not diminish the hero's welcome accorded to Castillo Armas. He received a twenty-one gun salute in Washington, a ticker-tape parade in New York City, and honorary degrees from Fordham and Columbia universities. Perhaps most significant, during his two-week tour of major cities he stopped in Denver, where Eisenhower greeted him from his bed at Fitzsimmons Army Hospital. The interview added great prestige to the frail-looking colonel from Guatemala.[66]

Nixon's toast at the White House dinner reflected the tenor of the welcome. "We in the United States," he said, "have watched the people of Guatemala record an episode in their history deeply significant to all peoples . . . Led by the courageous soldier who is our guest this evening, the Guatemalan people revolted against Communist rule, which in collapsing, bore graphic witness to its inherent shallowness, falsity and corruption."[67] These remarks encapsulate Washington's public position on the coup. It was not enough for the administration to deny the existence of PBSUCCESS, nor was it sufficient to rely on earlier statements by Eisenhower and Dulles. During these years of intense cold war, United States leaders deemed it essential that the populations of the world "record" the victory in Guatemala as "deeply significant to all peoples." A lesson had to be drawn for both the Free World and those living under Communist rule. What was needed was an official explanation of the events, an official cover-up.

Hence, by the end of 1954 both the House of Representatives Select Committee on Communist Aggression and the State Department had published independent investigations of the ten-year period of the Guatemalan revolution and its overthrow. It would be redundant to recapitulate their findings; the very titles of the publications—*Communist Aggression in Latin America* and *Penetration of the Political Institutions of Guatemala by the International Communist Movement*—indicate the results. The sole evidence presented was that of longtime Guatemalan opponents of both the Arévalo and Arbenz regimes and United States analysts who had consistently branded the revolutionary governments as Communist-dominated. Not only was there a marked absence of new information, but the witnesses merely repeated their previous conclusions. For example, after Peurifoy first spoke to Arbenz in December 1953, he reported to the State Department, "I am definitely convinced that if the President is not a Communist, he will certainly do until one comes along."[68] When questioned by the House committee concerning Arbenz's political beliefs, the ambassador responded: "I spent six hours with him one evening, and he talked like a Communist, he thought like a Communist, he acted like a Communist, and if he is not one, Mr. Chairman, he will do until one comes along."[69] Such programmed testimony typified the source material for both studies. Their findings totally exonerated the United States from any charges of complicity and left no room for any interpretation regarding the extent of the Communist threat in Guatemala.[70]

Still, the State Department found the conclusions unsatisfactory, at least concerning its own study. Dulles, in fact, had wanted a different kind of document. The day following the agreement between Castillo Armas and Monzón, when the final outstanding problem had been settled, the secretary phoned C. D. Jackson, who was vacationing in the Berkshire Mountains of Massachusetts. By this time Jackson had resigned his post at the White House and returned to work for Time, Incorporated. Dulles asked Jackson if the latter knew someone who might write a literary history of the Guatemalan affair. He had in mind "a sort of historical novel" with an "Uncle Tom's Cabin or Ida Tarbell touch." The writer would have access to all the relevant documents except, of course, the CIA material, and the documentation would be published separately. Dulles did not specify whether the State Department's name would appear on the "opus in question," but he did mention that it would be translated into Spanish and circulated throughout Latin America as well as the United States. Jackson considered the idea worth pursuing and promised Dulles he would get back to him if he thought of any names.[71]

Why the proposal came to naught is a matter for conjecture. Perhaps an appropriate author could not be found, or perhaps Dulles merely lost interest in the project as he moved on to other cold war battlefields. Whatever the reason, the 1954 State Department study was anything but literary. Indeed, as the Latin American expert Bryce Wood has carefully illustrated, it was so literal that it caused Foggy Bottom great concern. A research group prepared the publication, called the "Blue Book," and rather than trying to emulate Harriet Beecher Stowe it religiously adhered to the available documents.

It also included certain analyses that, while not contradicting Washington's official view, did on occasion hedge a bit. Consequently, in 1957 State ordered that a second study, *A Case History of Communist Penetration: Guatemala*, or the "Green Book," replace the initial one. The second study revised certain of its predecessor's evaluations. For example, as Wood notes, the "Blue Book" described the revolution's philosophy as "a glaze of nationalism and marxism, a scrambled compound which was short of the full strength of militant Communism." This description made Dulles and his colleagues uncomfortable, so the "Green Book" used the less ambiguous term "alien despotism." With such subtle revisions, Washington's case became airtight. The cover-up was complete.[72]

AN ALTERNATIVE EXPLANATION

The State Department's effort to rewrite the history of Guatemala stemmed from two interrelated yet independent objectives: to absolve the Eisenhower administration from any allegations of complicity in the coup and to demonstrate beyond any doubt that the Guatemalan government was dominated by Communists and part of the Soviet Union's international conspiracy. The objectives are interrelated because Washington's perceptions of the requisites of cold war defense demanded that the world believe that freedom-loving elements of the native population rose up to throw off the yoke of Communist oppression. They are independent because to prove United States complicity does not disprove the contention that Communists controlled Guatemala. Even after admitting the United States role, most of those involved in the operation maintain that PBSUCCESS worked so effectively because Arbenz was an agent of the Communists. The ends, they therefore conclude, justify the means.[73] To fully understand the consequences of United States policy toward Guatemala in 1954, therefore, one must reexamine not only the actual involvement in the coup but also the basis for that involvement and the causes of Arbenz's defeat.

A number of misperceptions contributed to Eisenhower's decision to authorize PBSUCCESS. The first was the consensus view that Guatemala was controlled by the Communists. As described in previous chapters, Washington predicated its evaluation of Guatemalans and the government programs on inferences, on syllogistic "duck tests" that consistently generalized from the particular. In the cold war ethos, it was a simple step to interpret the enactment of a long-overdue agrarian reform, official opposition to Yankee-supported

Latin American dictators, labor legislation, or other nationalistic policies that failed to coincide with those of the United States as proof of Communist intrigue. A closer look at the evidence, however, belies this interpretation. The agrarian reform, to take the most publicized example, called for the redistribution and private ownership of uncultivated land. United Fruit retained a vast amount of its property, and the legislation contained no provisions for nationalization or Communization. Yet the reform did damage UFCO's interests and thus came under the contemporary definition of a Communist program. Linked with other similar evidence, the agrarian reform convicted the revolutionary government.

Subjected to the same scrutiny, the other reform programs indicate what IBRD economist George Britnell described as a "green" revolution, not a "red" one.[74] Arévalo and Arbenz were neither Communists nor fellow travelers, nor would they, to paraphrase Peurifoy, do until a real Communist came along. Each was a nationalist, somewhat of an eclectic idealist whose philosophy could best be characterized as an amalgam of liberal reformism, democratic socialism, and a certain tinge of anti-Yankee sentiment. As mandated by the 1944 revolution, they vowed to modernize Guatemala, to create the conditions necessary for the country's self-sufficiency, and to increase the standard of living for the majority of the population. Each outlined his programs during his campaign for the presidency, and each adhered to his platform. In this regard, it must be noted that in both cases it was Guatemala's conservative opposition which first claimed that the two presidents were Communists, and only later did Washington reach the same conclusion. During the Ubico regime, it became common practice among Guatemala's wealthy minority to list as Communists all those who opposed the government's conservative policies. During the cold war, it became common practice within the United States to do the same.

To assert that Arévalo and Arbenz were not Communists does not imply that there were no Communists in Guatemala. There were indigenous Communists, some of whom played important roles in the labor movement, the educational programs, and even the government structure. By the time of Castillo Armas' invasion, their number had grown to as many as five thousand.[75] Five thousand, nevertheless, is a small percentage of a population of over three million. Eisenhower's friend William Prescott Allen, the publisher of the *Laredo Times*, put it another way. Telegramming the president after visiting Guatemala in 1954, he maintained, "Yes, Guatemala has a very small minority of Communists, but not as many as San Francisco."[76]

Numbers do not always tell the story. Analysts in the United States, familiar with the writings of Lenin and Mao as well as the Communist minorities' successes in Russia and China, feared that a similar potential existed in Guatemala. If the potential existed at all, it was extremely remote. The Communists' situation in Guatemala hardly paralleled their alleged models. There was no tightly knit organization, nor was there a leader capable of attracting a substantial following. The politically and culturally insulated Maya would be of little help in an attempted take-over. For Guatemalan Communists, the vehicle for expanding their power was the electoral process. Of the fifty-six seats in the National Assembly, at no time did members of the Guatemalan Labor party hold more than four, and the secretary general, José Manuel Fortuny, lost in his bid for election. Most important, Communist influence within the army and police, the key instruments for controlling the country, was negligible.[77]

Why then did Arbenz, who did not embrace the Communists' philosophy, choose to incur hostility by tolerating their presence and even legalizing their party? On numerous occasions government representatives explained the reasoning. Arbenz was interested in social and economic reform, which was an issue separate from that of winning the cold war. Certainly there were Communists in Guatemala, but they were but a small component of the coalition supporting the administration's program. As for Communist subversion, or what United States analysts called the "Guatemalan Way," Arbenz felt that the most effective way to prevent the spread of Communist influence was to alleviate the conditions that made Communism appear so attractive. Repression would only force the Communists underground, where they would be much more difficult to control. Let the government get on with its program, Arbenz's representatives pleaded, and there would be no need to fear the Communists.[78]

To members of the Eisenhower administration, such an explanation was, at best, naïve. What they did not understand, or would not admit, was that the Communists were a great asset to the reform program and that, for Guatemalan nationalists, the threat to the program came from the right, not the left. This does not mean that Arbenz depended on the Communists to the extent that they dominated him or his policies. Rather, it means only that the Communists supported the reforms and that the Washington-backed elements within Guatemala did not. The Communists promoted the agrarian legislation, worked hard on the literacy campaigns, and defended the rights of workers according to the Labor Code. They also supplied much needed administrative assistance. But they did not formulate the legislation, nor did they control the votes in congress. As Ronald Schneider writes in his critical study *Communism in Guatemala*, the Communists were "the truest interpreters of the wishes of the people . . . Arbenz favored the Communists more for their abilities and virtues than from any belief in communism."[79]

This last comment leads to the second and, perhaps, more serious misperception by cold war analysts. Alleging the monolithic nature of the international Communist movement, they assumed that the Guatemalan Communists took their orders from the Kremlin. Yet as early as 1950 such a highly respected Soviet expert as George Kennan wrote, "It is true that most of the people who go by the name of 'Communist' in Latin America are a somewhat different species than in Europe. Their bond with Moscow is tenuous and indirect."[80] In Guatemala, the bond was so tenuous and indirect that even the determined John Foster Dulles could not find it. A year after the coup, Dulles queried State's Assistant Secretary for Intelligence W. Park Armstrong as to whether his shop had ever found evidence of a connection between Guatemalan Communists and the Soviet Union. Armstrong could reply only that there was "nothing conclusive."[81]

Of course, the Soviet Union would have liked to see the Communists gain control of Guatemala. Yet, even before Stalin's death in 1953, Soviet foreign policy was characterized by conservatism, by moderation, by what would come to be called peaceful coexistence. Its foundation was the recognition that those geopolitical blocs where the Western alliance was strongest were off limits. In the words of two analysts from Georgetown University, "During the four decades following the [Russian] revolution . . . the majority of Moscow's foreign policy decision makers still held to the opinion that the region was the private domain of the United States which would not permit any large scale Soviet influence there." Moreover, during 1953 and 1954, Soviet leaders were more concerned with solving the problem of political succession than they were with expanding Communism. They feared the potential effect of an international crisis on their destabilized government apparatus. Logically, their foreign policy became more cautious. The Soviet Union did not impose its dogma on Guatemala from thousands of miles away, nor did it train the Guatemalan Communist leaders. This was the reason why Dulles was continually frustrated in his attempt to find evidence of a connection. Guatemalan Communism, or for that matter the idealism of the Guatemalan nationalists, developed from native conditions that pervaded national life long before the Russian Revolution. Unfortunately for the Guatemalan revolutionaries, their philosophy and their objectives could not be translated into the cold war vocabulary of absolutes.[82]

A fundamental cause for Arbenz's defeat can be found in the preceding analysis. It is obviously misleading to accept Washington's explanation that under the leadership of Castillo Armas the majority of Guatemalans overthrew a Communist-dominated government. It is also misleading to accept at face value the CIA's assessment that Arbenz lost when his nerve cracked, although this latter evaluation is closer to the truth and does describe the specific cause.[83] Nevertheless, by placing so much emphasis on Arbenz's personality, this explanation contributes little to a basic understanding. Why did Castillo Armas' victory come so easily? Why did the regular army fail to support the government adequately, and why did not Arbenz create a popular militia? In short, why was Arbenz virtually isolated within his own country and surrounded by hostile elements?

In 1955 Daniel Graham wrote in the *Nation,* "Deep down everyone in Guatemala knows that Communism was not the issue. Feudalism was the issue, and those who profited from feudalism won."[84] Therein lies the cause of Arbenz's defeat. He was a middle-class reformer who depended on the middle class for his survival. The 1944 revolution originated as a middle-class movement, and its character never changed.[85] The revolution's leadership attempted to overcome Guatemala's historically inequitable social and economic order by enacting relatively moderate reforms. In doing so, the government left untouched the "feudal" elements who benefited from the historic order. The same families owned the land and the same generals ran the army. Despite the improvements in their condition, the Indian majority remained powerless, leaving Arbenz little loyal support with which to fight the counterrevolution. The internal contradictions of the Guatemalan revolution planted the seeds for its defeat; Castillo Armas and the CIA simply reaped the harvest. Almost seven years later in Cuba, the story would be different.

8. Project PBSUCCESS: The Legacy

Whereas there are indications that the CIA operation in Guatemala influenced subsequent Third World developments,[1] its link to the Cuban revolution and the Bay of Pigs fiasco can be documented. The relationship between 1954 Guatemala and Cuba's 26th of July movement is best introduced by briefly sketching the career of Ernesto ("Che") Guevara. Learning of what was going on in Guatemala, Guevara decided to visit the country. He arrived on Christmas Eve 1953. Guevara took no part in the government, supporting himself by peddling encyclopedias, but he did talk to many national figures, including former President Juan José Arévalo. Once the Arbenz government was attacked, he immediately came to its defense—he encouraged government supporters and helped transport weapons from one place to another. This involvement was sufficient to make Guevara suspect to Castillo Armas, so after a short stay in the embassy of his native Argentina Che fled to Mexico City. There lived a small community of Latin American revolutionaries, many of whom had studied the Guatemalan reforms and coup in terms of their application to their own countries. One of their leaders was Raúl Castro, who brought the young medical student Che Guevara to the attention of his brother, Fidel.[2]

Guevara's experience in Guatemala was more than a mere opportunity to meet his future compatriots; it was also his chance to witness firsthand Guatemala's moderate reform program and the difficulties, internal and external, which he concluded such a program would inevitably encounter. This conclusion prompted him to develop his theories on revolutionary strategy. He later commented that "I was and still am an ardent admirer of the Arbenz government," and Fidel Castro's 1967 eulogy for his friend noted that the events in Guatemala had played a crucial part in Che's political development.[3] Guevara never lost the conviction that if Arbenz had repudiated his regular army and escaped to the mountains with a band of armed peasants, as he and Castro did in the Sierra Maestra, the Guatemalan president could have fought on indefinitely. The first article he wrote, "I Saw the Fall of Jacobo Arbenz," elaborated on this opinion. Unfortunately, the article has been lost, but Guevara's first wife, Hilda Gadea, tells us that it contained an outline of his emerging theories on guerrilla warfare and revolutionary strategy. The final sentence read, "The struggle begins now."[4]

THE BAY OF PIGS

In the early morning of April 17, 1961, nearly seven years after Arbenz's overthrow but less than five years after Castro and Guevara took to the Sierra Maestra, some fourteen hundred Cuban exiles, not unlike Castillo Armas' Army of Liberation, began to climb aboard landing boats to make their way toward the island's Bahía de Cochinos, the Bay of Pigs. Some of the members of the 2506 Brigade had been training for over a year, at camps in Guatemala and Nicaragua set up by the CIA. Their spirits were high; they had come to liberate their homeland. But many of the boats would not start because the outboard motors had been rusted by seawater. The landing was going to take much longer than planned. More disconcerting was a beacon coming from an unexpected lighthouse. Two days before, several B-26 bombers had conducted limited air strikes over the Cuban mainland. Would the alerted Castro government have stationed extra lookouts, capable of spotting the tiny armada as the beacon canvassed the water? The rebels remained confident. They thought that all they had to do was establish small lodgments on "Green," "Blue," and "Red" beaches and hold them for a week. Then the B-26s would have plenty of time to destroy Castro's air force and knock out the microwave communications network. Even if Castro's sentries had detected the invasion, it would take hours to move his troops through the swamp to the beaches. By the time they arrived, Playa Girón (the beach at the mouth of Bahía de Cochinos) would be teeming with thousands of Cubans who had been begging for the opportunity to take up arms against the Communists. CIA radio broadcasts and propaganda leaflets had been priming the native population for months, and that day the radio would announce the establishment of a new government. Castro's legions would refuse to fight. He would be finished. Operation ZAPATA could not fail.[5]

Abruptly the landing craft stopped; the ensuing tragicomedy of ineptitude is well known. Ahead was not a sandy approach but an obstacle course of protruding coral. The brigade had to wade ashore.

The footing was treacherous, especially since the inexperienced rebels had to carry their guns and ammunition high above their heads, as well as whatever supplies could be unloaded and transported by hand. There was no time to unstrap their wireless radios from their belts, for local militia had already started shooting at them from the beaches. They would have enough trouble making it to shore; they would worry about communications once they got there. Faced with the early resistance, Commander José Pérez ("Pepe") San Román decided to forego sending any troops to Green Beach and establish a single beachhead. He did not know that only one battalion had reached Red Beach and that it had lost most of its supplies. Nothing went according to plan. By morning Castro's regular troops had reinforced the local militia, and enemy T-33 fighter planes had begun to appear. Isolated on the beaches and quickly running out of supplies, the rebels waited for the promised strikes that would neutralize Castro's air force. They also waited for airdrops of ammunition, the arrival of native volunteers, and the opposition's cease-fire.

Two days later the survivors were still waiting. On D day, instead of waging a massive air strike, only thirteen B-26s left Nicaragua's Puerto Cabezas, and four of them were shot down. The T-33 sank the *Río Escondido,* damaged the *Houston,* and drove the *Caribe* and the *Atlántico* hundreds of miles south of Cuba. Castro's tanks and heavy artillery blocked all roads to and from the beaches. Although only a handful of the rebels had been trained for guerrilla warfare, they considered taking their battle into the Sierra Escambray. A vast, unprotected swamp prevented their passage. By April 20, they realized that all was lost. Hundreds had been killed and hundreds more captured. That night they made a desperate attempt to reach the destroyers that were cruising five miles off the coast, beyond the range of Cuban artillery fire. Only one group made it. "Most of our people feel we were in a way betrayed," one survivor complained, "we were sent in there to get slaughtered."[6]

"A WORLD OF THEIR OWN"

Just as there were hearings following Arbenz's overthrow, there were hearings following the Bay of Pigs, although they were of a different nature. President Eisenhower had wanted to dramatize how a small group of Guatemalan patriots thwarted the Communist threat to the hemisphere. President Kennedy wanted to know what had gone wrong. He therefore commissioned General Maxwell Taylor to establish the Paramilitary Study Group, informally called the Green

Study Group, to investigate the CIA failure. Whereas Congress' investigation of Guatemala totally concealed the role of the United States, the Taylor study group probed deeply into the CIA plot to eliminate Castro's government. As a consequence, the results of the hearings tell us more about the details of Operation ZAPATA than we will probably ever know about PBSUCCESS. These details suggest that the connection between the two covert projects was much closer than has been hitherto acknowledged and, moreover, that the CIA's easy success in 1954 significantly contributed to its downfall in 1961. Howard Hunt remarked, "If the Agency had not had Guatemala, it probably would not have had Cuba."[7] A brief examination of the Cuban venture illustrates his meaning.

There are a number of schools of thought regarding the reasons for the Bay of Pigs debacle, but none of them attribute much weight to the CIA's earlier triumph. Most explanations stem from the Taylor group's findings. After conducting twenty separate hearings between April 22 and May 25, Taylor concluded that the immediate causes were primarily tactical. First, there was a shortage of ammunition. The Cuban brigade itself exacerbated this problem, since its poor training and discipline led to excessive firing and waste. More serious was the loss of several of the freighters responsible for resupplying the rebels. For the surviving freighters to have come sufficiently close to shore to unload their cargo would have required jet cover or destroyer escort, alternatives that were impossible within the covert context of the operation.[8]

The other critical tactical failure, therefore, was the inability to neutralize Castro's air force. Taylor also blamed the covert character of the operation for this situation. The D-day strikes were canceled so as not to throw suspicion on the United States, and for a similar reason the White House ruled out the use of napalm and fragmentation bombs. Those strikes that were flown, moreover, originated from Nicaragua, because CIA strategists hoped that the Cuban population would believe that the planes were based on a landing strip adjacent to the Bay of Pigs. Owing to the five hundred miles the B-26s had to travel, it took them about nine hours to fly back and forth. The use of B-26s also contributed to the failure. Since the bombers were widely distributed throughout Latin America, they were considered the least likely plane to be linked to the United States. Unfortunately, they were no match for Castro's T-33s, which could easily outmaneuver the slower aircraft and shoot them down.[9]

Drawing upon these tactical considerations, Taylor reached more general conclusions. From the inception, his final memorandum read, the plan had too limited a chance for success. Its chances were further minimized by the overarching requirement that the operation be prepared and conducted in such a way that the United States could plausibly disclaim any connection with it. Too many restrictions had to be placed on the operation in order to satisfy this nonmilitary consideration. Compounding this inherent problem were poor planning and coordination. The project's leaders, in both the CIA and the military, never presented the strategy to the rest of the government with sufficient force and clarity for an adequate review. Furthermore, the executive branch was not organizationally prepared to oversee the program. Except for the president, the administration had no single authority capable of coordinating the activities of the CIA, the State and Defense departments, USIA, and the other involved departments and agencies. The Taylor group recommended that the administration establish a new governmental apparatus to carry out covert operations, a vital component of the United States strategy to win the cold war.[10]

While more recent assessments of the Bay of Pigs generally reinforce the Taylor group's findings, current analysts have advanced additional arguments. These writers are particularly interested in a question Kennedy asked his longtime friend and adviser Theodore Sorensen: "How could I have been so stupid to let them go ahead?"[11] The strategy for Operation ZAPATA had called for fourteen hundred Cuban exiles, many with but minimum training, to hold three separate beachheads against an army of at least thirty-five thousand. Even with increased air support and supplies, to many contemporaries the plan appears patently absurd. Coordination among the various departments and agencies was not the best, and not all responsible authorities were fully informed at all times. The project, nevertheless, received the approval of the CIA, the Joint Chiefs of Staff, the State and Defense departments, and the White House. From the evidence presented at the Taylor hearings, everyone involved—not just Kennedy—was stupid.

In an attempt to understand how the "best and the brightest" could have decided to go along with the CIA proposal, Yale psychologist Irving L. Janis examined the group dynamics of Kennedy's decision-making apparatus. By studying several foreign policy fiascoes, he came up with a phenomenon that he calls groupthink. According to Janis, the gross tactical miscalculations that plagued Operation ZAPATA at every stage resulted from the failure of Kennedy's advisers to carefully consider the various options and contingencies. Pressed for a decision due to the CIA's estimate that Castro's ability to repel an invasion increased each day, policy makers sought to avoid any substantive internal dissension. Firmly believing in United States superiority, they unquestionably accepted the agency's faulty analysis and proposal. Hence subordinates with serious misgivings, such as Secretary of State Dean Rusk, concurred with the majority and convinced themselves that the operation could succeed. Janis summarizes:

> The failure of Kennedy's inner circle to detect any of the false assumptions behind the Bay of Pigs invasion can be at least partially accounted for by the group's tendency to seek concurrence at the expense of seeking information, critical appraisal, and debate. The concurrence-seeking tendency was manifested by shared illusions and other symptoms, which helped the members maintain a sense of group solidarity. Most crucial were the symptoms that contributed to complacent overconfidence in the face of vague uncertainties and explicit warnings.[12]

In the latest and most penetrating treatment of the Bay of Pigs, Peter Wyden asserts that he, too, tried to uncover the mystery of Kennedy's seeming stupidity and found the groupthink hypothesis intriguing. Consequently, after cataloging the blunders that beset the ill-advised operation, he turned his attention to the policy makers themselves. His findings confirmed much of Janis' hypothesis, but, as Janis admits, groupthink can account only partially for the failure of the administration to reach a sound decision. The group dynamics of mutual reinforcement do not explain why Richard Bissell and the other CIA strategists conceived such a high-risk operation in the first place. In addition, the decisions to weaken or cancel planned air strikes, to give the final go-ahead, and not to try to salvage the situation by increasing United States support, even after it had become obvious that the deception could not be maintained, were made by the president almost unilaterally, outside of any group setting. If Kennedy had sought advice concerning these decisions, he certainly would have encountered stiff resistance.[13]

Although all the participants were to some degree culpable, Wyden believes that Kennedy and Bissell must assume primary responsibility. He writes that both were arrogantly ambitious, and both possessed an insatiable appetite for action. Kennedy perceived himself as the anointed one, blessed with a combination of ability and good fortune that could enable him to overcome all obstacles. He was going to awaken the United States from the doldrums of the Eisenhower years and lead it on to victory in the cold war. He would streamline the bureaucracy and relocate power where it belonged, in the Oval Office. He was prepared to take risks and would not tolerate the cautious or faint of heart. He wanted a dramatic victory in Cuba, and the CIA proposal promised him a shortcut to success. According to Wyden, Bissell was Kennedy's kind of man. Endowed with the same confidence and ambition as the president, he had already proven through his U-2 wizardry that he could achieve what others felt impossible.[14] If the White House or the State Department amputated any vital aspects of his plan, he would simply come up with an alternative. Once it had been realized, he would move up to the top echelon of Kennedy's advisers, succeeding Dulles as the CIA director. In short:

> The Bay of Pigs was a wild gamble. It was not mad. It failed because Kennedy and Bissell failed. They failed for altogether human reasons. The drive for gutsy action. The reluctance to cut losses except at the risk of a world war. The lure of a tar baby, whether called Cuba or Vietnam. Egos so tall that the eyes and ears can shut out whatever one prefers not to see or hear.[15]

Wyden's work as well as Janis' study and the release of the Taylor commission hearings have added greatly to our knowledge of the Bay of Pigs. Taken together, they explain a wide range of factors that contributed to the invasion's defeat. A number of critical questions, nevertheless, remain unanswered. Even if one accepts the analysis that Bissell's confidence and drive bordered on egomania—an analysis that is highly problematic—one cannot deny that the operation's leading strategist was extraordinarily intelligent. Knowing that his appointment as CIA director hinged on the project's success, how could he have staked his well-earned reputation on such a dubious plan? Kennedy, Rusk, Secretary of Defense McNamara, the Joint Chiefs of Staff were all bright, yet each still believed that the operation stood a fair chance of success, more than the 20 percent estimate that Allen Dulles gave Eisenhower during the Guatemalan venture.[16] This last point leads us to examine a factor largely overlooked in evaluations of Operation ZAPATA. McGeorge Bundy testified to Taylor's study group that "I don't think the failure was 'because of the want of a nail' . . . I think the men that worked on this got into a world of their own."[17] The parallels between ZAPATA and PBSUCCESS indicate that this world was that of 1954 Guatemala.

PBSUCCESS AND ZAPATA

On March 17, 1960, Richard Bissell received Eisenhower's authorization to produce "A Program of Covert Action against the Castro Regime."[18] The deputy director of plans was confident. His proposal would undergo numerous revisions over the next months; even the name changed from TRINIDAD to ZAPATA. What began as a limited program to recruit and train a cadre from among the Cuban exiles became a paramilitary invasion. Kennedy wanted the invasion to be less "spectacular," so Bissell had to eliminate certain of the military aspects and scale down others. He was not concerned. He had never relied on the military. He produced a plan that he thought would work—because it had worked before. From the time that he first received the Cuban assignment, Bissell had based his strategy on the precedent established in Guatemala. He realized that the circumstances required modifications, such as an amphibious attack, but he saw no reason to alter the essential blueprint. His scenario projected "a possibly protracted period of *psychological and political warfare*" (emphasis added).[19] "The chance of true success—that is the chance of toppling Castro—was predicated on the assumption that faced with that kind of pressure, he would suffer the *same loss of nerve* [as Arbenz]" (emphasis added).[20] Bissell considered the chance good. To him, PBSUCCESS had confirmed the legend of the CIA's invincibility.[21]

Bissell was not alone in this perspective. Into his world, to borrow Bundy's term, came a host of veterans from the 1954 operation. As Howard Hunt explained, "We had no trouble assuming our prior roles, knowing what it was all about, knowing what we could do and how to do it."[22] Indeed, virtually the entire PBSUCCESS apparatus was transplanted to ZAPATA. In addition to Bissell, Hunt, and of course Allen Dulles, the cast included Tracy Barnes, David Phillips, and J. C. King. Instead of the Voice of Liberation there was Radio SWAN; instead of F-47s there were B-26s; instead of Anastasio Somoza there was his son. Whiting Willauer initially served as the liaison among the CIA, the State Department, and the White House; later he was succeeded by Adolf Berle. State's chief advocate for ZAPATA was the assistant secretary for inter-American affairs, Thomas Mann. They were all proud of the part they had played in the victory against Arbenz and eager to duplicate it.[23]

Bissell and his colleagues failed. But, according to the criterion of Bay of Pigs analysts, if ZAPATA failed PBSUCCESS should also have failed. A greater number of rebels invaded Cuba, a greater number of bombs were dropped, and the Cuban brigade was better trained and equipped. It should not have made any difference that Kennedy diluted the military dimensions, because Bissell did not believe that Castro would resist. The Army of Liberation remained safely encamped by the Church of the Black Christ throughout the Guatemalan invasion, and radio broadcasts, not bombs, neutralized Arbenz's air force. When Bissell told Kennedy's National Security Council that the operation would demoralize Castro's government and militia, causing widespread defections, he merely paraphrased what Allen Dulles had told Eisenhower seven years earlier. The unexpected consequence was not that Bissell received Kennedy's approval; it was that Castro "reacted with speed and vigor." Castro's reaction, not Bissell's plan, destroyed the legend of the CIA's invincibility.[24]

During the summer of 1960, shortly after Bissell began developing Operation ZAPATA, Fidel Castro, having been in power for less than two years, hosted the Latin American Youth Congress in Havana. Among the speakers at the opening ceremonies was Che Guevara. Six years had passed since Guevara had watched the CIA's successful overthrow of Arbenz, but he had not forgotten. Arbenz was in the audience. Guevara paid him tribute:

> We would like to extend a special greeting to Jacobo Arbenz, president of the first Latin American country which fearlessly raised its voice against colonialism; a country which, in a far-reaching and courageous agrarian reform, gave expression to the hopes of the peasant masses. We would also like to *express our gratitude* to him, and to the democracy which gave way, for *the example* they gave us and for the *accurate estimate they enabled us to make of the weakness which that government was unable to overcome. This allows us to go to the root of the matter* and to behead those who hold power and their lackeys at a single stroke. (Emphasis added.)[25]

It would be an overstatement to assert that, had the events of 1954 not occurred in Guatemala, Operation ZAPATA would have succeeded. Too many other factors must be considered. Nevertheless, Guevara's speech reveals that the Guatemalan revolution served as an example for the Cubans. By studying Arbenz's government, they could make an "accurate estimate" of "the weakness which that government was unable to overcome." From their perspective, the weakness was Arbenz's failure to overcome the revolution's liberal, nationalist ideology. His moderate reforms failed "to go to the root of the matter and to behead those who hold power and their lackeys at a single stroke." This weakness left him vulnerable to United States intervention. Two years after Allen Dulles retired from the CIA in late 1961, he wrote Eisenhower, "In reviewing the 1954 incident, I was struck by the points of similarity with Cuba and felt there was an interesting lesson to be drawn."[26] Guevara, Castro, and the others who fought in the Sierra Maestras felt the same way.

Guevara's speech suggests that the defeat of the Guatemalan revolution influenced Cuba's revolutionaries to move beyond Arbenz's reformist programs. As a result, they were better prepared to meet the challenge at the Bay of Pigs. They did not enact legislation that merely redistributed the uncultivated land. Castro's 1959, and later 1962, agrarian reform effectively destroyed the foreign and national entrepreneurs who historically controlled Cuba's economy. Unlike Arbenz, Castro rose to power by relying on an irregular militia. Once in power he immediately dismantled the remainder of Batista's army, with its elite leadership, and organized the peasantry into a loyal fighting force. CIA planners did not appreciate this distinction. As Bissell testified at the Taylor hearings, they underestimated "Castro's capability in certain respects, mainly his organization ability, speed of movement and *will to fight*. We also underestimated his air capability. Example, contrary to our opinion, T-33's were armed and flown with *skill, loyalty and determination*" (emphasis added).[27] To list all of Castro's reforms and policies would require another book.[28] The point is that Richard Bissell drew on the lessons of Guatemala to construct a strategy for Cuba. He underestimated. Che Guevara also drew on the lessons of Guatemala to construct a strategy for Cuba. He estimated accurately.

The argument can therefore be made that the difference between United States and Cuban perceptions of the Guatemalan revolution contributed greatly to what happened at the Bay of Pigs. The CIA project in Guatemala had been a high-risk operation, and the ease with which it succeeded resulted largely from the nonmilitant nature of the 1944 revolution. Policy makers, ideologically entrenched in the cold war ethos, did not discern these favorable circumstances. They concluded that a strategy based on a mixture of military threats, covert operations, and alliances with indigenous client groups could thwart any movement for radical change. They not only underestimated these movements' ability and motivation to resist, but they actually increased that ability and motivation. By misconstruing Arbenz's nationalistic idealism as militant Communism, they failed to recognize Castro's true militancy. Eisenhower's last assistant secretary of state for inter-American affairs admitted, "I think I am safe in saying that the relative success in dealing with the Communist problem in Guatemala tended to blind a little bit the eyes of all of us . . . not so much to the fact that [Cuba] was a serious problem, but that maybe the problem, if it became an open sore, could be dealt with to some degree like the Guatemalan problem was dealt with."[29]

GUATEMALA'S REVOLUTION: YESTERDAY AND TODAY

More than a quarter century has passed since the overthrow of the Arbenz government. Over two decades have passed since the unsuccessful attempt to overthrow the Castro government. The final chapter of the legacy of PBSUCCESS, nevertheless, has yet to be written. Over the past several years, events in Central America have once again caused United States policy makers grave concern, giving rise to the familiar charge of Communist subversion. In July 1979, Nicaragua's Sandinista rebels overcame seemingly insurmountable odds and ended the dynasty of the Somoza family. A year later Anastasio Somoza, Jr., long considered the region's greatest bulwark against Communism, was brutally assassinated in Paraguay. Nearly every day there are new reports of violence in El Salvador and, perhaps more important, in Guatemala. Guatemala, still the most powerful of the Central American republics, has become the scene of a fierce battle between the right and the left, the results of which promise to have a profound effect upon similar struggles throughout the hemisphere. Washington can only watch and wait. NBC commentator Marvin Kalb remarked in a special broadcast that "the era of the Banana Republic is over. The era of the radical, Marxist Republic is now dawning, with the U.S. watching from the sidelines."[30] One State Department official conceded, "What we'd give to have an Arbenz now. We are going to have to invent one, but all the candidates are dead."[31]

The current dilemma facing the United States is, as the State Department comment accurately illustrates, the ultimate legacy of PBSUCCESS. It is a dilemma of Washington's own making. Jacobo Arbenz hoped to modernize Guatemala. By educating the Maya majority, by championing the cause of Guatemalan labor, by enacting agrarian legislation, and by advancing all the other reforms in his revolutionary program, he tried to break the stranglehold of his country's underdevelopment. In their attempt to avert what they perceived to be a threat to United States anti-Communist policies, cold warriors wedded their fate to that stranglehold—they returned to power the very elements of society that had created the conditions that the 1944 revolution tried to eradicate. Arévalo and Arbenz wanted Guatemala to become a model of democracy and progress; Castillo Armas and his successors made it a model of reaction and oppression. United States diplomat William O'Dwyer testified at the 1954 congressional hearings that "the foreign policy of the United States is . . . on trial in Guatemala."[32] Now the United States waits while the Guatemalan people bring in the verdict.

New York Times correspondent Alan Riding considers it ironic that the convulsions in Guatemala presently plaguing Washington should have resulted from the 1954 operation.[33] In retrospect, however, it is difficult to imagine any other consequence. From the time that it was installed by the CIA, the Castillo Armas government initiated policies to roll back the Guatemalan clock. In one of his first official acts, the new president returned to United Fruit over 99 percent of its expropriated land and abolished the tax on all interest, dividends, and other profits payable to foreign investors.[34] He restored the national farms to the state and abolished the cooperatives, in the process dispossessing, often forcibly, the peasants who had acquired their own plots under Decree 900. Then, with the help of United States advice and money, Castillo Armas enacted his own agrarian reform. Exempting private property, his legislation insured that only state-owned land or that which was generally undeveloped, inaccessible, or of poor quality could be made available for distribution. According to Gunder Frank, "At the rate at which land was distributed in Guatemala in the post-Arbenz years, it would take 148 years for all peasant families to receive some land—if there were no population growth in the meantime." Predictably, 2 percent of Guatemala's population still owns over half of the country's land.[35]

Fearful of the majority's response to his program, Castillo Armas methodically set out to eliminate any potential opposition. Since the bulk of the opposition had supported the 1944 revolution, the new president facilitated his task by branding them all Communists. Within days of his return to Guatemala City after signing the agreement with Monzón, he had arrested over two thousand alleged subversives. Concentration camps had to be established in order to accommodate the prisoners who could no longer fit into the already overloaded jails. He proclaimed July 12 Anti-Communist Day and announced his "personal intention that the full weight of the law shall fall without consideration on these criminals and that those directly responsible shall be executed in public vindication as an example to future generations which must know that crimes against freedom are crimes against the fatherland."[36] Acting upon the suggestion of Secretary of State Dulles, he detained hundreds of Guatemalans seeking to flee the country. "Communists," Dulles wrote at the end of July, "should be considered [a] class additional to common criminals not entitled asylum."[37]

No legal basis existed in Guatemala for prosecuting citizens suspected of holding alien political beliefs, so Castillo Armas changed the law. He summarily repealed the 1945 constitution and issued a "political statute" that invested in him all legislative and executive functions. He established a National Committee for Defense against Communism with extraordinary powers to conduct surveillance, arrest "dangerous persons," and deport without trial any foreigners. To assist the committee Castillo Armas formed a special police force under José Bernabe Linares, who had held the same post before the revolution. The Guatemalan president knew that he could rely on Bernabe Linares' thoroughness. As Ubico's "enforcer," he reputedly submerged his suspects in electric shock baths or applied a head-shrinking steel skullcap in order to "pry loose secrets and crush improper thoughts."[38]

Taking its orders directly from Castillo Armas and his committee, Bernabe Linares' police investigated virtually any Guatemalan who had ever joined a union, signed a petition, or accepted a homestead from the Arbenz government. *Hispanic American Report* estimated that the police files contained the names of over seventy thousand suspects. Thousands were arbitrarily imprisoned "for reasons of security." Many were executed; others simply disappeared. The vast majority of those arrested never faced a trial. Castillo Armas granted the national committee discretionary jurisdiction to place anyone in jail for up to six months while it investigated possible Communist affiliations. In most cases the allegations could not be substantiated, forcing the courts to set the individual free. On many occasions, however, the committee merely picked the suspect up again and held him or her another six months without trial. By this method, anyone could be kept in jail indefinitely without any legal means of recourse.[39]

In addition to utilizing gestapolike tactics, Castillo Armas initiated a series of political changes that codified the authoritarian nature of his rule. His 1956 constitution institutionalized the 1954 statute and insured that there would be no organized opposition to his governing party. Returning to the *caudillo* tradition, he replaced almost all the local administrators and magistrates with his personal representatives and disenfranchised over two-thirds of the population. He also decapitated the labor movement. Not only did he abrogate Arévalo's 1947 Labor Code and cancel the registration of more than five hundred unions, but he enacted a law requiring the National Committee for Defense against Communism to approve all future union charters. His government had the authority to declare any strike illegal at its own discretion and to sentence a participant to three years in prison. Incidents of workers being crushed to death by runaway trucks or accidentally shot reached epidemic proportions as Bernabe Linares' police carefully monitored labor activities. By the end of the decade, Guatemala's union membership had fallen to ten thousand, one-tenth of the total during Arbenz's last year in office. In all of Latin America, only Haiti had fewer organized workers.[40]

Castillo Armas did not live to see the final results of his policies. Two years after the conclusion of PBSUCCESS, a journalist predicted that "the Guatemalans are not likely to tolerate long their dictator, the man who handed labor over to the big landowners and foreign corporations—the man who is regarded by friends and enemies alike as the chief instrument of Yankee intervention."[41] They tolerated him one more year. On July 22, 1957, Romeo Vásquez Sánchez, Castillo Armas' previous bodyguard, assassinated the president in the National Palace. Eisenhower, calling the assassination a great loss to Guatemala and the world, sent his son John to attend the funeral. John Eisenhower remained in Guatemala City for three days, long enough to conclude that Vásquez Sánchez, who had committed suicide immediately after shooting Castillo Armas, had been acting under orders from Moscow. True to form, the Eisenhower administration had found more evidence of the Communist threat in Guatemala.[42]

There is convincing evidence to suggest that the Communists were not responsible for Castillo Armas' murder.[43] In retrospect, however, it makes little difference. Regardless of Vásquez Sánchez's political coloration, in the 1940s and 1950s the Communist movement in Guatemala was weak. Now it grows stronger. Castillo Armas was but the first in a line of Guatemalan presidents, all supported by the United States, who in the name of anti-Communism have ruled by terrorism and repression. Their effort to reverse the movement toward reform that began in 1944 has not produced the stability so eagerly sought in Washington. Rather, by pursuing programs inimical to the majority of Guatemalans, these modern-day *caudillos* have fueled the very Communist movement that the Eisenhower administration overestimated in 1954. As in the case of Cuba, it is now evident that United States policy makers underestimated the Guatemalans' will to resist.[44]

The guerrilla struggle going on in Guatemala, therefore, is the final irony—and legacy—of PBSUCCESS. Richard Gott is correct in asserting, "The history of the guerrilla movements in Latin America, indeed the contemporary Latin America, cannot be understood without reference to this cardinal event."[45] Ten years after the coup, when the descendants of those who fought against Castillo Armas met in the mountains to pledge their continued commitment, they acknowledged their debt to their forebears: "The experience [of the Arbenz government] has never been forgotten and it is the basis for the present revolutionary state in this country."[46]

Only time will reveal the eventual outcome. It took the Iranians a quarter century to reverse the CIA's success in 1953. They blame the United States for the shah's abuses. If the events in Nicaragua, and perhaps El Salvador, are any indication, strong-arm tactics can no longer control revolutionary change in Central America. Political violence has become endemic in Guatemala, with an estimated forty thousand people murdered since Arbenz's overthrow. President Romeo Lucas García, in power since 1978, has increasingly turned to death squads to stem the ever growing opposition. He has told the people that they must treat the government's terrorism campaign as a sort of "allergy" which they must "learn to live with."[47] They must also live with chronic unemployment, chronic malnutrition, high rates of illiteracy and infant mortality, and, for hundreds of thousands of peasants, little or no land. Even the traditionally docile Indians have joined the guerrilla bands to demonstrate, by their own use of force, that they will not live this way. Guatemala today resembles an occupied country. Government troops, in full battle gear, patrol both the city and the countryside. Yet, as NBC's Marvin Kalb explained, "Even with the most modern weapons of war, it is next to impossible to fight decades of social and economic injustice."[48] Arévalo and Arbenz sought to end this injustice through moderate reforms. The CIA's 1954 coup made moderation impossible.

Notes

1. Truman, Eisenhower, and the Cold War in Latin America

1. Mrs. John E. Peurifoy letter to Eleanor Lansing Dulles, quoted in Eleanor Lansing Dulles, *American Foreign Policy in the Making*, p. 243.
2. *New York Times*, 21 February 1954.
3. Ibid., 20 June 1954.
4. Ibid., 24 June 1954.
5. Henry Cabot Lodge, Jr., "The Guatemalan Complaint before the Security Council," *Department of State Bulletin* 31 (5 July 1954): 27. (Hereafter, this publication is referred to as *Bulletin*.)
6. John Foster Dulles, "International Communism," 30 June 1954, John Foster Dulles Papers, "re Guatemala 1954," Princeton University, Princeton, New Jersey.
7. Dwight D. Eisenhower, reply to Salazar upon the occasion of the presentation of his letter of credence, Dwight D. Eisenhower Papers as president, 1953–1961 (Whitman File), International Series, "Guatemala (1)," n.d., Dwight D. Eisenhower Library, Abilene, Kansas. (Hereafter, the Whitman File will be referred to as WF.)
8. United States House of Representatives, Subcommittee on Latin America of the Select Committee on Communist Aggression, *Ninth Interim Report of Hearings: Communist Aggression in Latin America*, pp. 2, 199.
9. WF, Press Conference Series, 19 January 1955.
10. Dwight D. Eisenhower, *The White House Years*, pp. 425–426.
11. There are numerous examples of the mainstream press coverage. Special attention should be paid to the articles in such popular magazines as *Time*, *Newsweek*, and the *Saturday Evening Post*, as well as to the newspaper columns in the *New York Times* and the *New York Herald Tribune*.

    For examples of the leftist press, see the articles of A. B. Magill in the *New York Daily Worker*, 1953–1954; Freda Kirchwey, "Guatemala Guinea Pig," *Nation* 179 (10 July 1954): 21–23; and Morris Siegel, "Perspective on Guatemala," *New Republic* 132 (19 July 1954): 10–14.
12. Shortly after the crisis in Guatemala in 1954, a number of books in both Spanish and English dealt with the subject. There were also several

U.S. government studies. However, none of these can be considered definitive or objective. For example, see Daniel James, *Red Design for the Americas*; Kalman H. Silvert, *A Study in Government: Guatemala*; Amy Elizabeth Jenkins, *Guatemala: A Historical Survey*; John D. Martz, *Communist Infiltration of Guatemala*; Ronald Schneider, *Communism in Guatemala, 1944–1954*; and Mario Rosenthal, *Guatemala*. Guatemalan works, which tend to take the extreme opposite view, include Guillermo Toriello Garrido, *La batalla de Guatemala* and *¿A dónde va Guatemala?*; Raúl Osegueda, *Operación Guatemala $ OK $*; Manuel Galich, *Por qué lucha Guatemala: Arévalo y Arbenz, dos hombres contra un imperio*; Luis Cardoza y Aragón, *La revolución Guatemalteca*; and Juan José Arévalo, *Guatemala, la democracia y el imperio* and *The Shark and the Sardines*.

For official U.S. sources see United States House of Representatives, Committee on Foreign Affairs, *Report of the Special Study Mission to Guatemala*; United States House of Representatives, Select Committee on Communist Aggression, *Report of the Subcommittee to Investigate Communist Aggression in Latin America*; and United States Department of State, *Penetration of the Political Institutions of Guatemala by the International Communist Movement* and *A Case History of Communist Penetration: Guatemala*.

Recent scholarship has improved. The best examples are Cole Blasier, *The Hovering Giant: U.S. Responses to Revolutionary Change in Latin America*, pp. 151–177; Max Gordon, "A Case History of U.S. Subversion: Guatemala, 1954," *Science and Society* 35 (Summer 1971): 129–155; José M. Aybar de Soto, *Dependency and Intervention: The Case of Guatemala in 1954*; and Stephen Schlesinger, "How Dulles Worked the Coup d'Etat," *Nation* 227 (28 October 1978): 1, 439–444. Schlesinger and Stephen Kinzer do use new documentation in their *Bitter Fruit: The Untold Story of the American Coup in Guatemala*, as does Blanche W. Cook in *The Declassified Eisenhower: A Divided Legacy of Peace and Political Warfare*, pp. 217–292.

Special mention should be made of unpublished studies other than my own dissertation, "The United States and Guatemala, 1954: A Cold War Strategy for the Americas." These include Marta Cehelsky, "Guatemala's Frustrated Revolution: The Liberation of 1954"; Richard Bruce Chardkoff, "Communist Toehold in the Americas: A History of Official United States Involvement in the Guatemalan Crisis, 1954"; and Susanne Jonas, "Test Case for the Hemisphere: United States Strategy in Guatemala, 1950–1974."

13. Details of Mussadegh's overthrow are now being made public by the CIA's principal operative in the project, Kermit ("Kim") Roosevelt. See his *Countercoup: The Struggle for the Control of Iran*. The 1979 takeover of the United States embassy in Tehran promises to elicit numerous other studies.

14. For example, see such diverse works as Walter LaFeber, *America, Russia, and the Cold War, 1945–1966*, pp. 158–160; Joyce Kolko and Ga-

briel Kolko, *The Limits of Power: The World and United States Foreign Policy, 1945–1954*, pp. 700–701; and John Lukacs, *A New History of the Cold War*, p. 119.

15. Representative exponents of the economic thesis are David Horowitz, *The Free World Colossus*, pp. 163–186; Richard J. Barnet, *Intervention and Revolution*, pp. 229–236; and Aybar de Soto, *Dependency and Intervention*.

16. The foremost example is David Wise and Thomas Ross, *The Invisible Government*. Mention should also be made of Andrew Tully, *CIA: The Inside Story*. More recently there have been references to the Guatemalan operation by former agents. Most notable are E. Howard Hunt, *Undercover: Memoirs of an American Secret Agent*; David Atlee Phillips, *Night Watch: Twenty Years of Peculiar Service*; and L. Fletcher Prouty, *The Secret Team*. Thomas Powers' excellent biography of Richard Helms devotes several pages to the operation, even though Helms was scarcely involved; see *The Man Who Kept the Secrets: Richard Helms and the CIA*, pp. 85–88. In *Bitter Fruit*, Kinzer and Schlesinger emphasize the influence of the United Fruit Company and then concentrate on the covert activity. Cook, in *Declassified Eisenhower*, underscores United Fruit's influence and the role of political warfare.

17. F. Parkinson, *Latin America, the Cold War, and the World Powers, 1945–1973*, p. 37.

18. *New York Times*, 5 March 1954; James, *Red Design for the Americas*, p. 26. Author of five books on Latin America, contributor to *Harper's*, the *Saturday Evening Post*, and other magazines, and former managing editor of the *New Leader*, James was a representative and influential writer. His reviewer in the *New York Times* called *Red Design* a "tour de force"; see Milton Bracker, "The Octopus Could Grow," *New York Times Book Review*, 24 October 1954, p. 45.

19. John E. Peurifoy, "The Communist Conspiracy in Guatemala," *Bulletin* 31 (8 November 1954): 696; Thomas Mann to Charles S. Murphy, memorandum, "Latin America and U.S. Policy," 11 December 1952, President's Secretary's File (hereafter, PSF), "Latin America," Harry S. Truman Papers, Harry S. Truman Library, Independence, Missouri.

20. There are too many studies of United States–Latin American relations and their economic interactions to begin to list them all here. Many appear in other notes and bibliography. For the differing perspectives on dependency theory, see Tony Smith, "The Underdevelopment of Development Literature: The Case of Dependency Theory," *World Politics* 31 (January 1979): 247–288, and Ronald H. Chilcote, "Dependency: A Critical Synthesis of the Literature," *Latin American Perspectives* 1 (Spring 1974): 4–29.

21. For details of the economic relationship, see Milton S. Eisenhower, "Report to the President, United States–Latin American Relations" (hereafter referred to as "Report to the President"), 18 November 1953, Milton S. Eisenhower Papers, Eisenhower Library; Mann to Murphy, "Latin America . . ."; George Kennan to Dean Acheson, 29 March

1950, *Papers Relating to the Foreign Relations of the United States* (hereafter referred to as *FRUS*), 2: 609–610.

22. Although it concentrates on the Roosevelt years, David Green's *The Containment of Latin America: A History of the Myths and Realities of the Good Neighbor Policy* provides keen insights into Truman's Latin American policy. See also Green's "The Cold War Comes to Latin America," in Barton J. Bernstein, ed., *Politics and Policies of the Truman Administration*, pp. 149–195. In addition to biographies of Eisenhower and Dulles, students of Latin American policies in the 1950s should consult Blasier, *Hovering Giant*.

23. NSC-68 was published as "A Report to the National Security Council by the Executive Secretary on United States Objectives and Programs for National Security," 14 April 1950, *Naval War College Review* 27 (May–June 1975): 51–108. See also Thruston B. Morton, "Foreign Policy in Perspective," *Bulletin* 31 (26 July 1954): 119–121.

24. John Foster Dulles, "Statement Introducing U.S. Draft Resolution on Communist Intervention," 8 March 1954, United States Department of State, *Tenth Inter-American Conference: Report of the Delegation of the United States of America with Related Documents*, p. 52.

25. Kennan to Acheson, 29 March 1950, *FRUS* 2: 604.

26. Daniel James, "Red Beachhead in America," *Saturday Evening Post* 226 (24 April 1954): 126; Kennan to Acheson, 29 March 1950, *FRUS* 2: 604; *New York Times*, 24 December 1950.

27. Quoted in Green, *Containment of Latin America*, p. 263; Dulles, "International Communism."

28. Kennan to Acheson, 29 March 1950, *FRUS* 2: 604–606; speech by Senator Alexander Wiley, 14 January 1954, *Congressional Record*, 83d Cong., 2d sess., 100, pt. 1: 249; testimony of Dean Acheson, 14 January 1949, United States Senate, *Executive Sessions of the Senate Foreign Relations Committee*, 81st Cong., 1st and 2d sess., 1949–1950, 2: 24.

29. Merwin L. Bohan, *Oral Interview*, Truman Library.

30. Green, *Containment of Latin America*, pp. 59–208.

31. Richard M. Bissell, Jr., *Oral History Interview*, 5 June 1967, Columbia Oral History Collection (hereafter referred to as COH).

32. NSC-141: "A Report to the National Security Council by the Secretaries of State and Defense [Dean Acheson and Robert Lovett] and the Director for Mutual Security [W. Averell Harriman] on Reexamination of United States Programs for National Security," 19 January 1953, Modern Military Branch Reference Section, Washington, D.C. Interestingly, representing Harriman on this report was Richard Bissell (Paul Nitze represented Acheson, and Frank Nash represented Lovett). A short time later, as a key CIA official, Bissell would be more involved in enacting United States foreign policy than analyzing it.

33. NSC-141.

34. Raymond Miller, *Oral Interview*, Truman Library, p. 40; Andrew F. Westwood, *Foreign Aid in a Foreign Policy Framework*, pp. 19–21.

35. It must be remembered that, in order to insure passage of the appropriations for the Truman Doctrine program, Truman went to great lengths to oversell the program ideologically. On the advice of such politically attuned advisers as Senator Arthur Vandenberg, who feared most United States citizens would be cool to such expenditures because they failed to understand the extent of the threat, Truman "scared hell out of the American people." LaFeber, *America, Russia, and the Cold War, 1945–1966*, pp. 37–47. LaFeber elaborates on the politics of the Truman Doctrine in his third edition, *America, Russia, and the Cold War, 1945–1975*, pp. 50–58.

36. Green, "The Cold War," pp. 160–175; Parkinson, *Latin America*, pp. 29–30; NSC-141.

37. The concluding chapter will argue that the Guatemalan reforms were not radical. In analyzing Point Four effectiveness, one must recall that Kennedy's Alliance for Progress was certainly much more ambitious than Truman's program, and its effects on Guatemala did not eliminate the severe poverty. See Jerome Levinson and Juan de Onis, *The Alliance That Lost Its Way*. A graphic picture of present conditions can be found in Alan Riding, "Guatemala Opening New Lands, but the Best Goes to Rich," *New York Times*, 5 April 1979.

38. "The Sources of Soviet Conduct," *Foreign Affairs* 25 (July 1947): 566–582; LaFeber, *America, Russia, and the Cold War, 1945–1975*, pp. 35–37; Dean Acheson, *Present at the Creation*, pp. 262–267.

39. The 1954 Declaration of Caracas, discussed in chapter 6, was an attempt to remedy this difficulty.

40. The use of a reform's adverse effect on U.S. interests as evidence of Communism will be expanded upon later in the text. A good illustration is Newbegin to Wilson, "Indications of Communism in Guatemala," 6 May 1948, National Archives 814.00B/5-648 (hereafter, NA 814 . . .).

41. Acheson, memorandum of conversation with the Mexican secretary of foreign relations, Manuel Tello, 22 March 1951, Acheson Papers, memos of conversations; Acheson testimony, *Executive Sessions of the Senate Foreign Relations Committee*, 82d Cong., 1st sess., 1951, 3, pt. 1: 347–348.

42. *New York Times*, 25 February 1953; *Nashville Banner*, 21 May 1954, in Eisenhower Records, General File (hereafter, GF) 122, "Guatemala," Eisenhower Library.

43. For example, see John Lewis Gaddis, *Russia, the Soviet Union, and the United States: An Interpretive History*, 208–212.

44. Often the Eisenhower administration's failure to help the Hungarian rebels in 1956 is cited to show the bankruptcy of "liberation."

45. Historiographical reviews of revisionist works on Eisenhower include Vincent DeSantis, "Eisenhower Revisionism," *Review of Politics* 38 (April 1976): 190–207, and Gary W. Reichard, "Eisenhower as President: The Changing View," *South Atlantic Quarterly* 77 (Summer

1978): 265–281. Of special interest is Fred I. Greenstein, "Eisenhower as an Activist President: A New Look at the Evidence," *Political Science Quarterly* 94 (Winter 1979–80): 575–599.

46. For a brief summary of the revisionist literature on Eisenhower's foreign policy before the opening of new archives, and its theoretical basis, see Barton J. Bernstein, "Foreign Policy in the Eisenhower Administration," *Foreign Service Journal* 50 (May 1973): 17–20, 29–30, 38.

47. For a review of the literature on Dulles, see Ole R. Holsti, "Will the Real Dulles Please Stand Up?" *International Journal* 30 (Winter 1974–75): 34–44. Major studies include John Robinson Beal, *John Foster Dulles: A Biography*; Andrew H. Berding, *Dulles on Diplomacy*; Mildred H. Comfort, *John Foster Dulles, Peacemaker*; Eleanor Lansing Dulles, *John Foster Dulles: The Last Year*; Roscoe Drummond and Gaston Coblentz, *Duel at the Brink: John Foster Dulles' Command of American Foreign Policy*; Herman Finer, *Dulles over Suez: The Theory and Practice of His Diplomacy*; Louis Gerson, *John Foster Dulles*; Michael A. Guhin, *John Foster Dulles: A Statesman and His Times*; Townsend Hoopes, *The Devil and John Foster Dulles*; and Hans Morgenthau, "John Foster Dulles (1953–1959)," in Norman Graebner, ed., *An Uncertain Tradition: American Secretaries of State in the Twentieth Century*, pp. 289–308.

48. Such phrases as "positive loyalty," "massive retaliation," and "brinkmanship" made almost any article on Dulles controversial reading.

49. Townsend Hoopes, "God and John Foster Dulles," *Foreign Policy* 13 (1973): 156.

50. Most noteworthy is the massive Whitman File in the Eisenhower Library. It contains thousands of pages of transcripts of the president's daily phone conversations, minutes of formal and informal meetings, memoranda and other written communications, and Eisenhower's personal diary. Also valuable are the summaries of Secretary Dulles' phone conversations, available at the Eisenhower Library and Princeton University.

51. For a revisionist critique of the conventional wisdom on Dulles and Eisenhower, see Richard H. Immerman, "Eisenhower and Dulles: Who Made the Decisions?" *Political Psychology* 1 (Autumn 1979): 21–38. The most thorough discussion of multiple advocacy can be found in Alexander George, "The Case for Multiple Advocacy in Making Foreign Policy," *American Political Science Review* 66 (September 1972): 751–785.

52. Milton S. Eisenhower, *Oral History Interview*, COH, and letter to author, 21 March 1978.

53. Interview with William B. Macomber, Jr., 7 August 1979; interview with Robert R. Bowie, 25 February 1981.

54. Sherman Adams, *Firsthand Report: The Story of the Eisenhower Administration*, p. 92.

55. Forrestal's extreme cold war attitudes, which contributed to his depression and eventual suicide, are examined in Arnold A. Rogow, *James Forrestal: A Study of Personality, Politics and Policy.*

56. Diary entry, 11 June 1949, Dwight D. Eisenhower Diaries, "December 1948 to July 1949," Eisenhower Library (hereafter, Eisenhower Diary). Most of the diary is published in Robert H. Ferrell, ed., *The Eisenhower Diaries.*

57. Lloyd C. Gardner, *Architects of Illusion: Men and Ideas in American Foreign Policy, 1941–1949,* p. 274.

58. Diary entry, 27 January 1949, Eisenhower Diary, "December 1948 to July 1949."

59. Diary entry, 11 June 1949, Eisenhower Diary, "December 1948 to July 1949."

60. Diary entry, 6 January 1953, Eisenhower Diary, "December 1952 to 19 August 1953 (4)."

61. Eisenhower to William Robinson, 4 August 1954, WF, Diary Series, "August 1954."

62. For Eisenhower's long involvement in intelligence activities, see Stephen E. Ambrose with Richard H. Immerman, *Ike's Spies: Eisenhower and the Espionage Establishment.*

63. Eisenhower to Lieutenant General James H. Doolittle, USAFR, 26 July 1954, WF, Administration Series, "Dulles, Allen (4)."

64. Eisenhower's staff secretary, Colonel (now General) Andrew Goodpaster, notes in his Columbia *Oral History Interview* how many times during his administration the president cited the Guatemalan project as an example of a well-planned operation. To Eisenhower the planning was crucial. On one occasion he vetoed a proposal to topple Egypt's Nasser because there was too much active hostility in 1956. "For a thing like this to be done without inflaming the Arab world," he cautioned, "a time free from heated stress holding the world's attention . . . would have to be chosen." See memorandum of conference with the president, 8 October 1956, WF, Diary Series, "Staff Notes, October 1956."

65. See the previously cited works on Dulles. Eisenhower viewed his foreign policy decision-making apparatus more as a team of numerous individuals than as a tandem of himself and the secretary of state. Nevertheless, he and Dulles were undoubtedly the two principle figures.

66. The intellectual foundation of Dulles' conduct as secretary of state is analyzed in Ole R. Holsti, "The 'Operational Code' Approach to the Study of Political Leaders: John Foster Dulles' Philosophical and Instrumental Beliefs," *Canadian Journal of Political Science* 3 (March 1970): 123–157. Dulles' attitudes toward McCarthy are a matter of controversy. Although this is not a proper forum to enter the debate, there is some indication that, believing himself vulnerable to McCarthy because he had recommended Alger Hiss to head the Carnegie Foundation, he sought to appease the junior senator from Wisconsin.

For an example see Immerman, "Eisenhower and Dulles," p. 31. I should add that the secretary's former associates play down the influence of Dulles' connection with Hiss.

67. Hoopes, "God and John Foster Dulles," pp. 165–166. See also Green, *Containment of Latin America*, p. 258.

68. The Eisenhower Papers are replete with detailed minutes of high-level conferences exploring in depth the relationship between financial considerations and United States defense policies. Representative are the "Goodpaster Briefings," "Staff Notes," and "Staff Meetings" folders in the Whitman File.

69. Though both Eisenhower and Dulles spent most of their public lives deeply involved with European and Asian affairs, they each had spent some formative years in Central America. As a young army officer not too long out of West Point, Eisenhower was stationed in the Panama Canal Zone from 1922 to 1924. In 1917 Dulles, also, went to Panama, at the request of Woodrow Wilson, to insure the cooperation of that government and its neighbors in protecting this vital area if the United States entered the war against Germany. Apparently Dulles' qualification for this mission was his association with the law firm of Sullivan and Cromwell, counsel for the government of Panama. Dulles' uncle, Robert Lansing, was Wilson's secretary of state.

70. Minutes of cabinet meeting, 6 October 1953, WF, Cabinet Series; "Purpose of Mission," attached to Eisenhower, message to Pan-American Union, 12 April 1953, Milton Eisenhower Papers, 1953, "Speeches, Articles (1)." In addition to having complete confidence in his brother, the president selected Milton to head the mission because of his awareness that their relationship would be of considerable advantage, for "Latin Americans have deep feelings of family loyalty and pride." See Milton Eisenhower, *The Wine Is Bitter*, p. 9.

71. Minutes of cabinet meeting, 5 March 1954, WF, Cabinet Series.

72. Milton Eisenhower, "Report to the President."

2. Underdevelopment, Repression, and Revolution

1. In this study, "revolution" will refer to the Guatemalan Revolution of 1944.

2. Leading Western economist W. S. Woytinsky, who fled the Russian Revolution in 1917, contends that the term "underdevelopment" should be replaced by "uneven development." He believes the problems with Third World development are more sociopolitical in nature than technical. The more leftist Gunder Frank agrees with Woytinsky in this regard. In taking issue with W. W. Rostow's classical model of development, Frank writes:

It is generally held that economic development occurs in a succession of capitalist stages and that today's underdeveloped countries are still in a state, sometimes depicted as an original state, of history through which we (the now developed countries) passed long ago. Yet even a modest acquaintance with history shows that underdevelopment is not original or traditional, and that neither the past nor the present of the underdeveloped countries resembles in any important respect the past of the now developed countries. The now developed countries were never *under*developed, though they may have been *un*developed.

See W. S. Woytinsky, *The United States and Latin America's Economy*, pp. 7–8; W. W. Rostow, *The Stages of Economic Growth: A Non-Communist Manifesto*; Andre Gunder Frank, *Latin America: Underdevelopment or Revolution: Essays on the Development or Underdevelopment and the Immediate Enemy*, p. 4.

3. In 1949 former United States Ambassador to Guatemala Edwin J. Kyle, an agricultural expert, described the country as the "Pearl of the Western World." A year later, *New York Herald Tribune* columnist Fitzhugh Turner did a special series on Communist infiltration in Guatemala—he wrote that the land was so fertile that "if you want to grow something you drop a seed in the ground and jump aside quickly." See Edwin J. Kyle, address upon receiving the award of the Order of the Quetzal by the government of Guatemala, February 22, 1949, Edwin J. Kyle Papers, Cornell University; *New York Herald Tribune*, 8 February 1950.

4. The early history of Guatemala can be found in most writings about the country. The definitive work remains Chester Lloyd Jones, *Guatemala: Past and Present*.

5. Galich, *Por qué lucha Guatemala*, p. 21; Thomas L. Karnes, *The Failure of Union: Central America, 1824–1960*, pp. 12–95; Hubert Howe Bancroft, *History of Central America*, vol. 3: *1801–1887*, pp. 60–144.

6. When the issue of a Central American union surfaced once more, in 1942, due to Nicaragua's President Somoza telling the Guatemalan ambassador in Managua that Roosevelt supported such a union, Undersecretary of State Sumner Welles wrote the president, "The project of a Central American Union has been the subject of bitter controversy over a period of many generations . . . I fear that if there is much public discussion of the project at this time it will arouse very strong feeling one way or the other and that it would consequently be better for this Government to let it be clearly understood that the United States regards this project as being a matter which only the Central American people themselves can determine." Consequently Welles drafted a telegram to this effect to Guatemala's President Ubico, which was repeated orally to the country's foreign minister. Roosevelt emphasized that he had not discussed the matter with any Central American leader. Welles to Roosevelt, 24 August 1942, Official File (hereafter, OF) 5110, Franklin D. Roosevelt Papers, Franklin D. Roosevelt Library, Hyde Park, New York; Roosevelt, memorandum for the undersecretary of state, 26 August 1942, OF 5110, FDR Papers.

7. Medardo Mejía, *Juan José Arévalo o el humanismo en la presidencia*, pp.

266–270; Marie-Berthe Dion, *Las ideas sociales y políticas de Aré-valo*, pp. 129–132. Arévalo's deep-seated Pan-Americanism, and its roots in Latin American history, is described in Pedro Alvarez Elizondo, *El presidente Arévalo y el retorno a Bolívar.*

8. Jonas, "Test Case for the Hemisphere," pp. 34–70; A. Fuentes-Mohr, "Land Settlement and Agrarian Reform in Guatemala," *International Journal of Agrarian Affairs* 2 (January 1955): 29; Mario Monteforte Toledo, *Guatemala—monografía sociológica*, pp. 255–264.

9. Schneider, *Communism*, p. 6; Marcel Niedergang, *Les vingt Amé-riques Latines*, pp. 20, 69; Juan Maestre Alfonso, *Guatemala: Subdesa-rrollo y violencia*, pp. 19–22; Lehman Fletcher et al., *Guatemala's Economic Development: The Role of Agriculture*, p. ·7.

10. International Bank for Reconstruction and Development (hereafter, IBRD), *The Economic Development of Guatemala*, p. 7; Susanne Jonas, "Guatemala: Land of Eternal Struggle," in Ronald H. Chilcote and Joel C. Edelstein, eds., *Latin America: The Struggle with Dependency and Beyond*, pp. 135–136; Fuentes-Mohr, "Land Settlement," p. 29; Leo A. Suslow, *Aspects of Social Reforms in Guatemala, 1944–1949*, p. 45.

11. Jonas, "Guatemala: Land of Eternal Struggle," pp. 135–137.

12. Merwin L. Bohan, draft manuscript "Guatemala," Merwin L. Bohan Papers, Truman Library.

13. John H. Adler, Eugene R. Schlesinger, and Ernest C. Olson, *Public Finance and Economic Development in Guatemala*, p. 25. It should be noted that, although there remained a wealthy native population, by this time it was a very small percentage. The largest economic concerns were owned and managed by foreign elements, the most important being the United Fruit Company. More on Guatemala's social and economic structure will follow.

14. Bohan, "Guatemala"; Gordon, "Subversion," pp. 132–133; Monteforte Toledo, *Guatemala*, p. 52; Eduardo H. Galeano, *Open Veins in Latin America*, p. 120.

15. Robert F. Woodward to secretary of state, 24 April 1945, NA 814.00/4-2445; Eric Wolf, *Sons of the Shaking Earth*, pp. 213–214.

16. A thorough analysis of Maya culture is beyond the scope of this study. For such an analysis, see Wolf, *Sons of the Shaking Earth*, and Monteforte Toledo, *Guatemala.*

17. Wolf, *Sons of the Shaking Earth*, pp. 224–228; Jonas, "Guatemala: Land of Eternal Struggle," p. 95; American University, Special Operations Research Office, *Case Study in Insurgency and Revolutionary Warfare: Guatemala, 1944–1954*, p. 28.

18. The finest work on race and class in Guatemala is Carlos Guzmán-Boeckler and Jean-Loup Herbert's *Guatemala, una interpretación his-tórico-social*. Richard Newbold Adams, *Crucifixion by Power: Essays on Guatemalan National Social Structure, 1944–1966*, should also be consulted.

19. Guatemala's upper class was overwhelmingly the landed aristocracy,

which also comprised the governing aristocracy. It did include a small number of wealthy professionals and business owners.

20. Maestre, *Guatemala*, pp. 49–50; Bohan, "Guatemala"; Toriello, *La batalla*, p. 17.

21. The role of the middle class in the defeat of Guatemala's revolution is discussed in the concluding chapter. For a general treatment, see Arno J. Mayer, *Dynamics of Counterrevolution in Europe, 1870–1956: An Analytic Framework*.

22. Germán Arciniegas, *The State of Latin America*, p. 292.

23. Monteforte Toledo, *Guatemala*, pp. 98–106; Jonas, "Guatemala: Land of Eternal Struggle," pp. 112–113.

24. Jonas, "Guatemala: Land of Eternal Struggle," pp. 121–123, 133–135.

25. Siegel, "Perspective on Guatemala," p. 11.

26. Guzmán-Boeckler and Herbert, *Guatemala*, pp. 99, 126–128, 146–150; American University, *Case Study*, p. 26; Monteforte Toledo, *Guatemala*, pp. 82–83.

27. Chardkoff, "Communist Toehold in the Americas," pp. 8–9.

28. Since many of the wealthy landowners were foreigners, it should also be added that a lot of the wealth generated by Guatemala's economy was exported.

29. Monteforte Toledo, *Guatemala*, pp. 75–81.

30. The classic analysis of feudalism is Marc Bloch, *Feudal Society*.

31. John Gillin and Kalman H. Silvert, "Ambiguities in Guatemala," *Foreign Affairs* 34 (April 1956): 473; Fredrick B. Pike, "Guatemala, The United States, and Communism in the Americas," *Review of Politics* 17 (April 1955): 236–237; Toriello, *La batalla*, pp. 38–39. So much land was left fallow because of the nature of such export crops as bananas. This problem will be explained in chapter 4.

32. Nathan L. Whetten, *Guatemala: The Land and the People*, pp. 92–97; idem, "Land Reform in a Modern World," *Rural Sociology* 19 (December 1954): 332; Donald M. Dozer, *Are We Good Neighbors?* p. 229; Fuentes-Mohr, "Land Settlement," p. 30; John R. Hildebrand, "Latin American Economic Development, Land Reform, and U.S. Aid with Special Reference to Guatemala," *Journal of Inter-American Studies* 4 (July 1962): 355.

33. Antonio Collart, "Problemas económico-sociales de Guatemala," in Alberto Ordóñez, ed., *Transformación económica de Guatemala: Hacia una reforma agraria*, p. 143; Rafael Piedrasante Arandi, *Análisis de la economía de Guatemala y política de desarrollo*, p. 20; Maestre, *Guatemala*, pp. 140–141; Fletcher et al., *Guatemala's Economic Development*, pp. 55–87; Whetten, *Guatemala*, p. 87.

34. Table reproduced in Fletcher et al., *Guatemala's Economic Development*, p. 23.

35. George E. Britnell, "Factors in the Economic Development of Guatemala," *American Economic Review* 43 (May 1953): 104.

36. Monteforte Toledo, *Guatemala*, pp. 50, 54–55, 108; Maestre, *Guate-*

mala, p. 149; Suslow, *Aspects of Social Reforms*, p. 100.

37. United Nations, *The Economic Development of Latin America in the Post-War Period*, p. 60; Donald Grant, "Guatemala and U.S. Foreign Policy," *Journal of International Affairs* 9 (1955): 66.

38. IBRD, *Economic Development*, p. 26; North American Congress on Latin America (hereafter, NACLA), *Guatemala*, ed. Susanne Jonas and David Tobis, p. 14.

39. Maestre, *Guatemala*, p. 132; Adams, *Crucifixion by Power*, p. 183; Piedrasante Arandi, *Análisis*, pp. 13–15; Adler, Schlesinger, and Olson, *Public Finance and Economic Development*, pp. 32–34.

40. Piedrasante Arandi, *Análisis*, pp. 33–43.

41. Ibid., pp. 52–54.

42. Jonas, "Guatemala: Land of Eternal Struggle," p. 148.

43. Kenneth J. Grieb, *Guatemalan Caudillo: The Regime of Jorge Ubico, Guatemala 1931–1944*, pp. 6–7, 17–18; J. Lloyd Mecham, *A Survey of United States–Latin American Relations*, p. 213; Jonas, "Guatemala: Land of Eternal Struggle," p. 146; Mario Efraín Nájera Farfán, *Los estafadores de la democracia (hombres y hechos en Guatemala)*, pp. 25–26.

44. Officials of both the United States government and the United Fruit Company indirectly aided in Ubico's election. This connection will be explained in chapter 4.

45. Lawrence Martin and Sylvia Martin, "Four Strong Men and a President," *Harper's Magazine* 185 (September 1942): 419; Arciniegas, *State of Latin America*, p. 291; Galeano, *Open Veins*, p. 126; "Guatemala: Heat on a Tyrant," *Time* 43 (26 June 1944): 45.

46. Schneider, *Communism*, pp. 7–13.

47. Grieb, *Guatemalan Caudillo*, pp. 17–18.

48. Schneider, *Communism*, pp. 7–13; Grieb, *Guatemalan Caudillo*, p. 34; Ruben E. Reina, "Chinautla: A Guatemalan Indian Community," in Richard Newbold Adams et al., *Community Culture and National Change*, p. 63; American University, *Case Study*, p. 4; Hubert Herring, *A History of Latin America*, p. 455; Martin and Martin, "Four Strong Men," pp. 418–419; Irma Gentry to United States Ambassador Boaz Long, 14 November 1944, NA 814.00/2-1345.

49. John Gerassi, *The Great Fear*, pp. 162–163 (this includes the García Granados quotation); "Guatemala: Heat on a Tyrant," p. 45; secret memo to State Department from U.S. embassy in Costa Rica, 30 June 1944, NA 814.00/6-3044; Grieb, *Guatemalan Caudillo*, p. 43.

50. "Guatemala: Heat on a Tyrant," p. 45.

51. Galich, *Por qué lucha Guatemala*, pp. 76–79; Ubico to Roosevelt and distinguished friends, 6 May 1943, OF 439, "1942–1945," FDR Papers.

52. John Gillin, "San Luis Jilotepeque: 1942–1955," in Adams et al., *Community Culture*, p. 23; Reina, "Chinautla," p. 64.

53. Reina, "Chinautla," p. 64.

54. Robert Ewald, "San Antonio Sacatepéquez, 1932–1953," in Adams et

al., *Community Culture,* p. 18; Morris Siegel, "San Miguel Acatan: 1938–1953," ibid., pp. 40–41.

55. Jonas, "Guatemala: Land of Eternal Struggle," p. 137; Suslow, *Aspects of Social Reforms,* p. 85; Galeano, *Open Veins,* p. 126. Grieb writes that Ubico's vagrancy laws were an improvement over the former peonage system. As I discuss in chapter 4, this may be true, but it was only a relative improvement which continued to oppress the Maya population. See Grieb, *Guatemalan Caudillo,* pp. 35–41.

56. John M. Cabot to Hull, strictly confidential, 4 December 1940, NA 814.00/12-440.

57. Dr. José Prado Romana, Dr. Gustavo A. Trangay, and Lic. Clemente Marroquín Rojas to Señior (sic) Dr. don Enrique Ruiz Guinazu, 12 January 1942, OF 439, "1942–1945," FDR Papers.

58. ALUSNA, Guatemala, coded message to War Department, 12 March 1943, MR 300-Warfare, "Warfare (Central America), 1942–1944, (sec. 1)," FDR Papers.

59. Jonas, "Guatemala: Land of Eternal Struggle," p. 149; Samuel Guy Inman, *A New Day in Guatemala,* p. 7; Cabot to Hull, 4 December 1940, NA 814.00/12-440; Martin and Martin, "Four Strong Men," p. 419.

60. Chardkoff, "Communist Toehold in the Americas," p. 44; Boaz Long to secretary of state, 27 June 1944, NA 814.00/6-2744.

61. Medardo Mejía, *Arévalo,* pp. 195–198, and *El movimiento obrero en la Revolución de Octubre,* pp. 5–7; Galich, *Por qué lucha Guatemala,* p. 110; Nájera, *Los estafadores de la democracia,* p. 33.

62. Galich, *Por qué lucha Guatemala,* pp. 75–76; Mejía, *El movimiento obrero,* p. 91.

63. Bernard Rosen, "Counter-Revolution: Guatemala's Tragedy," *Nation* 179 (31 July 1954): 87–89.

64. Herring, *Latin America,* pp. 455–456.

65. Jonas, "Guatemala: Land of Eternal Struggle," p. 151; Pike, "Guatemala, the United States, and Communism," p. 233.

66. Galich, *Por qué lucha Guatemala,* pp. 73–75; Mejía, *Arévalo,* p. 316; Robert L. Peterson, "Guatemala," in Ben G. Burnett and Kenneth F. Johnson, eds., *Political Forces in Latin America: Dimensions for the Quest for Stability,* p. 78.

67. For a full-length narrative, see Manuel Galich, *Del pánico al ataque.*

68. Professors, students, and writers had been the most outspoken critics of Guatemala's historical problems since the 1920s. The National University of Guatemala, after the fall of Estrada Cabrera, became a forum to debate such issues as Maya conditions, land and labor, illiteracy, and public health. See Walter A. Payne, "The Guatemalan Revolution, 1944–1954: An Interpretation," *Pacific Historian* 17 (Spring 1973), insert, 7–8.

69. Lawrence Duggan, memorandum to State Department, 26 June 1944, NA 814.00/6-2644; Mejía, *El movimiento obrero,* pp. 41–47.

70. Boaz Long to Secretary of State Hull, 23 June 1944, NA 814.00/6-2344;

Jonas, "Guatemala: Land of Eternal Struggle," pp. 150–151; Martz, *Communist Infiltration*, p. 11; Long to Hull, 21 June 1944, *FRUS* 7: 1132.

71. Long to Hull, 30 June 1944, NA 814.00/6-3044, and 1 July 1944, NA 814.00/7-144; Maestre, *Guatemala*, p. 160; J. M. Dougherty to Hull, 20 September 1944, NA 814.00/9-2044.

72. Austin F. MacDonald, *Latin American Politics and Government*, pp. 616–617; Nájera, *Los estafadores de la democracia*, pp. 40–41; Fedro Guillén, *Guatemala, prólogo y epílogo de una revolución*, p. 45; Mejía, *El movimiento obrero*, p. 81. Salazar became Castillo Armas' first ambassador to the United States.

73. Nájera, *Los estafadores de la democracia*, pp. 42–43; Antonio Valenzuela-Moreno to Hull, 18 November 1944, NA 814.00/11-1844.

74. American University, *Case Study*, pp. 4–5; Long to Hull, 7 July 1944, NA 814.00/7-744.

75. Nájera, *Los estafadores de la democracia*, p. 44; Mejía, *El movimiento obrero*, p. 84.

76. Suslow, *Aspects of Social Reforms*, p. 12; ALUSNA, Guatemala, coded message to War Department, 27 October 1944, MR 300-Warfare, "Warfare (Central America), 1942–1944 (sec. 1)," FDR Papers.

77. U.S. military attaché, Guatemala City, message to War Department, 23 September 1944, MR 300-Warfare, "Warfare (Central America), 1942–1944 (sec. 1)," FDR Papers.

78. Martz, *Communist Infiltration*, pp. 11–12; U.S. military attaché, Tegucigalpa, Honduras, message to War Department, 20 October 1944, MR 300-Warfare, "Warfare (Central America), 1942–1944 (sec. 1)," FDR Papers.

79. William C. Affeld telegram to Hull, 20 October 1944, NA 814.00/10-2044.

80. Marta de Ubico to Mrs. Roosevelt, 15 December 1944, President's Personal File (hereafter, PPF) 5157, FDR Papers; Summerlin to Grace Tulley, 3 January 1944, PPF 5157, FDR Papers; William R. Kavanaugh to Matthew J. Connelly, 28 January 1947, OF 439, Truman Papers; Stanley Woodward to Connelly, 4 February 1947, OF 439, Truman Papers.

81. Ponce telegram to FDR, enclosed in Hull to officer in charge of American mission, Mexico City, 15 November 1944, OF 439, "1942–1945," FDR Papers; Rolland Welch to Department of State, 12 January 1954, NA 714.00/1-1254.

82. ALUSNA, message to War Department, 27 October 1944, MR 300-Warfare, "Warfare (Central America), 1942–1944 (sec. 1)," FDR Papers.

83. William C. Affeld to Hull, 23 October 1944, enclosed in Long to Hull, 31 October 1944, NA 814.01/10-3144; Galich, *Por qué lucha Guatemala*, pp. 88–89.

3. The Revolutionary Governments: Communism or Nationalism?

1. For more on the military's role in Latin American politics, see two works by Edwin Lieuwen, *Arms and Politics in Latin America* and

Generals vs. Presidents: Neo-Militarism in Latin America. A more analytical study is José Nun, *Latin America: The Hegemonic Crisis and the Military Coup.*

2. American University, *Case Study*, p. 31.

3. Ibid., p. 32.

4. Long to Hull, 14 December 1944, NA 814.00/12-1444.

5. Guillén, *Guatemala*, pp. 44–45; Cardoza y Aragón, *Revolución Guatemalteca*, p. 48; Long to Hull, 18 December 1944, NA 814.00/12-1844; Long to Hull, 20 December 1944, *FRUS* 7: 1152; Ovidio Gondi, "Democracy in Latin America: Chaos on Our Doorstep," *Nation* 170 (28 January 1950): 81.

6. Suslow, *Aspects of Social Reforms*, p. 12; Long to Hull, 2 January 1945, NA 814.00/1-245.

7. Jonas, "Guatemala: Land of Eternal Struggle," pp. 151–152; Dion, *Las ideas de Arévalo*, pp. 10–15; Martz, *Communist Infiltration*, p. 35; Inman, *New Day*, p. 34; Juan José Arévalo, "Charla al clausurarse la campaña política," 16 December 1944, in his *Escritos políticos*, p. 158; Schneider, *Communism*, pp. 13–17; Archer Bush, *Organized Labor in Guatemala, 1944–1949*, p. 38.

8. Martz, *Communist Infiltration*, p. 35; Juan José Arévalo, "Inaugural Speech," 15 March 1945, in his *Escritos políticos y discursos*, pp. 15–20; Angela (Delli Sante) Arrocha, *Juan José Arévalo, pensador contemporáneo*, pp. 24–25; Arévalo, "Istmania," *Escritos políticos*, pp. 13–28; Inman, *New Day*, p. 1; Cardoza y Aragón, *Revolución Guatemalteca*, pp. 58–60; Nájera, *Los estafadores de la democracia*, pp. 76–77.

9. Arévalo, "Charla al clausurarse la campaña política," p. 162; idem, "Las cuatro raíces de servilismo," *Escritos políticos*, pp. 31–52; idem, "Nazismo Europeo y nazismo criollo," *Escritos políticos*, pp. 75–77; idem, "Gobiernos fuertes y gobiernos debiles," *Escritos políticos*, pp. 81–82.

10. Arrocha, *Arévalo*, pp. 36, 60–61; Dion, *Las ideas de Arévalo*, pp. 47, 71–76.

11. Arrocha, *Arévalo*, pp. 26–27, 59; Dion, *Las ideas de Arévalo*, pp. 52–54, 162; Arévalo, "Charla al clausurarse la campaña política," pp. 162–163.

12. Arrocha, *Arévalo*, pp. 13–19.

13. Arévalo, "Charla al clausurarse la campaña política," pp. 162–163; Arrocha, *Arévalo*, pp. 27–28; Dion, *Las ideas de Arévalo*, pp. 124–125, 166–167.

14. Long to Hull, 27 November 1944, NA 814.00/11-2744.

15. Arévalo, "Conservadores, liberales y socialistas," 1944, *Escritos políticos*, pp. 146–147; Dion, *Las ideas de Arévalo*, pp. 115–116; Arrocha, *Arévalo*, pp. 31–33; Selden Rodman, *The Guatemalan Traveler: A Concise History and Guide*, p. 56; Juan José Arévalo, *Informes al congreso*, 1946 and 1948, p. 32.

16. Mejía, *Arévalo*, pp. 59–68; Franklin D. Parker, *The Central American Republics*, p. 97; Monteforte Toledo, *Guatemala*, pp. 310–311; "The

Social Revolution in Guatemala," *World Today* 10 (July 1954): 280–281; Siegel, "San Miguel," p. 40; Reina, "Chinautla," p. 64; Jonas, "Guatemala: Land of Eternal Struggle," pp. 152–153.

17. Cardoza y Aragón, *Revolución Guatemalteca*, pp. 63–64; Mejía, *Arévalo*, pp. 237–242; C. Neale Ronning, *Law and Politics in Inter-American Diplomacy*, pp. 17–18.

18. The overthrow was led by José Figueres. Elected president in 1953, Figueres became one of Latin America's chief advocates of liberal reform.

19. Ismael González-Arévalo, *Statement Concerning the Conflict between Guatemalan Workers and the United Fruit Company*, pp. 3–4; Mejía, *Arévalo*, pp. 242–247; Fitzhugh Turner, part 4 of his special series "Communism in the Caribbean," *New York Herald Tribune*, 12 February 1950; United States Department of State memo, "To Assess Our Current Relations with Guatemala," 16 May 1950, Richard C. Patterson Papers, Truman Library, in Carrollton Press, Inc., *The Declassified Documents Quarterly Catalogue* 1 (January–December 1975): 180B; United States Department of State policy statement, 17 August 1948, NA 711.14/8-1748.

20. Dion, *Las ideas de Arévalo*, pp. 90, 152–155; Maestre, *Guatemala*, p. 161; Arrocha, *Arévalo*, pp. 67–68; Arévalo, "Inaugural Address," 15 March 1945, *Escritos políticos y discursos*, pp. 20–21; idem, "Cultura y posibilidades de cultura en la América Central," 1939, *Escritos políticos*, pp. 59–69.

21. Arévalo, "Inaugural Address," pp. 20–21; idem, "Radio Address on Visit to San Cristóbal," 22 May 1945, *Escritos políticos y discursos*, pp. 38–44; Mejía, *Arévalo*, pp. 232–234; Karnes, *Failure of Union*, pp. 233–236.

22. Dion, *Las ideas de Arévalo*, pp. 121–126; Arévalo, "El presidente electo al pueblo de Guatemala," *Escritos políticos y discursos*, pp. 165–166; George E. Britnell, "Problems of Economic and Social Change in Guatemala," *Canadian Journal of Economics and Political Science* 17 (November 1951): 472–473.

23. Toriello, *La batalla*, pp. 36–37; "Social Revolution in Guatemala," pp. 280–281; Jonas, "Guatemala: Land of Eternal Struggle," p. 154.

24. Galich, *Por qué lucha Guatemala*, pp. 161–167.

25. González-Arévalo, *Statement*, p. 2.

26. Monteforte Toledo, *Guatemala*, p. 434; Toriello, *La batalla*, p. 39; IBRD, *Economic Development*, p. 41. There is an extensive literature on the necessity of agrarian reform for Latin American development. For differing perspectives, see T. Lynn Smith, *Agrarian Reform in Latin America*, and James F. Petras and Robert LaPorte, Jr., *Cultivating Revolution: The United States and Agrarian Reform in Latin America*.

27. Fletcher et al., *Guatemala's Economic Development*, p. 136; Jonas, "Guatemala: Land of Eternal Struggle," pp. 154–155; Inman, *New Day*, pp. 26–28; Monteforte Toledo, *Guatemala*, pp. 433–434.

28. Cehelsky, "Guatemala's Frustrated Revolution," pp. 22–23; American University, *Case Study*, pp. 18–19.

29. Jonas, "Guatemala: Land of Eternal Struggle," pp. 152–153; Richard Allen LaBarge, "Impact of the United Fruit Company on the Economic Development of Guatemala, 1946–1954," in LaBarge et al., *Studies in Middle American Economics*, p. 48; Luis Cardoza y Aragón, "Land for the Many," *Nation* 176 (14 March 1953): 224.

30. Arévalo, *Informes al congreso*, pp. 53–54; LaBarge, "Impact of United Fruit," p. 48; Galich, *Por qué lucha Guatemala*, p. 97.

31. Britnell, "Problems of Economic and Social Change in Guatemala," pp. 477–478.

32. Toriello, *La batalla*, p. 37; Cardoza y Aragón, "Land for the Many," p. 224; memo of conversation by Edwin J. Kyle, Jr., 8 August 1947, *FRUS* 8: 111.

33. Galich, *Por qué lucha Guatemala*, pp. 158–160; Toriello, *La batalla*, pp. 33–34; Cardoza y Aragón, *Revolución Guatemalteca*, p. 86.

34. Inman, *New Day*, pp. 5, 28; Monteforte Toledo, *Guatemala*, pp. 47–50.

35. Luis Cardoza y Aragón, an active participant in the Arévalo administration, claims that members of the powerful landowners association advocated the perpetuation of rural illiteracy, contending that the education of peasants would foster a mass exodus from the land. See his "Land for the Many," p. 225.

36. United Nations, *Economic Development of Latin America*, p. 60; Maestre, *Guatemala*, pp. 27–28; Monteforte Toledo, *Guatemala*, pp. 251–252; Fletcher et al., *Guatemala's Economic Development*, pp. 7–8.

37. Inman, *New Day*, pp. 20–22; Galich, *Por qué lucha Guatemala*, pp. 126–129; NACLA, *Guatemala*, p. 31; Gordon, "Subversion," p. 136.

38. Reina, "Chinautla," p. 64; Rodman, *Guatemalan Traveler*, pp. 56–57; Monteforte Toledo, *Guatemala*, p. 121; Cardoza y Aragón, *Revolución Guatemalteca*, p. 81; Galich, *Por qué lucha Guatemala*, pp. 125–126; Inman, *New Day*, p. 31.

39. This attitude is well represented by former Assistant Secretary of Inter-American Affairs Spruille Braden. In an interview, he commented on the Guatemalan people's attitude toward the Arévalo government: "I don't think you can cover it by saying the Guatemalan people. It's only a few scattered, more intelligent, more educated people who ever had any thoughts about it. They were decent people, but the mass [the Indians] of the people really didn't know too much about it. They were concerned whether they were getting good wages and enough to eat." Interview with Braden, 16 November 1977.

40. Siegel, "Perspective on Guatemala," p. 13.

41. Reina, "Chinautla," pp. 76–77.

42. Jonas, "Guatemala: Land of Eternal Struggle," p. 155.

43. Guillén, *Guatemala*, p. 39; Jonas, "Guatemala: Land of Eternal Struggle," pp. 153–155.

44. Their analysis was valid. A comprehensive reform program in Guatemala required a complete overhaul of the existing social and economic order. Arévalo would not concede that the tiny elite which controlled

so much of the power and property would continually fight to maintain dominance.

45. There were so many attempts that no one seemed to be able to keep track. Estimates range from twenty-five to thirty-five. The *Hispanic American Report* (hereafter, *HAR*) stated that the uprising that followed Araña's assassination in July 1949 was the twentieth.

46. Edwin J. Kyle to secretary of state, 21 April 1948, NA 814.00/4-2148; Wilson to Wise and Newbegin, State Department office memorandum, "Indications of Communism in Guatemala," 6 May 1948, NA 814.00B/ 8-349; State Department memorandum, 30 June 1948, NA FW 814.00/ 6-2248.

47. Arévalo, *Informes al Congreso*, p. 8.

48. S. Walter Washington to secretary of state, 24 June 1947, NA 814.00/ 6-2447; Kyle to secretary of state, 9 October 1947, NA 814.00/10-947; Milton K. Wells to secretary of state, 3 August 1949, NA 814.00/8-349; State Department, secret policy statement, Guatemala, 17 August 1948, NA 711.14/8-1748.

49. See, for example, State Department memorandum of conversation, 6 October 1947, NA 814.00/10-647; Dr. Gustavo Adolfo Trangay to Secretary of State Marshall, July 1948, NA FW 814.00/7-48.

50. Miguel Ydígoras Fuentes, *My War with Communism*, p. 42; Milton K. Wells to secretary of state, 3 June 1949, NA 814.00/6-349; American University, *Case Study*, p. 93; House of Representatives, *Report of the Subcommittee to Investigate Communist Aggression*, p. 5; Pike, "Guatemala, the United States, and Communism," p. 235; Robert F. Woodward to secretary of state, 24 April 1945, NA 814.00/4-2445; Wells to secretary of state, 12 December 1947, NA 814.00B/12-1247.

51. Arciniegas, *State of Latin America*, p. 294; *HAR* 6 (September 1953): 14; H. Bradford Westerfield, *The Instruments of America's Foreign Policy*, p. 424; John J. Johnson, *The Military and Society in Latin America*, p. 143; Bush, *Organized Labor*, p. 12; Wells to secretary of state, 12 November 1948, NA 814.00/11-1248.

52. Cehelsky, "Guatemala's Frustrated Revolution," p. 30.

53. Wells to Ernest V. Siracusa, 22 July 1949, NA 814.00/7-2249; Capus M. Waynick to secretary of state, 26 September 1949, NA 814.00/ 9-2649; Turner, part 5 of "Communism in the Caribbean," 13 February 1950.

54. Wells to secretary of state, 18 July 1949, NA 814.00/7-1849; interview with E. Howard Hunt, 6 December 1977; William L. Krieg to Department of State, 14 July 1954, NA 714.00/7-1454.

55. Spruille Braden, "Syllabus on the Communist Threat in the Americas," pp. 6–7; Wells to secretary of state, 18 July 1949, NA 814.00/7-1849; Schneider, *Communism*, pp. 30–31.

56. Turner, "Communism in the Caribbean," 13 February 1950; William F. Lewis, colonel, USAF, U.S. Department of State dispatch, 22 July 1949, NA 814.00/7-2249; Central Intelligence Agency, *Review of the World*

Situation as It Relates to the Security of the United States, 1948–1950, 17 August 1949, PSF, Truman Papers.

57. We will see in the next chapter that the FBI, in 1948, believed that García Granados was a Communist.

58. Jonas, "Land of Eternal Struggle," p. 156.

59. Inman, *New Day,* p. 13.

60. Jonas, "Land of Eternal Struggle," p. 156; Schneider, *Communism,* pp. 32–34.

61. The three parties were the Party of Revolutionary Action, the Party of the Guatemalan Revolution, and the Party of National Renovation. Arbenz and Arévalo were both members of the largest, the Party of Revolutionary Action.

62. Although it remained silent in 1950, the United States government later claimed that the election was fraudulent, with Arbenz supporters harassing the opposition and stuffing ballot boxes. See House of Representatives, *Report of the Subcommittee to Investigate Communist Aggression,* p. 6. But the HAR, which had eyewitness reports, wrote that "the election was held in complete order, and the voting was free." See HAR 3 (December 1950): 13.

63. American University, *Case Study,* p. 6; Cardoza y Aragón, *Revolución Guatemalteca,* p. 139; Tapley Bennett, U.S. Department of State memo, "Some Aspects of Communist Penetration in Guatemala," 23 March 1950, in Carrollton Press, *Declassified Documents Quarterly Catalogue* 1: 179B; Wells to secretary of state, 15 November 1950, FRUS 2: 922; Parker, *Central American Republics,* p. 99; Inman, *New Day,* pp. 12–13; HAR 3 (December 1950): 13; HAR 3 (March 1950): 12.

64. HAR 4 (April 1951): 20; Sir Harold Mitchell, *Contemporary Politics and Economics in the Caribbean,* p. 376; Martz, *Communist Infiltration,* pp. 38–39; William C. Affeld to secretary of state, 26 October 1944, NA 814.00/10-2644; Galich, *Por qué lucha Guatemala,* pp. 221–223; Andrew E. Donovan II to secretary of state, 2 January 1947, NA 814.00/1-247; Maestre, *Guatemala,* pp. 167–168.

65. After Arbenz's overthrow, a number of critics in the United States claimed that María Arbenz was really the radical Communist and that the president was merely her puppet. In brief, these commentators concluded that Arbenz was a "lightweight thinker" and that it was María who "persuaded Arbenz to see in marxism the simple solution to everything that his direct and uncomplicated mind required." None of these critics, however, considers Arbenz's successful record prior to meeting María, nor do they explain his personal popularity throughout Guatemala. For example, Selden Rodman portrays Arbenz as "an introvert personality" who "delivered orders almost in a whisper from behind a visage as forbidding as Himmler's." To Rodman such a weak figure could be easily dominated by his ambitious, scheming wife. But eyewitnesses like Samuel Guy Inman wrote that Arbenz traveled openly among the Guatemalan villages, intelligently and congenially

discussing with his people their problems and his solutions. See Martz, *Communist Infiltration*, pp. 39–40; James, *Red Design for the Americas*, pp. 56–57; Rodman, *Guatemalan Traveler*, pp. 59–60; Inman, *New Day*, pp. 12–13.

66. Maestre, *Guatemala*, pp. 167–168; Niedergang, *Vingt Amériques Latines*, pp. 20, 76; M. Scully, "Inside Story of the Kremlin's Plot in Guatemala," *Reader's Digest* 66 (February 1955): 75.

67. Galich, *Por qué lucha Guatemala*, pp. 221–223; Jacobo Arbenz, "4 enfoques del programa administrativo actual," in Alberto Ordóñez, ed., *Transformación económica de Guatemala: Hacia una reforma agraria*, pp. 10–18.

68. IBRD, *Economic Development*, p. 40; Jacobo Arbenz, *Discursos*, p. 14.

69. Arbenz, "4 enfoques del programa administrativo," pp. 12–13; *Informe del Presidente Jacobo Arbenz Guzmán al congreso nacional en su primer período de sesiones ordinarias del año de 1953*, pp. v–vii; Cehelsky, "Guatemala's Frustrated Revolution," pp. 34–35; Jonas, "Guatemala: Land of Eternal Struggle," pp. 156–157; Arbenz, quoted in Ordóñez, *Transformación económica*, pp. 7–8.

70. Arbenz, "4 enfoques del programa administrativo," pp. 16–20.

71. Ibid., pp. 12–18; Arbenz, quoted in Ordóñez, *Transformación económica*, p. 8; Carlos Wyld Ospiña, "Consideraciones sobre la reforma agraria," in Ordóñez, *Transformación económica*, pp. 177–183; Collart, "Problemas económico-sociales," pp. 141–142.

72. Collart, "Problemas económico-sociales," pp. 143–145; Arbenz, "4 enfoques del programa administrativo," pp. 13–14.

73. Monteforte Toledo, *Guatemala*, p. 315; Guzmán-Boeckler and Herbert, *Guatemala*, p. 174; *Informe del Presidente Arbenz*, pp. v–xxxiii; Galich, *Por qué lucha Guatemala*, pp. 279–280; Alfonso Bauer Paíz, "La reforma agraria en Guatemala," in Ordóñez, *Transformación económica*, pp. 172–176.

74. Thomas Melville and Marjorie Melville, *Guatemala: The Politics of Land Ownership*, pp. 44–45; Whetten, *Guatemala*, pp. 132–156; Eduardo H. Galeano, *Guatemala, Occupied Country*, pp. 125–128; Toriello, *La batalla*, p. 41; Fuentes-Mohr, "Land Settlement," pp. 32–33.

75. Gordon, "Subversion," p. 138; Fuentes-Mohr, "Land Settlement," pp. 33–34; Aybar de Soto, *Dependency and Intervention*, pp. 171–179; Jonas, "Guatemala: Land of Eternal Struggle," pp. 158–159.

76. Maestre, *Guatemala*, p. 143; Whetten, *Guatemala*, pp. 162–163; Melville and Melville, *Guatemala*, p. 57; NACLA, *Guatemala*, p. 20; Fuentes-Mohr, "Land Settlement," p. 34; Toriello, *La batalla*, p. 42; HAR 5 (July 1952): 11.

77. Fuentes-Mohr, "Land Settlement," pp. 34–35; Toriello, *La batalla*, pp. 36–37.

78. The previously mentioned labor legislation played a substantial part in increasing per capita purchasing power. As noted, minimum salaries rose four- to five-fold during the ten-year revolutionary period.

79. Aybar de Soto, *Dependency and Intervention*, pp. 210–215; Jonas,

"Guatemala: Land of Eternal Struggle," pp. 158–159; Toriello, *La batalla*, p. 37; Karl M. Schmitt and David D. Burks, *Evolution or Chaos: Dynamics of Latin American Government and Politics*, p. 85.

4. The View from the North

1. For example, see John W. Fisher to Department of State, "Publication of Communist Newspaper *Octubre*," 28 June 1950, NA 714.001/6-2850; Nicholson to Bennett, "Communist Activities in Guatemala," 17 August 1950, NA 714.001/8-1750; Milton K. Wells to Department of State, "Communist Question into the Open," 27 September 1950, NA 714.001/9-2750.

2. Charles Morrow Wilson, *Empire in Green and Gold: The Story of the American Banana Trade*, pp. 36–68; Thomas P. McCann, *An American Company: The Tragedy of United Fruit*, pp. 15–17; César Jérez, S.J., "La United Fruit Co. en Guatemala," *Estudios Centro Americanos* 26 (March 1971): 118; Herbert Solow, "The Ripe Problem of United Fruit," *Fortune* 54 (March 1959): 99–100; Westerfield, *Instruments of America's Foreign Policy*, p. 423.

3. McCann, *American Company*, pp. 16–17; Wilson, *Empire*, pp. 91–92, 106–110.

4. Jérez, "La United Fruit Co.," pp. 118–119; McCann, *American Company*, p. 45; "Behind the Guatemalan Front," *New Statesman and Nation* 47 (26 June 1954): 821; Charles David Kepner, Jr., and Jay Henry Soothill, *The Banana Empire: A Case Study of Economic Imperialism*, p. 156.

5. Jonas, "Guatemala: Land of Eternal Struggle," pp. 142–143; Jérez, "La United Fruit Co.," p. 119; Wilson, *Empire*, pp. 122–123.

6. Jérez, "La United Fruit Co.," pp. 119–120; Toriello, *La batalla*, pp. 49–50; Stacy May and G. Plaza, *The United Fruit Company in Latin America*, pp. 162–164.

7. McCann, *American Company*, pp. 18–24; Wilson, *Empire*, pp. 245–265.

8. The United States State Department, particularly Ambassador Sheldon Whitehouse, contributed to Ubico's success. Also, rumors circulated that Ubico paid Orellana eighty thousand dollars to go off to Spain. See Kenneth J. Grieb, "American Involvement in the Rise of Jorge Ubico," *Caribbean Studies* 10 (April 1970): 5–21; Martin and Martin, "Four Strong Men," p. 419.

9. Alfonso Bauer Paíz, "How Yanqui Capital Works in Central America (The Case of Guatemala)," in Marvin D. Bernstein, ed., *Foreign Investment in Latin America: Cases and Attitudes*, pp. 252–253; "Guatemala: Heat on a Tyrant," p. 45; Jonas, "Guatemala: Land of Eternal Struggle," p. 142.

10. Jonas, "Guatemala: Land of Eternal Struggle," pp. 142–143; Melville and Melville, *Guatemala*, pp. 51–52; Adler, Schlesinger, and Olson, *Public Finance and Economic Development*, pp. 123–125; Ronning, *Law and Politics*, p. 42.

11. Jérez, "La United Fruit Co.," p. 120; Britnell, "Factors in the Economic Development of Guatemala," pp. 110–111; John D. Martz, *Central America, the Crisis and the Challenge*, pp. 49–50; May and Plaza, *United Fruit Company*, pp. 165–166; United States Department of Commerce, *Investment in Central America*, p. 142; Jonas, "Guatemala: Land of Eternal Struggle," p. 143; *New York Times*, 19 February 1953; LaBarge, "Impact of United Fruit," p. 15.

12. "Harassed u.f.," *Commonweal* 55 (9 November 1951): 108; Cardoza y Aragón, *Revolución Guatemalteca*, p. 44; Bush, *Organized Labor*, p. 7; Niedergang, *Vingt Amériques Latines*, p. 74; Blasier, *Hovering Giant*, p. 53; *United Fruit Company Annual Report*, 1951.

13. Solow, "Ripe Problem of United Fruit," pp. 99–100; *United Fruit Company Annual Report*, 1950–1955; Suslow, *Aspects of Social Reforms*, p. 90.

14. As noted previously, this is not a study of dependency theory as it applies to Guatemala, and I argue against the thesis that the preservation of United Fruit's interests determined the United States intervention. Thus my work is distinguished from the theoretical construct of Aybar de Soto's *Dependency and Intervention*.

15. Rodman, *Guatemalan Traveler*, p. 54; Suslow, *Aspects of Social Reforms*, pp. 90–93.

16. Schneider, *Communism*, pp. 48–49; Bush, *Organized Labor*, p. 38; Thomas U. Uzzell to John Cabot, 5 January 1945, NA 711.14/1-545; G. H. Butler to Uzzell, 17 April 1945, NA FW 711.14/3-2745.

17. Bush, *Organized Labor*, p. 18; American University, *Case Study*, pp. 20–21; Rodman, *Guatemalan Traveler*, p. 54; Braden interview; Edward L. Bernays, *Biography of an Idea: Memoirs of a Public Relations Counsel*, pp. 757–758.

18. Bush, *Organized Labor*, pp. 19–20; Galich, *Por qué lucha Guatemala*, p. 137; LaBarge, "Impact of United Fruit," pp. 43–45.

19. American University, *Case Study*, pp. 20–21.

20. "Guatemala: Stage Trick," *Time* 48 (18 November 1946): 38; Kenedon P. Steins, U.S. Department of State memorandum, 16 May 1950, *FRUS* 2: 893; John F. Fishburn to Edward Miller, 19 April 1950, *FRUS* 2: 880–881; Edwin Kyle to Robert Newbegin, 4 August 1947, 8 August 1947, *FRUS* 8: 707, 711; González-Arévalo, *Statement*, p. 1.

21. Ronning, *Law and Politics*, p. 43; Galich, *Por qué lucha Guatemala*, pp. 137–142; Samuel Zemurray, "La Frutera's Record," *Nation* 170 (25 March 1950): 228; Grieb, *Guatemalan Caudillo*, p. 184.

22. Galich, *Por qué lucha Guatemala*, p. 212; "Banana Bonanza," *Newsweek* 39 (24 March 1952): 62; *HAR* 4 (October 1951): 13; "Bananas and Politics," *New Republic* 126 (28 January 1952): 7; LaBarge, "Impact of United Fruit," pp. 49–50; *New York Times*, 3 March 1952.

23. *United Fruit Company Annual Report*, 1951.

24. "Banana Bonanza," p. 62; *Facts on File Yearbook*, 1952, pp. 10F, 82D; *United Fruit Company Annual Report*, 1952.

25. *HAR* 5 (February 1952): 11–12; American University, *Case Study*, pp.

22–23; Mclville and Melville, *Guatemala*, pp. 49–51; Jonas, "Test Case for the Hemisphere," p. 22.

26. *HAR* 4 (June 1951): 11–12; *Facts on File Yearbook*, 1951, p. 150G–H.
27. Bernays, *Biography of an Idea*, p. 760.
28. Bernays knows only that his suggestions were passed on to UFCO's representatives in Washington. Letter to author, 14 January 1980.
29. John F. Fishburn to Edward Miller, 19 April 1950, *FRUS* 2: 881.
30. Jonas, "Guatemala: Land of Eternal Struggle," p. 160; Fuentes-Mohr, "Land Settlement," p. 34.
31. Samuel Shapiro, *Invisible Latin America*, pp. 31–33; Clemente Marroquín Rojas, *La derrota de una batalla*, pp. 77–82; Toriello, *La batalla*, pp. 56–57; *HAR* 5 (January 1953): ii; Salvador de Madariaga, *Latin America between the Eagle and the Bear*, p. 110.
32. "Expropriation of United Fruit Company Property by the Government of Guatemala," *Bulletin* 29 (14 September 1953): 359–360.
33. The claim related only to the Tiquisate property. Of its total, $6,984,223 was for the expropriation, $8,737,600 for what the State Department termed "severance damages." See "Formal Claim Filed against the Guatemalan Government," *Bulletin* 30 (26 April 1954): 678–679. UFCO placed an additional claim for $3,500,000 for its holdings on the Caribbean coast, bringing the total claim to sixteen times the declared tax value.
34. Willard F. Barber to N. Leonard Jarvis, 25 August 1949, NA FW 814.00B/8-2549.
35. United States Department of State, memorandum of conversation, 25 May 1953, NA 611.14/5-2553; United States Department of State, memorandum of conversation, 26 June 1953, NA 611.14/6-2653; "Guatemala: Square Deal Wanted," *Time* 63 (3 May 1954): 36; May and Plaza, *United Fruit Company*, p. 215.
36. Dulles, news conference transcript, 8 June 1954, in United States Department of State, *American Foreign Policy, 1950–1955, Basic Documents*, 1: 1310.
37. Jonas, "Guatemala: Land of Eternal Struggle," pp. 144–145; Adams, *Crucifixion by Power*, pp. 138–141; Department of Commerce, *Investment in Central America*, p. 137; Jonas, "Test Case for the Hemisphere," pp. 25–26; Toriello, *La batalla*, p. 52; Cardoza y Aragón, *Revolución Guatemalteca*, p. 25.
38. Pike, "Guatemala, the United States, and Communism," pp. 237–239; Osegueda, *Operación Guatemala OK*, pp. 59–60; Alfonso Bauer Paíz, "The Third Government of the Revolution and Imperialism in Guatemala," *Science and Society* 34 (Summer 1970): 148.
39. Grant, "Guatemala and U.S. Foreign Policy," pp. 65–66; United States Department of State secret policy statement, "Guatemala," 17 August 1948, NA 711.14/8-1748; James, "Red Beachhead in America," p. 32.
40. Dr. José Prado Romana, Dr. Gustavo A. Trangay, and Lic. Clemente Marroquín Rojas to Señior (*sic*) Dr. don Enrique Ruiz Guinazu, 12 January 1942, OF 439, "1942–1945," FDR Papers.

41. Martin and Martin, "Four Strong Men," pp. 418–420. Kenneth Grieb's 1979 study of Ubico supports the view that he exhibited considerable concern for the Indians; it goes so far as to say that he was "unquestionably popular" in the countryside and enjoyed the Mayas' "enthusiastic support and loyalty." Grieb contends that they especially liked his trips to their villages and perceived his vagrancy laws as a vast improvement over the traditional system of debt peonage. It must be noted, however, that Grieb bases his conclusions on Guatemalan press coverage, which he admits was controlled by the general-president, on interviews with Ubico's supporters, and on reports by United States officials like Ambassador Sheldon Whitehouse, with whom Ubico was "particularly close." Grieb also writes that "the wily Caudillo sought to ingratiate himself with the Yankees," and certainly he succeeded. What is clear is that oppression of the Indians continued under Ubico. See Grieb, *Guatemalan Caudillo*, pp. 35–41, 67–75.

42. Long to Roosevelt, 2 September 1944, OF 439, "1942–1945," FDR Papers.

43. Long to Hull, 14 July 1944, *FRUS* 7: 1139.

44. Long to Roosevelt, 23 October 1944, OF 1898, FDR Papers. Less than a week after Ponce dissolved the National Assembly and engineered his election as president, Long, upon Hull's instructions, recognized the new government. See Hull to Long, 7 July 1944, *FRUS* 7: 1136; Long to Lic. Carlos Salazar, 8 July 1944, NA 711.14/7-1144.

45. Long to Edward Stettinius, 5 April 1945, NA 814.00/4-545.

46. Stettinius, circular telegram, 31 October 1944, *FRUS* 7: 1147; Stettinius to U.S. embassy in Guatemala, 4 November 1944, NA 814.00/10-3144; Long to Stettinius, 7 November 1944, *FRUS* 7: 1151; Braden interview; Edward L. Reed (chargé d'affaires ad interim, U.S. embassy in Guatemala) to secretary of state, 13 January 1945, NA 814.00/1-1345. It should be noted that there were also some scattered concerns that Arévalo had Nazi sympathies. See U.S. State Department memorandum, 24 October 1944, NA 814.00/10-644. Interestingly, Braden told me that he had not heard of Arévalo during his long, controversial experience in Argentina.

47. John F. Griffiths, memorandum sought by State Department, 8 January 1945, NA 814.00/1-1345.

48. Ibid.; Joseph Grew, memorandum to Roosevelt, 15 January 1945, PSF 13, "State Department, 1944–1945, II," FDR Papers; United States Senate, *Executive Sessions of the Senate Foreign Relations Committee*, 82d Cong., 1st sess., 1951, 3: 345. Unfortunately, the results of the State Department's recommendation to Roosevelt remain in doubt. Roosevelt's handwritten note on the top of Grew's memorandum indicated that he would receive Arévalo anytime after March 1, but the meeting never took place. Donald B. Schewe, the supervisory archivist at the Roosevelt Library, believes that Roosevelt died before any arrangements could be made.

49. Nelson Rockefeller to Edwin Kyle, 2, 6 July 1945, *FRUS* 9: 1084–1086.

50. U.S. Department of State memorandum to Guatemalan embassy, 28

May 1947, *FRUS* 8: 705–706; memo of conversation by U.S. public affairs officer in Guatemalan embassy, 9 January 1950, *FRUS* 2: 865.

51. Edward Miller to Patterson, 27 July 1949, *FRUS* 2: 656–657; CIA, *Review of the World Situation*, 17 August 1949.

52. Patterson memorandum of conversation with businessmen, 27 October 1948, Richard C. Patterson Papers, "Ambassador to Guatemala, 1948–1951," Truman Library.

53. Kyle to Truman, 21 February 1947, PPF, General File "K"; Truman to Kyle, 28 February 1947, PPF, General File "K"; Truman to Kyle, 20 March 1947, PPF, "3126"; Patterson to Truman, 17 December 1948, PSF, "Guatemala," all in the Truman Papers.

54. FBI reports to the State Department are extensive and have remained closed to the public until declassified under the Freedom of Information Act. For a sampling of their contents, see Hoover to Frederick B. Lyon (State Department's chief of the Division of Foreign Activity Correlation), 10 October 1945, NA 814.00B/10-1045; 16 May 1946, NA 814.00B/5-1646; 14 January 1946, NA 814.00B/1-1446; 5 April 1946, NA 814.00B/4-546; 19 April 1946, NA 814.00B/4-1946; 9 July 1946, NA 814.00B/7-946; 15 July 1946, NA 814.00B/7-1546; 17 September 1946, NA 814.00B/9-1746; 17 December 1946, NA 814.00B/12-1746.

The objectivity of the FBI's sources is suspect. Given that these informants cooperated fully with the United States under Ubico and that Arévalo enjoyed overwhelming support from Guatemala's intellectuals, armed forces, middle class, and Indian laborers, it is safe to conclude that the FBI's sources came primarily from Guatemala's traditional elite, which supported Ubico. As Grieb correctly writes, Ubico "exhibited a passionate hatred of communism," equating it with "criminality and political opposition" and judging that "anyone who disrupted the public order or opposed his regime was automatically espousing communism." Ubico treated such elements, chief among which were outlawed labor unionists, extremely harshly, with automatic imprisonment being the least severe penalty. The labor organizers comprised the majority of those Guatemalans whom former Ubico supporters were now identifying as Communists to the FBI. See Grieb, *Guatemalan Caudillo*, pp. 33–34.

55. Robert Wilson to Robert Newbegin (chief, Division of Caribbean Affairs), "Indications of Communism in Guatemala," 6 May 1948, NA 814.00B/5-648.

56. Edward D. Moffit to secretary of state, "Spanish Foreign Office Views on Communist Activities in Guatemala," 5 March 1948, NA 814.00B/3-548.

57. Robert Lovett to U.S. embassy in Guatemala, 7 October 1947, NA 814.00B/10-747.

58. Wells to the Honorable Secretary of State, "Communism in Guatemala," 6 May 1948, NA 814.00B/5-648.

59. Hoover to Lyon, 24 May 1946, NA 814.00B/5-2446; Andrew E. Donovan II to secretary of state, 2 January 1947, NA 814.00/1-247.

60. Wells to secretary of state, "Communism in Guatemala."
61. Hoover to Jack D. Neal, 8 January 1947, NA 814.00B/1-847; Moffit to secretary of state, "Spanish Foreign Office Views"; Bennett, "Some Aspects of Communist Penetration in Guatemala."
62. Bennett, "Some Aspects of Communist Penetration in Guatemala."
63. Guatemalan labor organized the Confederation of Workers of Guatemala immediately following the October revolution. In November 1945, the Syndical Federation of Guatemala, composed primarily of railway workers, split off to form another union. Pinto Usaga became the latter's secretary general in 1946 and, the following year, negotiated its reintegration with the parent organization. Later this combination became the National Committee of Union Syndicates, with Gutiérrez elected the secretary general.
64. Bennett, "Some Aspects of Communist Penetration in Guatemala"; interview with Luis Cardoza y Aragón, in NACLA, *Guatemala*, p. 55; House of Representatives, *Report of the Subcommittee to Investigate Communist Aggression*, pp. 7–8.
65. Bush, *Organized Labor*, p. 7; American University, *Case Study*, p. 45; Hoover to Lyon, 3 July 1946, NA 814.00B/7-346.
66. Wilson to Newbegin, "Indications of Communism in Guatemala."
67. George Meany, "The Last Five Years: How the American Federation of Labor Fights Communism around the World," p. 2.
68. House of Representatives, *Report of the Subcommittee to Investigate Communist Aggression*, pp. 4–5; Wells to secretary of state, 19 December 1947, FRUS 8: 718–719.
69. Woodward to secretary of state, 10 July 1945, NA 814.00/7-1045; Wells to secretary of state, 12 December 1947, NA 814.00B/12-1247.
70. Wells to secretary of state, 10 March 1949, NA 814.00B/3-1049; Department of State, *Case History*, introduction.
71. Wells to secretary of state, 12 December 1947, NA 814.00/12-1247.
72. Moffitt to secretary of state, "Spanish Foreign Office Views"; Jack D. Neal to Wilson, 19 March 1948, NA 814.00B/3-1948. When discussing the divided State Department thinking regarding the United States policy toward Palestine, Harry Truman lamented, "I am sorry to say that there were some among them who were also inclined to be anti-Semitic." See his *Memoirs by Harry S. Truman: Years of Trial and Hope*, p. 164. While García Granados was in exile in 1944, the State Department received a memorandum from the United States embassy in Costa Rica, describing him as "a democrat . . . as opposed to the Communists." See memorandum to State Department from embassy at Costa Rica, 30 June 1944, NA 814.00/6-3044. In 1950 he ran for president against Arbenz.
73. James C. Sappington 3d to secretary of state, 18 September 1946, NA 810.00B/9-1846; Wilson memorandum of conversation, 13 November 1947, NA 814.00B/11-1347; Wells to secretary of state, 29 April 1948, NA 814.00B/4-2948; Wells to secretary of state, "Communism in Guatemala"; Bursley to secretary of state, 27 April 1949, NA 813.00B/

4-2749. Guatemala's opposition to Franco's dictatorship makes the objectivity of the Spanish Foreign Office's condemnation of the Guatemalan government suspect. It should also be added that, under Ubico, Guatemala was the first nation to extend Franco's rebel government diplomatic recognition and to welcome a minister accredited by the generalissimo's regime.

74. Bennett, "Some Aspects of Communist Penetration in Guatemala."
75. *Facts on File Yearbook*, 1947, p. 277H-5; HAR 3 (August 1950): 13; United States House of Representatives, Committee on Foreign Affairs, *Inter-American Affairs*, pp. 131–138.
76. *New York Times*, 18 July 1950; speech by Mr. Ismael González-Arévalo, foreign minister and head of Guatemala's UN delegation to the UN General Assembly, 21 September 1950, OF 439, Truman Papers; Senate, *Executive Sessions*, 3: 355; CIA, *Review of the World Situation*, 16 August 1950.
77. Eisenhower, *White House Years*, pp. 421–422.
78. Braden, "Syllabus"; John Moors Cabot, *Toward Our Common American Destiny*, p. 87.
79. N. Leonard Jarvis to secretary of state, 15 July 1949, NA 814.00B/7-1549.
80. U.S. Department of State policy statement, 17 August 1948, NA 711.14/8-1748.
81. Memo of conversation by the director of the Office of American Republics (Daniels), 19 March 1948, FRUS 9: 495; U.S. Department of State memorandum, 13 May 1949, NA 711.14/5-1349; U.S. Department of State memorandum, 15 September 1949, NA 711.14/9-1549; memo by Ernest V. Siracusa of the Division of Central American and Pan American Affairs, 4 August 1949, FRUS 2: 455–457; C. Patterson to secretary of state, 12 May 1949, FRUS 2: 444.
82. Patterson to secretary of state, 12 May 1949, FRUS 2: 445.
83. CIA, *Review of the World Situation*, 12 May 1948, 15 June 1949, 19 October 1949. This divided alignment was nothing new. Prior to World War II, rumors circulated that a "Dictators' League" existed among Nicaragua's Somoza, El Salvador's Hernández Martínez, and Guatemala's Ubico. In fact the three did conduct negotiations, but their jealousies prevented any agreement. Nevertheless, the possibility of such a coalition explains, at least in part, the genesis of the Caribbean Legion and also the antidictator element of Arévalo's foreign policy. See Grieb, *Guatemalan Caudillo*, pp. 203–204.
84. Theodore Geiger, *Communism versus Progress in Guatemala*, p. 24.
85. "Informed public" refers to journalists and such advisory groups as the Council on Foreign Relations and the National Planning Association.
86. Wells to secretary of state, "Communism in Guatemala"; Wells to Department of State, 15 November 1950, FRUS 2: 922; *New York Times*, 17 April 1950. At the special request of *Times* publisher Arthur Sulzberger, Will Lissner, the paper's Soviet specialist, spent the next month in Guatemala. He stayed at the San Carlos Hotel, coincidentally in a

room right next to Neruda's. Lissner later wrote Edward Bernays that Neruda often lavishly entertained, at the Guatemalan government's expense, a host of Communists. Neruda invited Lissner to these gatherings, enabling the reporter to prepare file cards that "included several hundred names of [Communist] leaders, mostly nationals but a significant minority of foreigners." Lissner to Bernays, 24 October 1976. Both Mr. Lissner and Mr. Bernays kindly permitted me to acquire a copy of this letter.

87. In 1948 the Arévalo government dispatched missions to other American republics and the Balkan countries to study their land reform programs, intending to use the findings with respect to collectivizing the land expropriated from the Germans during World War II. United Fruit and other large Guatemalan landowners expressed the fear that this was only an initial step and that their properties would be placed in danger.

88. Wilson to Newbegin, "Indications of Communism in Guatemala."

89. Ibid.; State Department memorandum, 22 May 1947, NA 814.00B/5-2247.

90. Patterson confidential meeting with Dr. Bernardo Aldana, 18 August 1949, "Ambassador to Guatemala, 1948–1951, Crisis," Patterson Papers; Acheson to U.S. embassy in Guatemala, 28 February 1950, FRUS 2: 867–868.

91. "State Department's Dispute with Guatemala," *Nation* 170 (22 April 1950): 358–359.

92. *Who Was Who in America*, 1961–1968; Anna Rothe, *Current Biography*, 1946; Galich, *Por qué lucha Guatemala*, p. 208; J. P. McElvoy, "Trouble in Our Own Backyard," *Reader's Digest* 57 (August 1950): 7; Herbert L. Matthews, "Diplomatic Relations," in the American Assembly, Columbia University, *The United States and Latin America*, p. 142.

93. Inman, *New Day*, p. 4.

94. Ubico bestowed the Order of the Quetzal on Spruille Braden for his lengthy service in Latin America. After Braden's vitriolic attack on the Guatemalan government in 1953, the National Assembly decreed that the award be canceled. Braden never returned the medal, and it was "reinstated" following Arbenz's overthrow. AMEMBASSY, Guatemala, to Department of State, "Chronology of 1953 Events in Guatemala," 15 March 1954, NA 714.00/3-1554; Braden interview.

95. Address of the minister of foreign relations at the awarding of the Order of the Quetzal to Edwin J. Kyle by the government of Guatemala, 22 February 1949, Kyle Papers.

96. Extension of remarks by the Honorable Luther A. Johnson to the U.S. House of Representatives, 20 June 1946, Kyle Papers; Kyle to Professor Liberty Hyde Bailey, 29 March 1946, Kyle Papers.

97. Kyle to Truman, 20 April 1948, OF 301, Truman Papers; Kyle to Secretary of State George C. Marshall, 20 April 1948, Kyle Papers; Truman to Patterson, 29 September 1948, OF 558, Truman Papers.

98. Patterson to Ydígoras Fuentes, 28 February 1949, "Ambassador to Guatemala, 1948–1951, Appointment," Patterson Papers.
99. John A. Barnett (public relations officer) to Patterson, 3 January 1949, NA 711.14/1-349.
100. Patterson confidential meeting with Dr. Bernardo Aldana, 18 August 1949, "Ambassador to Guatemala, 1948–1951, Crisis," Patterson Papers.
101. U.S. Department of State, "Memorandum of Conversation," 24 March 1950, in Carrollton Press, *Declassified Documents Quarterly Catalogue* 1: 179C.
102. Inman, *New Day*, p. 45.
103. Department of State, "Memorandum of Conversation," 24 March 1950.
104. Nicholson (chief of the Division of Security) to Mann (director of the Office of Middle American Affairs), 5 April 1950, *FRUS* 2: 876; Acheson to Patterson, 25 March 1950, "Ambassador to Guatemala, 1948–1951, Crisis," Patterson Papers; Patterson to secretary of state, 26 March 1950, in Carrollton Press, Inc., *The Declassified Documents Retrospective Collection*, p. 489H; Edward Clark (Office of Middle American Affairs) to Edward Miller, 6 April 1950, *FRUS* 2: 877; *New York Times*, 6 April 1950.
105. In a later congressional hearing, John Peurifoy inaccurately testified that Patterson was declared *persona non grata*. See House of Representatives, *Ninth Interim Report of Hearings*, p. 135.
106. Undersecretary of State James A. Webb to Truman, 9 September 1950, *FRUS* 2: 913.
107. *Congressional Record*, 82d Cong., 1st sess., 1951, 97, pt. 3: 3803–3805.
108. Truman to Patterson, n.d., OF 558, Truman Papers.

5. From Truman to Eisenhower: The Road to Intervention

1. Wells to secretary of state, "Communism in Guatemala."
2. Diary entry, 11 June 1949, Eisenhower Diary, "December 1948 to July 1949."
3. In his previously cited 1945 memorandum on Arévalo, John Griffiths wrote, "I think we are sufficiently accustomed to the local practice of listing as Communists all those who are opposed to the present government [probably a reference to the Ubico administration]."
4. For example, shortly after his February 1950 West Virginia speech, McCarthy attacked the soon-to-be ambassador to Guatemala, John Peurifoy, then Dean Acheson's deputy undersecretary of state for administration. Nevertheless, testifying at the post-Arbenz congressional hearings, Peurifoy applied McCarthy-like inferences to the ousted Guatemalan president. See House of Representatives, *Ninth Interim Report of Hearings*, p. 124.
5. Patterson, fifth draft of speech to Rotary Club, 24 March 1950, "Ambassador to Guatemala, 1948–1951," Patterson Papers.
6. *Congressional Record*, 83d Cong., 2d sess., 1954, 100, pt. 1: 249.
7. Department of State memorandum, 26 June 1953, NA 611.14/6-2653.

8. Department of State, *Case History*, p. 35. The first page of this study states: "The significance of particular Communist movements and maneuvers in the Western hemisphere cannot be understood except in terms of the worldwide conspiracy which they represent and of which they form a part . . . Guatemalan Communist leaders are the servants of a foreign power which has its capital in Moscow." See also Peurifoy, "Communist Conspiracy in Guatemala," p. 692; *New York Times*, 22 June 1950; House of Representatives, *Report of the Subcommittee to Investigate Communist Aggression*, pp. 6–7. In 1953 Adolf Berle advised the Eisenhower administration that Soviet designs on Guatemala predated World War II, when the then Soviet ambassador to the United States, Constantine Oumansky, worked out a long-range strategy. See Beatrice Bishop Berle and Travis Beal Jacobs, eds., *Navigating the Rapids, 1918–1971: From the Papers of Adolf A. Berle*, p. 617.

9. Dulles kept a copy of Stalin's *Problems of Leninism* on his desk, and his repeated references to it illustrate that throughout these years United States analysts searched for a framework by which they could better understand Communists and their methods. A seminal work in this genre is Nathan Leites, *The Operational Code of the Politburo*. Begun while he was a research associate of the National Policy Committee at Yale University, under the financial sponsorship of the Carnegie Corporation, this study was completed for the Rand Corporation as part of its research program for the United States Air Force. Drawing on the writings of Lenin and Stalin, the volume attempts to provide a guide to Soviet behavior. The foreword reads, "It is hoped that other students of Soviet affairs will examine the rules of Soviet political conduct suggested in this book and test them against actual political and military events." Eudocio Racines' *The Yenan Way*, which appeared the same year, presented a more concrete analysis.

10. Racines, *Yenan Way*, pp. 113–163.

11. United States House of Representatives, Committee on Foreign Affairs, *Selected Executive Session Hearings of the Committee, 1951–1956*, vol. 16: *The Middle East, Africa, and Inter-American Affairs*, p. 403.

12. In fact, as will be discussed in chapter 6, an arms shipment from Czechoslovakia to Guatemala in May 1954 was the catalyst for the United States intervention.

13. House of Representatives, *Ninth Interim Report of Hearings*, p. 199.

14. Robert J. Alexander, "Guatemalan Communists," *Canadian Forum* 34 (July 1954): 81. See also James, *Red Design for the Americas*, pp. 20–22, and "Lessons of Guatemala," *New Leader* 37 (12 July 1954): 3; Johnston, "Some Principles of Communist Unconventional Warfare."

    In January 1954, the embassy in Guatemala telegrammed Secretary Dulles that unconfirmed press reports claimed that Arbenz's police had arrested Rubén Villatoro, president of Guatemala's National Union of Free Workers, and, after beating him, had deported him to Mexico without money or papers. The embassy suggested that the State Department notify Alexander, who would arrange with the American Federation of Labor to publicly protest the incident. An article by Villatoro appeared in the federation's journal. See Krieg to secretary of state, 29 January 1954, NA 714.00/1-2954; Rubén D. Villatoro, "Guatemala Smashes Free Unions," *American Federationist* 61 (May 1954): 23–24, 28.

15. Wells to secretary of state, "Communism in Guatemala."

16. Andrew E. Donovan II to secretary of state, 30 January 1946, NA 814.00B/1-3046; Thomas Mann to Willard Barber, 14 July 1950, *FRUS* 2: 908–909.

17. Edwin J. Kyle to secretary of state, 8 May 1946, NA 711.00/5-846; Andrew E. Donovan II to secretary of state, 10 May 1946, NA 814.00B/5-1046; U.S. Department of State memorandum, 1 September 1948, NA 814.00/9-148; James A. Webb to Truman, *FRUS* 2: 912; Wells to secretary of state, "Communism in Guatemala."

18. Wells to Department of State, "Speculation Regarding Arbenz's Attitude and Future Policy toward the Communists," 15 November 1950, NA 714.001/11-1550.

19. Senate, *Executive Sessions*, 3: 345.

20. Wells, "Speculation Regarding Arbenz's Attitude."

21. Bennett, "Some Aspects of Communist Penetration in Guatemala"; Patterson to Samuel Zemurray, 11 August 1949, "Ambassador to Guatemala, 1948–1951, American Interests," Patterson Papers; *New York Times*, 21 February, 23 June 1950; "Cold War in Our Tropic Supply Line," *Newsweek* 35 (17 April 1950): 46–47; *Intelligence Digest: A Review of World Affairs* 12, chap. 7 (June 1950): 9. I found this journal in the Truman Papers, OF 558. Also, on at least one occasion, UFCO executive John McClintock excerpted an article from *Intelligence Digest* on Communism in Guatemala and sent it to Thomas Mann. See McClintock to Mann and enclosure, 8 May 1952, NA 714.001/5-852.

22. Hunt interview; William F. Lewis, colonel, USAF, State Department dispatch, 22 July 1949, NA 814.00/7-2249; Jack D. Neal to Wilson, 19 March 1948, NA 814.00B/3-1948.

23. *HAR* 7 (August 1954): 12. For the later consensus view of Arbenz, see Department of State, *Case History*, and House of Representatives, *Report of the Subcommittee to Investigate Communist Aggression.*

24. United States Department of State, Division of Research for American Republics, Office of Intelligence Research, OIR Report No. 5123, "Guatemala: Communist Influence," 23 October 1950; Milton K. Wells to Department of State, "Guatemala: Communist Influence" and enclosures, 12 January 1951, NA 714.001/1-1251. For a related document, see Milton K. Wells to Department of State, "Communism in Guatemala" and enclosures, 27 November 1950, NA 714.001/11-2750.

25. W. Tapley Bennett, "A Review of Communist Influence in Guatemala," 31 May 1951, attached to Bennett to Nufer, Mann, and Miller, "Review of Recent Developments in Communist Penetration of Guatemala," 7 June 1951, NA 714.001/6-751.

26. Bennett, "Review of Communist Influence in Guatemala."

27. Miller to Bennett, "Review of Recent Developments in Communist Penetration of Guatemala," 7 June 1951, NA FW 714.001/6-751.

28. For example, see Andrew B. Wardlaw to Department of State, 30 May 1951, "Negotiations of New Labor Contracts between the United Fruit Company and the Unions at Tiquisate and Bananera," 30 May 1951, NA 814.062/5-3051; Krieg to secretary of state, 29 September 1951, NA 814.062/9-2951; Wardlaw to Department of State, "Informal Conciliation Hearing of Dispute between United Fruit Company and Its Employees," 5 October 1951, NA 814.062/10-551; Wardlaw to Department of State, "Interview of Representatives of the United Fruit Company with Minister of Economy and Labor Regarding Company Problems in Guatemala," 19 October 1951, NA 814.062/10-1951; Rudolf E. Schoenfeld to Department of State, "Message of President Arbenz to CGTG [General Confederation of Workers of Guatemala] Conference Regarding the United Fruit Company," 21 February 1952, NA 814.062/2-2152.

29. Memorandum of conversation by Ernest V. Siracusa, assistant officer in charge of Central American and Panamanian affairs, 29 December 1950, *FRUS* 2: 928–930; Department of State office memorandum, 21 May 1953, NA 611.14/5-2153.

30. Department of State policy statement, "Relations of the United States and Guatemala, with Special Reference to the Concern of the United States over Communist Activity in Guatemala," 2 May 1951, *FRUS* 2: 1428; Department of State memorandum of a conversation (Cabot, Fisher, Toriello), 25 March 1953, NA 611.14/3-2553.

31. Department of State memorandum from de Zengotita, 7 June 1949, NA 711.14/6-749; Department of State memorandum, 1 August 1949, NA 814.00/8-149; Department of State memorandum, "To Assess Our Current Relations with Guatemala," 16 May 1950.

32. Memorandum from de Zengotita, 7 June 1949; Acheson to U.S. embassy in Guatemala, 11 October 1950, *FRUS* 2: 917–918; Paul C. Daniels to Patterson, 14 June 1949, NA 711.14/6-1449; Department of State memorandum, 1 August 1949, NA 814.00/8-149; Department of State memorandum, "To Assess Our Current Relations."

33. State Department memorandum, 1 August 1949, NA 814.00/8-149; Congressional Quarterly Service, *Congress and the Nation: A Review of Government and Politics in the Postwar Years*, 1: 213–214.

34. Sanat Lahiri's address on presenting the 1979 International Public Relations Association President's Award to Dr. Edward Bernays, 7 November 1979, author's possession.

35. Lissner to Bernays, 24 October 1976.

36. Turner's series in the *New York Herald Tribune*, 8–10, 12, 13 February 1950, is of special interest. Other articles are cited throughout the notes of this study. See also Bernays, *Biography of an Idea*, pp. 760–761.

37. Interview with Edward L. Bernays, 25 August 1979.

38. Herbert L. Matthews to Leon Shimkin, 17 November 1966, author's

possession. Mr. Matthews reiterated his high regard for Mr. Bernays in a letter to me, 20 July 1977.

39. Bernays, *Biography of an Idea*, pp. 760–761; Matthews to author, 20 July 1977. Matthews' criticism of United States policy in Latin America reached its zenith during the early years of the Cuban revolution. His views on the Castro government prompted Whiting Willauer, the former United States ambassador to Honduras, to call him "Herbert Matthews of the Caribbean Communists." But, during the Guatemalan episode, Assistant Secretary of State Edward Miller wrote the *New York Times* editor, "It is something of a rarity in these days to have had the privilege of working with someone with such a high regard for accuracy and objectivity and such an ability to listen to the other fellow's point of view even though you do not agree with it." See United States Senate, Judiciary Committee, *Report of the Subcommittee to Investigate the Administration of the Internal Security Act and Other Internal Security Laws*; Miller to Matthews, 30 December 1952, Edward G. Miller, Jr., Papers, Assistant Secretary of State Correspondence File "M," Truman Library.

40. Bernays interview.

41. Arévalo, *Guatemala, la democracia y el imperio*, pp. 47–48.

42. An excellent representation of the reporting is Turner's previously cited series in the *New York Herald Tribune*. For examples of the *New York Times* reporting by Calhoun, Lissner, and Sydney Gruson, see the issues of 21 February, 22 June, 15 November 1950; 5, 8 June 1951; 25 February, 31 December 1952; 23 January 1953.

43. *New York Times*, 6 March, 4 August 1953; 15 March, 10 May, 4 June 1954.

44. *HAR* 7 (February 1954): 13; Department of State incoming telegram from Guatemala City to secretary of state, 9 February 1954, NA 714.00/2-954; Kirchwey, "Guatemala Guinea Pig," p. 21; *New York Times*, 13 March 1954. Arbenz permitted Gruson to return in May.

45. Bernays interview. Bernays' office, nevertheless, was an excellent source for reporters. For example, during the Castillo Armas invasion they huddled around the company's Boston headquarters to obtain almost hourly progress reports. See Tad Szulc, "US and ITT in Chile," *New Republic* 168 (30 June 1973): 21.

46. Inman, *New Day*, p. 48. For the text of the interview, see "Statement of the President of Guatemala, Juan José Arévalo, to Dr. Samuel Guy Inman," NA 714.001/"date unknown."

47. According to the journalist Harrison Salisbury, the United States government did on one occasion influence the *Times'* reporting. Salisbury's narrative, ironically, focuses on Gruson. Arbenz had permitted Gruson to return to Guatemala in May 1954, in time to witness the arrival of a shipment of arms from Czechoslovakia. As will be discussed in the next chapter, the arrival of the arms infuriated Washington, which condemned it as positive evidence of the Soviet conspiracy.

In reporting the events, Gruson expressed his concern that by reacting so strongly the United States might further arouse Guatemalan nationalism. His criticism upset Ambassador Peurifoy and, perhaps more important, the CIA's Allen Dulles and Frank Wisner. Evidently Wisner suspected Gruson of Communist leanings. Salisbury contends that Dulles had Wisner's suspicions passed on to Arthur Sulzberger, who ordered Gruson to cover Guatemalan developments from Mexico City. Given Gruson's record of opposing Arbenz, Salisbury's account, if accurate, reveals how deeply the cold war ethos skewed United States perspectives. See Harrison E. Salisbury, *Without Fear or Favor*, pp. 478–482.

48. Edward L. Bernays, *Propaganda*, p. 9.
49. Bernard C. Cohen, *The Press and Foreign Policy*, pp. 40–41, 134–135. For an extreme view that places much of the blame for the cold war on the leading publications, see James Aronson, *The Press and the Cold War*.

   Cohen's analysis should not be confused with that of such recent commentators as Carl Bernstein, who contend that during this period reporters for leading newspapers and magazines, in particular the *New York Times*, acted as agents for the CIA. While unable to discover the specific names of the cooperating correspondents or any connection with Guatemala, Bernstein asserts that Latin America was a leading area for this type of clandestine activity. Probably a more accurate description of the relationship between the press and intelligence gathering is that the CIA questioned reporters returning from assignments in certain regions about what information they were able to obtain or, in some cases where friendships existed, asked a journalist to keep an eye out for certain people or events. CIA operatives also might have used journalistic covers, although it is unlikely that a career journalist would have been turned into an undercover agent. See Carl Bernstein, "The CIA and the Media," *Rolling Stone* 250 (20 October 1977): 55–67; Bernstein to author, 16 November 1977. See also Peter Biskind, "How the CIA Manages the Media," *Seven Days* 2 (January 1978): 27; interview with Richard M. Bissell, Jr., 1 November 1977.
50. House of Representatives, *Executive Session Hearings*, 16: 397; McCann, *American Company*, pp. 56–57; Alexander Wiley to Theodore F. Green, 22 May 1950, in Carrollton Press, *Declassified Documents Retrospective*, p. 490B.
51. *Congressional Record*, 82d Cong., 2d sess., 1952, 98, pt. 2: 2279.
52. *Congressional Record*, 82d Cong., 2d sess., 1952, 98, pt. 3: 2977–2978.
53. McCann, *American Company*, p. 54; MHM memorandum for the president, 7 February 1939, OF 439, "1938–1941," FDR Papers; Bernays, *Biography of an Idea*, p. 770; Bernays interview.
54. Patterson to Zemurray, 11 January 1950, "Ambassador to Guatemala," Patterson Papers.
55. *Congressional Record*, 81st Cong., 1st sess., 1949, 95, pt. 1: 1172.
56. *Congressional Record*, 81st Cong., 1st sess., 1949, 95, pt. 2: 1464.

57. U.S. Department of State, notes of undersecretary's meeting, 15 June 1951, *FRUS* 2: 1441; *Congressional Record*, 81st Cong., 2d sess., 1950, 96, pt. 16: A5164–A5165; 82d Cong., 1st sess., 1951, 97, pt. 7: 9808–9809; *New York Times*, 26 February 1952.

58. Memorandum of Undersecretary of State Webb's meeting, 2 July 1950, *FRUS* 2: 902. Information on Braden, Cabot, and Miller can be obtained from the appropriate volumes of *Who's Who*. The connection of Sullivan and Cromwell will be discussed more fully with regard to John Foster Dulles.

59. Most of UFCO's correspondence contained the reports of William Taillon, the company's general manager in Guatemala, and press clippings dealing with Communist subversion. For example, see, with their attachments, John C. McClintock to Thomas Mann, 25 September 1950, NA 714.001/9-2550; McClintock to Ernest V. Siracusa, 29 May 1951, NA 814.062/5-2951; Kenneth H. Redmond to Edward G. Miller, Jr., 10 December 1951, NA 814.062/12-1051; Redmond to Mann, 5 February 1952, NA 814.062/2-552; Department of State memorandum of conversation, "United Fruit Company Difficulties in Guatemala," participants: John McClintock, Edward Clark, 5 March 1952, NA 814.062/3-552.

60. Mann to Murphy, "Latin America and United States Policy," 11 December 1952, PSF, "Latin America," Truman Papers; Mann, letter to author, 1 September 1978; memorandum of conversation by the director of the Office of Middle American Affairs (Mann), 15 May 1950, *FRUS* 2: 888–889.

61. In addition to Martin C. Needler's *The United States and the Latin American Revolution*, Walter LaFeber's crisp essay, "Latin American Policy," provides an excellent analysis of Mann and his now famous "Mann Doctrine." I thank Professor LaFeber for furnishing me with a copy of his essay, which appears in Robert Divine, ed., *Exploring the Johnson Years*, pp. 63–90.

62. Mann, memorandum of conversation, 15 May 1950; Mann to Murphy, "Latin America and U.S. Policy." Throughout 1951 State Department policy continued to rely on increasing economic pressure on Arbenz, although, as the Bureau of Inter-American affairs wrote in June, "It is considered important that we refrain from stating officially or privately that our actions [exerting economic pressure] are related to internal conditions in Guatemala." Paper prepared for the undersecretary's meeting, "Current Relations with Guatemala," 12 June 1951, *FRUS* 2: 1439. See also Department of State, "Relations of the U.S. and Guatemala."

63. Herbert L. Matthews, *A World in Revolution*, pp. 262–264; Matthews to author, 20 July 1977; Rolland Welch to John L. Ohmans, 11 May 1953, NA 714.00/5-1153.

64. For more on Somoza, his relations with the United Nations, and his opposition to the Guatemalan revolution, see Gondi, "Democracy in Latin America," p. 82; Martin and Martin, "Four Strong Men," p. 424; Braden interview; Fletcher Warren to secretary of state, 27 June 1945,

NA 814.00/6-2745; Wilson to secretary of state, 23 July 1947, NA 814.00/7-2347; Thorp to U.S. embassy in Guatemala, 19 March 1948, NA 814.00/3-1948; Capus Waynick to secretary of state, 29 July 1949, NA 814.00/7-2949.

Revealingly, when President Eisenhower attended the 1956 meeting of the Organization of American States in Panama, he thought that Somoza, along with Stroessner of Paraguay, "stood out"; see diary entry, 25 July 1956, Eisenhower Diary.

65. Matthews, *World in Revolution*, pp. 262–263; Welch to Ohmans, 11 May 1953.

66. Matthews, *World in Revolution*, pp. 263–264.

67. Welch to Ohmans, 11 May 1953.

68. For a good overview of McCarthy and McCarthyism, see Robert Griffith, *The Politics of Fear: Joseph R. McCarthy and the Senate*. A more specialized study that deemphasizes McCarthy's role in the politics of anti-Communism is Richard M. Fried, "Electoral Politics and McCarthyism: The 1950 Election," in Robert Griffith and Athan Theoharis, eds., *The Specter: Original Essays on the Cold War and the Origins of McCarthyism*, pp. 190–222.

69. In the Stouffer study of popular attitudes toward Communism, published in 1955, Eisenhower trailed FBI Director J. Edgar Hoover by only 3 percentage points in a poll to determine the individual in the United States most trusted to fight against the Communists. McCarthy ran third with only 8 percent (Hoover got 27 percent, Eisenhower 24 percent). Significantly, when asked whether their trust was based on their knowledge of the individual's opinions or just their confidence in him, only 19 percent responded that they knew Eisenhower's opinions; 65 percent had confidence in him as a person. In contrast, 33 percent based their trust in Hoover on their knowledge of his opinions, while only 55 percent did so because they had confidence in him. McCarthy scored 58 percent and 31 percent, respectively. See Samuel Stouffer, *Communism, Conformity and Civil Liberties*, pp. 330–331, reprinted in Frank J. Donner, *The Age of Surveillance: The Aims and Methods of America's Political Intelligence System*, p. 118.

70. See chapter 1 for these quotations from Eisenhower's diary. See also Eisenhower to William Robinson, 4 August 1954, WF, Diary Series, "August 1954"; Dwight D. Eisenhower, *Oral History Interview*, COH; Eisenhower, *White House Years*, pp. 421–427. Eisenhower's close aide, Andrew Goodpaster, comments that as a general and a president Eisenhower constantly thought in terms of move and countermove, anticipating game theorists by many years. See Goodpaster, COH.

71. Dulles headed the team responsible for the Republican foreign policy planks during the 1952 election and was Taft's choice for secretary of state as well as Eisenhower's. During his tenure he would brook no intrusions into his domain, as Nelson Rockefeller and Harold Stassen emphatically learned.

72. Immerman, "Eisenhower and Dulles," pp. 21–38.

73. Many of the previously cited works analyze the politics and policies of the Eisenhower administration. For additional information, see Herbert Parmet, *Eisenhower and the American Crusades*; Peter Lyon, *Eisenhower: Portrait of a Hero*; Charles C. Alexander, *Holding the Line: The Eisenhower Era, 1952–1961*; and William B. Ewald, Jr., *Eisenhower the President: Crucial Days, 1951–1960*.

74. Blasier, *Hovering Giant*, pp. 89–90.

75. In addition to his previously cited *Intervention and Revolution*, Richard J. Barnet's *Roots of War* provides an excellent analysis of United States foreign policy makers. See also Kolko and Kolko, *Limits of Power*.

76. Paul Hoffman, *Lions in the Street: The Inside Story of the Great Wall Street Law Firms*, pp. 22–23.

77. Ibid., p. 533. See also Hoopes, *The Devil and John Foster Dulles*, pp. 25–28; Melville and Melville, *Guatemala*, p. 77; NACLA, *Guatemala*, pp. 164–165.

78. For much of this information see *Who's Who*. See also Frederick J. Cook, "The CIA," *Nation* 192 (24 June 1961): 537–541; NACLA, *Guatemala*, pp. 164–165; Jonas, "Test Case for the Hemisphere," p. 40. For Dulles' conversations with Cutler, see telephone call to General Cutler, 26 May 1954, Dulles Papers, Telephone Conversations (hereafter, DPTC), "White House Telephone Memos, 1 January to 30 June 1954 (1)," Eisenhower Library.

79. McCann, *American Company*, pp. 50–58; Claude Julien, *America's Empire*, p. 344; Gordon, "Subversion," p. 141; Laurence H. Shoup and William Minter, *Imperial Brain Trust: The Council on Foreign Relations and United States Foreign Policy*, pp. 198–199; Geiger, *Communism versus Progress*.

80. *New York Times*, 23 January, 3 March, 1 August, 4 August 1953; 10 May, 4 June 1954. These are just representative samplings of the *Times'* coverage. Other leading newspapers and magazines echoed the analysis.

81. Matthews, *World in Revolution*, p. 261.

82. Braden to Dulles, 29 October 1953; Dulles to Ambassador William T. Pheiffer, 13 November 1953; Dulles to Braden, 13 November 1953; Braden to Dulles, 20 November 1953; Dulles to Braden, 18 December 1953; Braden to Dulles, 23 December 1953, Spruille Braden Papers, "Dulles, John Foster," Columbia University, New York City, New York. Ironically, the plaque characterized Braden and three Latin American political leaders as "despicable agents" of "international communism." The three others were Rómulo Betancourt, Ramón Grau San Martín, and, of all people, Juan José Arévalo. The grouping prompted Braden to write Dulles, "The coupling of my name with these three, of itself, is something which cannot be accepted with equanimity." Braden attributed the attack to Trujillo's "rage" engendered by "my firm defense of the interests of the United States."

83. Acheson, *Present at the Creation*, p. 160.

84. Adolf Berle to Louis Crane, 24 January 1955, Adolf Berle Papers, "Latin

America (General 1953–1956)," Franklin D. Roosevelt Library, Hyde Park, New York.

85. Spruille Braden, *Diplomats and Demagogues*, pp. 400–401.
86. Address by the Honorable Spruille Braden, former ambassador and assistant secretary of state, chairman, New York City Anti-Crime Committee, before the United States Inter-American Council, 24 April 1952, "Speeches, Miscellaneous, 1950s," Braden Papers.
87. Braden, "Syllabus."
88. *New York Times*, 26 March 1953; AMEMBASSY, Guatemala, to Department of State, "Chronology of 1953 Events in Guatemala," 15 March 1954, NA 714.00/3-1554. See also chapter 4, note 94.
89. Bernays interview.
90. For an analysis of the Council on Foreign Relations and its relationship to foreign policy, see Shoup and Minter, *Imperial Brain Trust*.
91. Spruille Braden circular, 30 September 1952, Archives of the Council on Foreign Relations, New York, Records of Groups, vol. 45 (1952–1953), "Political Unrest in Latin America" (hereafter, CFR-LA); discussion meeting report, 18 November 1952, CFR-LA; discussion meeting report, 15 October 1952, CFR-LA.
92. Discussion meeting report, 18 March 1953, CFR-LA; Adolf Berle, "For the Discussion Group on Political Unrest in Latin America," 15 May 1953, CFR-LA; discussion meeting report, 15 May 1953, CFR-LA.
93. 18 June 1952 entry, "Diary 1952" (hereafter, Berle Diary), Berle Papers. I cite the original diary because in almost all cases the editors of *Navigating the Rapids* have either omitted the relevant entries or deleted critical passages.
94. 17 October 1952, Berle Diary.
95. Rockefeller could not recall the entire incident. Hugh Morrow (assistant to Nelson A. Rockefeller), letter to author, 19 October 1977.
96. 17 October, 31 October, 2 December, 8 December 1952, Berle Diary.
97. Memorandum of conversation with José Figueres, 31 March 1953, Berle Diary.
98. C. D. Jackson memorandum to General Eisenhower, "Appraisal Survey of Our Cold War Effort," 21 November 1952, *Time* File, "Jackson Committee," C. D. Jackson Papers, Eisenhower Library; Eisenhower to James S. Lay, Jr., 24 January 1953, *Time* File, "Jackson Committee," Jackson Papers; 13 November 1952, Berle Diary; "Tentative Working Paper—Outline of Political Counterattack against Soviet Aggression," 17 November 1952, Berle Diary. For more on Jackson, the International Information Activities Committee, and psychological warfare, see Cook, *Declassified Eisenhower*, pp. 122–132, 176–183.
99. "Memorandum: The Guatemalan Problem in Central America," 31 March 1953, Berle Diary.
100. Ibid.
101. 1 April, 25 May 1953, 10 May 1954, Berle Diary; Ydígoras, *My War with Communism*, pp. 49–50.
102. Braden interview.

103. Hunt interview.

104. Cabot, *Our Common Destiny*, p. 119.

6. Project PBSUCCESS: The Preparation

1. Bernard Shanley Diary, entry for 11 March 1953, Eisenhower Library; AMEMBASSY, Guatemala, to Department of State, "Chronology of 1953 Events in Guatemala," 15 March 1954, NA 714.00/3-1554; U.S. Department of State memorandum, 21 May 1953, NA 611.14/5-2153; telephone conversation with Governor Dewey, 27 August 1953, DPTC, "Telephone Memoranda (Excepting to and from White House), 1 July to 31 October 1953 (4)"; minutes of cabinet meeting, 6 October 1953, WF, Cabinet Series; Milton Eisenhower, "Report to the President." Eisenhower's remarks at the 1953 cabinet meeting are given in chapter 1.

2. Mann to author, 1 September 1978; Sherman Adams, *Oral History Interview #3*, COH; Victor Marchetti and John D. Marks, *The CIA and the Cult of Intelligence*, pp. 297–298; Hunt, *Undercover*, p. 96; Greenstein, "Eisenhower as an Activist President," p. 578; Bissell interview; interview with Eleanor Lansing Dulles, 9 October 1979; interview with Milton S. Eisenhower (with Fred I. Greenstein), 1 November 1978.

3. Schlesinger and Kinzer write in *Bitter Fruit* that the official decision to move against Arbenz was made in early August 1953, at a meeting of the 54/12 committee. This date is reasonable, but the committee was not created until 1954. Records of its predecessor, the 10/2 committee, are not available.

4. Braden interview.

5. Hunt interview; Hunt, *Undercover*, pp. 83–85, 97.

6. Bill [Krieg] to Ray [Leddy], 10 November 1953, NA 714.00/11-1053; John Moors Cabot, *First Line of Defense: Forty Years' Experiences of a Career Diplomat.*

7. In *Countercoup* Roosevelt asserts that he refused the assignment of heading up the Guatemalan operation. Two years before his book's publication, however, Roosevelt wrote me that he had "nothing to do with the Guatemalan undertaking in any way," and his lack of experience in Central America makes it unlikely that he would have been offered the job. See Roosevelt, *Countercoup*, pp. 106–108, 210; Roosevelt to author, 1 December 1977.

8. Ydígoras, *My War with Communism*, pp. 50–51; Blasier, *Hovering Giant*, p. 161; William Krieg to Department of State, 29 January 1954, NA 714.00/1-2954.

9. U.S. Department of State draft press release, 1 February 1951, OF 1107, Truman Papers; Eisenhower to Schoenfeld, 11 January 1955, OF 8F, "Schoenfeld," Eisenhower Papers; telephone conversation with Eleanor Dulles, 1 August 1953, DPTC, "Telephone Memoranda (Excepting to and from White House), 1 July to 31 October 1953 (4)."

10. Entries for 3 April, 15 April, 2 May, 1953, *Time* File, "Log 1953 (1)" (hereafter, Jackson Log), Jackson papers; Jackson Log, "1953 (2)," 18 July 1953; memorandum for Robinson McIlvaine, assistant to the assistant

secretary of state, from James C. Hagerty, 8 October 1954, OF 8F, "Peurifoy," Eisenhower Papers; Hunt interview; memorandum for the president, "Chief of Mission Appointments," n.d., Dulles Papers, Subject Series (Eisenhower Library), "Personnel Matter 1953–1954 (2)."

11. *New York Times*, 8 November 1953.

12. Flora Lewis, "Ambassador Extraordinary: John Peurifoy," *New York Times Magazine*, 18 July 1954, pp. 9, 26; HAR 7 (1 August 1954): 12; Drew Pearson, *Diaries, 1949–1959*, p. 299.

13. For information on Peurifoy, see *Who's Who* and *Current Biography*. See also Lewis, "Ambassador Extraordinary," and Senate, *Executive Sessions*, 2: 13, 95.

14. House of Representatives, *Executive Session Hearings*, 16: 486.

15. U.S. Department of State memorandum of conversation, 29 October 1953, attached to AMEMBASSY, Guatemala, to Department of State, 2 November 1953, NA 611.14/11-253; Peurifoy to secretary of state, 19 November 1953, NA 611.14/11-1953; Peurifoy to secretary of state, 23 December 1953, NA 611.14/12-2353; confidential, "Subject: Caracas Meeting—1 March 1953" (sic), "Caracas," JFD Papers; "The Problem of Guatemala," *Time* 63 (11 January 1954): 27.

16. Bissell interview; Cehelsky, "Guatemala's Frustrated Revolution," p. 55; Richard M. Bissell, Jr., *Oral History Interview*, COH; Hunt interview; Hunt, *Undercover*, pp. 97–98.

17. Bissell interview. The transcripts of John Foster Dulles' telephone conversations, housed at the Princeton University and the Eisenhower Library, are replete with calls to and from Allen concerning Guatemala. Specific citations appear in later notes.

18. Bissell interview; Phillips, *Night Watch*, pp. 35–36; taped interview with E. Howard Hunt, 11 September 1979 (in this instance Mr. Hunt kindly sent a tape of his responses to questions I had posed); Wise and Ross, *Invisible Government*, p. 172.

19. Hunt, taped interview; Powers, *The Man Who Kept the Secrets*, p. 86; Bissell interview; Marchetti and Marks, *The CIA*, pp. 33–35.

20. Bissell interview; Hunt interview; Jonas, "Test Case for the Hemisphere," p. 62.

21. Wise and Ross, *Invisible Government*, pp. 167–168; Senate, *Report of the Subcommittee to Investigate the Administration of the Internal Security Act*, pp. 865–866; Hunt interview; transcript of "The Science of Spying," narrated by John Chancellor and produced by Robert Rogers, Ted Yates, and NBC News, originally broadcast 4 May 1965.

22. Whiting Willauer to C. L. Chennault, 27 May 1954, Whiting Willauer Papers, file 16, item 10, Princeton University.

23. Bissell interview; Hunt interview; "Guatemala: The New Junta," *Time* 64 (12 July 1954): 38; Lewis, "Ambassador Extraordinary," p. 9.

24. Dulles phone call to Senator Langer, 29 January 1953, DPTC, "Telephone Memoranda (Excepting to and from White House), 1 January to 30 April 1953 (4)"; Robert C. Hill, letter to author, 16 September 1977; memorandum of telephone conversation with Senator Saltonstall, 19

January 1954, DPTC, "Telephone Memoranda (Excepting to and from White House), 1 January to February 1954 (1)"; C. D. Jackson to Robert Salisbury, 11 April 1958, *Time* File, "Hill, Amb. Robert," Jackson Papers; Jackson memorandum to Emmet Hughes, 12 April 1958, *Time* File, "Hill, Amb. Robert," Jackson Papers.

25. Clark H. Galloway, "A Revolt the U.S. Couldn't Win," *U.S. News & World Report* 37 (2 July 1954): 22; Hunt, *Undercover*, pp. 97–99; Hunt interview.

26. Interview with Córdova Cerna, quoted in Cehelsky, "Guatemala's Frustrated Revolution," pp. 60–62; Hunt, *Undercover*, pp. 97–99; Arévalo, *Guatemala, la democracia y el imperio*, pp. 119–120.

27. *HAR* 7 (July 1954): 11–12; Cehelsky, "Guatemala's Frustrated Revolution," pp. 43, 66–68; Hunt interview. Evidence regarding Castillo Armas' escape is all hearsay. He might, in fact, have bribed a guard.

28. Cehelsky, "Guatemala's Frustrated Revolution," pp. 52–53; H. E. Urist to the ambassador (Peurifoy), 30 December 1953, NA 714.00/12-3053; John De. Erwin to Department of State, 5 November 1953, NA 714.00/11-553; Hunt interview; Braden interview; Bissell interview; *New York Times*, 16 June 1954.

29. Elmer B. Staats, memorandum for the Operations Coordinating Board, "Report on Actions Taken by the United States Information Agency in the Guatemalan Situation," 2 August 1954. (Unless indicated, recently declassified documents like this have no designated decimal file number.)

30. Incoming telegram from Guatemala City to secretary of state, 26 January 1954, NA 714.00/1-2654; AMEMBASSY, Guatemala, to Department of State, 27 January 1954, NA 714.00/1-2754; William Krieg to secretary of state, 29 January 1954, NA 714.00/1-2954; Villatoro, "Guatemala Smashes Free Unions," p. 23.

31. Samuel Guy Inman, *Inter-American Conferences, 1826–1954*, p. 258; Gordon Connell-Smith, *The Inter-American System*, p. 161; José Figueres, *Oral Interview*, Truman Library.

32. Minutes of cabinet meeting, 26 February 1954, WF, Cabinet Series.

33. Organization of American States, *Annals*, 5: 106, 297; OAS, *Agenda of the Tenth Inter-American Conference*; OAS, *Annals*, 6: 10–11.

34. Department of State, *Tenth Inter-American Conference*, pp. 3–4; *Congressional Record*, 83d Cong., 2d sess., 1954, 100, pt. 2: 2306.

35. Confidential, "Subject: Caracas Meeting—1 March 1953" (sic), "Caracas," JFD Papers.

36. Incoming telegram from Guatemala City to secretary of state, 12 February 1954, NA 714.00/2-1254; Burrows to Cabot, draft memorandum on handling of Guatemala at Caracas, 10 February 1954, NA 714.00/2-1054.

37. Department of State, *Tenth Inter-American Conference*, p. 8; telephone conversation with Mr. Allen Dulles, 25 February 1954, DPTC, "Telephone Memoranda (Excepting to and from White House), 1 January to February 1954 (1)"; interview with Herman Phleger, 12 April

1980; report of the proceedings of the U.S. Senate Committee on Foreign Relations, 16 March 1954, "Caracas," JFD Papers; Hickenlooper to Eisenhower, 17 March 1954, OF 116-J (2), Eisenhower Papers.

38. Department of State, *Tenth Inter-American Conference*, pp. 8–9.

39. *New York Times*, 7, 9 March 1954; Dulles, draft of statement, 13 March 1954, "Caracas," JFD Papers.

40. Department of State, *Tenth Inter-American Conference*, p. 9; tenth Inter-American Conference, *Documents of the Plenary Sessions*, 8 March 1954, p. 6, quoted in Connell-Smith, *Inter-American System*, pp. 230–231; Dulles, statement proposing an additional paragraph to U.S. draft resolution on Communist intervention, 11 March 1954, in Department of State, *Tenth Inter-American Conference*, pp. 59–60.

41. Toriello, *La batalla*, p. 76.

42. Dulles, "Intervention," 8 March 1954, PR 121, "Caracas," JFD Papers.

43. Louis M. McDermott, "Guatemala 1954: Intervention or Aggression?" *Rocky Mountain Social Science Journal* 9 (January 1972): 82; Arévalo, *Guatemala, la democracia y el imperio*, pp. 52–55; *New York Times*, 6 March 1954; House of Representatives, *Executive Session Hearings*, 16: 501; tenth Inter-American Conference, *Plenary Sessions*, 5 March 1954, quoted in Connell-Smith, *Inter-American System*, pp. 162–163.

44. Shortly after Arbenz's overthrow, the new Guatemalan minister of foreign affairs informed the secretary general of the OAS that his government adhered to the resolution and withdrew any statements and reservations that had formerly been made. See Department of State, *Tenth Inter-American Conference*, p. 9.

45. Ibid.; Gerassi, *The Great Fear*, pp. 223–224; John C. Dreier, *The Organization of American States and the Hemisphere Crisis*, p. 50.

46. Roy R. Rubottom, Jr., *Transcript of a Recorded Interview*, John Foster Dulles Oral History Project (hereafter, DOH), Princeton University; Aybar de Soto, *Dependency and Intervention*, p. 238; telephone conversation with Senator Wiley, 2 February 1954, DPTC, "Telephone Memoranda (Excepting to and from White House), 1 January to February 1954 (2)."

47. Philip B. Taylor, Jr., "The Guatemalan Affair: A Critique of United States Foreign Policy," *American Political Science Review* 50 (September 1956): 791–792; Inman, *Inter-American Conferences*, pp. 258, 265; John Moors Cabot, *Transcript of a Recorded Interview*, DOH.

48. Quoted in United Nations Security Council, *Official Records* (hereafter, UNSCOR), *Ninth Year, 675th Meeting*, 20 June 1954; HAR 7 (February 1954): 39.

49. Quoted in UNSCOR, *675th Meeting*.

50. Dulles, remarks on return from Caracas, 14 March 1954, PR 133, "Caracas," JFD Papers; James C. Hagerty Diary (hereafter, Hagerty Diary), entry for 26 April 1954, James C. Hagerty Papers, Eisenhower Library; Eisenhower, *White House Years*, p. 423.

51. Staats, "Report on Actions Taken by the United States Information

Agency in the Guatemalan Situation"; *New York Times*, 14 March 1954.

52. Arévalo, *Guatemala, la democracia y el imperio*, pp. 59–62.
53. Rubottom, DOH; U.S. Department of State, "OAS Action against Communism in Guatemala," 10 May 1954, NA 714.00/5-1054.
54. C. D. Jackson to Dulles, 26 February 1954, "Caracas," JFD Papers; telephone conversation with Mr. Allen Dulles, 7 April 1954, DPTC, "Telephone Memoranda (Excepting to and from White House), 1 March to 30 April 1954 (1)."
55. Bissell interview; telephone interview with Gordon Gray, 14 August 1980; Hunt interview; John W. Fisher to Holland, 19 April 1954, NA 714.00/4-1954.
56. *HAR* 7 (March 1954): 12; *Congressional Record*, 83d Cong., 2d sess., 100, pt. 2: 1475.
57. *Congressional Record*, 83d Cong., 2d sess., 1954, 100, pt. 18: A3908.
58. For a discussion of the Bricker Amendment, see Gary W. Reichard, "Eisenhower and the Bricker Amendment," *Prologue: The Journal of the National Archives* 6 (Summer 1974): 88–91.
59. Eisenhower phone conversation with Knowland, 2 February 1954, WF, Diary Series, "Phone Calls January–May 1954."
60. Telephone conversation with Senator William Knowland, 15 March 1954, DPTC, "Telephone Memoranda (Excepting to and from White House), 1 March to 30 April 1954 (3)."
61. Eisenhower phone conversation with Bedell Smith, 26 April 1954, WF, Diary Series, "Phone Calls January–May 1954."
62. Memorandum for Mr. Sherman Adams, 24 April 1954, NA 714.00/4-2454; "Memorandum on Guatemalan Situation," WF, Legislative Leaders Series, "March–April 1954 (2)."
63. Shanley Diary, 24 May 1954.
64. Memo on Guatemala, enclosed in R. L. O'Connor, memorandum for ARA—Mr. Holland, re congressional reaction on the Guatemalan situation, 25 June 1954, NA 714.00/6-2554.
65. O'Connor, memorandum for ARA—Mr. Holland; Jack D. Neal, MID, to Holland, ARA, 5 May 1954, NA 714.00/5-554; U.S. Department of State, "OAS Action against Communism in Guatemala," 13 May 1954, NA 714.00/5-1354.
66. Telephone conversation with Mr. Holland, 11 May 1954, DPTC, "Telephone Memoranda (Excepting to and from White House), 1 May to 30 June 1954 (3)."
67. *New York Times*, 29 May 1954; Eisenhower, *White House Years*, p. 424; telephone call to Mr. Allen Dulles, 13 May 1954, DPTC, "Telephone Memoranda (Excepting to and from White House), 1 May to 30 June 1954 (3)"; John Foster Dulles, "General Strike in Honduras," *Bulletin* 30 (24 May 1954): 801.
68. U.S. Department of State office memo, 21 May 1954, NA 611.14/5-2154; Barry Blechman and Stephen Kaplan, *Force without War: U.S.*

Armed Forces as a Political Instrument, pp. 47–51; *New York Times*, 23–28 May and 2, 19 June 1954.

69. United States Department of State, memorandum of conversation (Toriello, Cabot, Fisher), 25 March 1953, NA 611.14/3-2553; William L. Krieg to Department of State, 23 November 1953, NA 714.00/11-2353.

70. Incoming telegram from Guatemala City to secretary of state, 9 February 1954, NA 714.00/2-954; Dulles to AMEMBASSY, Guatemala, 9 February 1954, NA 714.00/2-954.

71. Telephone call to Mr. Wisner, 18 May 1954, DPTC, "Telephone Memoranda (Excepting to and from White House), 1 May to 30 June 1954 (3)"; telephone call to Mr. Wisner, 17 May 1954, DPTC, "Telephone Memoranda (Excepting to and from White House), 1 May to 30 June 1954 (3)."

72. Richard Harkness and Gladys Harkness, "America's Secret Agents: The Mysterious Doings of CIA," *Saturday Evening Post* 227 (30 October 1954): 19–20; Hunt interview; Hagerty Diary, 20 May 1954; telephone call to Mr. Wisner, 17 May 1954, DPTC, "Telephone Memoranda (Excepting to and from White House), 1 May to 30 June 1954 (3)."

73. Telephone conversation with Mr. Allen Dulles, 17 May 1954, DPTC, "Telephone Memoranda (Excepting to and from White House), 1 May to 30 June 1954 (3)"; telephone call to Mr. Allen Dulles, 18 May 1954, DPTC, "Telephone Memoranda (Excepting to and from White House), 1 May to 30 June 1954 (3)"; telephone call from Senator Knowland, 18 May 1954, DPTC, "Telephone Memoranda (Excepting to and from White House), 1 May to 30 June 1954 (3)"; telephone call to Mr. Wisner, 18 May 1954, DPTC, "Telephone Memoranda (Excepting to and from White House), 1 May to 30 June 1954 (3)."

74. Telephone conversation with Mr. Allen Dulles, 18 May 1954, DPTC, "Telephone Memoranda (Excepting to and from White House), 1 May to 30 June 1954 (3)"; *New York Times*, 19, 21 May 1954.

75. Hagerty Diary, 19 May 1954; telephone call to Mr. Holland, 19 May 1954, DPTC, "Telephone Memoranda (Excepting to and from White House), 1 May to 30 June 1954 (3)"; *Public Papers of the Presidents of the United States: Dwight D. Eisenhower, 1954* (hereafter, *PPP*), p. 493; Eisenhower, *White House Years*, p. 424.

76. Telephone conversation with Mr. Allen Dulles, 17 May 1954, DPTC, "Telephone Memoranda (Excepting to and from White House), 1 May to 30 June 1954 (3)"; United States Department of State, "Arms Shipment to Guatemala from Soviet-Controlled Area," *Bulletin* 30 (31 May 1954): 835; John Foster Dulles, "Communist Influence in Guatemala," *Bulletin* 30 (7 June 1954): 874.

77. Hagerty Diary, 24 May 1954.

78. Robert Cutler, "Memo for President for Leaders' Meeting, May 24/53" (*sic*), 22 May 1954, WF, Legislative Leaders Series, "1954 (3), May–June"; NSC-5419 and NSC-5419/1, "U.S. Policy in the Event of Guatemalan Aggression in Latin America," 24 May and 28 May 1954, White House Office of the Special Assistant for National Security Affairs: Records, 1952–1961, Eisenhower Library.

79. Willauer to secretary of state, 21 May 1954, NA 714.00/5-2154.

80. For examples of the State Department's delaying tactics, see the following documents, none of which has yet received a decimal file number: U.S. Department of State memorandum, 3 June 1954; meeting of the Guatemalan group, 4 June 1954; meeting of the Guatemalan group, 14 June 1954; U.S. Department of State intelligence report, 17 June 1954; Guatemalan group, agenda for Wednesday, 23 June 1954; meeting of the Guatemalan group, 25 June 1954.

81. Consistent with his other positions, Holland appeared, at least initially, to earnestly want the meeting, and at one point he became upset. Dulles, however, was concerned that he would have to attend such a meeting, which would occupy two or three valuable days. After Castillo Armas launched his invasion, Dulles expressed the additional concern that if the invasion failed a resolution condemning Arbenz would probably be rejected. Telephone conversation with Mr. Holland, 9 June 1954, DPTC, "Telephone Memoranda (Excepting to and from White House), 1 May to 30 June 1954 (2)"; telephone calls to Mr. Murphy, 10 and 11 June 1954, DPTC, "Telephone Memoranda (Excepting to and from White House), 1 May to 30 June 1954 (2)"; meeting of the Guatemalan group, 25 June 1954.

82. U.S. Department of State, "OAS Action against Communism in Guatemala," 29 May 1954, NA 714.00/5-2954; John C. Hill to Peurifoy, 30 May 1954, NA 714.00/5-3054; Raymond G. Leddy to Peurifoy, 5 June 1954, NA 714.00/6-554.

83. Telephone conversation with Mr. Holland, 29 June 1954, DPTC, "Telephone Memoranda (Excepting to and from White House), 1 May to 30 June 1954 (1)."

84. Staats, "Report on Actions Taken by the United States Information Agency in the Guatemalan Situation."

85. "Guatemala: Plot within a Plot," *Time* 63 (31 May 1954): 30.

86. Keith Monroe, "Guatemala, What the Reds Left Behind," *Harper's Magazine* 211 (July 1955): 63.

87. Staats, "Report on Actions Taken by the United States Information Agency in the Guatemalan Situation"; telephone call to Frank Wisner (instead of AWD), 12 June 1954, DPTC, "Telephone Memoranda (Excepting to and from White House), 1 May to 30 June 1954 (2)."

88. Telephone call to Mr. Allen Dulles, 18 May 1954, DPTC, "Telephone Memoranda (Excepting to and from White House), 1 May to 30 June 1954 (3)"; telephone call to Mr. Holland, 19 May 1954, DPTC, "Telephone Memoranda (Excepting to and from White House), 1 May to 30 June 1954 (2)"; telephone conversation with Sec. Robert Anderson, 19 May 1954, DPTC, "Telephone Memoranda (Excepting to and from White House), 1 May to 30 June 1954 (2)"; telephone call to Mr. Allen Dulles, 19 May 1954, DPTC, "Telephone Memoranda (Excepting to and from White House), 1 May to 30 June 1954 (2)."

89. English to Holland, 20 May 1954, NA 714.00/5-2054; Cutler, "Memo for President for Leaders' Meeting, May 24/53" (*sic*).

90. Murphy to secretary, 25 May 1954, NA 611.14/5-2554.
91. U.S. Department of State, memorandum of conversation, 25 May 1954, NA 714.00/5-2554; Anthony Eden, *Full Circle: The Memoirs of Anthony Eden*, pp. 151–153; *New York Times*, 24 June 1954; HAR 7 (July 1954): 12.
92. Hunt interview; telephone call to Mr. Holland, 19 May 1954, DPTC, "Telephone Memoranda (Excepting to and from White House), 1 May to 30 June 1954 (3)"; telephone call to Mr. Allen Dulles, 19 May 1954, DPTC, "Telephone Memoranda (Excepting to and from White House), 1 May to 30 June 1954 (3)."
93. Telephone call to Mr. Allen Dulles, 19 May 1954, DPTC, "Telephone Memoranda (Excepting to and from White House), 1 May to 30 June 1954 (3)"; Hunt interview; quoted in HAR 7 (August 1954): 12.

7. Project PBSUCCESS: The Coup

1. Hunt interview; Wise and Ross, *Invisible Government*, pp. 176–177; U.S. Department of State circular, 22 June 1954, NA 714.00/6-2254; *Facts on File Yearbook*, 1954, p. 206D–F; K. W. McMahan, acting assistant director current intelligence [of CIA], memorandum for the president, "The Situation in Guatemala as of 20 June," WF, Administrative Series, "Dulles, Allen (4)" (emphasis in original).
2. Bissell, COH. For Eisenhower's reliance on psychological and political warfare, see Cook, *Declassified Eisenhower*, pp. 149–292.
3. Martz, *Central America*, p. 60; Bernays, *Biography of an Idea*, p. 771.
4. Bissell interview; Bissell, COH; Cehelsky, "Guatemala's Frustrated Revolution," p. 57; Ernst Halperin, "The National Liberation Movements in Latin America," p. 54; Blasier, *Hovering Giant*, pp. 172–174.
5. Grant, "Guatemala and U.S. Foreign Policy," pp. 69–70; Szulc, *Compulsive Spy*, p. 69; Westerfield, *Instruments of America's Foreign Policy*, p. 434; Julien, *America's Empire*, pp. 338–339.
6. As early as April 1953, following an antigovernment uprising at Salamá, Arbenz's government formally notified the UN General Assembly that elements within the United States and the Central American nations were conspiring to foment a counterrevolution. See *New York Times*, 8 April 1953; HAR 6 (May 1953): 12–13.
7. Bissell interview; Blechman and Kaplan, *Force without War*, pp. 47–51.
8. Hunt, *Undercover*, pp. 98–99. For the church's influence in Guatemala and throughout Latin America, see Penny Lernoux, *Cry of the People*. Lernoux notes how the church's attitudes have changed in recent years.
9. Hunt, *Undercover*, p. 99; Martin F. Herz, "Some Psychological Lessons from Leaflet Propaganda in World War II," in Society for the Study of Social Issues, ed., *Public Opinion and Propaganda*, pp. 543–553.
10. ...ips, *Night Watch*, pp. 40–46.
    ...l., Guatemala City to secretary of state, 1 June 1954, NA 714.00/
    ...inc. tel., Guatemala City to secretary of state, 2 June 1954, NA
    ...5-254; telephone call from Mr. Hagerty, 2 June 1954, DPTC,

"Telephone Memoranda (Excepting to and from White House), 1 May to 30 June 1954 (1)"; the president's news conference of 2 June 1954, *PPP*, pp. 526–533.

12. John Foster Dulles, "U.S. Policy on Guatemala," *Bulletin* 30 (21 June 1954): 950–951; idem, "International Unity," *Bulletin* 30 (21 June 1954): 938–939; telephone call to Frank Wisner, 12 June 1954, DPTC, "Telephone Memoranda (Excepting to and from White House), 1 May to 30 June 1954 (2)"; telephone call to Mr. Allen Dulles, 15 June 1954, DPTC, "Telephone Memoranda (Excepting to and from White House), 1 May to 30 June 1954 (2)"; telephone call to A. W. Dulles, 15 June 1954, DPTC, "Telephone Memoranda (Excepting to and from White House), 1 May to 30 June 1954 (2)"; John Foster Dulles, "News Conference Statement by Secretary Dulles: Guatemalan Situation," *Bulletin* 30 (21 June 1954): 981.

13. Hagerty Diary, 14 June 1954; telephone call to Mr. Allen Dulles, 15 June 1954, DPTC, "Telephone Mcmoranda (Excepting to and from White House), 1 May to 30 June 1954 (2)"; Hagerty Diary, 15, 16 June 1954; telephone call with Mr. Hagerty, DPTC, "Telephone Memoranda (Excepting to and from White House), 1 May to 30 June 1954 (2)"; draft of statement or comment for the president re Guatemalan situation, n.d., WF, Press Conference Series, "16 June 1954."

14. The president's news conference of 16 June 1954, *PPP*, p. 573.

15. Hagerty Diary, 18 June 1954.

16. McMahan, "The Situation in Guatemala as of 20 June"; 19 June speech of Arbenz, attached to AMEMBASSY, Guatemala, to Department of State, 29 June 1954, NA 714.00/6-2954.

17. Peurifoy to secretary of state, 28 June 1954, NA 714.00/6-2854; Wise and Ross, *Invisible Government*, pp. 173–175; Bissell, COH; Phillips, *Night Watch*, p. 47. Referring to the *Springfjord* incident, Bissell explained, "You can't take on operations of this scope, draw boundaries of policy around them, and be absolutely sure that those boundaries will not be overstepped." Quoted in Marchetti and Marks, *The CIA*, p. 298.

18. Halperin, "National Liberation Movements," pp. 13–14, 54–55; Niedergang, *Vingt Amériques Latines*, p. 83; Peurifoy to secretary of state, 8 June 1954, NA 714.00/6-754; Krieg to secretary of state, 6 August 1954, NA 714.00/8-654.

19. Bissell, COH; Phillips, *Night Watch*, p. 44; AMEMBASSY, Guatemala, to Department of State, 6 May 1954, NA 714.00/5-654; Guillén, *Guatemala*, pp. 62–64.

20. McMahan, "The Situation in Guatemala as of 20 June"; Phillips, *Night Watch*, pp. 43–44.

21. Peurifoy to secretary of state, 20 June 1954, NA 714.00/6-2054; Eisenhower, *White House Years*, pp. 425–426.

22. UNSCOR, supplement, April, May, and June 1954, document S/3232, "Cablegram Dated 19 June 1954 from the Minister for External Relations of Guatemala to the President of the Security Council," pp. 11–13; Toriello to secretary of state, 19 June 1954, NA FW 714.00/

6-1954; Great Britain, Parliament, Cmd. 9277, *Report on Events Leading up to and Arising out of the Change of Regime in Guatemala, 1954*, appendix 1: "The Guatemalan Chargé d'Affaires at Washington to the Chairman of the Inter-American Peace Committee, 19 June 1954," pp. 100–101.

23. Toriello to secretary of state, 19 June 1954, NA FW 714.00/6-1954; William L. Krieg to Department of State, 2 November 1953, NA 714.00/11-253.

24. Department of State, *Tenth Inter-American Conference*, p. 172.

25. Lodge, "The Guatemalan Complaint before the Security Council," pp. 26–31; UNSCOR, "Cablegram Dated 19 June 1954"; Toriello to secretary of state, 19 June 1954, NA FW 714.00/6-1954; Peurifoy to secretary of state, 23 June 1954, NA 714.00/6-2354; Murphy (acting) to AMEMBASSY, Managua and Tegucigalpa, 21 June 1954, NA 714.00/6-2154.

26. UNSCOR, *675th Meeting*, pp. 1–13.

27. Ibid., pp. 13–32.

28. Ibid., p. 37; Parliament, *Report on Events*, pp. 8–9; message from the minister of foreign relations of Guatemala to the president of the Security Council of the United Nations, 20 June 1954, attached to EMBASSY of Guatemala to Department of State, 21 June 1954, NA FW 714.00/6-2154; UNSCOR, supplement, document S/3241, "Letter Dated 22 June 1954 from the Representative of Guatemala to the Secretary General," pp. 14–15; telephone conversation with Ambassador Lodge (NY), 22 June 1954, DPTC, "Telephone Memoranda (Excepting to and from White House), 1 May to 30 June 1954 (1)"; meeting of the Guatemalan group, 23 June 1954; telephone call from Amb. Lodge, 24 June 1954, DPTC, "Telephone Memoranda (Excepting to and from White House), 1 May to 30 June 1954 (1)."

29. Telephone call from Amb. Lodge, 24 June 1954, DPTC, "Telephone Memoranda (Excepting to and from White House), 1 May to 30 June 1954 (1)"; telephone call to Amb. Lodge, 25 June 1954, DPTC, "Telephone Memoranda (Excepting to and from White House), 1 May to 30 June 1954 (1)"; Bryce Harlow, *Transcript of a Recorded Interview*, DOH.

30. Hagerty Diary, 24 June 1954.

31. Telephone call to Amb. Lodge, 24 June 1954, DPTC, "Telephone Memoranda (Excepting to and from White House), 1 May to 30 June 1954 (1)."

32. Robert Murphy, *Diplomat among Warriors*, pp. 372–373; Parliament, *Report on Events*, annex (a), United Nations Charter, p. 13.

33. Lodge to secretary of state, 24 June 1954, NA 714.00/6-2454.

34. Lodge to secretary of state, 25 June 1954, NA 714.00/6-2554.

35. Eden, *Full Circle*, pp. 153–154; Hagerty Diary, 25 June 1954.

36. Telephone call to Amb. Lodge, 25 June 1954, DPTC, "Telephone Memoranda (Excepting to and from White House), 1 May to 30 June 1954 (1)."

37. Hagerty Diary, 26 June 1954; telephone interview with Henry Cabot Lodge, Jr., 28 July 1980; Eden, *Full Circle*, p. 155; telephone call to Amb. Lodge, 25 June 1954, DPTC, "Telephone Memoranda (Excepting to and from White House), 1 May to 30 June 1954 (1)"; telephone call to

Amb. Bonnet, 25 June 1954, DPTC, "Telephone Memoranda (Excepting to and from White House), 1 May to 30 June 1954 (1)"; UNSCOR, *676th Meeting*; Brian Urquhart, *Hammarskjöld*, pp. 88–94.

38. Minutes of cabinet meeting, 8 July 1954, WF, Cabinet Series.

39. Murphy (acting) to AMEMBASSY, Managua and Tegucigalpa, 21 June 1954, NA 714.00/6-2154; Parliament, *Report on Events*, pp. 92–97; memorandum of telephone conversation, participants: Ambassador Peurifoy, Guatemala, Mr. Holland, 29 June 1954, NA 714.00/6-2954; W. G. Bowdler to Mr. Pearson, ARA monthly report for July, "Political Summary: Guatemala," 4 August 1954, NA 714.00/8-454.

40. Telephone conversation with Mr. Allen Dulles, 24 June 1954, DPTC, "Telephone Memoranda (Excepting to and from White House), 1 May to 30 June 1954 (1)"; telephone call from Senator Knowland, 24 June 1954, DPTC, "Telephone Memoranda (Excepting to and from White House), 1 May to 30 June 1954 (1)"; telephone conversation with Sen. Knowland, 26 June 1954, DPTC, "Telephone Memoranda (Excepting to and from White House), 1 May to 30 June 1954 (1)"; telephone call to Sen. Johnson, 26 June 1954, DPTC, "Telephone Memoranda (Excepting to and from White House), 1 May to 30 June 1954 (1)"; telephone call to Lyndon Johnson, 28 June 1954, DPTC, "Telephone Memoranda (Excepting to and from White House), 1 May to 30 June 1954 (1)"; *Congressional Record*, 83d Cong., 2d sess., 1954, 100, pt. 7: 8921–8927, 9065–9066.

The margin in the Senate was 69 to 1, while the House version passed unanimously. North Dakota Senator William Langer cast the lone dissenting vote. Langer, a maverick Republican, invariably followed Robert La Follette's old progressive line and opposed internationalist foreign policies. In the case of the Guatemalan resolution, his vote excited so much comment that he felt compelled to issue an explanation. Emphasizing that he had no quarrel with those who feared the threat of international Communism, he took the unique position that "the true nature of the conflict in Guatemala is not yet clear." Consequently, "I do not think we ought to jump into the Guatemalan situation, a sensitive, and very grave threat to world peace, with such elephant indelicacy." See "For Immediate Release by Senator William Langer," 28 June 1954, William Langer Papers, Orin G. Libby Manuscript Collection, University of North Dakota, Grand Forks, North Dakota. For more on Langer and his record, see Robert Griffith, "Old Progressives and the Cold War," *Journal of American History* 66 (September 1979): 334–347, and Gary W. Reichard, *The Reaffirmation of Republicanism: Eisenhower and the Eighty-Third Congress*, pp. 88, 116, 250.

41. Phillips, *Night Watch*, pp. 47–50; NBC News, "The Science of Spying"; Halperin, "National Liberation Movements," p. 56; Cook, "CIA," p. 530; Peurifoy to secretary of state, 27 June 1954, NA 714.00/6-2754; Willauer to C. L. Chennault, 30 June 1954, Willauer Papers, file 16, item 10.

42. Peurifoy to secretary of state, 23 June 1954, NA 714.00/6-2354; Peurifoy to secretary of state, 27 June 1954, NA 714.00/6-2754.

43. Peurifoy to secretary of state, 27 June 1954, NA 714.00/6-2754; incoming telegram, Guatemala City to secretary of state, 28 June 1954, NA 714.00/6-2854; memorandum of telephone conversation, Holland and Peurifoy, 28 June 1954, NA 714.00/6-2854; Peurifoy to secretary of state, 29 June 1954, NA 714.00/6-2854; telephone call to Mr. Allen Dulles, 28 June 1954, DPTC, "Telephone Memoranda (Excepting to and from White House), 1 May to 30 June 1954 (1)."

44. Ralph de Toledano, "Unconventional Ambassador," *American Mercury* 79 (October 1954): 32; Peurifoy to secretary of state, 29 June 1954, NA 714.00/6-2854. In his resignation speech, Arbenz had reiterated his charges of United States complicity.

45. Peurifoy to secretary of state, 30 June 1954, NA 714.00/6-2954; quoted in "Guatemala: The New Junta," pp. 38–39; *Facts on File Yearbook,* 1954, p. 213C–F.

46. Pearson, *Diaries,* p. 323.

47. John (Peurifoy) to Ray (Leddy), 4 January 1954, NA 714.00/1-454.

48. Peurifoy to secretary of state, 30 June 1954, NA 714.00/6-3054.

49. Memorandum of telephone conversation, participants: Ambassador Peurifoy, Guatemala, Mr. Holland, 29 June 1954, NA 714.00/6-2954; telephone call to Mr. Allen Dulles, 30 June 1954, DPTC, "Telephone Memoranda (Excepting to and from White House), 1 May to 30 June 1954 (1)"; Department of State, memorandum of conversation, telephone, participants: Ambassador John E. Peurifoy, Guatemala; Assistant Secretary Holland; Ambassador Thomas E. Whelan, Managua; Ambassador Michael J. McDermott, San Salvador; Ambassador Héctor David Castro, president of COAS (Council of the Organization of American States) 29 June 1954, NA 714.00/6-2954.

50. Telephone call to Mr. Allen Dulles, 30 June 1954, DPTC, "Telephone Memoranda (Excepting to and from White House), 1 May to 30 June 1954 (1)"; Peurifoy to secretary of state, 20 June 1954, NA 714.00/6-2054; memorandum of telephone conversation (Holland), 29 June 1954, NA 714.00/6-2954; Department of State, memorandum of conversation (overseas telephone), participants: the Honorable John E. Peurifoy, United States Ambassador to Guatemala, Mr. Raymond G. Leddy, officer of Middle American Affairs, 30 June 1954, NA 714.00/6-3054; Dulles telegram to AMEMBASSY, Guatemala (Peurifoy), 29 June 1954, NA 714.00/6-2954; Department of State, memorandum of conversation—TELEPHONE—participants: Ambassador Michael J. McDermott—San Salvador, Assistant Secretary Henry F. Holland, 30 June 1954, NA 714.00/6-3054.

51. Department of State, memorandum of conversation—TELEPHONE—participants: Ambassador Michael J. McDermott—San Salvador, Assistant Secretary Henry F. Holland, 30 June 1954, NA 714.00/6-3054; confidential, "Mr. Holland dictated . . . ," 30 June 1954, NA 714.00/6-3054.

52. Telephone call to Amb. Peurifoy in El Salvador, 1 July 1954, DPTC, "Telephone Memoranda (Excepting to and from White House), 1 July to 31 August 1954 (5)"; AMEMBASSY, Guatemala, to Department of State, 7 July 1954, NA 714.00/7-754. Dulles' secretary, Phyllis Bernau, transcribed the words as "put a couple of heads together."

53. Michael J. McDermott to Department of State, 5 July 1954, NA 714.00/7-554; Peurifoy to secretary of state, 7 July 1954, NA 714.00/7-754; AMEMBASSY, Guatemala, to Department of State, 7 July 1954, NA 714.00/7-754.

54. Blasier, *Hovering Giant*, pp. 174–177; Julio Castro, *Bombas y dolares sobre Guatemala*, p. 23; *London Times*, 9 October 1954; HAR 7 (October 1954): 10; *Facts on File Yearbook*, 1954, p. 366A–B3; Wise and Ross, *Invisible Government*, pp. 176–177; *New York Times*, 28 January 1971.

55. Telephone call from Mr. Armour, 31 July 1954, DPTC, "Telephone Memoranda (Excepting to and from White House), 1 July to 31 August 1954 (3)"; telephone call to Mr. Holland, 31 July 1954, DPTC, "Telephone Memoranda (Excepting to and from White House), 1 July to 31 August 1954 (3)"; telephone call to Sen. Knowland, 19 August 1954, DPTC, "Telephone Memoranda (Excepting to and from White House), 1 July to 31 August 1954 (1)."

56. Telephone calls to Allen Dulles, 20 July 1954, DPTC, "Telephone Memoranda (Excepting to and from White House), 1 July to 31 August 1954 (4)"; Westerfield, *Instruments of America's Foreign Policy*, p. 439; Hunt interview; memorandum of telephone conversation with the president, 12 August 1955, DPTC, "White House Telephone Memoranda, 7 March to 29 August 1955 (1)."

57. Telephone call from Mr. Hagerty, 30 June 1954, DPTC, "White House Telephone Memoranda, 1 January to 30 June 1954 (1)"; press conference material, "June 30, 1954," Hagerty Papers; the president's news conference of 30 June 1954, PPP, p. 605; address at the Illinois State Fair in Springfield, 19 August 1954, PPP, p. 731.

58. Dwight D. Eisenhower, reply to Salazar upon the occasion of the presentation of his letter of credence, n.d., WF, International Series, "Guatemala (1)."

59. Telephone call to Mr. Allen Dulles, 26 June 1954, DPTC, "Telephone Memoranda (Excepting to and from White House), 1 May to 30 June 1954 (1)"; telephone call to Mr. Holland, 28 June 1954, DPTC, "Telephone Memoranda (Excepting to and from White House), 1 May to 30 June 1954 (1)"; telephone call to Mr. Holland, 29 June 1954, DPTC, "Telephone Memoranda (Excepting to and from White House), 1 May to 30 June 1954 (1)."

60. Telephone call with Mr. McCardle, 29 June 1954, DPTC, "Telephone Memoranda (Excepting to and from White House), 1 May to 30 June 1954 (1)."

61. For a description of how Eisenhower and Dulles coordinated their public pronouncements, see Carl McCardle, *Oral History Interview*, COH.

62. John Foster Dulles, "International Communism in Guatemala," *Bulletin* 31 (12 July 1954): 43–45.
63. Eisenhower to Herbert Swope, 6 July 1954, WF, Name Series, "Swope, Herbert"; memorandum for the secretary of state, 7 July 1954, Subject Series, "Guatemala 1954," Dulles Papers.
64. Wiley to Mr. President, 1 June 1955, OF 185, "Guatemala (1)," Eisenhower Papers.
65. Eisenhower to Wiley, suggested reply, 13 June 1954, OF 185, "Guatemala (1)," Eisenhower Papers; Herbert Hoover, Jr., memorandum for the president, 21 June 1954, OF 185, "Guatemala (1)," Eisenhower Papers.
66. Jonas, "Test Case for the Hemisphere," pp. 151–152; Toriello, *¿A dónde va Guatemala?* pp. 25–26.
67. Suggested toast to President Carlos Castillo Armas by Vice-President Nixon, n.d., OF 185, "Guatemala (1)," Eisenhower Papers.
68. Peurifoy, memorandum of conversation, 17 December 1953, NA 611.14/12-1853.
69. House of Representatives, *Ninth Interim Report of Hearings*, p. 2.
70. Ibid.; Department of State, *Penetration of the Political Institutions*.
71. Telephone conversation with C. D. Jackson, 3 July 1954, DPTC, "Telephone Memoranda (Excepting to and from White House), 1 July to 31 August 1954 (5)."
72. Bryce Wood, "Self-Plagiarism and Foreign Policy," *Latin American Research Review* 3 (Summer 1968): 184–191.
73. One exception is Richard Bissell. He now believes that Arbenz, albeit unwisely, tried to use the Communists for his own purposes, and "with hindsight I am inclined to believe that we exaggerated at that time the strength of the Communist party." Bissell interview.
74. Britnell, "Factors in the Economic Development of Guatemala," p. 113; see also "Social Revolution in Guatemala," pp. 279–282.
75. Schneider estimates that from May 1950 to May 1954 Communist strength grew from a few dozen Guatemalans to nearly four thousand. Castillo Armas placed the figure at five thousand. See Schneider, *Communism*, pp. 44–47; Carlos Castillo Armas, "Damage Reds Do" (interview with Clark H. Galloway), *U.S. News & World Report* 37 (6 August 1954): 38.
76. William Prescott Allen to Eisenhower, 24 June 1954, GF 122, "Guatemala," Eisenhower Records.
77. Blasier, *Hovering Giant*, pp. 155–157; Halperin, "National Liberation Movements," pp. 10–13. The most comprehensive treatment of the Communists is Schneider, *Communism*. For the military's role in Latin American politics, see Lieuwen, *Arms and Politics in Latin America*; idem, *Generals vs. Presidents*; and Nun, *Latin America*.
78. See, for example, U.S. Department of State memorandum, 8 December 1952, NA 611.14/12-852; Rudolf Schoenfeld to Edward Clark, 19 December 1952, NA 611.14/12-1952; U.S. Department of State memorandum of conversation, 26 June 1953, NA 611.14/6-2653.

79. Pike, "Guatemala, the United States, and Communism," pp. 242–244; Monteforte Toledo, *Guatemala*, pp. 315–317; Schmitt and Burks, *Evolution or Chaos*, p. 168; Siegel, "Perspective on Guatemala," p. 13; Schneider, *Communism*, pp. 196–197. Schneider based his assessment on the more than fifty thousand documents concerning the Arbenz government collected in July 1954 by the Guatemalan National Committee for Defense against Communism. These documents detail Arbenz's relations with the Communists. Thanks to the efforts of Blanche Cook, the documents are now available for scholarly research at the Library of Congress. For a concise analysis of the coalitional character of Latin American politics, see Charles W. Anderson, "The Latin American Political System," in John D. Martz, ed., *The Dynamics of Change in Latin American Politics*, p. 292.

80. George Kennan memorandum to Acheson, 29 March 1950, FRUS 2: 603.

81. Telephone call to Mr. Armstrong, 19 May 1955, DPTC, "Telephone Conversations, General, 2 May to 31 August 1955 (6)."

82. Marshall Shulman, *Stalin's Foreign Policy Reappraised*; T. Stephen Cheston and Bernard Loeffke, *Aspects of Soviet Policy toward Latin America*, p. 8; Adam B. Ulam, *Expansion and Coexistence: The History of Soviet Foreign Policy, 1917–67*, pp. 539–560; *New York Herald Tribune*, 9 February 1950; Bush, *Organized Labor*, pp. 36–37; Joseph Maier and Richard W. Weatherhead, eds., *Politics of Change in Latin America*, p. 9.

83. See, for example, Bissell, COH.

84. Daniel Graham, "Castillo's Guatemala," *Nation* 180 (21 May 1955): 440.

85. Guatemalan revolutionaries rejected the Soviet and Chinese models, preferring to view themselves as the heirs of the liberal revolution in Mexico that lasted from 1911 to 1940. See Guillén, *Guatemala*, pp. 26–28, 37–44; Betty Kirk, "United States in Latin America—Policy of the Suction Pump," *Nation* 185 (5 October 1957): 214–222; "Social Revolution in Guatemala," p. 279.

8. Project PBSUCCESS: The Legacy

1. For example, Leonard Mosley wrote that in 1955, after learning that Kim Roosevelt was coming to Egypt, the Egyptian ambassador to the United States warned President Nasser, "Remember Guatemala, remember Guatemala." Mosley's allegation cannot be substantiated, but the coup in Guatemala certainly dramatized the CIA's potential to Third World leaders. See Leonard Mosley, *Dulles: A Biography of Eleanor, Allen and John Foster Dulles and Their Family Network*, pp. 384–392.

2. John Gerassi, ed., *Venceremos: The Speeches and Writings of Ernesto Che Guevara*, pp. 9–12; Ricardo Rojo, *My Friend Che*, pp. 45–55; Richard Gott, *Rural Guerillas in Latin America*, p. 67.

3. Gerassi, *Venceremos*, p. 11; eulogy delivered by Major Fidel Castro

Ruz, in memory of Major Ernesto Che Guevara, 18 October 1967, in ibid., pp. 433–434.

4. Hilda Gadea, *Ernesto: A Memoir of Che Guevara,* pp. 53–57.

5. The accounts of the Bay of Pigs invasion rely primarily on the Taylor Report (Paramilitary Study Group), National Security Files, John F. Kennedy Library, Boston, Massachusetts. The report, contained in eleven folders, consists of the memoranda and minutes of hearings that resulted from General Maxwell D. Taylor's commission to investigate the Bay of Pigs. With editorial modifications, it is now published in *Operation* ZAPATA: *The "Ultrasensitive" Report and Testimony of the Board of Inquiry on the Bay of Pigs.* See also Peter Wyden, *Bay of Pigs: The Untold Story.*

6. Memorandum for the record, Paramilitary Study Group, 17 May 1961, "Taylor Report (10)."

7. Hunt interview.

8. Memorandum 2, "Immediate Causes of Failure of the Operation ZA-PATA," 13 June 1961, "Taylor Report (1)."

9. Ibid.

10. Ibid.; memorandum 3, "Conclusions of the Cuban Study Group," 13 June 1961, "Taylor Report (1)."

11. Quoted in Wyden, *Bay of Pigs,* p. 8.

12. Irving L. Janis, *Victims of Groupthink: A Psychological Study of Foreign Policy Decisions,* pp. 48–49.

13. Wyden, *Bay of Pigs,* pp. 311–316. At the Taylor hearings, representatives of both the military and the CIA testified that they had opposed canceling the strikes.

14. For Bissell and the U-2, see Ambrose with Immerman, *Ike's Spies,* pp. 265–292.

15. Wyden, *Bay of Pigs,* p. 326.

16. Rusk's estimate went as high as 50 percent. See his testimony, 4 May 1961, 10th meeting, "Taylor Report (8)."

17. 1 May 1961, 7th meeting, "Taylor Report (7)."

18. A full chronology of the Bay of Pigs can be found in the Taylor Report.

19. Memorandum 1, "Narrative of the Anti-Castro Cuban Operation ZA-PATA," 13 June 1961, "Taylor Report (1)"; Bissell, letter to author, 1 November 1979.

20. Bissell, COH.

21. For a CIA veteran's appraisal of the impact of PBSUCCESS on the legend, see Ray S. Cline, *Secrets, Spies, and Soldiers: Blueprint of the Essential CIA,* pp. 132–133.

22. Hunt interview.

23. Taylor Report. See also E. Howard Hunt, *Give Us This Day,* p. 26; Phillips, *Night Watch,* pp. 86, 89.

24. Taylor Report, "Narrative of the Anti-Castro Cuban Operation ZAPATA."

25. Quoted in Gott, *Rural Guerillas,* p. 40.

26. Allen Dulles to Eisenhower, n.d., "re Guatemala, 1963," Allen W. Dulles Papers, Princeton University, Princeton, New Jersey.

27. 25 April 1961, 3d meeting, "Taylor Report (5)."
28. For a balanced appraisal of Castro's revolutionary program, see Jorge I. Domínguez, *Cuba: Order and Revolution.*
29. Rubottom, DOH.
30. Transcript of "NBC White Paper: The Castro Connection," narrated by Marvin Kalb and produced by Robert Rogers and NBC News, originally broadcast 3 September 1980.
31. Quoted in Marlise Simons, "Guatemala: The Coming Danger," *Foreign Policy* 43 (Summer 1981): 103.
32. House of Representatives, *Ninth Interim Report of Hearings*, pp. 162–163.
33. Alan Riding, "Guatemala: State of Siege," *New York Times Magazine*, 24 August 1980, p. 67.
34. Despite the return of its property, UFCO considered it imprudent to continue its Guatemalan operations. Before the end of 1954, it began negotiations with Castillo Armas to sell the government its holdings. By 1958 the company had divested itself of all its interests, including its stock in IRCA.
35. Jonas, "Test Case for the Hemisphere," pp. 204–205; Daniel Graham, "Liberated Guatemala," *Nation* 183 (14 July 1956): 34; Whetten, *Guatemala*, p. 30; Department of Commerce, *Investment in Central America*, pp. 168–169; Frank, *Latin America*, p. 270; *New York Times*, 5 April 1979.
36. *New York Times*, 6 July 1954; *Facts on File Yearbook*, 1954, pp. 225C3–226A1; translation of Castillo Armas' speech enclosed in William L. Krieg to Department of State, 14 July 1954, NA 714.00/7-1454.
37. Dulles to AMEMBASSY, Guatemala, 27 July 1954, NA 714.00/7-2754.
38. U.S. Department of State memorandum, "Guatemala," 2 September 1954, NA 714.00/9-254; Cehelsky, "Guatemala's Frustrated Revolution," p. 78; *New York Times*, 31 July 1954; HAR 7 (August 1954): 10–14.
39. HAR 7 (December 1954): 12; Monteforte Toledo, *Guatemala*, p. 320; Graham, "Castillo's Guatemala," p. 441.
40. Cehelsky, "Guatemala's Frustrated Revolution," p. 78; *Facts on File Yearbook*, 1954, pp. 225C3–226A1; Jonas, "Guatemala: Land of Eternal Struggle," pp. 169–171; Gordon, "Subversion," pp. 149–150; Maestre, *Guatemala*, p. 127; Graham, "Castillo's Guatemala," p. 441; Martin C. Needler, ed., *Political Development in Latin America: Instability, Violence, and Evolutionary Change*, p. 96; Ernest Feder, *The Rape of the Peasantry: Latin America's Landholding System*, p. 164; Whetten, *Guatemala*, pp. 104–105; Hildebrand, "Latin American Economic Development," p. 357.
41. Graham, "Liberated Guatemala," p. 37.
42. Gerassi, *The Great Fear*, p. 223; Eisenhower to Mrs. Joseph B. Kavanaugh, 7 August 1957, OF 185, "Guatemala (2)," Eisenhower Papers; John Eisenhower, report to the president on trip to Guatemala, 29–31 July 1957, WF, International Series, "Guatemala."

43. John Eisenhower based his conclusion on a photostat of a letter alleged to have been found by the Guatemalan government on Vásquez Sánchez's body. Guatemalan authorities, while never producing the photostat, maintained that it was the bodyguard's correspondence to Moscow confirming his assignment to assassinate Castillo Armas. Major Eisenhower did not question the photostat's authenticity, despite the unlikelihood of the Kremlin copying such damaging evidence and returning it to Guatemala and Vásquez Sánchez carrying it with him on his dangerous mission. From information gathered in interviews years later, Marta Cehelsky believes that Trujillo, with the aid of Guatemalan dissidents, plotted the murder. See John Eisenhower, report to the president; Cehelsky, "Guatemala's Frustrated Revolution," pp. 110–113.

44. J. Michael Luhan, "The Next El Salvador," *New Republic* 182 (11 April 1981): 23–25.

45. Gott, *Rural Guerillas*.

46. John Gerassi, ed., *The Coming of the New International*, pp. 467–468; Yon Sosa et al., "First Declaration of Sierra de las Minas," in ibid., p. 494.

47. Quoted in Stephen Kinzer, "Guatemala: The Hard Line," *Atlantic* 245 (January 1980): 6.

48. NBC News, "The Castro Connection."

Bibliography

UNPUBLISHED PAPERS AND DOCUMENTS

Acheson, Dean, Harry S. Truman Library, Independence, Missouri.
Archives of the Council on Foreign Relations, New York, New York.
Berle, Adolf, Franklin D. Roosevelt Library, Hyde Park, New York.
Bohan, Merwin L., Harry S. Truman Library, Independence, Missouri.
Braden, Spruille, Columbia University, New York, New York.
Dulles, Allen W., Princeton University, Princeton, New Jersey.
Dulles, John Foster, Dwight D. Eisenhower Library, Abilene, Kansas.
———, Princeton University, Princeton, New Jersey.
Eisenhower, Dwight D., Dwight D. Eisenhower Library, Abilene, Kansas.
Eisenhower, Milton S., Dwight D. Eisenhower Library, Abilene, Kansas.
Hagerty, James C., Dwight D. Eisenhower Library, Abilene, Kansas.
Jackson, C. D., Dwight D. Eisenhower Library, Abilene, Kansas.
Kyle, Edwin Jackson, Jr., Cornell University, Ithaca, New York.
Langer, William, University of North Dakota, Grand Forks, North Dakota.
Miller, Edward G., Jr., Harry S. Truman Library, Independence, Missouri.
Patterson, Richard C., Jr., Harry S. Truman Library, Independence, Missouri.
Roosevelt, Franklin D., Franklin D. Roosevelt Library, Hyde Park, New York.
Shanley, Bernard, Dwight D. Eisenhower Library, Abilene, Kansas.
Smith, Walter Bedell, Dwight D. Eisenhower Library, Abilene, Kansas.
Taylor Report (Paramilitary Study Group), National Security Files, John F. Kennedy Library, Boston, Massachusetts.
Truman, Harry S., Harry S. Truman Library, Independence, Missouri.
United States National Archives, Diplomatic Branch, Central Decimal File, Record Group 59, Washington, D.C.
———, Modern Military Branch Reference Section, Washington, D.C.
White House Office of the Special Assistant for National Security Affairs, Records, 1952–1961, Dwight D. Eisenhower Library, Abilene, Kansas.
Willauer, Whiting, Princeton University, Princeton, New Jersey.

PERSONAL INTERVIEWS AND CORRESPONDENCE

Bernays, Edward L., interview, 25 August 1979.
———, letter to author, 14 January 1980.

Bernstein, Carl, letter to author, 16 November 1977.
Bissell, Richard M., Jr., interview, 1 November 1977.
————, letter to author, 1 November 1979.
Bowie, Robert R., interview, 25 February 1981.
Braden, Spruille, interview, 16 November 1977.
Dulles, Eleanor Lansing, interview, 9 October 1979.
Eisenhower, Milton S., interview (with Fred I. Greenstein), 1 November 1978.
————, letter to author, 21 March 1978.
Gray, Gordon, interview, 15 October 1979.
————, telephone interview, 14 August 1980.
Hill, Robert C., letter to author, 16 September 1977.
Hunt, E. Howard, interview, 1 November 1977.
————, interview, 6 December 1977.
————, taped interview, 11 September 1979.
Lissner, Will, letter to Edward L. Bernays, 24 October 1976 (copy in author's possession).
Lodge, Henry Cabot, Jr., telephone interview, 28 July 1980.
Macomber, William B., Jr., interview, 7 August 1979.
Mann, Thomas C., letter to author, 1 September 1978.
Matthews, Herbert L., letter to author, 20 July 1977.
————, letter to Leon Shimkin, 17 November 1966 (author's possession).
Morrow, Hugh, assistant to Nelson A. Rockefeller, letter to author, 19 October 1977.
Phleger, Herman, interview, 12 April 1980.
Roosevelt, Kermit, letter to author, 1 December 1977.

PUBLISHED RECORDS AND OFFICIAL SOURCES

Beaulac, Willard L. "The Communist Effort in Guatemala." *Department of State Bulletin* 31 (16 August 1954): 235–237.
Cabot, John Moors. "Inter-American Cooperation and Hemispheric Solidarity." *Department of State Bulletin* 29 (26 October 1953): 554–559.
Carrollton Press, Inc. *The Declassified Documents Quarterly Catalogue.* Vol. 1 (January–December 1975). Washington, D.C., Inverness.
————. *The Declassified Documents Retrospective Collection.* Vols. 1–2. Washington, D.C., Inverness, 1976.
Central Intelligence Agency. *Review of the World Situation as It Relates to the Security of the United States, 1948–1950.* Truman Papers, Truman Library.
Congressional Record, 1944–1954. Washington, D.C.
Curl, Peter V., ed. *Documents on American Foreign Relations, 1954.* New York, 1955.
Dreier, John C. "The Guatemalan Problem before the OAS Council." *Department of State Bulletin* 31 (12 July 1954): 45–47.
Dulles, John Foster. "Communist Influence in Guatemala." *Department of State Bulletin* 30 (7 June 1954): 873–874.

———. "General Strike in Honduras." *Department of State Bulletin* 30 (24 May 1954): 801.

———. "International Communism in Guatemala." *Department of State Bulletin* 31 (12 July 1954): 43–45.

———. "International Unity." *Department of State Bulletin* 30 (21 June 1954): 938–939.

———. "News Conference Statement by Secretary Dulles: Guatemalan Situation." *Department of State Bulletin* 30 (21 June 1954): 981.

———. "U.S. Policy on Guatemala." *Department of State Bulletin* 30 (21 June 1954): 950–951.

Great Britain, Parliament, Cmd. 9277. *Report on Events Leading up to and Arising out of the Change of Regime in Guatemala, 1954.* Presented by the Secretary of State for Foreign Affairs to Parliament by Command of Her Majesty, London, 1954.

Key, David McK. "The Organization of American States and the United Nations: Rivals or Partners?" *Department of State Bulletin* 31 (26 July 1954): 115–118.

Lodge, Henry Cabot, Jr. "The Guatemalan Complaint before the Security Council." *Department of State Bulletin* 31 (5 July 1954): 26–31.

Morton, Thruston B. "Foreign Policy in Perspective." *Department of State Bulletin* 31 (26 July 1954): 119–121.

NSC-68: "A Report to the National Security Council by the Executive Secretary on United States Objectives and Programs for National Security," 14 April 1950. *Naval War College Review* 27 (May–June 1975): 51–108.

Organization of American States. *Agenda of the Tenth Inter-American Conference.* Washington, D.C., 1953.

———. *Annals* 5–6 (1953–1954). Washington, D.C., 1953–1954.

Peurifoy, John E. "The Communist Conspiracy in Guatemala." *Department of State Bulletin* 31 (8 November 1954): 690–697.

———. "Meeting the Communist Challenge in the Western Hemisphere." *Department of State Bulletin* 31 (6 September 1954): 333–336.

Public Papers of the Presidents of the United States: Dwight D. Eisenhower, 1954. Washington, D.C., 1960.

United Nations. *The Economic Development of Latin America in the Post-War Period.* New York, 1964.

United Nations Security Council. *Official Records.*

United States Department of Commerce. *Investment in Central America.* Washington, D.C., 1956.

United States Department of State. *American Foreign Policy, 1950–1955, Basic Documents.* Vol. 1. Washington, D.C., 1957.

———. "Arms Shipment to Guatemala from Soviet-Controlled Area." *Department of State Bulletin* 30 (31 May 1954): 835.

———. *A Case History of Communist Penetration: Guatemala.* Washington, D.C., 1957.

———. "Declaration of Caracas." *Department of State Bulletin* 30 (22 March 1954): 420.

———. "Expropriation of United Fruit Company Property by the Government of Guatemala." *Department of State Bulletin* 29 (14 September 1953): 337–360.

———. "Formal Claim Filed against the Guatemalan Government." *Department of State Bulletin* 30 (26 April 1954): 678–679.

———. *Papers Relating to the Foreign Relations of the United States, 1944–1951.* Washington, D.C., 1967–1979.

———. *Penetration of the Political Institutions of Guatemala by the International Communist Movement.* Washington, D.C., 1954.

———. *Tenth Inter-American Conference: Report of the Delegation of the United States of America with Related Documents.* Washington, D.C., 1955.

United States House of Representatives, Committee on Foreign Affairs (92d Cong., 2d sess.). *Inter-American Affairs.* Washington, D.C., 1972.

———, Committee on Foreign Affairs (85th Cong., 1st sess.). *Report of the Special Study Mission to Guatemala.* Washington, D.C., 1957.

———, Committee on Foreign Affairs. *Selected Executive Session Hearings of the Committee, 1951–1956.* Vol. 16: *The Middle East, Africa, and Inter-American Affairs.* Washington, D.C., 1980.

———, Select Committee on Communist Aggression (83d Cong., 2d sess.). *Report of the Subcommittee to Investigate Communist Aggression in Latin America.* Washington, D.C., 1954.

———, Subcommittee on Latin America of the Select Committee on Communist Aggression (83d Cong., 2d sess.). *Ninth Interim Report of Hearings: Communist Aggression in Latin America.* Washington, D.C., 1954.

United States Senate, Committee on Appropriations (86th Cong., 1st sess.). *Review of the United States Government Operations in Latin America, 1958,* by Allen J. Ellender, 19 February 1959. Washington, D.C., 1959.

———, Committee on Foreign Relations, *Executive Sessions of the Senate Foreign Relations Committee* (Historical Series). Vol. 2 (81st Cong., 1st and 2d sess.), 1949–1950. Washington, D.C., 1976.

———, Committee on Foreign Relations, *Executive Sessions of the Senate Foreign Relations Committee* (Historical Series). Vol. 3 (82d Cong., 1st sess.), 1951. Washington, D.C., 1976.

———, Judiciary Committee (87th Cong., 1st sess.). *Report of the Subcommittee to Investigate the Administration of the Internal Security Act and Other Internal Security Laws.* Washington, D.C., 1962.

———, Special Committee to Study the Foreign Aid Program. *Compilation of Studies and Surveys: Survey #9, Central America and the Caribbean Area.* Washington, D.C., 1957.

PUBLISHED ORAL HISTORIES AND INTERVIEWS

Adams, Sherman. *Oral History Interview #3.* Columbia Oral History Collection, Columbia University.

Bissell, Richard M., Jr. *Oral History Interview.* Columbia Oral History Collection, Columbia University.
———. *Transcript of a Recorded Interview.* John Foster Dulles Oral History Project, Princeton University.
Bohan, Merwin L. *Oral Interview.* Harry S. Truman Library.
Cabot, John Moors. *Transcript of a Recorded Interview.* John Foster Dulles Oral History Project, Princeton University.
Eisenhower, Dwight D. *Oral History Interview.* Columbia Oral History Collection, Columbia University.
Eisenhower, Milton S. *Oral History Interview.* Columbia Oral History Collection, Columbia University.
Figueres, José. *Oral Interview.* Harry S. Truman Library.
Goodpaster, Andrew. *Oral History Interview.* Columbia Oral History Collection, Columbia University.
Harlow, Bryce. *Transcript of a Recorded Interview.* John Foster Dulles Oral History Project, Princeton University.
McCardle, Carl. *Oral History Interview.* Columbia Oral History Collection, Columbia University.
Miller, Raymond. *Oral Interview.* Harry S. Truman Library.
Rubottom, Roy R., Jr. *Transcript of a Recorded Interview.* John Foster Dulles Oral History Project, Princeton University.

TELEVISION TRANSCRIPTS

"NBC White Paper: The Castro Connection." A television documentary narrated by Marvin Kalb and produced by Robert Rogers and NBC News, originally broadcast 3 September 1980.
"The Science of Spying." A television documentary narrated by John Chancellor and produced by Robert Rogers, Ted Yates, and NBC News, originally broadcast by NBC on 4 May 1965.

PRIMARY BOOKS AND RECORDS

Acheson, Dean. *Present at the Creation.* New York, 1969.
———. *This Vast External Realm.* New York, 1973.
Agee, Philip. *Inside the Company: CIA Diary.* Great Britain, 1975.
Arbenz, Jacobo. *Discursos.* Guatemala City, 1951.
Arévalo, Juan José. *Anti-Kommunism in Latin America.* Trans. Carleton Beals. New York, 1963.
———. *Discursos en la presidencia, 1945–1947.* Guatemala, 1947.
———. *Escritos políticos.* Guatemala, 1945.
———. *Escritos políticos y discursos.* Havana, 1953.
———. *Guatemala, la democracia y el imperio.* Havana, 1960.
———. *Informes al congreso.* Guatemala, 1948.
———. *The Shark and the Sardines.* Trans. June Cobb and Raúl Osegueda. New York, 1961.
Berle, Beatrice Bishop, and Travis Beal Jacobs, eds. *Navigating the Rapids, 1918–1971: From the Papers of Adolf A. Berle.* New York, 1973.

Bernays, Edward L. *Biography of an Idea: Memoirs of a Public Relations Counsel.* New York, 1965.

———. *Propaganda.* New York, 1928.

Braden, Spruille. *Diplomats and Demagogues.* New Rochelle, 1971.

Cabot, John Moors. *First Line of Defense: Forty Years' Experiences of a Career Diplomat.* Washington, D.C., n.d.

———. *Toward Our Common American Destiny.* New York, n.d.

Cardoza y Aragón, Luis. *La revolución Guatemalteca.* Mexico, 1955.

Cline, Ray S. *Secrets, Spies, and Soldiers: Blueprint of the Essential CIA.* Washington, D.C., 1976.

Congressional Quarterly Service. *Congress and the Nation: A Review of Government and Politics in the Postwar Years.* Vol. 1: *1945–1964.* Washington, D.C., 1965.

Daniels, Walter M., ed. *Latin America in the Cold War.* New York, 1952.

Dreier, John C. *The Organization of American States and the Hemisphere Crisis.* New York, 1962.

Dulles, Allen. *The Craft of Intelligence.* New York, 1963.

Dulles, Eleanor Lansing. *John Foster Dulles: The Last Year.* New York, 1963.

Eden, Anthony. *Full Circle: The Memoirs of Anthony Eden.* Boston, 1960.

Eisenhower, Dwight D. *The White House Years: Mandate for Change, 1953–1956.* Garden City, N.Y., 1963.

Facts on File Yearbook. 1944–1954. New York, 1945–1955.

Ferrell, Robert H., ed. *The Eisenhower Diaries.* New York, 1981.

Gadea, Hilda. *Ernesto: A Memoir of Che Guevara.* Trans. Carmen Molina and Walter I. Bradbury. New York, 1972.

Galich, Manuel. *Del pánico al ataque.* Guatemala, 1949.

———. *Por qué lucha Guatemala: Arévalo y Arbenz, dos hombres contra un imperio.* Buenos Aires, 1956.

Gerassi, John, ed. *The Coming of the New International.* New York and Cleveland, 1971.

———, ed. *Venceremos: The Speeches and Writings of Ernesto Che Guevara.* New York, 1968.

González-Arévalo, Ismael. *Statement Concerning the Conflict between Guatemalan Workers and the United Fruit Company.* Washington, D.C., 1949.

Guillén, Fedro. *Guatemala, prólogo y epílogo de una revolución.* Mexico, 1964.

Hunt, E. Howard. *Give Us This Day.* New Rochelle, 1973.

———. *Undercover: Memoirs of an American Secret Agent.* New York, 1974.

Informe del Presidente Jacobo Arbenz Guzmán al congreso nacional en su primer período de sesiones ordinarias del año de 1953. Guatemala, 1953.

Inman, Samuel Guy. *A New Day in Guatemala: A Study of the Present Revolution.* Wilton, Conn., 1951.

International Bank for Reconstruction and Development. *The Economic Development of Guatemala.* Washington, D.C., 1951.

Marchetti, Victor, and John D. Marks. *The CIA and the Cult of Intelligence.* New York, 1974.

Marroquín Rojas, Clemente. *La derrota de una batalla.* Guatemala, 1956.

Mejía, Medardo. *El movimiento obrero en la Revolución de Octubre.* Guatemala, 1949.

Murphy, Robert. *Diplomat among Warriors.* Garden City, N.Y., 1964.

Nájera Farfán, Mario Efraín. *Los estafadores de la democracia (hombres y hechos en Guatemala).* Buenos Aires, 1956.

Osegueda, Raúl. *Operación Guatemala OK.* Mexico, 1955.

Pearson, Drew. *Diaries, 1949–1959.* Ed. Tyler Abell. New York, 1974.

Phillips, David Atlee. *Night Watch: Twenty Years of Peculiar Service.* New York, 1977.

Pollan, A. A. *The United Fruit Company in Middle America.* New York, 1944.

Primer Congreso contra la Intervención Soviética en América Latina. *El libro negro del comunismo en Guatemala.* Mexico, 1954.

Prouty, L. Fletcher. *The Secret Team.* Englewood Cliffs, N.J., 1973.

Rojo, Ricardo. *My Friend Che.* Trans. Julian Casart. New York, 1968.

Ronning, C. Neale, ed. *Intervention in Latin America.* New York, 1970.

Roosevelt, Kermit. *Countercoup: The Struggle for the Control of Iran.* New York, 1979.

Salisbury, Harrison E. *Without Fear or Favor: The New York Times and Its Times.* New York, 1980.

Samoya Chincilla, Carlos. *El quetzal no es rojo.* Mexico, 1956.

Stebbins, Richard P., and the Research Staff of the Council on Foreign Relations. *The United States in World Affairs, 1954.* New York, 1956.

Toriello Garrido, Guillermo. *¿A dónde va Guatemala?* Mexico, 1956.

———. *La batalla de Guatemala.* Mexico, 1955.

Truman, Harry S. *Memoirs by Harry S. Truman: Years of Trial and Hope.* Garden City, N.Y., 1956.

United Fruit Company Annual Report. 1950–1955. Boston.

Woytinsky, W. S. *The United States and Latin America's Economy.* New York, 1958.

Ydígoras Fuentes, Miguel, with Mario Rosenthal. *My War with Communism.* Englewood Cliffs, N.J., 1963.

ARTICLES, SPEECHES, AND NEWSPAPERS

Adolfo Rey, Julio. "Revolution and Liberation: A Review of Recent Literature on the Guatemalan Situation." *Hispanic American Historical Review* 38 (May 1958): 239–255.

"After the Vote." *Time* 63 (29 March 1954): 32.

Alexander, Robert J. "Guatemalan Communists." *Canadian Forum* 34 (July 1954): 81–83.

———. "The Guatemalan Revolution and Communism." *Foreign Policy Bulletin* 33 (April 1954): 5–7.

Alvarez del Vayo, J. "Aggression Is the Word: The Guatemalan Crisis." *Nation* 178 (26 June 1954): 537–538.
Anderson, Charles W. "The Latin American Political System." In John D. Martz, ed., *The Dynamics of Change in Latin American Politics*, pp. 289–318. Englewood Cliffs, N.J., 1971.
Arbenz, Jacobo. "4 enfoques del programa administrativo actual." In Alberto Ordóñez, ed., *Transformación económica de Guatemala: Hacia una reforma agraria.* Guatemala City, 1951.
"Banana Bonanza." *Newsweek* 39 (24 March 1952): 62.
"Bananas and Politics." *New Republic* 126 (28 January 1952): 7.
Bauer Paíz, Alfonso. "La reforma agraria en Guatemala." In Alberto Ordóñez, ed., *Transformación económica de Guatemala: Hacia una reforma agraria*, pp. 172–176. Guatemala City, 1951.
———. "The Third Government of the Revolution and Imperialism in Guatemala." *Science and Society* 34 (Summer 1970): 146–165.
"Behind the Guatemalan Front." *New Statesman and Nation* 47 (26 June 1954): 821.
Bernstein, Barton J. "Foreign Policy in the Eisenhower Administration." *Foreign Service Journal* 50 (May 1973): 17–20, 29–30, 38.
Bernstein, Carl. "The CIA and the Media." *Rolling Stone* 250 (20 October 1977): 55–67.
Biskind, Peter. "How the CIA Manages the Media." *Seven Days* (January 1978): 26–27.
Bracker, Milton. "The Octopus Could Grow." *New York Times Book Review*, 24 October 1954, p. 45.
Braden, Spruille. "Syllabus on the Communist Threat in the Americas." Lecture before the great issues course at Dartmouth College, 12 March 1953.
Britnell, George E. "Factors in the Economic Development of Guatemala." *American Economic Review* 43 (May 1953): 104–114.
———. "Problems of Economic and Social Change in Guatemala." *Canadian Journal of Economics and Political Science* 17 (November 1951): 468–481.
Cardoza y Aragón, Luis. "Land for the Many." *Nation* 176 (14 March 1953): 224–225.
Castillo Armas, Carlos, with Clark H. Galloway. "Damage Reds Do." *U.S. News & World Report* 37 (6 August 1954): 38–40.
Chilcote, Ronald H. "Dependency: A Critical Synthesis of the Literature." *Latin American Perspectives* 1 (Spring 1974): 4–29.
"Cold War in Our Tropic Supply Line." *Newsweek* 35 (17 April 1950): 46–47.
Collart, Antonio. "Problemas económico-sociales de Guatemala." In Alberto Ordóñez, ed., *Transformación económica de Guatemala: Hacia una reforma agraria*, pp. 135–150. Guatemala City, 1951.
Cook, Frederick J. "The CIA." *Nation* 192 (24 June 1961): 529–572.
Cumberland, Charles C. "Guatemala: Labor and the Communists." *Current History* 24 (March 1953): 143–148.

DeSantis, Vincent. "Eisenhower Revisionism." *Review of Politics* 38 (April 1976): 190–207.

de Toledano, Ralph. "Unconventional Ambassador." *American Mercury* 79 (October 1954): 28–32.

Draper, Theodore. "How Red Is Guatemala?" *Reporter* 3 (7 November 1950): 23–26.

———. "The Minutemen of Guatemala." *Reporter* 3 (24 October 1950): 32–35.

Dulles, Allen. "Progress of Freedom Abroad." *Vital Speeches* 21 (1 December 1954): 869–871.

"End of a Twelve Day Civil War." *Life* 37 (12 July 1954): 20–22.

Fuentes-Mohr, A. "Land Settlement and Agrarian Reform in Guatemala." *International Journal of Agrarian Affairs* 2 (January 1955): 26–36.

Galloway, Clark H. "A Revolt the U.S. Couldn't Win." *U.S. News & World Report* 37 (2 July 1954): 22–24.

George, Alexander. "The Case for Multiple Advocacy in Making Foreign Policy." *American Political Science Review* 66 (September 1972): 751–785.

Gillin, John, and Kalman H. Silvert. "Ambiguities in Guatemala." *Foreign Affairs* 34 (April 1956): 469–482.

Gondi, Ovidio. "Democracy in Latin America: Chaos on Our Doorstep." *Nation* 170 (28 January 1950): 81.

Gordon, Max. "A Case History of U.S. Subversion: Guatemala, 1954." *Science and Society* 35 (Summer 1971): 129–155.

Graham, Daniel. "Castillo's Guatemala." *Nation* 180 (21 May 1955): 440–442.

———. "Liberated Guatemala." *Nation* 183 (14 July 1956): 34–37.

Grant, Donald. "Guatemala and U.S. Foreign Policy." *Journal of International Affairs* 9 (1955): 64–72.

Green, David. "The Cold War Comes to Latin America." In Barton J. Bernstein, ed., *Politics and Policies of the Truman Administration*, pp. 149–195. Chicago, 1972.

Greenstein, Fred I. "Eisenhower as an Activist President: A New Look at the Evidence." *Political Science Quarterly* 94 (Winter 1979–80): 575–599.

Grieb, Kenneth J. "American Involvement in the Rise of Jorge Ubico." *Caribbean Studies* 10 (April 1970): 5–21.

Griffith, Robert. "Old Progressives and the Cold War." *Journal of American History* 66 (September 1979): 334–347.

"Guatemala: Heat on a Tyrant." *Time* 43 (26 June 1944): 45.

"Guatemala: The New Junta." *Time* 64 (12 July 1954): 38–39.

"Guatemala: Plot within a Plot." *Time* 63 (31 May 1954): 30.

"Guatemala: The Reds Lose a Round." *Time* 44 (17 March 1952): 36.

"Guatemala: Square Deal Wanted." *Time* 63 (3 May 1954): 36.

"Guatemala: Stage Trick." *Time* 48 (18 November 1946): 38.

"Guatemala: Unifruit under Fire." *Time* 58 (12 November 1951): 36.

"Guatemalan Revolution That Everybody Expected." *Life* 36 (28 June 1954): 12–15.

"Guatemalan War." *New Republic* 130 (28 June 1954): 3.

Halperin, Ernst. "The National Liberation Movements in Latin America." Center for Internal Studies, MIT, Cambridge, Mass., Report #A/69-6 (June 1959).

"Harassed U.F." *Commonweal* 55 (9 November 1951): 108.

Harkness, Richard, and Gladys Harkness. "America's Secret Agents: The Mysterious Doings of CIA." *Saturday Evening Post* 227 (30 October 1954): 19–20.

Herz, Martin F. "Some Psychological Lessons from Leaflet Propaganda in World War II." In Society for the Study of Social Issues, ed., *Public Opinion and Propaganda*, pp. 543–553. New York, 1954.

Hildebrand, John R. "Latin American Economic Development, Land Reform, and U.S. Aid with Special Reference to Guatemala." *Journal of Inter-American Studies* 4 (July 1962): 351–361.

Hispanic American Report.

Holsti, Ole R. "The 'Operational Code' Approach to the Study of Political Leaders: John Foster Dulles' Philosophical and Instrumental Beliefs." *Canadian Journal of Political Science* 3 (March 1970): 123–157.

———. "Will the Real Dulles Please Stand Up?" *International Journal* 30 (Winter 1974–75): 34–44.

Hoopes, Townsend. "God and John Foster Dulles." *Foreign Policy* 13 (1973): 154–177.

"How Reds Use Terror near U.S." *U.S. News & World Report* 36 (28 May 1954): 26–32.

Immerman, Richard H. "Eisenhower and Dulles: Who Made the Decisions?" *Political Psychology* 1 (Autumn 1979): 21–38.

"In the Shadow of the Volcano." *Commonweal* 60 (2 July 1954): 308–309.

Intelligence Digest: A Review of World Affairs 12, chap. 7 (June 1950): 7–16.

James, Daniel. "Guatemala's Warning to U.S. Business." *Fortune* 48 (July 1953): 73.

———. "Lessons of Guatemala." *New Leader* 37 (12 July 1954): 3–5.

———. "Red Beachhead in America." *Saturday Evening Post* 226 (24 April 1954): 32–34, 125–128.

Jérez, César, S.J. "La United Fruit Co. en Guatemala." *Estudios Centro Americanos* 26 (March 1971): 117–128.

Jonas, Susanne. "Guatemala: Land of Eternal Struggle." In Ronald H. Chilcote and Joel C. Edelstein, eds., *Latin America: The Struggle with Dependency and Beyond*, pp. 89–215. New York, 1974.

"Keeping Communists Out." *Time* 63 (15 March 1954): 30.

Kinzer, Stephen. "Guatemala: The Hard Line." *Atlantic* 245 (January 1980): 4–14.

Kirchwey, Freda. "Guatemala Guinea Pig." *Nation* 179 (10 July 1954): 21–23.

Kirk, Betty. "United States in Latin America—Policy of the Suction Pump." *Nation* 185 (5 October 1957): 214–222.

Kobler, John. "Sam the Banana Man." *Life* 30 (19 February 1951): 83–94.

Krehm, William. "Victory for the West in Guatemala?" *International Journal* 9 (Fall 1954): 295–302.

LaBarge, Richard Allen. "Impact of the United Fruit Company on the Economic Development of Guatemala, 1946–1954." In LaBarge et al., *Studies in Middle American Economics*, pp. 1–72. New Orleans, 1968.

LaFeber, Walter. "Latin American Policy." In Robert A. Divine, ed., *Exploring the Johnson Years*, pp. 63–90. Austin, 1981.

"Left-Wing Alliance." *Time* 59 (25 February 1952): 40.

"Letter to the President of Guatemala." *American Federationist* 61 (February 1954): 91.

Lewis, Flora. "Ambassador Extraordinary: John Peurifoy." *New York Times Magazine*, 18 July 1954, pp. 9, 26.

London Times.

Luhan, J. Michael. "The Next El Salvador." *New Republic* 182 (11 April 1981): 23–25.

McDermott, Louis M. "Guatemala 1954: Intervention or Aggression?" *Rocky Mountain Social Science Journal* 9 (January 1972): 79–88.

McElvoy, J. P. "Trouble in Our Own Backyard." *Reader's Digest* 57 (August 1950): 7–11.

McMahon, P. "Man Who Kicked the Reds out of Guatemala." *American Mercury* 79 (September 1954): 21–23.

Martin, Lawrence, and Sylvia Martin. "Four Strong Men and a President." *Harper's Magazine* 185 (September 1942): 418–427.

Matthews, Herbert L. "The U.S. and Latin America." Headline Series, Foreign Policy Association, no. 100 (July–August 1953).

Meany, George. "The Last Five Years: How the American Federation of Labor Fights Communism around the World." Address delivered before the Catholic Labor Alliance, Chicago, 13 March 1951.

"Middleman in a Successful Revolution." *U.S. News & World Report* 37 (9 July 1954): 46–49.

Monroe, Keith. "Guatemala, What the Reds Left Behind." *Harper's Magazine* 211 (July 1955): 60–65.

Nashville Banner.

Newbold, Stokes [Richard Newbold Adams]. "Receptivity to Communist-Fomented Agitation in Rural Guatemala." *Economic Development and Cultural Change* 5 (July 1957): 338–361.

New York Daily Worker.

New York Herald Tribune.

New York Times.

Ogle, Ellis. "Communism in Guatemala?" *Nation* 170 (18 March 1950): 246–247.

Ospina, Carlos. "Consideraciones sobre la reforma agraria." In Alberto Ordóñez, ed., *Transformación económica de Guatemala: Hacia una reforma agraria*, pp. 177–183. Guatemala City, 1951.

Payne, Walter A. "The Guatemalan Revolution, 1944–1954: An Interpretation." *Pacific Historian* 17 (Spring 1973), insert, 1–32.

Pike, Fredrick B. "Guatemala, the United States, and Communism in the

Americas." *Review of Politics* 17 (April 1955): 232–261.

"The Problem of Guatemala." *Time* 63 (11 January 1954): 27.

"The Red Outpost in Central America." *Life* 35 (12 October 1953): 169–177.

"Red Shadow in Election." *Newsweek* 36 (13 November 1950): 52.

"The Reds Must Get No American Beachhead." *Saturday Evening Post* 226 (20 March 1954): 10.

Reichard, Gary W. "Eisenhower and the Bricker Amendment." *Prologue: The Journal of the National Archives* 6 (Summer 1974): 88–91.

———. "Eisenhower as President: The Changing View." *South Atlantic Quarterly* 77 (Summer 1978): 265–281.

Riding, Alan. "Guatemala: State of Siege." *New York Times Magazine*, 24 August 1980, pp. 17–29, 66–67.

———. "Guatemala Opening New Lands, but the Best Goes to Rich." *New York Times*, 5 April 1979.

Romualdi, Serafino. "Report on Guatemala." *American Federationist* 61 (September 1954): 26–31.

Rosen, Bernard. "Counter-Revolution: Guatemala's Tragedy." *Nation* 179 (31 July 1954): 87–89.

St. Louis Post-Dispatch.

Schlesinger, Stephen. "How Dulles Worked the Coup d'Etat." *Nation* 227 (28 October 1978): 1, 439–444.

Scully, M. "Inside Story of the Kremlin's Plot in Guatemala." *Reader's Digest* 66 (February 1955): 73–78.

"Showdown in Guatemala." *Business Week*, 8 December 1951, pp. 177–178.

Siegel, Morris. "Perspective on Guatemala." *New Republic* 132 (19 July 1954): 10–14.

Simons, Marlise. "Guatemala: The Coming Danger." *Foreign Policy* 43 (Summer 1981): 93–103.

Smith, Tony. "The Underdevelopment of Development Literature: The Case of Dependency Theory." *World Politics* 31 (January 1979): 247–288.

"The Social Revolution in Guatemala." *World Today* 10 (July 1954): 279–282.

Solow, Herbert. "The Ripe Problem of United Fruit." *Fortune* 54 (March 1959): 97–100.

"The Sources of Soviet Conduct." *Foreign Affairs* 25 (July 1947): 566–582.

"Soviets Cross the Atlantic." *U.S. News & World Report* 37 (9 July 1954): 17–19.

"State Department's Dispute with Guatemala." *Nation* 170 (22 April 1950): 358–359.

Szulc, Tad. "US and ITT in Chile." *New Republic* 168 (30 June 1973): 21–23.

Talmadge, I.D. "Guatemala: Bananas and Bolshevism." *Scholastic Teacher* 63 (14 October 1953): 11–13.

Taylor, Philip B., Jr. "The Guatemalan Affair: A Critique of United States

Foreign Policy." *American Political Science Review* 50 (September 1956): 787–806.

Tobis, David. "United Fruit Is Not Chiquita." NACLA *Newsletter* (October 1971).

Villatoro, Rubén D. "Guatemala Smashes Free Unions." *American Federationist* 61 (May 1954): 23–24, 28.

Whetten, Nathan L. "Land Reform in a Modern World." *Rural Sociology* 19 (December 1954): 329–337.

Whitaker, Arthur P. "Guatemala, OAS, and U.S." *Foreign Policy Bulletin* 33 (1 September 1954): 4–7.

Wood, Bryce. "Self-Plagiarism and Foreign Policy." *Latin American Research Review* 3 (Summer 1968): 184–191.

Zemurray, Samuel. "La Frutera's Record." *Nation* 170 (25 March 1950): 287–289.

DISSERTATIONS AND THESES

Cehelsky, Marta. "Guatemala's Frustrated Revolution: The Liberation of 1954." M.A. thesis, Columbia University, 1967.

Chardkoff, Richard Bruce. "Communist Toehold in the Americas: A History of Official United States Involvement in the Guatemalan Crisis, 1954." Ph.D. dissertation, Florida State University, 1967.

Immerman, Richard H. "The United States and Guatemala, 1954: A Cold War Strategy for the Americas." Ph.D. dissertation, Boston College, 1978.

Johnston, William Franklin. "Some Principles of Communist Unconventional Warfare: Lessons from the Yenan and Guatemalan 'Ways.'" M.A. thesis, Georgetown University, 1958.

Jonas, Susanne. "Test Case for the Hemisphere: United States Strategy in Guatemala, 1950–1974." Ph.D. dissertation, University of California, Berkeley, 1974.

SECONDARY BOOKS AND RECORDS

Adams, Richard Newbold. *Crucifixion by Power: Essays on Guatemalan National Social Structure, 1944–1966.* Austin and London, 1970.

———. *Social Change in Latin America.* New York, 1960.

———, et al. *Community Culture and National Change.* New Orleans, 1972.

Adams, Sherman. *Firsthand Report: The Story of the Eisenhower Administration.* New York, 1961.

Adler, John H., Eugene R. Schlesinger, and Ernest C. Olson. *Public Finance and Economic Development in Guatemala.* New York, 1952.

Alexander, Charles C. *Holding the Line: The Eisenhower Era, 1952–1961.* Bloomington, 1975.

Alexander, Robert J. *Communism in Latin America.* New Brunswick, 1957.

———, and C. O. Porter. *The Struggle for Democracy in Latin America.* New York, 1961.

Alvarez Elizondo, Pedro. *El Presidente Arévalo y el retorno a Bolívar.* Mexico City, 1947.

Ambrose, Stephen E., with Richard H. Immerman. *Ike's Spies: Eisenhower and the Espionage Establishment.* Garden City, N.Y., 1981.

American Assembly, Columbia University. *The United States and Latin America.* Englewood Cliffs, N.J., 1963.

American University, Special Operations Research Office. *Case Study in Insurgency and Revolutionary Warfare: Guatemala, 1944–1954.* Washington, D.C., 1964.

Arciniegas, Germán. *The State of Latin America.* Trans. Harriet de Onis. London, 1953.

Aronson, James. *The Press and the Cold War.* Indianapolis and New York, 1970.

Arrocha, Angela (Delli Sante). *Juan José Arévalo, pensador contemporáneo.* Mexico, 1962.

Aybar de Soto, José M. *Dependency and Intervention: The Case of Guatemala in 1954.* Boulder, Colo., 1978.

Bailey, Norman A., ed. *Latin America: Politics, Economics, and Hemispheric Security.* New York, 1962.

Bancroft, Hubert Howe. *History of Central America.* Vol. 3: *1801–1887.* San Francisco, 1887.

Barnet, Richard J. *Intervention and Revolution: The United States in the Third World.* New York, 1968.

———. *Roots of War.* New York, 1972.

———, and Ronald E. Mueller. *Global Reach.* New York, 1974.

Beal, John Robinson. *John Foster Dulles: A Biography.* New York, 1957.

———. *John Foster Dulles, 1888–1959.* New York, 1959.

Berding, Andrew H. *Dulles on Diplomacy.* Princeton, 1965.

Bernstein, Barton J., ed. *Politics and Policies of the Truman Administration.* Chicago, 1972.

Bernstein, Marvin D., ed. *Foreign Investment in Latin America: Cases and Attitudes.* New York, 1966.

Blasier, Cole. *The Hovering Giant: U.S. Responses to Revolutionary Change in Latin America.* Pittsburgh, 1976.

Blechman, Barry, and Stephen Kaplan. *Force without War: U.S. Armed Forces as a Political Instrument.* Washington, D.C., 1978.

Bloch, Marc. *Feudal Society.* Trans. L. A. Manyon. London, 1961.

Burnett, Ben G., and Kenneth F. Johnson, eds. *Political Forces in Latin America: Dimensions for the Quest for Stability.* Belmont, Calif., 1970.

Burr, Robert, ed. *The Annals of the American Academy.* Vol. 334 (March, 1961).

Bush, Archer. *Organized Labor in Guatemala, 1944–1949.* Hamilton, N.Y., 1950.

Castro, Julio. *Bombas y dolares sobre Guatemala.* Montevideo, 1954.

Cheston, T. Stephen, and Bernard Loeffke. *Aspects of Soviet Policy toward Latin America.* New York, 1974.

Cohen, Bernard C. *The Press and Foreign Policy*. Princeton, 1963.

Comfort, Mildred H. *John Foster Dulles, Peacemaker*. Minneapolis, 1960.

Connell-Smith, Gordon. *The Inter-American System*. London, 1966.

――――. *The United States and Latin America*. London, 1974.

Cook, Blanche Wiesen. *The Declassified Eisenhower: A Divided Legacy of Peace and Political Warfare*. Garden City, N.Y., 1981.

Davis, Harold, ed. *Government and Politics in Latin America*. New York, 1958.

DeGramont, Sanche. *The Secret War*. New York, 1962.

Dion, Marie-Berthe. *Las ideas sociales y políticas de Arévalo*. Santiago, 1958.

Domínguez, Jorge I. *Cuba: Order and Revolution*. Cambridge, Mass., and London, 1978.

Donner, Frank J. *The Age of Surveillance: The Aims and Methods of America's Political Intelligence System*. New York, 1980.

Dozer, Donald M. *Are We Good Neighbors?* Gainesville, Fla., 1959.

Drummond, Roscoe, and Gaston Coblentz. *Duel at the Brink: John Foster Dulles' Command of American Foreign Policy*. Garden City, N.Y., 1960.

Dulles, Eleanor Lansing. *American Foreign Policy in the Making*. New York, Evanston, London, 1968.

Eisenhower, Milton S. *The Wine Is Bitter*. Garden City, N.Y., 1963.

Ewald, William B., Jr. *Eisenhower the President: Crucial Days, 1951–1960*. Englewood Cliffs, N.J., 1981.

Feder, Ernest. *The Rape of the Peasantry: Latin America's Landholding System*. Garden City, N.Y., 1971.

Finer, Herman. *Dulles over Suez: The Theory and Practice of His Diplomacy*. Chicago, 1964.

Fletcher, Lehman, et al. *Guatemala's Economic Development: The Role of Agriculture*. Ames, Iowa, 1970.

Foner, Philip S. *History of the Labor Movement in the United States*. Vol. 5. New York, 1965.

Frank, Andre Gunder. *Latin America: Underdevelopment or Revolution: Essays on the Development or Underdevelopment and the Immediate Enemy*. New York and London, 1969.

Gaddis, John Lewis. *Russia, the Soviet Union, and the United States: An Interpretive History*. New York, 1978.

Galeano, Eduardo H. *Guatemala, Occupied Country*. Trans. Cedric Belfrage. New York, 1969.

――――. *Open Veins in Latin America: Five Centuries of the Pillage of a Continent*. Trans. Cedric Belfrage. New York and London, 1973.

Gardner, Lloyd C. *Architects of Illusion: Men and Ideas in American Foreign Policy, 1941–1949*. Chicago, 1970.

Geiger, Theodore. *Communism versus Progress in Guatemala*. New York, 1953.

Gerassi, John. *The Great Fear: The Reconquest of Latin America by Latin Americans*. New York, 1963.

Gerson, Louis. *John Foster Dulles.* New York, 1967.

Gollas, Manuel. *Surplus Labor and Economic Development: The Guatemalan Cases.* N.p., 1970.

Goold-Adams, Richard. *John Foster Dulles: A Reappraisal.* New York, 1962.

Gott, Richard. *Rural Guerillas in Latin America.* Middlesex, Eng., 1973.

Green, David. *The Containment of Latin America: A History of the Myths and Realities of the Good Neighbor Policy.* Chicago, 1971.

Greene, Felix. *The Enemy: What Every American Should Know about Imperialism.* New York, 1971.

Grieb, Kenneth J. *Guatemalan Caudillo: The Regime of Jorge Ubico, Guatemala 1931–1944.* Athens, Ohio, 1979.

Griffith, Robert. *The Politics of Fear: Joseph R. McCarthy and the Senate.* New York, 1970.

———, and Athan Theoharis, eds. *The Specter: Original Essays on the Cold War and the Origins of McCarthyism.* New York, 1974.

Guhin, Michael A. *John Foster Dulles: A Statesman and His Times.* New York and London, 1972.

Gurtov, Melvin. *The United States against the Third World: Antinationalism and Intervention.* New York, 1974.

Guzmán-Boeckler, Carlos, and Jean-Loup Herbert. *Guatemala, una interpretación histórico-social.* Mexico, 1970.

Herring, Hubert. *A History of Latin America.* 2d rev. ed. New York, 1961.

Hirschman, Albert O., ed. *Latin American Issues—Essays and Comments.* New York, 1961.

Hoffman, Paul. *Lions in the Street: The Inside Story of the Great Wall Street Law Firms.* New York, 1973.

Hoopes, Townsend. *The Devil and John Foster Dulles.* Boston, 1973.

Horowitz, David. *The Free World Colossus.* New York, 1955.

Inman, Samuel Guy. *Inter-American Conferences, 1826–1954.* Washington, D.C., 1965.

James, Daniel. *Red Design for the Americas.* New York, 1954.

Janis, Irving L. *Victims of Groupthink: A Psychological Study of Foreign Policy Decisions.* Boston, 1972.

Jenkins, Amy Elizabeth. *Guatemala: A Historical Survey.* New York, 1955.

Johnson, John J. *The Military and Society in Latin America.* Stanford, 1964.

Jones, Chester Lloyd. *Guatemala: Past and Present.* New York, 1966.

Julien, Claude. *America's Empire.* Trans. Renaud Bruce. New York, 1971.

Karnes, Thomas L. *The Failure of Union: Central America, 1824–1960.* Chapel Hill, N.C., 1961.

Kepner, Charles David, Jr., and Jay Henry Soothill. *The Banana Empire: A Case Study of Economic Imperialism.* New York, 1935.

Kinzer, Stephen, and Stephen Schlesinger. *Bitter Fruit: The Untold Story of the American Coup in Guatemala.* Garden City, N.Y., 1981.

Kolko, Joyce, and Gabriel Kolko. *The Limits of Power: The World and United States Foreign Policy, 1945–1954.* New York, 1972.

Krasner, Stephen D. *Defending the National Interest: Raw Materials, Investments and U.S. Foreign Policy.* Princeton, 1978.

LaFeber, Walter. *America, Russia, and the Cold War, 1945–1966.* New York, London, Sydney, Toronto, 1967.

———. *America, Russia, and the Cold War, 1945–1975.* 3d ed. New York, London, Sydney, Toronto, 1976.

Leites, Nathan. *The Operational Code of the Politburo.* New York, London, Toronto, 1951.

Lernoux, Penny. *Cry of the People.* Garden City, N.Y., 1980.

Levinson, Jerome, and Juan de Onis. *The Alliance That Lost Its Way.* Chicago, 1970.

Lieuwen, Edwin. *Arms and Politics in Latin America.* Rev. ed. New York, 1965.

———. *Generals vs. Presidents: Neo-Militarism in Latin America.* New York, 1964.

Lukacs, John. *A New History of the Cold War.* 3d ed. Garden City, N.Y., 1966.

Lyon, Peter. *Eisenhower: Portrait of a Hero.* Boston, 1974.

McCann, Thomas P. *An American Company: The Tragedy of United Fruit.* Ed. Henry Scammell. New York, 1976.

MacDonald, Austin F. *Latin American Politics and Government.* 2d ed. New York, 1954.

Madariaga, Salvador de. *Latin America between the Eagle and the Bear.* New York, 1962.

Maestre Alfonso, Juan. *Guatemala: Subdesarrollo y violencia.* Madrid, 1969.

Maier, Joseph, and Richard W. Weatherhead, eds. *Politics of Change in Latin America.* New York, 1964.

Manfred, A. Z. *A Short History of the World.* Moscow, 1974.

Martz, John D. *Central America, the Crisis and the Challenge.* Chapel Hill, N.C., 1959.

———. *Communist Infiltration of Guatemala.* New York, 1956.

———, ed. *The Dynamics of Change in Latin American Politics.* Englewood Cliffs, N.J., 1971.

Matthews, Herbert L. *A World in Revolution.* New York, 1971.

May, Stacy, and G. Plaza. *The United Fruit Company in Latin America.* Washington, D.C., 1958.

Mayer, Arno J. *Dynamics of Counterrevolution in Europe, 1870–1956: An Analytic Framework.* New York, Evanston, San Francisco, London, 1971.

Mecham, J. Lloyd. *A Survey of United States–Latin American Relations.* Boston, 1965.

Mejía, Medardo. *Juan José Arévalo o el humanismo en la presidencia.* Guatemala, 1951.

Melville, Thomas, and Marjorie Melville. *Guatemala: The Politics of Land Ownership.* New York, 1971.

Mendez Montenegro, Julio César. *444 Años de legislación agraria, 1513–1957*. Guatemala, 1960.

Mikesell, Raymond F. *Foreign Investments in Latin America*. Washington, D.C., 1955.

Mitchell, Sir Harold. *Contemporary Politics and Economics in the Caribbean*. Athens, Ohio, 1967.

Monteforte Toledo, Mario. *Guatemala—monografía sociológica*. Mexico, 1959.

Morgenthau, Hans. "John Foster Dulles (1953–1959)." In Norman Graebner, ed., *An Uncertain Tradition: American Secretaries of State in the Twentieth Century*, pp. 289–308. New York, Toronto, London, 1961.

Morris, George. *CIA and American Labor*. New York, 1967.

Mosley, Leonard. *Dulles: A Biography of Eleanor, Allen and John Foster Dulles and Their Family Network*. New York, 1978.

Needler, Martin C., ed. *Political Development in Latin America: Instability, Violence, and Evolutionary Change*. New York, 1968.

———. *The United States and the Latin American Revolution*. Boston, 1972.

Niedergang, Marcel. *Les vingt Amériques Latines*. Vol. 3. Paris, 1969.

North American Congress on Latin America. *Guatemala*. Ed. Susanne Jonas and David Tobis. New York and Berkeley, 1974.

Nun, José. *Latin America: The Hegemonic Crisis and the Military Coup*. Berkeley, 1969.

Operation ZAPATA: The "Ultrasensitive" Report and Testimony of the Board of Inquiry on the Bay of Pigs. Frederick, Md., 1981.

Pan American Union. *Guatemala*. Washington, D.C., 1967.

Parker, Franklin D. *The Central American Republics*. London, 1964.

Parkinson, F. *Latin America, the Cold War, and the World Powers, 1945–1973*. Beverly Hills and London, 1974.

Parmet, Herbert. *Eisenhower and the American Crusades*. New York, 1972.

Petras, James F., and Robert LaPorte, Jr. *Cultivating Revolution: The United States and Agrarian Reform in Latin America*. New York, 1971.

———, and Maurice Zeitlin, eds. *Latin America, Reform or Revolution*. Greenwich, Conn., 1968.

Piedrasante Arandi, Rafael. *Análisis de la economía de Guatemala y política de desarrollo*. Guatemala, 1952.

Pierson, William, and Federico Gil. *Governments of Latin America*. New York, 1957.

Powers, Thomas. *The Man Who Kept the Secrets: Richard Helms and the CIA*. New York, 1979.

Ra'anan, Uri. *The USSR Arms the Third World: Case Studies in Soviet Foreign Policy*. Cambridge, Mass., and London, 1969.

Racines, Eudocio. *The Yenan Way*. New York, 1951.

Reichard, Gary W. *The Reaffirmation of Republicanism: Eisenhower and the Eighty-Third Congress*. Knoxville, Tenn., 1975.

Rodman, Selden. *The Guatemalan Traveler: A Concise History and Guide*. New York, 1967.

Rogow, Arnold A. *James Forrestal: A Study of Personality, Politics and Policy.* New York, 1963.

Ronning, C. Neale. *Law and Politics in Inter-American Diplomacy.* New York, 1963.

Rosenthal, Mario. *Guatemala.* New York, 1962.

Rostow, W. W. *The Stages of Economic Growth: A Non-Communist Manifesto.* Cambridge, Mass., 1962.

Schmitt, Karl M., and David D. Burks. *Evolution or Chaos: Dynamics of Latin American Government and Politics.* New York, 1963.

Schneider, Ronald. *Communism in Guatemala, 1944–1954.* New York, 1958.

Shapiro, Samuel. *Invisible Latin America.* Boston, 1963.

Sharp, Gene. *The Politics of Nonviolent Action.* Boston, 1973.

Shoup, Lawrence H., and William Minter. *Imperial Brain Trust: The Council on Foreign Relations and United States Foreign Policy.* New York and London, 1977.

Shulman, Marshall. *Stalin's Foreign Policy Reappraised.* Cambridge, Mass., 1963.

Silvert, Kalman A. *The Conflict Society.* New York, 1966.

———. *A Study in Government: Guatemala.* New Orleans, 1954.

Smith, T. Lynn. *Agrarian Reform in Latin America.* New York, 1966.

Suslow, Leo A. *Aspects of Social Reforms in Guatemala, 1944–1949.* Hamilton, N.Y., 1949.

Szulc, Tad. *Compulsive Spy: The Strange Career of E. Howard Hunt.* New York, 1974.

———. *The Winds of Revolution.* New York, 1963.

Torrez Rivas, Edelberto. *Procesos y estructuras de una sociedad dependiente (Centroamérica).* Santiago, 1969.

Tully, Andrew. *CIA: The Inside Story.* New York, 1962.

Ulam, Adam B. *Expansion and Coexistence: The History of Soviet Foreign Policy, 1917–67.* Cambridge, Mass., 1968.

Urquhart, Brian. *Hammarskjöld.* New York, 1972.

Veliz, Claudio, ed. *Latin America and the Caribbean.* New York, 1968.

von Lazar, Arpad, and Robert R. Kaufman, eds. *Reform and Revolution: Readings in Latin American Politics.* Boston, 1969.

Westerfield, H. Bradford. *The Instruments of America's Foreign Policy.* New York, 1963.

Westwood, Andrew F. *Foreign Aid in a Foreign Policy Framework.* Washington, D.C., 1966.

Whetten, Nathan L. *Guatemala: The Land and the People.* New Haven, 1961.

Wilson, Charles Morrow. *Empire in Green and Gold: The Story of the American Banana Trade.* New York, 1947.

Wise, David, and Thomas Ross. *The Invisible Government: The CIA and U.S. Intelligence.* New York, 1964.

Wolf, Eric. *Sons of the Shaking Earth.* Chicago, 1959.

Wyden, Peter. *Bay of Pigs: The Untold Story.* New York, 1979.

Index